JUSTICE
RUTLEDGE
and
The Bright Constellation

by

FOWLER V. HARPER

THE **BOBBS-MERRILL** COMPANY, INC.
A SUBSIDIARY OF HOWARD W. SAMS & CO., INC.
Publishers • INDIANAPOLIS • NEW YORK

To
Miriam

INTRODUCTION

IN this book on the contribution of Wiley Blount Rutledge to American law and judicial history, "the Bright Constellation" is composed of the first eight amendments to the Constitution. If the term were applied, as it could be no less appropriately, to members of the Supreme Court who have gleamed as stars of the first magnitude, Justice Rutledge assuredly would find a place among them. Great services do not depend on long tenure. But the thought of being classed among the great never would have occurred to him. Among the felicitations he received after the Senate confirmed him as Associate Justice was a note from a colleague bidding him "welcome to the fellowship of Holmes, Brandeis and Cardozo." In his acknowledgment of it he said he had no aspiration to be ranked with that high fellowship, but would be well content with the pleasant associations that lay ahead. If there was just a hint in this reply that the fellowship had already been made too inclusive, it was no more than saying that appointment to the nation's highest tribunal did not turn men into supermen.

As a wearer of judicial robes Wiley Rutledge was exactly what he had been before—a man who held himself on an exact level with humanity in general without thinking about the fact that he was doing so. Nobody realized this better than the employes of the Supreme Court, from GS-4 to the top of the salary scale. Every floor swabber, every elevator operator, every messenger, every court policeman, every librarian who worked in the "marble palace" from 1943 to 1949 will carry the memory of Justice Rutledge in his heart for the rest of his life. Just as an experiment I asked an elevator operator some weeks ago, "Were you here when Rutledge was on the Court?" His face (a black one) lit up: "Oh, there was a fine man. Did you know him? The finest man I ever knew."

The same question put to a court policeman from the Deep South brought the same reaction. What stood out in his recollection was Rutledge's refusal to be treated as an Associate Justice, but only as an associate, when they were in casual contact. "I remember," he said, "that on one awfully hot day I was resting in a chair outside the north door when Justice Rutledge came out. I stood up and he said, 'Sit down, I've been sitting on my rump all day and just came out to have a smoke.' So he stood and I sat, and we had the kind of talk we always had, just the kind I have with any friend." Rules governing the Supreme Court police, it may be worth noting, require them to stand when any person—not just a member of the Court—comes up to speak to them when they are on duty.

I mentioned these incidents to the veteran holder of a higher position on the Supreme Court staff. "I've known them all for thirty years," he said. "There have been a lot of fine men, but never another one like Rutledge. Once in a while a judge comes on who is all wapsy with the staff for thirty days and that's an end of it. But Rutledge was the same the last day he was here as the day he came. Everything he believed in, he was."

One of today's staff members grew up in the Court. He was a page boy when Justice Rutledge was appointed, and his work gave him a more varied contact with the judges than some high officers of the Court would have had. Whenever a lawyer newly admitted to the federal bar was to argue his first case, he was likely to be nervous and almost always was given pointers on the probable attitude of the justices. The former page repeated the advice he had heard given over and again in the barristers' room:

> Justice Frankfurter likes to needle new lawyers. He will ask questions to catch you up. Don't let that worry you. Do the best you can and go on with your argument. But when Justice Rutledge asks a question, pay close attention. Answer him and answer him straight.

This young page was stationed during court sessions to carry messages for members sitting to the left of the Chief Justice. This put him close to the chair of Justice Rutledge and gave him an opportunity to observe his treatment of lawyers. "He put his questions in a quiet, considerate manner," as the former page recalled it, "and almost never came down hard on a lawyer, but when he did it was something to watch." One such occurrence he would never forget:

"Justice Rutledge asked the lawyer a question and got a round-about answer that didn't mean anything. The lawyer turned back to his notes and said, 'And now as I was saying,' and he went on while Rutledge leaned back in his chair. When the lawyer got through with his first sentence Rutledge said quietly, 'Perhaps I should have worded my question differently.' He then repeated the question in a new form. The lawyer passed it off as before with some meaningless evasion and went back to his argument. He just got far enough to repeat, 'As I was saying,' when Rutledge leaned forward, pointed a finger at the lawyer and said, 'I asked you a question. I want an answer to it, and I want it now.' He got the answer."

Wiley loved to talk with young Court employes, to draw them out about their activities and attitudes. He related with relish, one day, his conversation with a Negro messenger who was "moonlighting" as a taxi driver. After a discussion of that with its demands on evening hours, their talk got around to recreation, including gambling. "Do you shoot craps?" asked the Justice. "I used to," replied the young man. "Why did you quit?" "Well," said the youth, "I got to thinking about it, and I concluded that if I won enough money to be worth winning, I'd never get home with it."

Things like this may seem to play small part in the qualifications of a Justice of the Supreme Court, but in the case of Wiley Rutledge they were fundamental to his outlook on life. In 1938, when he was under close consideration for appointment to succeed Justice Cardozo, his photograph was the nearest approach to personal acquaintance on the part of anybody at the White House. Professor Harper quotes my comment to Wiley, after his nomination to the Supreme Court four years later, that one of the President's aides said this photo "was what sold me on that fellow." I did not pass along to Wiley the comment made by the President's aide when he first looked at the photograph: "This is the kind of man we need on the Court. He has bulldog strength and is a human being." A dozen years of close association could not have produced a truer appraisal.

It has commonly been assumed that the approval Dean Rutledge gave to the President's court-enlargement bill in 1937 contributed heavily to his nomination to the Supreme Court. Certainly if he had been active on the other side that would have eliminated any possibility of it. But it was in February 1936, a year before Congress was asked to enlarge the Court, that President Roosevelt asked me to prepare a dossier on Rutledge for possible appointment to it. And almost three years passed before Wiley had the slightest inkling that he was being considered for the judicial post.

It may be worth while to relate how Rutledge's attitude toward the court bill came into the picture. In the spring of 1937, in St. Louis, I received a call from the White House requesting me to telephone to Dean Rutledge at Iowa City, where he had gone a year earlier to head the University of Iowa's law school, and ask him whether he would be willing, should the need develop, to testify in support of the court bill. Though disliking the chosen plan of reform, he had already approved the measure as a necessity, in informal talks before service clubs. His answer was that he would appear before the Senate committee if asked to do so. He considered the country's situation so critical that it overrode all other considerations. Some weeks later came the great about-face of the Court's swing men, Chief

Justice Hughes and Justice Roberts, resulting in the validation of New Deal legislation. That ended the hearings. Dean Rutledge expressed deep disappointment to me that the President did not drop the bill at this point. The fight, he said, was won.

From first to last, Dean Rutledge's attitude toward the court bill bespoke his courage, independence and irreverence toward artificially exalted human institutions. His basic position on the bill was about the same as my own, that it was a faulty approach to an imperative reform, and once proposed, could not be abandoned until the objective was achieved. But when he took a public stand in support of it, he was doing so in a section of the country which, in spite of a recent political swing to the Democratic party, was ultra-conservative in every other way, especially in professional and business ranks. In the past, fear of financial reprisals in the Iowa legislature had carried a feeling of restraint into academic circles. Entering upon his duties as dean of law, Wiley Rutledge did not hesitate to make public speeches in support of the New Deal. Faculty colleagues waited for something to happen, and nothing did. "His coming," the head of the history department (Professor Root) told me afterward, "was like a fresh wind sweeping through." Inhibitions left over from a former university administration vanished. But to speak in favor of the court bill, in the state of Iowa—that was challenging the whole commonwealth. No curb was laid on the dean, but he got the feeling of repression in the atmosphere. This is what he wrote about restrictive tendencies on January 30, 1939:

> I made up my mind to do what I could to break down that attitude. The court bill gave me my chance—one of course in which I could act honestly, because I then believed the Constitution would be set in irrefragable mold, if something were not done and done quickly. I did not like the apparent reasons given as arguments for the bill, but I understood its real purpose from the beginning and approved that. I did not myself realize how violent would be the reaction against the statement of my position.

It was a statewide reaction that was at its height when the inquiry was relayed from the White House, asking whether he would testify for the bill if invited to do so. He answered "yes," knowing that the tumult would be doubled if he did testify. A period followed in which the good people of Iowa looked upon Rutledge as an odd bird; a fine fellow presonally, a splendid law dean, but having ideas that, well, that people of the Hawkeye State just didn't have. (I am an Iowan.) Then came the news, in November 1938, that Rutledge was a possible appointee to the Supreme Court. His stock shot up like a suddenly discovered blue chip on Wall Street. Why, he wrote to me, "I can make a near New Deal speech now *before bar associations* without being run out of town." And he added, in this letter written after the appointment of Frankfurter appeared to end his judicial prospects:

> Now I do not regard a person as any different because of the fact he has been "mentioned" for the Supreme Court. He's just what he was before and no more. But some people, poor souls, do. The appearance of success or distinction takes the place of real qualities of character and ability with many people, and unfortunately some of these are people who count. So great is the reverence of some people for the Court, that any one whose name has been even remotely associated with it, acquires a weight and a dignity he could not achieve otherwise, however great an ass he may be in reality.

Professor Harper tells in detail the story of Rutledge's appointment to the United States Court of Appeals of the District of Columbia in 1939 and his elevation to the Supreme Court in 1943. To that let me add a footnote. When Dean Rutledge learned late in 1938 that Senator Gillette of Iowa had formally recommended him to the President to succeed Justice Cardozo, he wrote to the Senator and asked him to go to the White House and withdraw his name. He was unwilling to be placed in a position that would militate against the appointment of Felix Frankfurter, who deserved the place because of his legal qualifications and public services. The place did go to Frankfurter, the decisive factor being the advice of Senator George Norris of Nebraska to the President to forget all about choosing a man from west of the Mississippi. When a subsequent vacancy (not the next one) brought Rutledge once more into the forefront of possible appointees, I talked about his qualifications with Senator Norris and told of his refusal to be considered for the position when his appointment would prevent that of Frankfurter. "That is enough for me," said Norris. "A man who will do that is the man for the place." And he wrote at once to the President urging the nomination of Rutledge.

A great deal happened between those two actions by the Nebraska liberal. Two weeks after Frankfurter was sworn in, Justice Brandeis resigned, and the choice of a successor lay chiefly between William O. Douglas and Wiley B. Rutledge. The former was named to the Supreme Court, the latter to the most important Court of Appeals in the country. Following these simultaneous nominations, the strongest White House backer of Douglas told me that after the consecutive appointments of two professors of law it would be impossible to nominate a third justice directly from a law school. (There were protests against Yale-man Douglas on that account, as it was.) The naming of Rutledge to the Court of Appeals, this presidential aide predicted, would lead to the Supreme Court. After a few years on the appellate bench, Rutledge could be presented not as a law dean but as a judge with a proven record of merit. And so it turned out, with abundant evidence of fitness to support the action.

During three years in the United States Court of Appeals, Judge Rutledge had ample opportunity to discover that his advance to the Supreme Court would not produce the expected degree of unity with Justice Frankfurter. The two men had basically different approaches to judicial review, especially in the realm of constitutional law. Justice Frankfurter was an ardent and volubly proclaimed advocate of judicial self-restraint. The Court should defer to the judgment of the co-ordinate branches of the federal government and to state courts and legislatures, unless what they did was so shocking to the fundamental sense of justice, so contrary to long-established "canons of decency," that it must on that account be overruled. Thus the meaning of the Constitution, in matters affecting rights and liberties, depended less on the wording of that document than on how easily five members of the Supreme Court could be shocked. Fitting closely into this concept was the rule of *stare decisis*—i.e., adherence to previous decisions. The rule of *stare decisis* is one which all English and American judges follow in substantial measure, and which they must follow if the law is to maintain integrity and continuity. But some Justices—Justice Frankfurter among them—have tended to place greater emphasis on the rule than others. And too close a devotion to the rule of *stare decisis*—especially in the realm of constitutional law—can result in judicial perpetuation of unjust and unwise doctrines for no better reason than that an earlier Court erred years or decades ago.

I once asked Justice Rutledge how he approached the job of deciding a case. His reply suggested a judicial method quite unlike that of Justice Frankfurter. The law, said Justice Rutledge, seldom presented a single clearly marked and unmistakable channel. When the opposing briefs of litigants came before him, he studied them to determine if possible on which side justice lay. If that was clear, he searched the law for a legitimate means of rendering justice. It was usually possible, he said, to find a route that satisfied both the requirements of the case and sound principles of law. A route that never failed was the Bill of Rights, faithfully upheld.

In the application of these policies to human rights, Justice Frankfurter best pleased the supporters of those rights when he deviated from his own rule, which he did with moderate frequency. The result was to make "canons of decency" look less like a genuine test of "due process of law" than a process under which decisions resulting in injustice won the plaudits of the legal profession for the manner in which they were reached. The system followed by Justice Rutledge made law and justice coincide in almost 100 per cent of the cases, although more often than not he had to express his opinion in dissent. When it was also the opinion of a majority of the Court, the right thus obtained for the individual was carried on into the future, to the benefit of all.

With two such thorough legal scholars on the Court, and with so extreme a divergency in their ways of thinking, it was inevitable that they should come to grips in the conference chamber whenever they were divided and the decision hung in the balance. Justice Frankfurter was a master of the fine art of ratiocination, and could build a high edifice to support his argument. Justice Rutledge, devoting similar resources to plainer ends, had a talent for thrusting a hand into the Frankfurter edifice and pulling out the principal supporting timber. This frequently raised quite a cloud of dust. Not often, perhaps, did it determine the outcome of a case, but the nature and extent of it can be measured wherever their views were carried into separate opposing opinions. Much of that will be found in the pages of Fowler Harper's book.

One result hoped for by some from the Rutledge appointment did not materialize. That was the establishment of a bond between him and Chief Justice Stone that might possibly help to draw the Chief Justice back toward the liberalism (though he always objected to its being called that) from which he seemed to have been deviating in the previous two or three years. Stone contributed to the appointment of Rutledge at least to the extent of making it perfectly clear that it would please him, but he was not given to advocacy. Twice to my knowledge he used all his efforts, through indirect channels, to prevent appointments that were much talked about and which if made would have given the Court a strong push in the pro-corporation direction or to a lower level of competency. Yet in the very act of telling me that he would welcome the appointment of Rutledge he said that he regretted the resignation of Justice Byrnes, who did not differ markedly in his views from one of the men whose possible appointment had worried Stone a few years earlier. Byrnes, he said, had been on the Court too short a time to be thoroughly broken in to the work, "but if he had stayed I think he would have proved a valuable member. Of course," he added, "he was rather conservative."

Coming from one who was himself moving in that direction, both in economics and in his legal philosophy, this was indeed an enlightening remark. Between Chief Justice Stone and Justice Rutledge there was the utmost cordiality and mutual regard. But the Chief Justice, as was evident both in his court opinions and in conversation, was feeling the traumatic effects of the sitdown strikes in the automobile industry. After they began, and were brought before the Supreme Court, Harlan Fiske Stone never was the same person he had been when he so vigorously affirmed the power of the federal government to engage in economic experiments to cope with the great depression of the 1930s. During the first five years of the Roosevelt presidency Stone's great fear was that the Supreme Court would paralyze the power of the government to deal with the problems before it. This might convert the economic crisis into one endangering the government and the whole society. The sitdown strikes produced an apprehension of similar results, but altered the source and reversed the direction from which the hazard was to come. However great or small that danger may have been, it vanished with the disappearance of the assembly-line conditions that produced the sitdowns—conditions that never reached the press or the Court. But that change did not take place within the lifetimes of Stone and Rutledge.

Professor Harper tells the story of one bit of teamwork between Chief Justice Stone and Justice Rutledge immediately after Wiley came upon the high Court. Two cases involving freedom of conscience had lately been decided against the freedom claimed, with the Chief Justice leading the four dissenters. These cases were set for reargument and went five to four the other way, Rutledge's vote making the difference. If this had involved a major question of national policy, and if an appointment to the Court had been made for the specific purpose of reversing the decisions, it might have produced a shock like the one that attended the reversal of the Legal Tender decisions in 1871. But in this instance it was a mere matter of correcting a false step while one foot was still in the air.

Justice Rutledge had a very keen awareness of the need to protect the Court from this particular variety of shock to its standing with the public. That occupied first place in his mind when (Justice Jackson being in Nuremberg and Chief Justice Stone having died) seven members of the Court were called upon to decide whether the malapportionment of population in congressional districts violated various provisions of the Constitution. Aside from Rutledge the Court was divided three to three. Roberts, Reed and Frankfurter regarded it as a political question that should not be decided by the Court. Black, Douglas and Murphy wanted to declare such lopsidedness unconstitutional.

Rutledge joined the first three, thus making a court, but did not accept Frankfurter's opinion. He wrote in concurrence that a decision on the constitutional question should be avoided, particularly because the shortness of time before the Illinois election made it doubtful whether the petitioners could receive the benefit they wanted from a decision favorable to them. Justice Rutledge told me that if the question had come before the full Court, he would have stood with Justices Black, Douglas and Murphy in declaring malapportionment to be a violation of the constitutional right of equal representation. But he was unwilling to have so grave a decision made by a majority that was a minority of the whole Court. His apprehension was that when a nine-man Court was restored, it might order the case reargued and reverse the decision. Such an occurrence, he thought, would inflict a deep wound upon the Court. That can be called the understatement of the century, judging from the furore that developed in Congress when the decision then sidestepped was made in 1964 by a clear majority of the Court.

Justice Rutledge produced something of a furore against himself, though tempered with the approval of a gratifying number of law journals, legal writers, newspaper editors and public men, when he and Justice Murphy dissented from the condemnation of Japanese General Yamashita to death by an American military commission. This commission, as Professor Harper makes clear, violated almost every element of due process of law involved in the case except the right to counsel. The story of the Rutledge dissent in that case, as presented in this book, should be read and reread a dozen times. It is a story not only of General Yamashita and the commission, but of Rutledge himself, the Court, the American people, and humanity. But this much can be hoped for. If that unconstitutional condemnation threw the "Bright Constellation" into obscurity, the revelation of the truth about it may serve to double the brilliance of those re-emerging stars.

Fowler Harper has done far more than present a record of Wiley Rutledge's work upon the Supreme Court. He has told the story of the Court itself during six years of kaleidoscopic change in the status of human rights, both for the better and for the worse. He brings into view the greatness and the frailties of judges, and makes it clear above all that they are men, faithfully performing their duty as they see it, but with different ideas of how that duty is to be performed. They are men of good will who struggle with the problems before them and in varying degrees gain wisdom and insight from the struggle.

This book reaches back to give historical perspective to the period of Justice Rutledge's service. It carries the story forward to the present day, when many of the positions taken by him in dissent have become the law of the land. The great cases recounted are not mere italicized names divided by the letter "v." The story is told in human terms, of rights upheld and rights denied, of men to whom writs of *certiorari* marked the road to life or death, and of the judges who decided which way they should go upon that road. Of the four members who worked so closely together in the 1940s—Justices Black, Douglas, Murphy and Rutledge—only the two who came first upon the Court remained to win and witness the belated acceptance of so much that all of them stood for. In spirit and moral effect the alliance never was broken.

In 1939, after the clearing up of the uncertainties that attended the offer of a place on the Court of Appeals, Wiley Rutledge wrote to a friend: "I'd have given a half dozen years from the end of my life to have your opinion." Had those years been so given, it would have left just four months of his life span for active work upon the Supreme Court. In those last half dozen years which seemed so distant when he wrote, he did the work of a lifetime. The record of it will not perish as long as the Bright Constellation continues to shine in the American sky.

Irving Brant

ACKNOWLEDGMENTS

I am in the debt of a number of persons for assistance in the writing of this book. First are the Justice's widow, Annabel, his son, Neal and his two daughters, Mary Louise and Jean Ann. They made available to me the Justice's papers and files which had been stored in the Supreme Court building from the time of his death until the fall of 1961. The Justice's halfbrother, Dwight Rutledge, and Mrs. Frank Smith of Cloverport also contributed information about the family. I am especially grateful to Irving Brant for access to his correspondence with and about the Justice in regard to his appointment to the Court of Appeals and to the Supreme Court.

Next is Francis X. Dineen, a graduate of the Yale Law School who acted as my research assistant. I do not know how I could have produced this volume without his exacting and uncompromising scholarship. I should also mention Gary Weatherford, a Yale law student and Laurie Pouzzner McManus, a Sarah Lawrence student, for research help; Louise Montanaro who patiently typed and retyped the manuscript; and Nathaniel Gozansky, a Yale law graduate student and his wife, Esther, for other necessary editorial assistance. As always, my wife, Miriam, was most helpful with her critical judgment and constant encouragement.

Last, but by no means least, I am indebted to the Louis Rabinowitz Foundation for making this project possible by its generous financial contribution; and, of course, to the Yale Law School for its liberal policy in encouraging scholarly writing.

Fowler V. Harper

A JUSTICE IN THE GREAT TRADITION

Cartoon by Fitzpatrick, reproduced by permission of the St. Louis Post-Dispatch
© *1949.*

JUSTICE RUTLEDGE

and

The Bright Constellation

EPITAPH

ON September 10, 1949, President Franklin D. Roosevelt's eighth and last appointee to the Supreme Court of the United States died after a brief illness at a hospital in Maine. He was fifty-five years old. The death of Justice Wiley B. Rutledge of a cerebral hemorrhage came within a few weeks after the death of Justice Frank Murphy.

Rutledge and Murphy had for a half dozen years been closely associated in controversial civil rights cases with Justices Black and Douglas, frequently in dissent, sometimes a majority when one or more of the other Justices joined with them.

The death of these two Justices did indeed mark the end of an era in American constitutional history. "Where," asked Irving Dilliard, a close observer of the Court, "will President Truman find another Murphy and Rutledge?" Where indeed!

At the first session of the fall term after their death, Chief Justice Vinson in his memorial remarks concluded: "Saddened by our losses, but inspired by their examples of devotion to duty which Mr. Justice Murphy and Mr. Justice Rutledge have provided . . . , we turn to the work before us." Of this, John Frank has ironically observed, "Within six weeks the country knew that the 'work before us' consisted in large part of rejecting the civil-rights views of the late Justices."

Early in his adult years Wiley Rutledge chose the life of the professor and scholar. He so lived until he accepted the lonely lot of the judge. His death terminated a brief but amazing tenure on the Supreme Court. Perhaps, because of the short span of his service, his great contributions to constitutional law have not been generally recognized. Had he lived, he would already have seen, as did a great dissenter of a previous generation, many of his minority views accepted as the law of the land. History is writing Wiley Rutledge into the slender volume of "Justices in the Great Tradition."

TABLE OF CONTENTS

ILLUSTRATIONS

". . . freedom of religion; freedom of the press; freedom of the person under the protection of the habeas corpus; and trial by juries impartially selected —these principles form the bright constellation which has gone before us, and guided our steps. . . ."

Thomas Jefferson
First Inaugural Address

ACROSS THE OHIO RIVER FROM CLOVERPORT

CHAPTER I

THE BOY AND THE MAN

The Early Years

IN Breckenridge County, Kentucky, on the south bank of the Ohio River is a picturesque little village of less than fifteen hundred souls, including men, women and children. It was first settled in 1804 when the country in that area was a vast wilderness. It was formerly called Joeville, presumably for some reason, but the flatboat rivermen renamed it Cloverport because of the extensive patches of clover that grew along the banks of the river. Also nearby, in the distant past, some gigantic convulsion of nature had thrown up hundreds of acres of earth in which were buried thousands of tons of cannel coal. It was here that the first coal oil was produced in 1851. A few years later this fuel was manufactured commercially for home use.

Cloverport claims that it was there that Thomas Lincoln, his wife Nancy Hanks Lincoln, their daughter Sarah and seven year old son, Abraham, were ferried across the river on a log raft to Indiana by Jacob Weatherholt. Whether or not this claim is valid, there is no doubt that in the summer of 1894 a son, who was later to sit on the Supreme Court of the United States, was born to a Baptist clergyman and his wife in Cloverport.

His father, Wiley B. Rutledge, Sr., was born and reared on a farm in western Tennessee. He attended the schools in that locality and eventually went to the Baptist Theological Seminary in Louisville, Kentucky.

The Justice's grandfather, Thomas, or perhaps his Scotch-Irish great-grandfather, Jackson Rutledge, had moved from North Carolina and settled in the Sequachie Valley in eastern Tennessee where Thomas worked at his trade as a cooper. Thomas was twice married and had nine children by each marriage. Wiley, Sr., the youngest of the eighteen, was born in 1861 and died eighty-three years later. Little is known of the early Rutledges and information about the family

1

largely begins with the Justice's father. Whether the Tennessee and the distinguished South Carolina Rutledges were of the same family is not known but is a natural matter for speculation. Two Rutledge brothers, Edward and John, were conspicuous in public affairs before the birth of the nation and for the first few years of its life. Both were lawyers. Edward was Governor of South Carolina and John was twice nominated for the Supreme Court of the United States by President Washington. He was appointed Associate Justice on the first Court in 1790. Although he served on circuit, as Supreme Court Justices did in those days, he never attended a session of the Court. He resigned to accept the office of Chief Justice of his state supreme court, a position then regarded as of greater distinction, and with less arduous duties. When Chief Justice Jay was elected Governor of New York, the President again turned to John Rutledge and nominated him as Chief Justice. It was a recess appointment and Rutledge took his seat. When the Senate next met, Washington again nominated Rutledge, but he was never confirmed. He had attacked the treaty with Great Britain which Chief Justice Jay had negotiated, with the result that, in spite of his professional reputation, the northern Federalists were able to bring about his rejection. The position eventually went to Oliver Ellsworth of Connecticut.[1] It was the opinion of Wiley, Jr. that he probably was neither a descendant of John Rutledge nor collaterally related to him.

Of his mother's side much more is known. Mary Louise Wigginton, born July 16, 1870, was one of four children born to George Washington Wigginton and Georgia Lovell. The latter was the daughter of Robert Lovell and Susan Dale. She had had a prior marriage to a man named Finley but apparently no issue had been born of that union. George Washington also had been previously married to Ann Marie Birkhead who died in 1864 after giving birth to nine children. He had originally lived on a farm near Plum Creek and later moved to Mt. Washington.

The Lovells came from Virginia. Georgia's father, Robert, hauled oysters from Virginia as far as Kentucky to be sold there as a great luxury. Whether or not it was the reason for his moving, his wife Susan was born and living in Kentucky when they married. They had four children, Mary Louise being the third.

The Wigginton family can be directly traced back to Elijah, born in 1778 in Stafford County, Virginia, near the courthouse. He died on his farm on Simpson Creek, Spencer County, Kentucky, in 1855. He had married in 1801 to Ann Riley who died a year after Elijah's death. Both are buried under the same stone in the Little Union Churchyard. Elijah was called Squire Wigginton, wore knee britches and silver buckles, carried a riding whip, and was followed by his dogs. At first he lived in a stone house in front of the church. Later he owned a large frame house with a two-story veranda beside the church. He owned many slaves whose births and deaths were recorded in the family Bible. This, with the names and birth dates of his children, was buried in the bottom drawer of his desk in the possession of his great-granddaughter, Marguerite McAffee. In 1807 the tax book showed that he owned 160 acres of land. In 1861, before the outbreak of the war, his real property was valued at $14,000 which was considerable wealth at that time.

Elijah was descended from William Wigginton who came to Manhattan in 1654. He migrated to Virginia the following year and settled in Westmoreland County which, at the time included Stafford, Prince William and several other counties. Some years later he received a land grant in Stafford County bordering Aequia Creek in Overwharton Parish. A farm, still known as Wigginton Farm is located near the Yeon Pico Bay church in Cople Parish. The church records were burned but the name appears in the early seventeen hundreds in Westmoreland and it is probable that some parts of the family lived both there and in Stafford. William's son, Roger, later lived in Fairfax County. It was a grandson, Elijah, who followed the Ohio River to Kentucky and settled in Spencer County. And it was Elijah's son, George Washington Wigginton, born in 1822, who married Georgia Lovell, Wiley's devoted grandmother, after the death of his first wife.

Several of the Wiggintons still live in northern Kentucky. When Wiley Rutledge was first widely reported as being under consideration for Supreme Court appointment in 1939, the *Louisville Courier-Journal* published a feature story in its issue for Sunday, March the 5th. The reporter had been able to interview several of the members of the Wigginton family, but was unable to obtain precise information even of the exact place of Wiley's birth. The best guess from relatives indicates a small cottage called Tar Springs in Cloverport. He was, however, able to find a maternal uncle who dug up a picture of Wiley, his baby sister and their parents, and one of the family standing in front of the parsonage in Cloverport. He found the pictures in a small trunk in the hayloft of the barn. "I been meaning to get at these pictures for some while," Farmer Wigginton said, "ever since Wiley was through here last summer, when there was so much hay I couldn't get at the trunk." He told of the maternal grandmother's devotion to the children, how she would travel by carriage and horses from Mt. Washington to Cloverport (a two-day journey) to see them. On the death of their mother, she took them into her own home in Mt. Washington where they had several of their first years in a one-room schoolhouse. He also recalled how the aunts and uncles doted on the motherless children and particularly Aunt Cora's remark about Wiley that, "If that boy lives long enough, he will be President of the United States some day." Mr. Wigginton reflected on how pleased Aunt Cora would be "to hear about Wiley now." "If he gets to the Supreme Court," he said, "that will be pretty near as good as being President."

It seems that the village of Mt. Washington was the first pastorate served by the senior Rutledge. It was close to Louisville and he preached there while attending the seminary. It was in Mt. Washington that he met and successfully courted Mary Wigginton. Shortly after their marriage, the couple moved to Cloverport, some forty miles west of Louisville where the Reverend Rutledge preached and rode circuit. When Wiley was three years old his sister Margaret was born. Margaret never married and died at the age of thirty-nine after a prolonged illness. Mary Louise Wigginton Rutledge died in Cloverport in 1903 when Wiley was nine years old and his sister six. Some years later, Preacher Rutledge married Miss Tamsey Cate of Cleveland, Tennessee, who was twenty years younger than her husband. Three children were born to this union, Ivan in 1915, while his father was a minister at White Pines, Kentucky; Dwight in 1919 at Bearden, Tennessee, a small village near Knoxville. A sister was born and died between the births of the two boys. Ivan Rutledge is at present a professor of law at Ohio State University in Columbus, Ohio, while Dwight lives in New Haven, Connecticut, and is associated with the Pratt-Whitney Engineering Company in North Haven.

The elder Rutledge, it appears, was a typical product of his times and environment. He was, from all accounts, a dedicated clergyman with a complete and uncomplicated doctrinaire belief in his religion. He had the confidence of the fundamentalist in the literal infallibility of the Scriptures. He had the simple faith that moved William Jennings Bryan during the Scopes trial in Dayton so fanatically to attack the heresy of the young school teacher who professed a belief in the evolutionary process of life on the earth. As was to be expected, he shared the views of many of his Protestant clerical colleagues concerning a certain religious creed differing from their own. He is quoted by one of his sons as declaring that "he would vote for the blackest man in Africa before voting for Al Smith." Of his sincerity, however, and dedication to his faith there can be little doubt. His sense of humor also helped to endear him to those who knew him. He commanded tremendous respect and affection from his parishioners and neighbors as well as from his sons.

The local weekly newspaper in January of some year while the Reverend Rutledge was living in Cloverport, but before Wiley, Jr. was born, carried the following notice:

> On Thursday evening Jan. 7th., an exciting "storm" struck the parsonage of the Cloverport Baptist Church, and came dangerously near producing a panic among the inmates.
>
> Where the cloud came from was difficult to discern, as the pastor and his wife were totally unconscious of its approach until it struck the house with such tremendous force, as to capsize the best judgment of the whole family except the mother-in-law, who is always prepared for the best. She, too, might have taken fright if she had not fired a bale of paper and sent it whizzing up the chimney, illuminating the earth beneath and the heavens above until she could see the gathering tempest.
>
> The cloud burst in copious showers filling the kitchen and dining-room with the most delicious fruits, meats, flour, sugar, coffee, sweet spices and other groceries, dry goods and kitchenware.
>
> The delightful refreshments, that were served without regard to the wishes or directions of the pastor or his wife, were by no means the least enjoyable feature of this eventful evening.
>
> It is not always pleasant for a family to be compelled to surrender home with all its privileges, but for once the people took possession of the parsonage, and the shepherd became submissive to the will of the sheep.
>
> May we be permitted to extend our sincerest thanks to all, not only of the Baptist church but to the Methodist church also for the enjoyment of the evening and for the many tokens of kindness and appreciation. May God abundantly bless you both in heart and in storehouse.
>
> W. B. RUTLEDGE and WIFE.

Another like letter appeared in the paper in December after Wiley was born:

> At about 7 o'clock on Monday night, Dec. 5th, a sudden drumming on the door of the new parsonage betokened the

presence of a large crowd of men, women and children, well laden with divers kinds of good things for the comfort of the pastor and his family. For five successive years have we been thus substantially remembered, and each time we think, "Well, we will not be surprised the next time they come." But the last was one of the greatest surprises we have ever had. These tokens of love and friendship make us feel like singing with Mr. Fawcett—

> Blest be the tie that binds
> Our hearts in Christian love,
> The fellowship of kindred minds
> Is like to that above.

We cannot express our gratitude in words, but shall ever remember with warm and tender affection those who love not in word only, but in deed and in truth. It makes us want to do more for the spiritual edification of those to whom we minister. May the Giver of every good and every perfect gift abundantly reward those cheerful givers.

W. B. RUTLEDGE and FAMILY.

Not to be outdone in writing grateful thanks for blessings received, the young son at the age of six months wrote to Santa Claus:

DEAR SANTA:—You were so very kind to me on Christmas morning as to bring me a nice suit of warm clothes, a pretty little red chair, some money and other nice trinkets.

Now, I must thank you for making my first Christmas in this world so very bright and happy.

I only wish I could have given some of the pleasure that you gave me to some of my brother babies that never heard of you and don't know there is any Santa Claus.

Mamma and papa want to thank you for the many good things you brought them also. They say this is the second time you have overwhelmed them with showers of blessings for which they are not able to express their gratitude but will, in their feeble way, try to do you good.

Wishing you, dear Santa, a happy New Year, I am your devoted little friedd [sic],

BABY RUTLEDGE.

On Preacher Rutledge's departure from Cloverport, the weekly *Breckenridge News* for April 20, 1901, reported the fact with the following comment which indicates how the community regarded him:

> Rev. Rutledge has always been ready and willing to tender his services toward the advancement of the town's welfare and the cause of Christianity. His leaving is a sad blow to many as he has formed the friendship and love of nearly each inhabitant of this town. He was not an idle man but a man whose labors were constant. Rev. Rutledge delivered his farewell sermon Wednesday night. A large membership of the church as well as non-members turned out to hear his discourse. Half the audience was in tears as his departure came to them as a realization.

The reason for departure from Cloverport was to look for a healthier climate for Wiley's mother who had contracted tuberculosis. They visited in Texas and Louisiana but finally moved to Asheville, North Carolina, where Wiley, Sr. accepted a pastorate. They remained there until sometime in 1903 when Mary Wigginton Rutledge died. The family then returned to Kentucky and buried the wife and mother in Mt. Washington, her old home. Reverend Rutledge held pastorates in Pikesville and perhaps other communities in the state before moving to Maryville when Wiley was of high school age. Wiley in 1910 entered the preparatory school of small Maryville College and two years later the college division where he met and fell in love with his Greek teacher whom he married in 1917.

From all accounts, Wiley was a typical high school and college boy participating in athletics and extracurricular activities in no way different from that of his fellow students. He was a member of the Athenian Literary Society and was reputed to be the best student speaker on the campus. He was captain of the college debating team which he was said to have led to a number of victories in intercollegiate contests. His hobbies were hiking through woods and trout fishing, a sport which he enjoyed all his life. Maryville President Lloyd in his citation for an honorary degree conferred on Rutledge in 1945 recalls a class football game in which Wiley made a "flying tackle" for his team in the middle of the field, a play which made him an outstanding star. He also recalled a three-way debate during the presidential campaign of 1912. Wiley was for Wilson, he (Lloyd) for Teddy Roosevelt and another for Taft. All claimed victory, "but the election in November indicated that Rutledge had influenced the nation most widely."

Tobacco and liquor, of course, were out of bounds in the Rutledge household and although drinking was not prevalent among his schoolmates, the use of tobacco was apparently not uncommon. There is evidence that Wiley took up smoking and that he indulged clandestinely from time to time in the manly habit of chewing tobacco.

He was also reported to have enjoyed a practical joke as much as anyone else. There is a story that on one occasion he invited a classmate to spend the Christmas vacation with him at his home in Knoxville. Of course, he had no home in Knoxville. His friend, however, did not know that he lived in Maryville where his father was a clergyman. After the last class the two boys took the train to the capital city thirty miles away. On arrival Wiley managed to leave his empty suitcase in the station while they climbed into a horse-drawn hack to go to his "home." Wiley directed the driver to a fashionable and wealthy suburb where they drove in the curved driveway to the front door of one of the finest homes in the city. At that point Wiley recalled that he had forgotten his suitcase at the station. "You get out," he said to his friend, "and go right on into the house. My mother and father are expecting us. Just tell them that I drove back to the station to pick up my suitcase. I'll be back in a few minutes." He then returned to the station, paid the hack driver and took the next train back to Maryville. This, of course, was a typical college boy's sense of humor. But Wiley Rutledge enjoyed a good joke to the end of his life.

It was during Wiley's sophomore college year that he had the young and attractive Annabel Person as his professor of Greek. She was fresh from college where she had majored in the classics. She had even begun the study of Greek in high school. Being much farther advanced than her classmates, she received what practically amounted to private tutoring from Dr. Oliphant who recommended her for teaching positions in several colleges. Maryville appealed to her, as a small co-educational college. She lived in a rooming house in the town but took her meals at the girl's dormitory. Young single teachers seldom "dated" with students, but through the importunities on his behalf by a male faculty friend and his own perseverance, Wiley managed to "keep company" with Annabel until the end of his junior year when he transferred to the University of Wisconsin— but not until the young professor had promised to become his wife.

The Person (sometimes called Pearson) family were also early settlers in this country. Annabel Person Rutledge is of the tenth generation, the youngest of four children. A sister, thirteen years her senior, was a kindergarten teacher. One brother was accidentally killed by a discharge of his own rifle when Annabel was ten years old. A second brother lived in Lansing, Michigan. He was a lawyer and former Republican Congressman from that state. It was he who was largely responsible for his sister's serious study of the ancient languages. She attended Olivet College fifty miles from the farm on which she was born. It was there that she met and studied Greek under Dr. Oliphant who became a life-long friend and influence in her life.

On Annabel's mother's side, Edward Howe, born in England, settled in Lynn, Massachusetts, in 1635. He and his wife, Elizabeth, were sixty years old when they arrived. Some years later the Howes moved to New Haven, Connecticut. Their descendants lived in various Connecticut and New York communities. Annabel's grandparents lived in western New York where her mother, Martha Ann Howe, was born. When Martha was three or four years old, the family moved to Howell, Michigan.

The earliest Pearson to come to the New World was John from Yorkshire, England. He arrived in Lynn, Massachusetts, in 1637 but moved to what became Reading, Massachusetts, two years later. He was one of the founders of the town. Annabel's great-grandfather moved to Iosco Township, Michigan, in 1863. Her paternal grandmother, Lucinda Stafford, also came from an old New England family which settled there about 1680, later moving to Michigan.

Annabel's uncle, her father's only brother, sat on the Supreme Court of Michigan for a number of years and at least several of her forebears were clergymen. Cornelius Gray Pearson was an early Universalist minister and the name "Cornelius" appears in every generation of Pearsons. "Neal" Pearson Rutledge, the Justice's and Annabel's only son, continues the name in contracted form in the present generation.

Wiley graduated from the University of Wisconsin in the summer of 1914. In the spring of that year his father had remarried and written that he could no longer help him financially with his education. This made it impossible for Wiley to attend the University of Wisconsin Law School as he had hoped to do. Having a good knowledge of shorthand, he decided to go to the home of an aunt in Bowling Green, Kentucky, for a few weeks to attend the business college there in order to brush up on shorthand so that he could teach it and earn money to help with his law course. He soon finished his "refresher" course and accepted a position in the Bloomington, Indiana, High School where, at the same time he could attend Indiana University

Law School. This, however, became overburdensome and the following year he gave up law school for full-time teaching of business subjects as well as coaching basketball in Connersville, Indiana. Annabel,
in the meantime, had left Maryville College and followed her Greek
professor, Dr. Oliphant, to Grove City College, a Presbyterian institution in Grove City, Pennsylvania. She remained there teaching
Greek until her marriage on August 28, 1917.

During the summer vacation in 1916, while visiting Annabel at
her home, Wiley contracted influenza. He became seriously ill and was
persuaded by Mrs. Person to go to Battle Creek for a checkup. There
it was discovered that he had incipient tuberculosis and needed a
long period of rest and care. On the advice of friends he went to the
North Carolina state sanitarium in Asheville. The medical director
had been his mother's physician and was the father-in-law of his good
friend, Dr. Paul McCain, who was also on the medical staff there.
At the hospital Wiley gradually improved. He was an excellent patient
and loved by all the staff. In August 1917 Annabel went to visit him.
He was then well along in his cure. While she was there, a telegram
arrived inviting him to teach business subjects in the high school in
Albuquerque, New Mexico. They decided to be married immediately.
Wiley's father performed the ceremony. Wiley at once left for the
West to take up his school work and find a place for them to live.
Annabel remained for a while with Wiley's sister Margaret, who was
also ill in a sanitarium in Asheville, and later, after returning home,
followed on to Albuquerque to start life as Wiley's wife at last.

Some of Rutledge's feelings about his illness are recalled by his
remarks, less than a year before his death, in a tribute to Dr. McCain
at the Asheville hospital:

> It was thirty-two years last July since I first came to this
> place and to Paul McCain's ministry. Then it was just well be-
> gun. I came fearfully, seriously stricken in body, downcast in
> mind and hope. Then, in the twenties, I learned that it is hard
> for the young especially with all of life before them to face
> slow death, worse perhaps to stand in dread of lingering illness
> and pain. . . . It was due largely to his [Dr. McCain's] in-
> fluence that "the San," as we called it then, became a place of
> cheerfulness, not of despondency . . . . I remember with what
> surprise I so shortly discovered this after being sentenced, as I
> had thought, by one of his friends, Dr. Pritchard of the Battle
> Creek Sanitarium, to a term of months, if not years or the
> remainder of my life, in an institution hardly less attractive
> than a prison. . . .

The Teacher

In Albuquerque the newlyweds rented a small house with only a coal stove to which the fuel had to be carried by hand. It was a rough year for the young couple, particularly as Wiley's health was still somewhat precarious. However, the altitude and dry air, plus loving care, helped him "over the hump" and he began to take on greater strength. With their meager savings they bought a piece of land on the outskirts of town, intending to build on it. But shortly thereafter, a brick and adobe furnished house close by the school was offered them in exchange for their land. They accepted and settled in, comfortably and happily. Here Wiley gradually regained his strength, and within a relatively short time, no longer needed to be concerned about his health.

After three years in Albuquerque, during which he not only taught classes but acted as Secretary to the Board of Education, Wiley was again ready to resume his study of law. He had never lost his interest and resolve to enter this field. Colorado attracted him largely by reason of its climate and in 1920 the couple decided to move to Boulder where Wiley could put full time into law study. In 1922 he finally obtained his law degree.

The years between Wisconsin and Colorado were not wasted years for Wiley's intellectual and emotional growth. Coming from the South, like his father he quite naturally had some of the prejudices of that region. Several incidents indicate changes. In Maryville Annabel had spoken of her laundress as "Mrs. A." Wiley corrected her, asserting that, as a Negro, she should be called by her first name. Annabel insisted that this would be improper, that it was discrimination and a product of the caste system in the South. (On Monday, March 31, 1964, the Supreme Court of the United States affirmed Annabel in a six to three decision when it reversed the conviction for contempt of an Alabama State court of a Negro woman who had refused to answer questions addressed to her as "Mary." She had insisted that the State prosecutor address her as "Miss Hamilton.")[2] Wiley soon recognized that this was right. Later at the Connersville High School, in a state north of the Ohio River but with a strong southern influence, he found the same practice but soon stopped it. And when he was the dean at Washington University in St. Louis, a meeting of law professors brought Negroes and Whites together. There was some excitement about the problem of eating. Rutledge quickly settled the matter with instructions to put the Negro teachers at his table. No doubt it was Annabel's attitude which influenced him initially, but it fell on fertile ground with her husband's ideas of democracy and individual dignity.

When Rutledge was widely rumored as a probable appointee to the Court in 1939, the *Des Moines Register* ran several editorials and feature articles about him. One front page Sunday edition story was in the form of a "letter" to President Roosevelt containing "a few tips about Iowa's Rutledge." "Let's go back a ways, first," the article went, "and see where Dean Rutledge came from." It then continued:

> About the time Peter Stuyvesant was storming and fuming at the King of England and your own ancestors were puffing their meerschaum pipes on the banks of the Hudson River, some Scotch-Irish settlers came over to this country. Because they were poor people they pushed back into the Appalachian mountains where at least they could live as free men. The descendants of these isolated mountain folk have stayed in the hills and have changed very little since colonial times. Dean Rutledge comes from those hillbillies in the mountains of Tennessee. . . . Talk about social evolution, why, Mr. President, Dean Rutledge of the State University of Iowa is a walking social evolution.

The writer then went on to describe the Rutledge home in Iowa City and noted a picture of Abraham Lincoln hanging on the wall. "Do you realize what that means," he asked the President, "a grandson of the old South, suh, with a picture of Abraham Lincoln hanging in the parlor? I told you Dean Rutledge was social evolution in the flesh."[3]

After graduation from the University of Colorado, Wiley practiced law in Boulder for two years. He and Annabel then planned to move to California where Wiley was to take up practice. Annabel had taken their young daughter, Mary Lou, back East so that she could "show her off" to her relatives in Howell, Michigan, when Wiley was offered a place on the faculty at the University of Colorado. Professor Bryant Smith was resigning to go to Washington University in St. Louis. Interestingly, two years later Wiley again took Smith's place at Washington University when the latter accepted a professorship at the University of Texas in Austin. The decision for Wiley to go into the academic profession was undoubtedly an important turning point in the career of the future Supreme Court Justice. In 1926 the Rutledges moved to St. Louis, but later often returned to their familiar and beloved haunts in Colorado as visiting professor of law.

Rutledge became Acting Dean at Washington University in 1930 and Dean in 1931. Four years later he went to the State University of Iowa to serve as Professor of Law and Dean until 1939 when he was appointed to the United States Court of Appeals for the District of Columbia.

Throughout his academic career Rutledge was known as an inspiring teacher, beloved by his students.   They realized that his interest in them was genuine. Throughout the war, when his judicial duties were heaviest, Rutledge carried on an extensive correspondence with a large number of students all over the world.   To them, notwithstanding his high office, he was Dean Rutledge, their teacher and friend.[4] He believed in humanizing the rules of law and dealing with students as people.   His home was always open to friends—and there were myriads of them—and to students.   He loved a hot argument and spirited debate. Like a good teacher, he eschewed "spoon feeding" methods.   He wanted his students to find out for themselves.

Willard Wirtz, later Secretary of Labor, one of his ex-colleagues and close friends, speaking at the "Proceedings of the Bar in Memory of Wiley Blount Rutledge," said on that occasion:

> He [Rutledge] spoke out repeatedly against the impersonalness of legal education and against the reflections of that same quality in the profession itself. . . . He pointed out the inevitability of false emphasis resulting from climaxing of each semester with a series of examinations which reveal only clinical accomplishment. We train artisans, he said, while a democratic society pleads for architects. His answers to the problem were all reflections of his basic quality of simple humanity. This meant, first, treating his students as human beings, getting to know them as individuals. He did this, seemingly oblivious to the other demands upon his time, by opening his office door and his home, inviting students in, singly and in groups of two or three, and then sitting and talking with them. The conversation would be personal at first, as teacher and student found out what underlay the other's reactions. Then it would broaden out, proceeding with an awareness of assumptions, predilections and biases. Now the human heart of the subject matter of the day's lecture could be taken up intelligently, and that of the morning's headlines. The subject would become not just a particular case or a news story but how a decent, honest, intelligent man approaches any subject coming within the competence and obligations of the lawyer. . . .
>
> The dean offered, by his own performance of innumerable public services, an example of what seemed to him the lawyer must do in full discharge of his professional obligations. Few in

Boulder and St. Louis and Iowa were so active as he in the public service programs of the bar associations in sponsorship of new legislation, in the organization of discussion groups, the setting up of student forums, the affairs of innumerable committees. He contributed tirelessly to the work of the Commission on Uniform State Laws, spoke willingly and often before campus, town, state and national group. He recognized the responsibilities of the citizen, the lawyer and the educator and spared no effort to meet them all.

However casual, informal and friendly Dean Rutledge was outside the classroom, he was all business inside. There was no nonsense tolerated there. Question after question was hammered at the student. Searching, relentless questioning was the order of the hour as he led or pushed students to explore every aspect of a problem. He was known as a "tough" teacher but respected the more for his rigorous intellectual discipline. He had no time for the unprepared student. In his handling of the case system of law teaching, he assumed that the cases had been read and studied and the students were prepared to discuss them. He started from that point.

His relations with his fellow faculty members were cordial, friendly and in many cases extremely close. He never sought to impose his own methods and teaching techniques on them for he recognized that there was no formula, simple or complex, for good and effective classroom performance. Good teaching was an art which must be developed by each individual for himself. There were no textbooks and no schools of education for law professors.

For all his seriousness in his classes, the Dean was never unkind and was ever careful not to hurt a student's feelings. He welcomed disagreement if a student had reasons and could defend his position. Although his method was usually Socratic—constant questioning, seldom what students call a "lay out"—occasionally he would lecture for an hour to pull together loose ends, explain apparent conflicts and dispel confusion. It is reported that once when the bell rang at the close of such a performance, the students to a man, stood up and applauded. He was never content with a purely technical legal analysis of cases or problems. Although he was himself an excellent craftsman and insisted on his students acquiring technical skills, he was forever probing into the social and economic implications of legal rules and court decisions. In other words, he was interested primarily in the living law and its effect on people. He had what might be called an instrumental philosophy of law. Law was an instrument for the attainment of justice and freedom—his favorite trinity.

The period of Rutledge's law teaching and administration was from the early twenties to the late thirties. This was a time of sharp reaction in the field of legal education to the conceptualism which had characterized the earlier generations of legal and juristic thinking. It was the period of developing realism with its down-grading of a technique of deductive logic from assumed major premises which concealed the conclusion to be reached. It was an era of emphasis on the factual aspects of the issues and an identification and balancing of the values involved.

Judge Jerome Frank's book, *Law and the Modern Mind,* was published in 1930 and made a tremendous impact on the young generation of law teachers. It was, indeed, the challenge of realism to the platitudes and pious generalizations of a jurisprudence which, in one way or another, was rooted in some kind of "natural law." It was a time when Cook, Hamilton, Bohlen, Llewellyn, Moore and others were developing fresh approaches and new teaching materials to replace the stereotype Harvard casebook. Although most middle western law schools were fashioned after the Harvard model which had dominated the field for so long, they were alert to new trends, new ideas and new methods. Rutledge's disposition, personality and experience made him especially hospitable to these recent movements in legal thought and education.

While at Iowa, he started a summer school for police officers which was one of the first of its kind in the country. He also developed a program whereby the class in criminal law sat each week with members of the Department of Psychiatry.

During the war, the Association of American Law Schools suspended its regular annual meetings, but there were enough law professors in the government or around Washington in the service that it was possible to have a meeting on an informal, but nonetheless a very large scale, in Washington. Such a meeting was held in the Harrington Hotel, probably in the spring of 1943 shortly after the Rutledge appointment, although it may have been a few months later.

The meeting was extremely well attended. The intense wave of applause which filled the room when Rutledge entered was spontaneous evidence of his personal popularity with his fellow law teachers. There was something altogether warmly emotional about it. Most of those attending came from west of the Alleghenys, and somehow almost everyone had a vague sense of personal identification with Rutledge.

The principal speaker that evening was James Landis, then Dean of the Harvard Law School, who was discussing plans for legal education after the war. His remarks were depressingly retrograde. It was quite apparent that post-war Harvard was to be as identical with pre-war Harvard as the Dean could make it. Since, in fact, the administration of post-war Harvard fell to Dean Erwin Griswold, it turned out that something of an education revolution occurred there, and under Griswold the school became one of the most progressive in the country. But this was something no one could foresee in 1943. The extremely conservative nature of the discussion was intensified by Professor Barton Leach of Harvard, who attended in military uniform, and who, in his colorful way, spoke glowingly of the great days of Harvard during the twenties. It was apparent that the Harvard plan for the future was to turn the clock as far back as possible.

After the meeting Rutledge and his friend, John Frank, left together. In Frank's own words this conversation took place:

> I said something to the effect that this has been a terribly discouraging experience. Here is the largest and most influential law school in the country, and it is clearly going to use its whole great weight to move education backwards, not forward. What can be expected from the smaller schools of the country with such leadership from this one?
>
> Rutledge stopped right there in the middle of the corridor of the Hotel Harrington and turned on me with mock indignation. He said: "You young teachers have no right to be discouraged. The rest of us in legal education have been carrying Harvard as an albatross around our necks for years. It seems that this is part of the burden which has to be borne for the sake of progress in legal education in the United States. So you get in there and pick up your share of the load and carry it."

On the walls of the offices of the professor, the Dean and the Justice were photographs of three men who, he would say, had especially influenced his professional life and thinking. One was George Norlin, President of the University of Colorado for a number of years and former professor of Greek. Another, John D. Flemming, Dean of the University of Colorado Law School when Wiley taught there and a prominent Colorado lawyer in the important fields of mining and water rights. The third was Hurbert Hadley, one time Governor of Missouri. Hadley later became a prominent Colorado Republican and regarded by party leaders as presidential timber until he suffered a severe breakdown in health. While recuperating, he accepted a position on the law faculty of the university. He was a law professor when Wiley was a student and a warm friendship developed between them. Later Hadley became Chancellor of Washington University in St. Louis. He took his colleague Bryant Smith with him and later replaced Smith with Rutledge.

Rutledge was always a stout defender of academic freedom and understood its relation to education and public information. He also recognized the necessity of the uncensored distribution of news, free from "management," either by government or private interests. In a speech at Indiana University in 1946, he expressed these views:

> Wherever the great agencies of public enlightenment become subservient to men in political power, to that extent, they become instruments for perverting the democratic process. The same thing is true, and to the same degree, when they fall under domination of any private, selfish interest or group or institution. Being not free themselves, they cannot create, they can only distort and in the end tear down the framework of freedom. Special interests of all sorts must have voice and the freedom to speak. But such voices are not adequate to sustain the democratic institution, for they are biased and prejudiced, one-sided and unrepresentative. However, honest—and not all will be honest—truth becomes distorted in their presentation. Facts are half-told or wholly suppressed in their advocacy.
>
> This is as true of schools, colleges and universities, of the press and the radio, of all the great agencies of public enlightenment as of any other, when they become slaves to special and more particularly to selfish interests.
>
> . . . There must be great independent agencies for full information and enlightenment, free from all such influences, devoted only to the interest of the whole community and dominated alone by that devotion, for the democratic process to work. It cannot live in our time upon a diet exclusively composed of privilege-supported propaganda, biased and one-sided. There must be great instrumentalities of impartial information and disinterested opinion and judgment, governed alone by that sincere regard for truth which requires all available facts before judgment and renders it with an eye single to the general welfare, not that of some special interest.[5]

The Association of American Law Schools is the accrediting body for schools of law. It has been such for many years and its authority in the field of legal education is unchallenged. Its annual meeting takes place each year between Christmas and New Year's, much to the understandable distress of law professors' wives and children. Educational policy as well as technical legal problems are considered during the three days of round table, executive sessions and bar room meetings of the delegates. The proceedings of the Association for December 28, 29, and 30, 1933, record certain goings-on. President of the association, Dean Charles E. Clark of Yale Law School, called for the Report of the Executive Committee. It was delivered by one Rufus Harris, then Dean of the Tulane Law School. After certain routine matters, Chairman Harris reported:

> Shortly after the last meeting of the association, the Executive Committee received an invitation from The Foundation Press, Inc. to act as host for an informal dinner for the association on the second day of its meeting.
>
> Upon some informal investigation of the sentiment of law teachers, it appeared that this would not only increase the attendance at our informal dinner but this would also show a disposition on our part to reciprocate without discrimination the courtesies of all law book publishers. The committee realized also that there had occurred a closer connection of the association with one particular company than others, namely, the West Publishing Company, through the official directory of the association, the publication of the handbook, and otherwise, and accordingly, voted to accept the invitation.
>
> Since the appearance of our program, the faculty of one member school has made protest against this action and has inquired of representatives of other schools as to whether this action was supported. The committee has been informed that some other law teachers appear to be more or less in accord.
>
> It is the purpose of the committee to make its meetings attractive to the delegates and it does not wish to cause embarrassment to any one. No permanent policy has been established. It has not been able to see, however, how it is at all inappropriate for the association to meet the courtesies shown by the various publishers in the spirit in which they have been tendered, provided no discrimination is made among them.

The "member law school" was Washington University, St. Louis, Wiley B. Rutledge, Dean. The Report of the Executive Committee was put to the vote by President Clark who reported, somewhat sadly, "the ayes seem to have it."

The Foundation Press was an important publisher of legal case books and texts used in law schools as the basic materials for class preparation. All students were required to buy the books prescribed for the courses in which they were enrolled. For many years another law book publisher, the West Publishing Company of St. Paul, had enjoyed a near monopoly with relatively light competition in a few areas of the law. Foundation was headed by up-and-coming promoters and was threatening to become a serious rival for the law school trade. West had, from time to time, acted as genial dinner host to the assembled professors who now saw no harm in enjoying the largess of Foundation. But Rutledge did. As Judge Clark explained at Proceedings of the Bar and Officers of the Supreme Court in Memory of Justice Rutledge: "He [Rutledge] regarded the offer as a seduction to and by commercialism which would inevitably, even if by hardly perceptible degrees, bias the teacher in his important calling. So almost single handed, except for his own faculty, he gallantly staged a protest against our accepting such a patent bribe."

Rutledge was a dedicated family man—a loving husband and affectionate father. He was always close to his three children, Mary Lou, the eldest daughter, Jean Ann and Neal, the son. There was a very real comradeship between them. He was interested in their school work, their social life and their love affairs. He was never too busy to give time and thought to their problems and he took a father's proper pride in their achievements. Neal is now a successful lawyer in Miami, the father of four children and both girls are happily married, the one to a Washington nuclear physicist, the other to a law professor at the University of North Carolina.

But Wiley Rutledge did not limit his attention and affection to his immediate family. Even when he was sitting on the High Court, bedevilled by harrassing technical problems and a heavy work load, he somehow found time to keep up a far-flung correspondence with aunts, uncles, cousins, nephews, and so forth; and to respond, when he could, to their questions, requests and greetings with the warmth which charterized his relations, generally, with close friends, associates and admirers.

If he was asked for a favor which he thought he could not with propriety grant, he was careful to explain the reasons. "Here in the Court," he once wrote to a "cousin" or other relative, "we are not able to bring inflence to bear on matters of this sort as Senators and Congressmen quite often do. That is because the Court has to keep itself apart from any political activity, since it sits in judgment on laws affecting these agencies including the Civil Service Commission. We can hardly do that and at the same time ask the Commission for favors." Rutledge was always considerate of others, whether they be relatives, friends or strangers. There was in him no want of human kindness.

There is a small Jewish delicatessen and liquor store in the shopping center at 4855 Massachusetts Avenue in Washington. Anyone who drops in can hardly fail to notice a single framed picture on the wall in the dining area. It is a photograph of the Supreme Court of the United States with the reproduced autographs of all the Justices. Beneath that of Mr. Justice Rutledge, in his original hand, is a personal greeting to "my good friend, Sammy Wagshal."

Wiley Rutledge and Sam Wagshal were, indeed, good friends. Wagshal tells something about it—and a great deal about Rutledge—in the *Reader's Digest* shortly after the Justice's death.[6]

> How did I get to know the Justice? The fact is, that I, Sam Wagshal, turned him away from my store one night. My dining section closes at 7:45. And, look, here he comes at 8:45.
>
> He asks me, "May I have a ham sandwich, Smithfield ham?" "No," I said, "No sandwiches. Too late. I'll sell you the bread, I'll sell you the ham. Take it home and you can make your own sandwiches."
>
> That's right. I'm independent. Say, listen, if I can't do what I like—what's the use of being your own boss?
>
> Several times he came late and I had to tell him, plain talk: Nothing doing. I wouldn't wait on him. No exceptions. That's my policy.
>
> He used to say: "I'm sorry. I forgot. All right." . . . But believe me, he got used to coming in on time—and staying late.
>
> Then, we got to having big talks. With the Smithfield ham, the sour cream, the herrings—we also discussed issues.
>
> I remember the time he said: "Well, Sammy—so you're a Republican. What's the matter—you got it so bad under the New Deal? Look at Sammy, the New Deal did him dirt. It brought him a lot of customers. It sure is tough for you, Sammy, isn't it?" That's the way he used to kid me.
>
> Well, I used to say to him: "Justice"—I used to call him "Justice"—"Justice, you've got your principles and I've got my prejudices. So I remain Republican." . . . .
>
> Last January, the day before inauguration, suddenly my telephone rings. "Mr. Wagshal?"—"Yes, yes, what is it?"—"Just a minute please, I'll put Mr. Justice Rutledge on."
>
> He never telephoned before. "Sammy, do you want to go to to the inauguration?" I thought a moment. "Sure, sure"—What a question. Then by messenger, in an auto, he sent me the whole engraved fancy business, with the invitations and pictures of Truman and Barkley. All right, even though I'm a Republican, I said, "Yes, I'll go."

Next morning, Inauguration Day, his car came around, with his nice wife and children—and all of us drive to the Supreme Court. I never been there before. I sat with them right up there in the Capitol, watching a President get inaugurated. I can't begin to tell you what a thrill!

Here I am, Sam Wagshal, delicatessen businessman—frankly speaking, not a bad one—sitting right up there with the Supreme Court judges. Justice introduced me to them all. "Yes, yes—how do you do." Mr. Murphy says: "Oh, hello, Mr. Wagshal, I remember your name."

. . .

One time, my boy Ben was complaining—you know the way young fellows naturally complain—about how hard we have to work in our business, and other people are making more money, and bellyaching like that.

Well, Justice heard him. And he and the boy sat down for an hour. He told my son how proud he should be of his father— and of what I'm doing—an independent man—a small businessman, if you please. I know my customers, I am proud to take care of them. That's what makes America great, Justice said to my boy. It will be a different America when men can't work and live independent.

That was a beautiful thing for him to say to my boy. And I felt mighty proud, I can tell you. Justice sure handed down a mighty fine decision that time. . . .

In December 17, 1947, the Supreme Court heard arguments in an injunction suit brought by one Wagshal against a local union of Bakery Drivers which had picketed and boycotted the plaintiff's delicatessen. Wagshal won, Rutledge, J., not participating. Justices Black, Douglas and Murphy dissented. It is not hard to guess how Rutledge would have voted had he not disqualified himself. The result, of course, would have been the same by a five to four instead of a five to three vote.[7]

Rutledge was for the most part an uncomplicated character. There was little or no vacillation about him as to principle. He never forgot his father's admonition to him that "the best policy is loyalty to principle and devotion to conviction." He had simple but excellent tastes. He was modest but extroverted. He hated sham, hypocrisy and simulation of any kind. One of his former students and close, academic friend, Professor Clarence Morris of the University of Pennsylvania, has described an incident which is typical. Morris said that he happened to be in Washington when Rutledge was sworn in for the Court of Appeals in 1939.

He asked me to come to his chambers. The other persons there were Senator George Norris, Senator Gillette of Iowa, and Frank Murphy. I was the only other visitor. We chatted for a few minutes before Court came into session and returned to the chambers afterwards. I do not remember any of the conversation. Wiley had left his family in Iowa City at this time and was living in Washington alone while looking for a house and, I suppose, allowing the children to finish out the school year. The night before he was sworn in, he and my son Bob, who was then eleven, had a date for dinner. When we went to his modest hotel, which was in back of the Mayflower, he suggested that we go to the Tidal Basin and take our supper by getting hot dogs at a hot dog stand. Spring was bourgeoning and it was a lovely evening. Thus the three of us celebrated his coming elevation to the bench.[8]

MARY LOUISE WIGGINTON RUTLEDGE
(Wiley's Mother)

PASTOR RUTLEDGE, WILEY, MARGARET
AND THEIR MOTHER

BAPTIST CHURCH. MT. WASHINGTON

BAPTIST PARSONAGE, CLOVERPORT

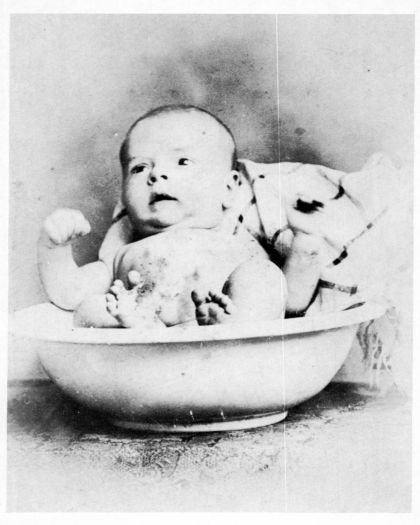

MR. JUSTICE RUTLEDGE AT AGE SIX MONTHS

CLASS FOOTBALL TEAM, MARYVILLE COLLEGE

(Rutledge, Captain)

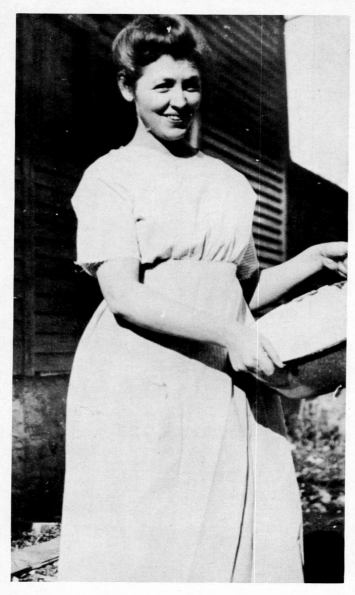

ANNABEL, YOUNG HOUSEWIFE

DEAN RUTLEDGE, IOWA CITY

RUTLEDGE FAMILY IN WASHINGTON

CHAPTER II

". . . HE SHALL NOMINATE . . . JUDGES . . . ."

W HEN Justice Byrnes resigned from the Court on October 3, 1942 to become Director of War Mobilization, after but a year of service, the usual political maneuvering began. Much pressure was brought to bear upon the President and the Attorney General for the appointment, among others, of Judge Learned Hand of the Second Circuit Court of Appeals. Hand was highly regarded by the bar and had had a long and distinguished career on the federal bench. Mason reports[1] that Chief Justice Stone favored Hand, thought that his appointment "would greatly strengthen the Court," and that it would make him "very happy." Stone had been consulted and had so expressed himself.

Whether Hand would have fulfilled the promise Stone thought he had, as a potential member of the Court, is doubtful although in the declining years of the Chief Justice the two would probably have seen eye to eye on many matters. In any event, Stone must have been pleased with Rutledge's early performance. He could scarcely have failed to have been gratified when the new Justice cast the deciding vote in the Jehovah Witnesses cases about which Stone felt so strongly. And he could have been no less pleased with Rutledge's dignified behavior and attitude in connection with the personal feuds which rocked the Court from time to time and which caused the Chief Justice so much distress and embarrassment. Rutledge had the quality, not always prominently displayed by some of his colleagues, of being able to disagree without hostility. While by no means making a fetish of judicial self-restraint, he showed admirable personal self-restraint. Had all of his brethren disciplined their emotions to the same degree, the dignity of the Court would have suffered less on several occasions.

According to Francis Biddle, who was Attorney General at the time of the Rutledge appointment, President Roosevelt took his time about appointing judges and never considered there was any particular hurry about filling a vacancy.[2] During the short service of Justice Byrnes, it was well known that he was giving less attention to his judicial duties than to his consultation with the President on matters of the war effort. Indeed, at the time of his resignation, he had in effect been on leave of absence from the Court for several months. Biddle is authority for the statement that the President appeared little concerned with the fact that the Supreme Court was operating shorthanded with a constantly increasing load of work. The President, in his devotion to Byrnes, wanted to keep open the seat on the Court for him until the war was over. He even suggested to Biddle that they might appoint some "nice solid Republican" who would be willing to resign when he had reached the age of seventy so that Byrnes could "be brought back." After consultation with the Chief Justice, the Attorney General succeeded in convincing the President that this sort of monkeyshine would not do and that what the Court needed was a working Justice who would pull his weight in the boat.

Hand had strong support, particularly from Justice Frankfurter who, it was reported, brought pressure from many sources in support of Hand's appointment. But Hand was close to seventy years of age, and Biddle reminded the President that he had vowed to appoint no Justice over the age of sixty. If, however, as Ralph Waldo Emerson observed, consistency is the hobgoblin of small minds, the President's mind was not small.

Rutledge, too, had strong support from several quarters and Biddle asked Professor Herbert Wechsler of Columbia University Law School to make an analysis of Rutledge's more important opinions on the Court of Appeals. The result met with favorable reaction from Biddle, from several members of the Court, and, to a lesser degree, perhaps, from the Chief Justice himself. "Outside of Hand, who is far more distinguished than any of the others," Biddle thought, "Rutledge seemed the most promising."

> His views were sound, carefully reasoned and lawyer-like. He was apt to be long-winded, probably because he suffered from a sense of obligation to answer everything in the case. He was a liberal who would stand up for human rights, particularly during a war when they were apt to be forgotten. But there was nothing extreme or messianic about his approach. He was certainly not a "nice, solid Republican."

A law clerk to one of the Justices has recalled the reactions of several members of the Court at that time.

The first time the Rutledge appointment came into discussion for the seat which he finally got was the day Justice Byrnes resigned. On that day there was immediate talk at the Supreme Court Building concerning the possibility that Rutledge might be appointed. I can also recall the day on which Attorney General Biddle came up to the Court to ask some of the Justices their opinions as to who would be the most desirable addition. I remember that he called on Justices Black, Douglas and Murphy. My impression at that time was that those were the only Justices he called on, although conceivably there were others. However, I expressly remember the day he came to call on those three. Each expressed the hope that Rutledge would be appointed. At least some of them had very carefully reviewed all of his work on the Court of Appeals up to that time.[3]

It was clear that at "least some of them" had read the Wechsler memorandum.

There is no doubt that Judge Hand was the "runner up." The President asked Biddle his opinion of Hand. The Attorney General repeated the appraisal of the Chief Justice that Hand was "head and shoulders above the others." Nevertheless, the President chose Rutledge. It was reported that he had resented what he regarded as "organized pressure" on behalf of the venerable dean of Circuit Court judges. But Rutledge, too, was a federal judge with several years' experience. There were many letters and endorsements for him sent to the Attorney General and to the President. It seems that the President did not regard this as an "organized pressure" group. And he had direct information from his friend, Brant, that Rutledge had not personally sought the appointment and that he had discouraged his friends and admirers from seeking it for him. Moreover (and this seemed important to the President) as he observed at the time, Rutledge had "geography."

The appointment was made public on January 11th. The Associated Press on January 17th announced that "Rutledge's appointment was favorably received in the Senate and speedy confirmation is indicated." As to "geography," Senator Gillette, Democrat of Iowa, commented that the appointment "recognizes a man coming from west of the Mississippi River, a section that has been neglected in court appointments in the recent past." On February 9th, the same press association reported as follows:

The Senate confirmed the nomination of Wiley B. Rutledge to the Supreme Court yesterday, restoring the Court's full strength of nine Justices following the resignation of James F.

Byrnes to be Stabilization (sic) Director.

Rutledge probably will take his seat by next Monday, the Court's next order day. At that time orders may be issued for the reargument of several pending cases to permit Rutledge to ' participate in their decision.

The long pendency of some of these cases led to speculation among Court observers that the eight Justices might be evenly divided over the decisions and reluctant to dispose of them on that basis in view of the prospect that a ninth Justice would be available to break the tie.

Senator Langer (Rep., North Dakota) made the only speech against Rutledge, formerly a Justice of the District of Columbia Court of Appeals. Langer contended that a lawyer of wide practical experience rather than a "second best" Justice should be appointed to the Supreme Court, and said that Rutledge, "so far as I can ascertain, never has practiced law inside a courtroom."

The man who more than any other single person was responsible for Rutledge's judicial career was the distinguished Madison biographer, Irving Brant. Brant was a newspaperman in St. Louis during a number of years when Rutledge was the Dean of the Law School at Washington University. Rutledge had attracted Brant's attention by several speeches and articles which he had written concerning the burning issues of the New Deal of which Brant was an ardent advocate. In one such article, Rutledge had taken the Supreme Court to task for its disposition of child labor legislation. "Congress," he wrote, "three times has overwhelmingly declared the regulation of child labor to be an appropriate function of the federal Government. But this view has been overruled by the views of five men who happen to constitute a majority of the Court." Rutledge also had attracted attention by engaging in a spirited controversy with one Clarence E. Martin, President of the American Bar Association in 1933. The association was strongly opposed to child labor legislation, a position which Rutledge characterized as based upon "legal and political dogmas of the 18th Century, behind which all forms of commercialized greed have sought to establish their interests out of the reach of government control."

In another speech he proposed a national incorporation law to supersede the state chartering system, at least for corporations in interstate commerce. During the depression years he was a firm supporter of strong federal action to meet the economic problems of the period. "If our national Government is without the power to control production, to place limits upon the scope and methods of unfair competition and to regulate all phases of industrial and commercial life which fundamentally affect these problems," he stated in 1933, "the only alternative is continuance of the economic disorder with which we have struggled for four years."[4] In discussing national control of corporations he said, in the same year:

> The philosophy of competition remains, but the basis of its creation is gone. There must be one or two things done, voluntary self-regulation by corporation managers or effective governmental regulations, which we have never had. We will absolutely have to have controlled production. We have tried private control during the last 100 years or more. The result you see. It seems evident that we will eventually have some sort of government regulation.

In May of 1935, Dean Rutledge published a feature article in the Sunday edition of the *St. Louis Post Dispatch* on holding companies and pending legislation to control them. "There is no doubt," he wrote, "that the holding company is the most pliable and facile instrument for the concentration of wealth and economic power which history has devised."

> Within twenty-five years it has assembled into national systems eighty per cent of all power distributed in the United States. In the power field it has issued more than two billion dollars in securities, controlling thereby investments of ten billion dollars in operating companies. Prior to 1929, a single company with $750,000,000 capitalization had control of corporations with over three billion dollars in assets, and capitalists dominated the holding company with less than $300,000,000 investment. The holding company has accomplished what the "corner", the "pool" and the "trust" of previous generations sought but were unable to achieve.

Public statements and articles of this character were sure to catch the eye and ear of Brant. After Rutledge had indicated his sympathy with the President's plan to "pack" the Supreme Court, Brant began to take a more active interest in him. But it was Rutledge's reaction to the "Triple A" decision, holding processing taxes unconstitutional as a source of federal aid to agriculture, which apparently impressed Brant most. On the day of the decision, he relates, Rutledge addressed a luncheon club of business and professional men in St. Louis. Without having read the dissenting opinions, Rutledge gave a devastating rebuttal to the majority arguments. "For me," Brant has written, "it was a sudden and startling introduction to the power of Rutledge's mind and the depth of feeling behind his devotion to the public welfare."[5]

In the meantime, Rutledge had left St. Louis to accept the deanship of the School of Law of the University of Iowa. Shortly after the luncheon club speech, on February 15th, Brant wrote to the Dean at Iowa City mysteriously, as follows:

> I am going to do a little exploring in the relationship between law deanships and constitutional exposition and would like to begin with you, if you are willing. Can you give me citations of articles you have written on the Constitution, or the work of the Courts, or any addresses you have delivered on the subject? . . .
>
> Inclosed is an article which I wrote for the Peoples' Lobby on the large carrying capacity of the buggy used in horse and buggy days, compared with the Baby Austin which the Supreme Court now permits us to drive.

A few days later Rutledge replied as follows:

> Unfortunately I have never had the pleasure of teaching constitutional law, and, quite modestly, I make no special pretentions to any competence in that vast field. . . .
>
> "I was very much interested in your essay on Government Monopolies. I hope you (or the Peoples' Lobby) have seen to it that copies have been placed in the hands of the Justices of the Supreme Court. What gripes me (you will pardon the vulgarity) about the AAA decision is that when the verbiage is boiled down to the real issue, the Court does nothing more than *assert* the invalidity of the act. There is no reasoning about the scope and content of the general welfare! There is no intimation that the whole process of production (agricultural or otherwise) can ever under any conceivable circumstances have any relation to the national interest or the general welfare. There is the bold assertion that agricultural production is a matter reserved (by implication only) to the states, and therefore denied to the federal Government, and there is the end of the matter. Even if we are going to have a Baby Austin, as you say, we should get it by rational process, not by mere fiat.

Brant was clearly thinking of Rutledge in connection with the Supreme Court and his enthusiasm was not dampened by Rutledge's subsequent sympathetic reaction to the Roosevelt Court bill. Brant's relationship with the President was such that he saw him not infrequently and that he was in a position to offer suggestions and advice in respect to judicial appointments as well as other matters of state. But Brant was also a strong admirer of Frankfurter and on November 12, 1938, wrote to Rutledge as follows:

> It looks very much as if Felix Frankfurter would be named to the Supreme Court vacancy. I urged it strongly on the President a few weeks ago. He virtually said that the only deterrent was the demand of trans-Mississippi Senators that the post go to a westerner, but he indicated that this consideration was an important one. I told him that present conditions inside the Court were such that the influence of Frankfurter would be decisive, as to personal factors, and that this was much more important at the moment than geographical distribution. Yesterday I was told that the outlook for Frankfurter was good. What I wish is that there were more of a western call for him.

Ten days later Rutledge replied:

> I was interested in your comments on Frankfurter's chances for appointment. To me, of course, that would be an ideal selection notwithstanding the geographical qualification. I am inclined to think that this is a situation in which this factor should be disregarded just as Hoover did with Cardozo's appointment. In fact, Hoover's final decision in that case seems to me to have involved an even greater disregard of geographical factors than would this. I suspect that the principal thing for which Mr. Hoover's presidency will be remembered in a favorable light fifty years from now will be that he appointed Justice Cardozo. Furthermore, it should be remembered that the Cardozo appointment was received with universal acclaim. When appointments of such character are made, geographical considerations become insignificant, not only in the professional and political mind but also in that of the public. Nor is there anyone west of the Mississippi that I know who would be even within close distance to Frankfurter on the basis of qualification with the possible exception of Joseph C. Hutcheson of Texas.

Rutledge was totally unaware of it, of course, but during this period Brant's plans were further maturing in his own mind with respect to the Supreme Court. On November 30th in a letter to Dr. George Norlin, President of the University of Colorado, he revealed the results of his ground work:

Wiley Rutledge does not know it, but he is being personally considered for appointment to the United States Supreme Court. It is considered certain that there will be two places to fill on the Court by next June, and possibly three. The appointment of Felix Frankfurter is taken for granted. The other place is practically certain to go to somebody west of the Mississippi. A survey of possible appointees from that part of the country, made at the request of the President by some of his close advisors, has put Rutledge right at the top of the score on fitness for the place.

The first admission of his operations behind Rutledge's back was made in his letter to him of December 27th:

I suppose you have read, by this time, that you are being considered for appointment to the Supreme Court. The first reference I have seen to it was in the inclosed column of Alsop and Kintner.

Since that has been published, I can terminate a mild dissimilation. I suggested your name to the President, for future consideration three years ago, and he asked me to get some material together about you for his private files. That was why I wrote to ask for your published writings and addresses on constitutional subjects, in the Spring of 1938. But instead of turning these in to the White House, partly through inertia and perhaps a little more because I thought political conditions were unfavorable when the first two vacancies occurred, I held them back.

A couple of months ago I urged the President to appoint Frankfurter to the Cardozo vacancy, on account of cleavages inside the Court which he might remedy, and because of his fitness. He said that the one thing which might deter him was the demand for an appointment from west of the Mississippi.

At that, I prepared a digest of your address on Social Changes and the Law, and a symposium of your 1936 letters to me on the reactionary decisions of the Supreme Court, and sent them to the President, along with your article on child labor, and some accompanying comment. The President had typewritten copies made of everything you had written, with identifying marks omitted, and sent them to a number of advisors for comment, they not knowing who the subject was.

Indications are that there will be either two or three vacancies on the Court by next October, including the present one, but there is no certainty that Frankfurter will be nominated next week. I know that you are being very seriously considered for the place, if it goes West, and for later appointment otherwise because one of the President's right hand men asked me if I could get a good indorsement of you from Colorado. Dr. Norlin wrote one. On the other hand, there is terrific pressure on the President to appoint somebody from the West who will make up in political strength what he may lack in judicial qualifications. And there is the tactical disadvantage of appointing two law school men to the Court in succession.

In sending the material about you to the President, I told him that I hoped he would name Frankfurter to the present vacancy and consider you for the next one. One of the exhibits was a tough-looking picture of you which I clipped out of your Press-Citizen review of my book. One of the men to whom the material was submitted saw this photograph and said to me afterward that it "was what sold me on that fellow."

I told one of the President's advisors what you said in praise of Judge Hutcheson and he replied: "That's good argument for Rutledge. I like men who talk about the merits of other men rather than their own."

Everything in this letter, of course, is confidential, though there is no need of my saying so.

Rutledge replied on December 29th with his usual modesty:

I do not deserve such confidence from my friends however highly I value it. I fear you have, for once, allowed your friendship to get the better of your judgment. Some here and at home feel that I should ask others to support your suggestion but of course any such thing is out of the question. I have never sought office or position, and do not intend doing so now. Further, despite your good offices, I shall not build hope upon an eventuality so remote. I still think Frankfurter is *the* man, & perhaps the only one, worthy to succeed Cardozo. . . .

A few days later, Brant wrote to Professor Ralph Fuchs of Washington University School of Law, a colleague, close friend and admirer of Rutledge, that "he felt reasonably confident that the appointment would go to Frankfurter." He indicated, however, that the next vacancy would be filled by a man from the western part of the country. There was still an outside possibility he thought that the order of appointments could be reversed and the westerner appointed first. He thought the President was uncertain as to Justice Brandeis' intentions.

If the latter were to retire in the near future, the President might with-hold the Frankfurter appointment, presumably because he could im-mediately appease the westerners and at the same time make what everyone would regard as a thoroughly appropriate replacement for the Brandeis vacancy. He concluded his letter by declaring that, "there seems no doubt that he [Rutledge] rates and is rated at the White House, as the best Court material west of the Mississippi. What he needs is some endorsements that would off-set his lack of political strength."

The date of the letter to Fuchs was December 31, 1938. A few days earlier the President had in fact consulted Frankfurter about Rutledge. The account is given by the Justice in his *Reminiscences*:

> It was a day or two after Christmas [1938], maybe two days af-ter that I had a phone call. The phone rang, long distance, and there was the President of the United States, and he said that another suggestion had been made to him, and he wanted to know what I thought of it: Dean Wiley Rutledge of the Law School of the University of Iowa, what did I think of him? I said, "I do not know him. I've never met him, and therefore I have no opinion, but if you want me to find out from people in whose judgment I have confidence, what they think about him, it's very easy for me to do so because all the law professors are now meeting in Chicago."
>
> It was the meeting of the American Association of Law Schools, and he said, "I wish you would."
>
> I then got on the phone and got hold of T. R. Powell in Chicago, who was one of our delegation, (that is of the Harvard Law School) that year, and I told him absolutely nothing about the inquiry of FDR and the Supreme Court, but I put him the questions on which I wanted light on Wiley Rutledge which would reveal the intellectual and moral content of the man. He knew Rutledge somewhat. I said, "You ask fellows like Lloyd Garrison and so on—just wrastle around and call me back collect and tell me what the results of your inquiries are."
>
> He knew it was something important. Men who had the kind of relations he and I had understood each other without spelling it out, and in due course Powell called me back and gave me a very detailed report, detailed estimate, assessment as to why he liked Rutledge's qualities and potentialities on the basis of which I wrote a memorandum to the President, the up-shot of which was that if I had to act on the information my net inquiry had fished up I would think that Rutledge was quali-fied for the Court and would be a properly appointed man.[6]

About a week later, on January 4, the President notified Frankfurter by telephone that his appointment would go to the Senate the following day. It did.[7]

On the same day that the news was announced, Rutledge expressed his satisfaction in a letter to Brant. "Word has just come of Frankfurter's nomination. The President has done the right and courageous thing. No other designation would have been fitting to the successor of Holmes and Cardozo." In another letter he congratulated Brant on his "objectivity" in recommending Frankfurter first. "In the face of his qualifications, geographical considerations and those of personal friendship should count for nothing."

Brant sent excerpts from several of Rutledge's letters expressing similar sentiments to Frankfurter because, as he said, "they reflect credit in both directions." In explaining and commenting upon Rutledge's qualifications for the Court, he wrote that Rutledge was "so intolerably modest (despite a combative dispositon where justice is concerned) that he has not a public repute commensurate with his character and attainments."

Brant, of course, continued his efforts on Rutledge's behalf, knowing that the Brandeis seat could be vacant at any time. Already, of course, speculation was high as to the successor of the venerable Justice. On February 19 Brant wrote Rutledge that, "the President took with him to the South a dossier on each of several men under consideration, prepared by the Attorney General."

> From all I can learn they point to the complete fitness and availability of yourself and Schwellenbach, to the complete fitness and partial availability of William O. Douglas, to the fitness and doubtful availability of Dean Garrison of Wisconsin; to a mixed record for Judge Hutcheson and thumbs pretty well down on Judge Stephens and Judge Bratton.

The reference to "Schwellenbach" was to Lewis B. Schwellenbach, then United States Senator from Washington, subsequently Secretary of Labor in the Truman cabinet. Both he and Rutledge were geographically "available," coming as they did from "west of the Mississippi." Presumably the partial availability of Douglas, originally from Oregon, referred to his years in the East as a Yale law professor and member of the S.E.C. Why Dean Lloyd Garrison of the University of Wisconsin School of Law was of "doubtful availability" is not clear, but might be ascribed to his eastern origin and limited tenure in the West. Judge Joseph C. Hutcheson of the Court of Appeals, Fifth Circuit, Judge Harold M. Stephens of the Court of

Appeals, District of Columbia and Judge Sam A. Bratton of the Tenth
Circuit, were apparently not taken seriously by those responsible for
advising the President on judicial appointments.

It appears that Senator Schwellenbach was indeed considered seriously and was an early favorite. Rumor had it that he lost out when
he voted against the confirmation of a nominee for a federal judgeship in Virginia whom Senator Carter Glass had opposed. This, of
course, was merely "senatorial courtesy." Schwellenbach had plenty
of company as the vote was 72 to 9 against confirmation. Nevertheless, it was reported that the President regarded it as a vote of confidence between Glass and himself. He was irritated.

Brant guessed that the choice would be between Rutledge and
Douglas, both of whom would normally be considered to have superior
qualifications to any of the other candidates. On March the 3rd, he
wrote to Attorney General Murphy his evaluation of the two. "About
the only material distinction I would draw between him [Douglas]
and Rutledge is that Rutledge reaches instantaneously right moral
conclusions, Douglas reaches ultimately right moral conclusions." A
week later he wrote to President Roosevelt his analysis of the constitutional state of the union.

> There are two tasks immediately ahead. One is to win back
> Justice Stone to the liberal wing. . . . The other task is to bottle
> up the conservative lawyers of the country. This can be done
> by naming somebody for your key appointment whose legal
> scholarship, integrity and aloofness from politics will force
> them to silence when they contemplate his liberalism. . . . Of
> the men under consideration I think that Rutledge is the one
> who would perfectly reinforce Frankfurter in winning Stone
> back. Rutledge has the economic beliefs and liberal attitude of
> Black, a nationalism possibly exceeding Frankfurter's and the
> same attitude toward administrative law as Frankfurter. He has
> in addition a philosophical ground work and broad knowledge
> *which is the only enduring basis of liberalism,* and which would
> win the complete respect of Stone; plus courage and resource-
> fulness. . . . [Emphasis original.]

Perhaps Brant's predictions with respect to the Rutledge-Frank-
furter-Stone triumvirate were as good as any that could be made at
that time. It is true that Stone had vacillated in his attitude toward
judicial review, economic matters and civil liberties, and he continued to do so until his death. As to Frankfurter's position in relation
to those of Rutledge and Stone, it was not infrequent that Rutledge
and Stone on the one hand were opposed by Frankfurter on important

controversial issues, and, more frequently, Frankfurter and Stone stood together against Rutledge and those with whom he agreed. Two years later, Rutledge apparently somewhat disenchanted with both the Chief Justice and the man he had thought the most worthy successor to Justice Cardozo, wrote Brant, referring to two then recent free speech decisions:[8]

> I was more surprised that Stone went with the majority in those cases than I was that Frankfurter did so. Since that Gobitus [*sic*] business [the first flag salute case, upholding the law], I have begun to wonder just where he [Frankfurter] stands on free speech, free conscience and free religion. As I have been watching his decisions lately, it seems to me that where there has been a sharp issue between downright liberalism and a tempered variety, he has fallen rather consistently on the latter side. I'm afraid, too, that I notice a change in Stone since he became Chief Justice, but I hope that it isn't true.

Whatever the final and decisive factors were in the President's judgment, on March the 20th, he sent to the Senate the nominations of William O. Douglas to the Supreme Court of the United States and the following day the nomination of Wiley B. Rutledge, Jr., to the United States Court of Appeals for the District of Columbia.

Immediately after the reading of the announcement of the Douglas nomination, Rutledge, on March 20, wrote to his close friend Clay Apple of Greely, Colorado. He indicated his satisfaction with the President's choice and was confident that Douglas would make an excellent member of the Court. He then went on:

> There is another matter which I want to tell you in the strictest confidence. . . . Last Wednesday afternoon I had a telephone call from Attorney General Murphy. It was extremely cordial in tone, told me of the many evidences he had received of my various qualities, expressed his and the President's very high opinion of me, etc., stated that my name "was still in every picture," but wound up with the request that I indicate whether, if the Supreme Court decision should be favorable to another, I would accept an appointment to the Court of Appeals of the District of Columbia.
>
> It was a very tough spot for me, and I replied that I was greatly honored by the suggestion, but always took counsel with my wife about such matters, and asked to be permitted to do so in this. He replied that he was going to Baltimore for a con-

cert that evening, and asked me to call him at the White House at midnight.

Rutledge then told of his conversations with his wife and her brother, two colleagues on the Iowa law faculty, Professors Philip Meechem and Willard Wirtz, and Professor Ralph Fuchs of Washington University. The result was, he decided that he would accept such an appointment notwithstanding his brother-in-law's advice of "Supreme Court or nothing."

Rutledge's call to Murphy did not go through that night, but the following morning he gave his answer to the Attorney General. At the time of this letter, of course, he did not know whether he would be offered the place on the Supreme Court, on the Court of Appeals, or no place at all. He had merely expressed his willingness to accept the lesser judgeship if it were offered to him after the appointment of another to the Supreme Court. He had weighed the matter carefully and recognized that the move to Washington with his family at a salary of $12,500.00 per year would involve some financial hardship as compared with life in the university town at a time when his children were approaching college age. It was also well known that Rutledge was in line for the Presidency of the University of Iowa on the retirement of President Gillmore which was shortly to come. However, he had no stomach for the university presidency and, as he put it to Apple, "I suspect I have done about all I will be able to do here in the way of constructive achievement, with an Old Guard 'economy' stricken legislature which will not increase materially the reduced university budget."

The following day Rutledge again wrote to Apple. "This morning about 10:30 a reporter walked in my office and asked what I intended to do about the Court of Appeals. That bowled me over and then struck me dumb. What in H— could I say? No official tender, yet an AP report marked, 'Hold for Release' this afternoon." Murphy called about three quarters of an hour later.

Apparently it had been a nip-and-tuck affair between Douglas and Rutledge, with the President's advisors split in their choice. The Pearson-Allen column for March 6th carried the following gossip which was later substantiated.

The inner circle, which was unanimous behind Justice Felix Frankfurter, is divided regarding the successor to Brandeis.

Tommy Corcoran, Ben Cohen and most of the other "downtown" militants are beating the drum for Douglas. Secretary Henry Wallace and Midwestern New Dealers are pulling wires for Wiley Blount Rutledge, outstanding dean of the Iowa University Law School, while various administrationites in the Senate are rooting for Senator Louis Schwellenbach.

The rivalry is vigorous, but not acrimonious. The boys aren't calling each other names, but they are missing no bets to boost their candidates.

It was also well known that Senator Borah of Idaho, long time staunch liberal, favored Douglas and was actively backing him, publicly and privately. It may well be that this Republican support for the Chairman of the Securities and Exchange Commission tipped the scales in his favor.

During the period of speculation, Tennessee and Kentucky newspapers took pride in the publicity given to Rutledge's candidacy. The Breckenridge county weekly *News* for February 15th carried a large front page headline: "WILEY B. RUTLEDGE, JR., POSSIBLE SUCCESSOR TO CHIEF JUSTICE BRANDEIS."

On March 21, the same day that the Rutledge appointment was announced, Brant wrote to Professor Ralph Fuchs in St. Louis.

The appointment of Wiley Rutledge to the D.C. Court of Appeals was a complete surprise to me, but it clarified some matters which had had me greatly puzzled.

For the last ten days there have been indications that Douglas was "in" as far as the Supreme Court appointment was concerned, yet statements were made to me which indicated that Rutledge was not "out." The double appointments makes them understandable.

As nobody knows whether there will or will not be further vacancies on the Supreme Court during the Roosevelt administration, there is no use speculating on that subject, but it may be noted that the appointment to the D.C. Court puts Rutledge in a far better position than he was before, in connection with any future vacancy. Roosevelt could not name a third law school man in succession to the Supreme Court, [Frankfurter, from Harvard; Douglas, former Yale professor] but if Rutledge should be considered in connection with such a vacancy, it will be on the basis of whatever he proves to be as a federal judge. . . .

The President did not appoint a third ex-professor in succession. Indeed, there were three intervening appointments before he named Rutledge. Justice Butler died in Washington on November 3, 1939, and Attorney General Frank Murphy was named to his seat on the Court. Chief Justice Hughes and Justice McReynolds both retired in 1941. On June 12 of that year, President Roosevelt nominated Justice Stone to be Chief Justice, and Senator James F. Byrnes of South Carolina and Attorney General Robert H. Jackson to the two vacancies. Byrnes was confirmed by the Senate on the same day; the other two nominations in due course.

Justice Byrnes left the Court on October 3, 1942 to become Director of War Mobilization. Brant immediately went into action once more. He had a number of influential friends in Washington and always kept his ear constantly to the ground on matters affecting the Court in which his vital interest continued unabated. The same day he wrote to Luther Ely Smith, prominent St. Louis lawyer and strong Rutledge admirer, as follows:

> There is a better chance at this moment that Wiley Rutledge will be appointed to the Supreme Court than on any previous occasion. As nearly as I can learn, the present field of real possibilities includes Rutledge, Senator Barkley, Solicitor General Fahy, Judge Parker and Dean Acheson, with Rutledge leading on merit, Barkley in political support, and your old friend and ex-liberal Felix Frankfurter plugging for Fahy or Acheson, either of whom he thinks he can control. Wiley, as you know, has made a splendid record as a judge, jumping in two years time to the very top in the estimation of leading members of the bar.
>
> Do you feel like writing a letter to Attorney General Francis Biddle and seeing if any group bar endorsements can be made within the next week? Or the Washington U. law faculty? It would be useful if they asked for appointment of a Justice identified with the part of the country west of the Mississippi, as well as indorsing Rutledge personally. . . .

Of course, Smith's "ex-liberal" friend had been Brant's first choice for Cardozo's seat. His suggestion that Frankfurter thought he could "control" Fahy or Acheson is an interesting one. It may well be that the Justice did so think. If he did, it requires great credulity to believe that he was right. Those who are familiar with Fahy's work as Solicitor General and his subsequent career on the Court of Appeals are confident that his kindly and gentle manner in no sense reflects an indecisive mind or weak character. As for Acheson, it is true that he and Frankfurter were for many years close friends. Acheson, after graduating at Yale had gone to Harvard Law School and had thereafter clerked for Justice Brandeis. Regardless of these ties and others of personal friendship, it is hard to believe that anyone could "control" the man who subsequently became the forceful Secretary of State in the Truman cabinet and has since been a positive personality in connection with matters of high policy whenever he has had an opportunity to participate in government affairs.

As to the situation respecting Barkley, Drew Pearson's "Merry-Go-Round" for November 6th was probably reasonably accurate except as to Rutledge being "the candidate of Chief Justice Stone."

The President told advisers that he wanted to put off filling Justice Byrnes' vacancy on the Supreme Court until after elections. Meanwhile the pressure from the Senate to appoint Senator Alben Barkley of Kentucky has become so great that FDR almost wishes he had not delayed.

Roosevelt is extremely fond of Barkley, values his services in the Senate and feels grateful to him. But there are two handicaps in the path of Barkley's appointment: (1) his age, 65, which is contrary to the President's 1937 thesis that the Court should be staffed with younger men; (2) a Kentuckian already is on the Supreme Court.

In fact, there are already two justices from the South, Hugo Black of Alabama and Stanley Reed of Kentucky, while there is none from west of Michigan.

Therefore, the White House has been subject to pressure to appoint Judge Wiley Rutledge of the United States Court of Appeals in the District of Columbia, former dean of law at the State University of Iowa.

Though Felix Frankfurter is opposed to him, Rutledge happens to be the candidate of Chief Justice Stone, who would like to see a judge rather than a Senator appointed. . . .

Among the many letters Brant sent to various well-known lawyers and educators in Missouri, Iowa, and Colorado, and other western states, was one to John C. Prior, the President of the National Conference of Commissioners on Uniform State Laws, an important position in legal circles. His reply throws a significant light on the selflessness and humility of Rutledge's personality. "I was pleased and yet perplexed," Prior wrote, "to get your letter of November 2, 1942."

Right after Justice Byrnes resigned, I wrote Wiley about the matter and expressed my desire to be of assistance. He replied at once and very emphatically discouraged any such assistance. He expressed his conviction that the appointment should go to a Republican and asked me to use such influence as I might have in favor of Judge John J. Parker of North Carolina, pointing out that a distinct injustice had been done Judge Parker by the Senate's failure to confirm his previous appointment. Wiley's thought as to the appointment of a Republican was that it would promote unity at a time when it was most needed. . . .

As a result of Brant's work, more letters and recommendations poured into the offices of the Attorney General and the President, and St. Louis and Iowa newspaper editorials began to take account of the situation and to stress Rutledge's availability. On November 10, the *St. Louis Star Times* commented:

> The Star Times said of him [Rutledge] three years ago, in discussing his possible appointment to succeed Justice Brandeis, that in St. Louis Wiley Rutledge was equally well known as a scholar in the field of law, a courageous liberal in the field of scholarship. . . . Time has vindicated this judgment and there is more reason than ever to believe that Justice Rutledge would be a valuable addition to the high court.

As time wore on with no action from the White House, further favorable editorial comment appeared from time to time. On December 17 the *Post Dispatch* pointed out the desirability of the promotion of qualified judges in the lower federal courts.

> The President has a three-fold opportunity in making his eighth Supreme Court appointment. He can recognize the fine work of the long-neglected lower court judges.
>
> He can select a Justice who measures up to the great responsibility ahead of him, in view of the present even division of the Court on important questions.
>
> He can contribute to national unity by making an appointment which is not personal in the sense that all his Supreme Court appointments have been.

The suggestion that a competent federal judge be promoted was a popular one which the President had never before followed. After the appointment, the *Washington News* commended him: "First because this eighth Roosevelt nominee to the highest court is being promoted for able service on a lower Federal bench, in recognition of a sound principle heretofore ignored."[9] The *New York Times* of the same date made the same point, observing that it was the first time the President had elevated a lower federal judge to the Supreme Court. It predicted prompt confirmation.

As noted, the President did not act until January 11, 1943, more than three months after the resignation of Byrnes and during a term of Court when eight Justices were handling a tremendous volume of litigation. Indeed, it was another month after the nomination that Rutledge was confirmed by the Senate and not until February 15, that he took his seat.

There was some newspaper gossip and speculation with respect to Senate confirmation. The *Indianapolis Times* in a story by its Washington correspondent, reported that Indiana Democrat, Senator Van Nuys of the Senate Judiciary Committee thought that Rutledge's position on the court-packing plan might have an important bearing on his confirmation. Van Nuys appointed to the subcommittee on the Rutledge nomination Senator O'Mahoney, Democrat of Wyoming, Chairman; and Senators McCarran, Democrat of Nevada, and Austin, Republican of Vermont, as the other members. All three were actively in opposition to the Roosevelt court plan and had signed a blistering committee report against it. When asked why he chose these particular Senators to cross-examine Rutledge, Van Nuys is reported to have smilingly said, "Well, you see, his name was sent up here as that of a Westerner, so I thought he ought to have two Western Democrats to handle it."

The alleged excitement about Rutledge and his views never materialized. The Associated Press for February 1 reported the approval of the nomination by the Judiciary Committee by a vote of 11 to 0 with four Senators abstaining. The four were Senators Wheeler, Democrat of Montana; Langer, Republican of North Dakota; Ferguson, Republican of Michigan; and Revercomb, Republican of West Virginia. Ferguson told reporters that he had raised the question of Rutledge's stand on the court enlargement bill and had not received "a satisfactory answer." The eleven who approved the nomination included seven Democrats and four Republicans, among whom were Chairman Van Nuys and Senator Austin of Vermont.

Actually, the Rutledge appointment was generally regarded as a splendid, nonpolitical and nonpersonal selection. As previously noted, the only voice raised in the Senate against him was the futile one of Senator Langer. As reported in the *Chattanooga Times* for February 14, "The appointment to the Supreme Court was widely praised by members of the National and District Bar Associations and by Congressmen of Western states who consider him an authority on matters affecting their sections of the country." The newspaper also remarked that the legal profession from the President of the conservative American Bar Association to members of the liberal National Lawyers Guild joined in the near-universal approval of what *Time Magazine*[10] characterized as "Everybody's Justice." The magazine commented that the President usually made important government appointments with an eye to geography and Rutledge certainly had it. "But," it continued, "stocky, rugged Justice Rutledge, 48, had more than geography to recommend him." *Time's* judgment here was better than it has been on some other occasions.

Press comment was almost universally laudatory and largely of the same nature. "He is a grand man . . . unostentatious and kindly." He "can disagree without offending . . . is forthright, but never gets overly heated in argument." If he was not "everybody's Justice," his capacity for friendship was unlimited. His friends "included waiters and governors, laborers and lawyers, janitors and musicians." A press association correspondent wrote, "Acclaimed as a man of great social sympathies and one who possesses more interest in human welfare than in abstract facts of law, he has made extensive studies of the social and economic aspects of his profession."

The *American Bar Association Journal* described him as "a man of simple tastes, modest disposition, discreet manner and sympathetic understanding."

> He is a courteous, listening judge, tolerant of contrary viewpoints, unhurried at arriving at conclusions and resourceful in maintaining them. He is a skillful technician in legal writing and his skill is purposefully devoted to the evolution of a dynamic law. He is . . . committed, among other things, to the proposition that, under the Constitution, the general welfare is as much a concern of the Federal government as the common defense. . . .

This was high praise, indeed, from an organization not always characterized by its advocacy of liberal constitutional policies or support of liberal judges.

There were also expressions of approval which, no doubt, left Rutledge somewhat less than flattered. A Tennessee newspaper, after characterizing him as coming from "fine old American stock," a graduate of Maryville College, declared that:

> He is said to be an able jurist and has not been connected with the fellow travelers of the "isms" as have several other Roosevelt appointees. Judge Rutledge should grace the Supreme Bench, and it is a relief to have him follow in the wake of the "specimens" who preceded him since the "nine

old men" began to fade out in the course of nature and left the Court a Roosevelt organization.[11]

A few, but very few dissonant voices were raised, aside from Senator Langer's Senate speech in which he suggested as an alternative ground for Rutledge's disqualification, the fact that he came from Iowa City, "the home of Harry Hopkins." The *New York Herald Tribune* was much distressed. It deplored the "inability of the President to infuse even into his own policies the strength and realism which can be achieved only through the choice of effective officers, with reputations and talents consonant with the practical tasks to which they are approved."[12] Along with Stone, Frankfurter and Douglas, Rutledge made the fourth former law professor on the Court. And so, the newspaper lamented, Rutledge "would add to the academic cast which is already too pronounced."

It was a compliment with considerable point when Luther Smith in a congratulatory letter to Brant declared, "It is very clear to me that the first requisite of anyone desiring to become a member of the Supreme Court is to look around and see if he numbers among his friends an Irving Brant."

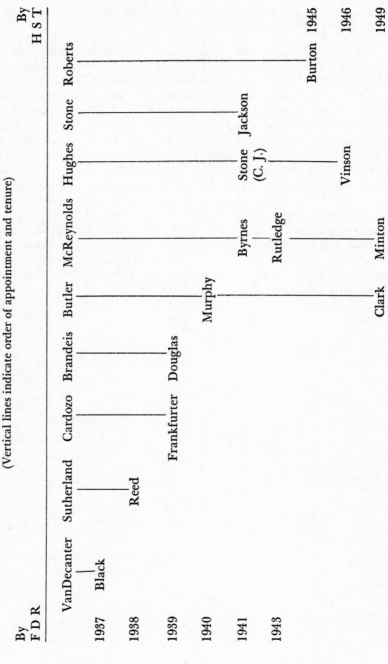

SUPREME COURT—ROOSEVELT AND TRUMAN APPOINTMENTS
(Vertical lines indicate order of appointment and tenure)

CHAPTER III

"...RESPECTING AN ESTABLISHMENT OF RELIGION, OR PROHIBITING THE FREE EXERCISE THEREOF...."

"Ye Are My Witnesses"

THE religions of the world have been organized in many forms and their faiths reflected in numerous creeds. It is probably not too much to say that all societies in all ages have had some more or less systematic way of explaining life's mysteries which could be called religion. This is, indeed, a believing world. Western Europe and the Americas have for centuries been religiously dominated by Christianity with slight Judaic overtones. Catholics and Protestants compete for ascendency in the various nations, the former more numerous in South America and Southern Europe, the latter predominating, with minor exceptions, elsewhere.

Protestantism is divided into a dozen or more major denominations, with minor offshoots, differing on lesser matters of discipline, ceremony, and faith. In addition, it has from time to time, been plagued with small crackpot sects or movements, some merely fanatically motivated, others originating from political and financial considerations, with varying degrees of moral and intellectual dishonesty in their leaders. But as Justice Jackson pointed out in the "I Am" cult case:

> The chief wrong which false prophets do to their following is not financial. . . . The real harm is on the mental and spiritual plane. There are those who hunger and thirst after higher values which they feel wanting in their humdrum lives. They live in mental confusion or moral anarchy and seek vaguely for truth and beauty and moral support. When they are deluded and then disillusioned, cynicism and confusion follow. . . . But that is precisely the thing the Constitution put

45

beyond the reach of the prosecutor, for the price of freedom of religion or of speech or of the press is that we must put up with, and even pay for, a good deal of rubbish.[1]

In one of the most sensitive areas of human thought, where tolerance is least to be found, this is strong doctrine. But so far as the law is concerned, it "knows no heresy, and is committed to the support of no dogma, the establishment of no sect."[2]

Jehovah's Witnesses is a fanatical, fundamentalist religious organization founded in 1872 by a man named Charles Taze Russell of Pennsylvania. It seems that at first this was an informal group which gathered together to study the scriptures. Apparently they became fascinated with the idea of the second coming of Christ and the end of the world. Some years later the group incorporated and established headquarters in Brooklyn, New York. The movement grew and expanded. It has been claimed that "since 1938, with the adoption of a Theocratic organization extending all the way down to the congregational level, Jehovah's Witnesses have made their most amazing increase. In the ten years following that date new ministers were being baptized and entering the field at the rate of a thousand a week."[3] Today, the organization carries on its programs in England, Europe, and other parts of the world. It is essentially an evangelical organization, "preaching" the "word" in the streets and engaging in door to door canvassing to sell or give away the numerous tracts and pamphlets put out by the Watchtower Bible and Tract Society, its Pennsylvania corporate publishing house.

Little is known of the finances of the Society. Presumably most of its revenues are derived from sales of its literature and the contributions of its members, who, although for the most part of small income, are of great faith and devotion. The Society has acquired some real estate over the years and several radio stations, but as income producers these are probably of comparatively little value.

In addition to literature, the Society has used portable phonographs extensively in its recruiting and proselyting activities. It also manufactures records for sale as well as for street use. From time to time it uses sound trucks with amplifiers sufficient to reach audiences of considerable size.

The bulk of its evangelistic activities is carried on by the rank and file who carry the message, personally, to the public. The words of Isaiah (43:10) are taken literally and personally: "Ye are my Witnesses." These colporteurs consist of men, women and children, "thoroughly consecrated to the program and eager to sacrifice everything, if necessary, for the work to which they believe Jehovah has called them."[4] This work is not carried out on a hit or miss basis. It is carefully organized, the preachers being assigned to definite areas by direction of a local central organization.

The Witnesses who work in the streets were originally called "Pioneers." Stroup, writing in 1945, reported that the Pioneers received full maintenance (room, board and clothing), travel expenses and ten dollars a month as an allowance—"the same as any full-time worker in the Brooklyn factory or on the farms. Missionaries sent abroad by the Society work on the same basis as do the Pioneers at home."[5]

The *Watchtower* for January 1, 1962, contains a summary of the widespread activities of this group. It reported that the average number of "publishers," that is, colporteurs who devote a substantial amount of their time to "preaching" on the streets and public places for the United States was 248,681. The total pieces of literature distributed annually was 6,240,290 in 37,232,858 hours of canvassing. It also disclosed activities, varying in number and extent, in 175 different countries as divergent as the Islands of Tobago, Taiwan, the Azores and Iceland, and the Argentine, Sudan, China, India, Pakistan, France, Great Britain and Sweden. The grand total of "publishers" all over the world came to 851,378. That this sect is still active and growing in the United States is evidenced by the fact, as reported in the *New York Times*, July 13, 1963, that in a single ceremony, 2,251 converts were baptized at Orchard Beach in the Bronx.

Persecution of the Witnesses in small cities and towns in the United States was nothing new to them. Their fanatical attacks upon Catholicism had brought them many violent reprisals in Italy and other European countries. With the advent of the Hitler dictatorship in 1933, their troubles in Germany increased. Their property was seized, their printing plant closed, their meetings and activities forced underground.[6] As might be expected, the Witnesses fared no better under Communist rule. They report in *Jehovah's Witnesses in the Divine Purpose*:

> The expansion in Europe following World War II was not accomplished without great difficulties. This was especially true in those countries where Communist influence was strongly felt. As Russia gradually lowered the Iron Curtain in Europe after 1948, thousands of Witnesses found themselves subjected to persecution, in many ways, worse than that which they had experienced under Nazi rule. After only three or four years of freedom from concentration camps, thousands again found

themselves forced back into such devilish institutions or were
sent to work as slaves in Russian mines, or, worse still, were
banished to Siberia. . . . In 1948, there were 440 still in
prison.[7]

In 1941, the American Civil Liberties Union published a pamphlet
outlining the troubles of violence suffered by the Witnesses in the
United States. Not since the persecution of the Mormons, it noted,
had any religious minority been subjected to such lawless attacks by
irresponsible mobs. The worst outbreak occurred after the 1940
decision in the *Gobitis* case[8] in which the Supreme Court upheld the
compulsory flag-salute regulation of a local school board. The Gobitis
children had refused to comply because of their conscientious objections and those of their parents.

Most of the attacks were made on helpless house-to-house canvassers in small communities. Legionnaires and other self-proclaimed
"patriots" insisted that they "salute" the flag. Men and women were
beaten, jailed, and chased out of town. Instance after instance was
recorded of shameless and cowardly assaults with police protection
refused. Their literature was seized and destroyed repeatedly and
their property damaged. In few cases were attorneys for the Witnesses able to obtain warrants for the arrest of members of the
mob whom they had positively identified. The situation became so
scandalous that in June 1940, Attorney General Biddle addressed
the nation on a radio network. "A religious sect known as Jehovah's
Witnesses," he said, "have been repeatedly set upon and beaten.
They had committed no crime; but the mob adjudged they had,
and meted out punishments . . . . We shall not defeat the Nazi
evil by emulating its methods."[9]

At about this time a series of cases, eventually to reach the
Supreme Court, were in the making, challenging official restrictions
on the behavior of members of the Society. The Court had already
decided three cases[10] involving basically the same issue but there
was dissension and conflict ahead.

In one, *Lovell* v. *Griffin* a unanimous Court, in an opinion by Chief
Justice Hughes, held void a sweeping ordinance which required a
license to distribute any kind of literature. The City Manager was
given authority to grant such licenses in his discretion. Although
the convicted Witness had been distributing religious pamphlets,
the case was decided solely on the freedom of the press issue. This
was in March, 1938.

Mr. Justice Roberts delivered the opinion in the *Schneider* case
in November 1939. Only Justice McReynolds dissented. Again the

decision turned on freedom of the press rather than freedom of religion. Ordinances of several cities were involved, either prohibiting pamphlet distribution on the streets or requiring a permit from the police. All were struck down, the Court holding that neither the purpose of keeping the streets clean nor the prevention of fraudulent advertising was sufficient to justify invasion of the privilege of freedom of the press. There are other obvious methods of protection against such evils which are reasonable and less restrictive. The *Cantwell* case, decided the following May (1940), involved both freedom of speech and religion. Justice Roberts again speaking for the Court, held invalid a Connecticut statute requiring the approval of a state official for any religious or philanthropic cause as a condition to the solicitation of money from persons other than members of the soliciting organization.

Almost two years later these issues got to the Supreme Court all over again. On February 15th, 1943, the *New York Times*[11] carried a news story, in part as follows:

> Wiley Blount Rutledge, Jr. was sworn in today as an Associate Justice of the Supreme Court and within half an hour the Court issued two unexpected orders aimed at speedy disposition of important cases affecting civil liberties.
>
> One order, rare in the tribunal's history, granted rearguments in three cases in which the Court decided 5 to 4 last June that Jehovah's Witnesses must obey city ordinances prohibiting distribution of literature without a license.
>
> Some observers who have followed the cases of Jehovah's Witnesses in the Supreme Court believe that with Justice Rutledge upon the bench, the Jurists may now reverse themselves not only in the literature-peddling cases, but also in the *Gobitis* decision of three years ago that school children of that sect must salute the American flag regardless of religious convictions.

The previous June the Court had upheld city ordinances of cities in Alabama, Arkansas, and Arizona imposing license taxes on the sale of printed matter, as applied to Jehovah's Witnesses' itinerant street evangelists. The case is commonly referred to as the *Opelika* case.[12] The ordinances had been attacked as in violation of the free speech and press provisions as well as the free practice of religion clause of the First Amendment made applicable to the states through the Fourteenth Amendment. The decision was five to four, Chief Justice Stone and Justices Black, Douglas, and Murphy dissenting. As reported in the *Times,* rehearing was ordered on the day Rutledge took his seat on the Court. After argument, the decision was reversed on the same day that the Court handed down decisions in three other related cases involving activities of this particular sect. Rutledge, of course, cast the deciding vote. The remaining four Justices of the former majority dissented.[13]

It is almost impossible to find a rational explanation for the series of Supreme Court decisions involving the Witnesses during these years. To be sure there were slight differences in the city ordinances involved in these various cases, but it is hard, indeed, to find constitutional distinctions. Nor does the changing personnel of the Court clarify things until the Rutledge appointment and the second *Opelika* decision. In the 1938 case, Justice Cardozo took no part because of illness but he no doubt would have joined in the opinion of Chief Justice Hughes, as did the other seven Justices, in invalidating the city law. In 1939 Justice McReynolds was a lone dissenter in the *Schneider* case. Justices Frankfurter and Douglas, who had replaced Justices Cardozo and Brandeis, joined the four other Justices in supporting Roberts' opinion that the ordinance involved was unconstitutional. Justice Butler had died a week before and had not participated in the judgment. In the Connecticut case, Justice Murphy had taken Butler's seat and the decision was again unanimous. Within two weeks after this decision came the first flag salute case. A law requiring children of the Witnesses to salute the flag in public schools was upheld by the same Court, Stone being the only dissenter. Two years later, with Byrnes filling McReynolds' place after the latter's retirement, the first *Opelika* decision came down, upholding the license ordinance by a five to four vote.

There is much to be explained. How did Justice McReynolds come to hold unconstitutional the ordinances in the *Lovell* and Connecticut cases? He failed to explain his dissent in the *Schneider* case. Indeed he said nothing in any of these cases. Why did Butler so vote in *Lovell?* How to explain Frankfurter's votes in the *Schneider* case and his contrary vote in both *Opelikas,* not to mention the flag salute case? Finally, who would have supposed that Douglas and Black would have upheld the flag salute law? Stone's position throughout this series of cases appears to be the only consistent one of the various Justices involved.

The original *Opelika* opinion had been written by Justice Reed. The city ordinance had required a ten dollar yearly license fee for book agents and a five dollar fee for transient agents or distributors. The licenses were subject to revocation in the discretion of the licensing commission, with or without notice. The two other cases,

decided at the same time, involved slightly different license requirements or city ordinances. Appellants, convicted for noncompliance,
relied both on the free press and freedom of religion clauses of the
First Amendment. Reed's opinion pointed out the difference between
"censorship and complete prohibition" on the one hand, and "regulation of the conduct of individuals in the time, manner and place
of their activities." He placed emphasis upon the fact that since the
appellants' evangelism was also used as a source of funds, "the
financial aspects of their transactions need not wholly be disregarded."

> To subject any religious or didactic group to a reasonable
> fee for their money-making activities does not require a finding
> that the licensed acts are purely commercial. . . . If we were
> to assume, as is here argued, that the licensed activities
> involve religious rites, a different question would be presented.
> These are not taxes on free will offerings. But it is because
> we view these sales as partaking more of commercial than reli-
> gious or educational transactions that we find the ordinances,
> as here presented, valid.[14]

Stone's dissent was powerful. He started with *Lovell* v. *Griffin*[15] in
which a unanimous Court had held void on its face the requirement
of a license for the distribution of pamphlets to be issued in the
sole discretion of an administrative officer.

> That purpose [freedom from previous restraint upon pub-
> lication] cannot rightly be defeated by so transparent a subter-
> fuge as the pronouncement that, while a license may not be
> required if its award is contingent upon the whim of an ad-
> ministrative officer, it may be if its retention and the enjoyment
> of the privilege which it purports to give are wholly contin-
> gent upon his whim.

He then blasted the argument that the ordinances merely regulated
the "time, place and manner" of appellant's activities. "None of the
ordinances, if complied with," he wrote, "purports to, or could, control
the time, place or manner of the distribution of the books and pamphlets concerned."

> None has any discernible relationship to the police protec-
> tion or the good order of the community. The only condition
> and purpose of the licenses . . . is suppression of the specified
> distributions of literature in default of the payment of a sub-
> stantial tax fixed in amount and measured neither by the

extent of the defendants' activities under the license nor the amounts which they receive for and devote to religious purposes in the exercise of the licensed privilege.

He thought that if such taxes as those involved in the three cases before them were sustained, the way was open for the effective suppression of speech, press and religion. "In its potency," he concluded, "as a prior restraint on publication, the flat license tax falls short only of outright censorship or suppression."

Another case,[16] decided the same day as the second *Opelika* decision, invalidated a city ordinance requiring a license for which the licensee paid a reasonable fee to canvass, take orders or deliver any merchandise within the city. Several Witnesses had been arrested for noncompliance. The opinion of the Court was rendered by Justice Douglas, with the same dissenters as in *Opelika*. He pointed out that the cases involved no unlawful act during the solicitation, nor any question of registration of solicitors. "The cases present a single issue," he wrote, "the constitutionality of an ordinance which as construed and applied requires religious colporteurs to pay a license tax as a condition to the pursuit of their activities." The activity of the Witnesses "is more than preaching; it is more than distribution of religious literature. It is a combination of both. Its purpose is as evangelical as the revival meeting."

He distinguished the situation before the Court from one involving purely commercial activities. The mere fact that the colporteurs "sold" or gave away their literature did not make it a business enterprise. "If it did, then the passing of the collection plate in church would make the church service a commercial project. The constitutional rights of those spreading their religious beliefs through the spoken and printed word are not to be gauged by standards governing retailers or wholesalers of books." Douglas hammered away at his theme:

> [A]n itinerant evangelist however misguided or intolerant he may be, does not become a mere book agent by selling the Bible or religious tracts to help defray his expenses or to sustain him. Freedom of speech, freedom of the press, freedom of religion are available to all, not merely to those who can pay their own way.

In his dissent, Justice Reed insisted upon the right of the states to tax publishing houses and religious organizations. "It may be concluded," he wrote, "that neither in the state or the federal constitutions was general taxation of church or press interdicted. Is there anything in the decisions of this Court which indicates that church or press is free from the financial burdens of government? We find nothing."[17] To which Douglas answered:

> We do not mean to say that religious groups and the press are free from all financial burdens of government. . . . We have here something quite different, for example, from a tax on the income of one who engages in religious activities or a tax on property used or employed in connection with those activities. It is one thing to impose a tax on the income or property of a preacher. It is quite another thing to exact a tax from him for the privilege of delivering a sermon. The tax imposed by the City of Jeannette is a flat license tax, the payment of which is a condition of the exercise of these constitutional privileges. The power to tax the exercise of a privilege is the power to control or supress its enjoyment. . . . Those who can tax the exercise of this religious practice can make its exercise so costly as to deprive it of the resources necessary for its maintenance. Those who can tax the privilege of engaging in this form of missionary evangelism can close its doors to all those who do not have a full purse. Spreading religious beliefs in this ancient and honorable manner would thus be denied the needy. Those who can deprive religious groups of their colporteurs can take from them a part of the vital power of the press which has survived from the Reformation.[18]

Here Douglas may have pushed a good argument too far. As Justice Frankfurter in his dissent pointed out, "the power to tax is the power to destroy only in the sense that those who have power can misuse it." He then quoted Justice Holmes, as disposing of this "smooth phrase," when he added "not while this Court sits." But Holmes' dictum in this context may also be too "smooth." The real issue is when, if ever, may a state impose a tax on the exercise of a right guaranteed by the Constitution of the United States?

A third case decided the same day as the *Opelika* decision involved a municipal ordinance of the Ohio town of Struthers[19] which made it unlawful for any person distributing handbills, circulars or advertisements, to ring doorbells, sound doorknockers or otherwise summon householders to the door to receive them. The ordinance was held unconstitutional by the usual five to four decision. Mr. Justice Black wrote for the Court. Mr. Justice Murphy wrote a concurring opinion in which Justices Rutledge and Douglas joined.

Justice Rutledge's file on this case discloses a curious sequence of events. The original vote had been for upholding the ordinance; Black, Jackson, Roberts, Frankfurter, and Reed constituting the majority, with Stone, Murphy, Douglas, and Rutledge dissenting. Black was to write the opinion for the Court. Black wrote his opinion and circulated it. His position, briefly, was as follows: While the Constitution assures to everyone the right to believe and worship in accordance with his individual conscience, it does not grant an unrestrained liberty to engage, even in the name of religion, in conduct which may seriously jeopardize the rights of others. Religious liberty is not a license to interfere in the affairs of another who does not share his beliefs. There was evidence that Struthers was an industrial community near Youngstown where the iron and steel mills operated swing shifts around the clock. This meant that many workers slept in the daytime. Black thought that callers selling pots and pans or distributing leaflets could interfere with the peaceful enjoyment of a home as much as a neighborhood glue factory or a railroad yard. The rubric "a man's home is his castle" is no mere rhetorical phrase.

At this point both Stone and Rutledge wrote and circulated dissenting opinions. The Rutledge draft pointed out that the record was meager as to the extent of swing shifts and the number of night workers. "Neither common knowledge nor unsupported assertions of counsel can supply foundation in fact for belief that handbill distributors are more disturbing than others." He denounced the law as altogether arbitrary. "The ordinance, as written, includes everyone who knocks or rings the bell with paper in hand and intends to give it to the occupant. It excludes all who come without the circular. The prohibition is not confined to the nuisance who rings pestiferously or persistently. One knock is enough." The thrust of this opinion was the discriminatory character of the ordinance although it also pointed out that the law was broad enough to exclude circular distributors who were welcome to the householder and thus to usurp the owner's "right to control his property."

Stone's opinion made somewhat the same point as Rutledge's. Further, he could not accept a decision which could open the way to complete suppression in every town and city in the land, of all personal communication of ideas by a stranger to the people in their homes, however willing they might be to receive them. Such ordinances would have stamped out the form of evangelism—to say nothing of political appeals by handbills and pamphlets—which has been the historic means of communicating ideas to people in their homes, both in Europe and in the United States. He pointed out that a community which today, if moved to do so, could by the use of this device suppress the house-to-house communication of ideas and solicitations of funds by Jehovah's Witnesses, could in other days have similarly suppressed the collection of funds and the dissemination of ideas in the support of Protestantism and Catholicism and many another faith now accepted and cherished by millions. If only accepted causes, which no longer need the house-to-house appeal, are entitled to enjoy the benefits of the First Amendment, he thought, its guarantees serve little purpose and could as well not have been written.

Neither Black's opinion referred to above, nor Stone's and Rutledge's was ever published. Black switched his vote to join the dissenters who then constituted the majority to invalidate the ordinance. He then wrote the opinion for the Court as it eventually appeared. Stone was content with the reasons expressed therein while Rutledge joined in a concurring opinion by Murphy. Reed wrote a dissenting opinion in which Roberts and Jackson joined; Frankfurter wrote a short opinion which he characterized as neither "concurring nor dissenting."

The last of the May 3rd Jehovah Witnesses cases was *Douglas* v. *City of Jeannette*,[20] in which the Court held an injunction not available to prohibit city officials from enforcing an ordinance requiring a license, for which a tax must be paid, to solicit orders for any kind of merchandise. It was the usual manifestation of the reluctance of the federal courts to interfere with or embarrass proceedings in state courts except to prevent irreparable and imminent injury. There was no reason to believe that the complainants were threatened with injury other than that incidental to any criminal prosecution brought in good faith. Adequate relief, if their claims were justified, would be available by resort to normal appellate procedure, that is, if convicted, they could appeal through the state courts to the Supreme Court of the United States.

The *Prince*[21] case, decided the following term of Court, involved the validity of the Massachusetts Child Labor Law as applied to a nine-year-old Jehovah Witness girl selling or offering for sale religious literature on the streets of Brockton. The law forbade boys under twelve and girls under eighteen to "sell, expose or offer for sale any newspapers, magazines, periodicals or any other articles of merchandise of any description, or exercise the trade of boot-black," and so forth on the streets.

The girl, accompanied by her aunt, had violated this statute, making the usual claim that this was a part of a religious duty, to worship God and "engage in preaching work." The aunt, Mrs.

Prince, was prosecuted and convicted under the provision of the law which made parents or guardians violators by compelling or permitting violation by under age children. Against her First Amendment plea, the state court affirmed her conviction. "We think that freedom of the press and of religion," the court said, "is subject to incidental regulation to the slight degree involved in the prohibition of the selling of religious literature in streets and public places by boys under twelve and girls under eighteen and in the further statutory provisions herein considered, which have been adopted as means of enforcing that prohibition."22

Rutledge, writing for the Court, affirmed the state court in upholding the law. Actually the only point in issue was the free-practice-of-religion clause. Appellant did not stand on freedom of speech or press. She conceded that Massachusetts might regulate the distribution of secular literature by these means, but not religious matter. She also sought to buttress her position with a claim of parental right under the due process clause of the Fourteenth Amendment. But as Rutledge pointed out, in the circumstances of the case before the Court, "all that is comprehended in the former [due process] is included in the latter [freedom of religion]."

"It is in the interest of youth itself," wrote Rutledge, "and of the whole community, that children be both safeguarded from abuses and given opportunities for growth into free and independent, well-developed men and citizens." "And," he added, "neither rights of religion nor rights of parenthood are beyond limitation." He continued:

> Acting to guard the general interest in youth's well being, the state as parens patriae may restrict the parent's control by requiring school attendance, regulating or prohibiting the child's labor, and in many other ways. Its authority is not nullified merely because the parent grounds his claim to control the child's course of conduct on religion or conscience.23

It was conceded by the opinion that a statute identical in terms would be invalid as applied to adults.

> The state's authority over children's activities is broader than over like actions of adults. This is peculiarly true of public activities and in matters of employment. . . . It is true children have rights, in common with older people, in the primary use of highways. . . . Street preaching, whether oral or by handing out literature, is not the primary use of the

highway, even for adults. While for them it cannot be wholly prohibited, it can be regulated within reasonable limits in accommodation to the primary and other incidental uses.[24]

While the presence of parent or guardian might protect the child against some street risks, it could not forestall all of them. Zealously propagandizing the community in public places, Rutledge thought, whether politically or religiously, creates situations difficult for adults, much more so for children including emotional excitement and psychological, as well as physical, harm. "Parents may be free to become martyrs themselves. But it does not follow they are free, in identical circumstances, to make martyrs of their children. . . ."

But, the appellant argued, for Jehovah's Witnesses and their children, the streets were their church, and to deny them access for religious purposes is on the level with the exclusion of altar boys, choir boys, and other children from their places of worship. To this, Rutledge replied that "the public highways have not become their religious property merely by their assertion. And there is no denial of equal protection in excluding their children from doing there what no other children may do." In one of the relatively few cases involving First Amendment issues, Justice Murphy here found himself in disagreement with Rutledge.

The Justice's papers disclose traces of kindly but serious badinage on the issue in which eight members of the Court were in agreement on a highly controversial issue. "Frank wants the solitary glory of dissent," wrote one of the Justices to Rutledge. In a scribbled note, Frankfurter explained why he had left the conference on this case. He had to see an old friend who had a personal problem "and so could not enter into talk when you began to say some joshing thing to me. I came later to listen to you at length and to rejosh, if I could."

"Solitary glory" or not, Murphy's opinion was a strong one, both from the heart and the mind. After the circulation of Rutledge's draft opinion, he, too, in a penciled note, wrote: "Wiley—I am never happy disagreeing with you. And there is so little I can contribute here but I am a profound if not an adequate Jeffersonian on freedom of conscience. So I will write a note—inoffensive I'm sure— in the *Prince* case when it comes down."

In fact, although his "note" was inoffensive as they invariably were, Murphy made points which Rutledge did not answer to the satisfaction of many "profound," if not "adequate Jeffersonians." Relying on the "preferred position" of First Amendment rights, Murphy pointed out that, "we are not aided by any strong presumption of the constitutionality of such legislation. . . .

> On the contrary, the human freedoms enumerated in the First Amendment and carried over into the Fourteenth Amendment are to be presumed to be invulnerable and any attempt to sweep away those freedoms is prima facie invalid. . . . The burden was therefore on the state of Massachusetts to prove the reasonableness and necessity of prohibiting children from engaging in religious activity of the type involved in this case. The burden in this instance, however, is not met by vague references to the reasonableness underlying child labor legislation in general. . . . The vital freedom of religion. . . cannot be erased by slender references to the state's power to restrict the more secular activities of children.

It can hardly be denied that the facts, as revealed in the Court's opinion, indicate little more than "slender references" to the state's power to protect children from the evils of activities in the streets. During oral argument it appears that the Chief Justice had made some remark to the effect that the Court would take judicial notice of street dangers to children. Counsel for the Witnesses later wrote a letter asking the Court to take judicial notice of a study by the Metropolitan Life Insurance Company concluding that "the home is relatively more dangerous than the public sidewalks." Nevertheless, to many readers and critics who may be as "profound," and perhaps, more "adequate Jeffersonians," the decision may appear to be a common sense, pragmatic accommodation of the power of the state, as *parens patriae* to the right of the free practice of religion in a situation created by a fanatical, though consecrated minority.

The Court's position and Murphy's position in this case are perfectly clear regardless of one's point of view as to the merits. But there was another opinion—characterized as "separate," by Justice Jackson. He had joined in Frankfurter's dissent in *Murdock* v. *Pennsylvania*. In his *Prince* opinion, he dissented from *Murdock* all over again, but in fact concurred in the child labor decision. "I have no alternative," he said, "but to dissent from the grounds of affirmance of a judgment which I think was rightly decided, and upon right grounds, by the Supreme Judicial Court of Massachusetts."

It is not too clear just what it was that troubled Jackson. Apparently, it was the accent on youth of the Rutledge position. He quoted from Douglas' *Murdock* opinion that the street evangelism of the Witnesses occupies the same high estate under the First Amendment as does "worship in the churches and preaching from the pulpits" and stressed the Court's refusal to regard it as a commercial enterprise. In some curious way, he then arrived at the non-sequitur that, "if the Murdock doctrine stands along with today's decision, a foundation is laid for any state intervention in the indoctrination and participation of children in religion, provided it is done in the name of their health or welfare."[25]

After the circulation among the Justices of this opinion, Rutledge received a scribbled complaint from the irked Douglas, suggesting that Jackson's point be somehow met. The result was the addition of the final paragraph of the opinion, to which Douglas agreed, as follows:

> Our ruling does not extend beyond the facts the case presents. We neither lay the foundation "for any [that is, every] state intervention in the indoctrination and participation of children in religion" which may be done "in the name of their health and welfare" nor give warrant for "every limitation on their religious training and activities." The religious training and indoctrination of children may be accomplished in many ways, some of which, as we have noted, have received constitutional protection through decisions of this Court. These and all others except the public proclaiming of religion on the streets, if this may be taken as either training or indoctrination of the proclaimer, remain unaffected by the decision.[26]

Two days before opinion day Rutledge received a note from Frankfurter to the effect that he wished to withdraw his previously indicated concurrence with the Court's opinion. Since the Jackson opinion was based on approval of the grounds taken by the Massachusetts Supreme Judicial Court and since he thought those were the right grounds, he had decided to join Jackson. Roberts had already indicated that he would concur with the Jackson opinion. Both Justices had dissented in *Murdock*.

The opinion of the Massachusetts court was mostly devoted to an interpretation of the provisions of the child labor law and the question of self-incrimination involved when appellant refused to give the child's name to the school attendance office, for which she was convicted on the first count of the indictment. Scarcely more than a page of the opinion dealt with the First Amendment constitutional issue. The grounds for decision on the point may be summed up in one sentence. "These provisions belong to a type of legislation long regarded as within the duty of the State to protect the health, morals, and welfare of its people."[27] When Justice Black re-

turned the Rutledge draft with his approval, he added that he liked
its "clarity, force and brevity." It is not obvious that the opinion of
the Massachusetts court was superior in any of these respects, unless
it was "brevity."

It appears that a majority of the Court had originally favored
dismissal of the appeal for want of a substantial federal question and
a typewritten "Per Curiam" memorandum to that effect was circulated. Murphy, who dissented, and Jackson who had his axe to
grind over *Murdock*, circulated memoranda urging that the appeal
be granted. Jackson's argument was substantially that which appeared in his "separate" opinion.

Rutledge worked hard on his opinion and was, as always, open
to criticism and suggestions from his brethren although he did not,
of course, invariably follow them. Sometimes, however, he made too
many concessions. For example, he accepted a suggestion from the
Chief Justice which actually weakened his *Prince* opinion. The
draft of the opinion as originally circulated, contained the following:

> The fallacy of the (appellants) argument is obvious. It as-
> sumes a child's freedom to practice his religion is coextensive
> with an adult's and the parent's to aid and encourage him to do
> so in public is as broad as his own. In other words, the
> state's power to limit what the child may do under a claim
> of practicing religion is no broader than in the case of a ma-
> ture person.

This paragraph was omitted. "You seem to say," the Chief
Justice wrote, "that the First Amendment, standing by itself, makes
a difference between the religious freedom guaranteed to an infant
and that guaranteed to an adult. This does not seem to me to be
strictly accurate. The difference, it seems to me, is not to be found
in any distinction to be derived from the First Amendment but from
the fact that other provisions of the Constitution have conferred the
power on the state . . . to forbid the employment of children
in the streets. . . ." Stone thought the point important and Rutledge
followed his suggestion.

A law review commentator argued:

> It cannot be denied that the *Prince* decision in part qualifies
> the *Murdock* decision. It is one thing for the Court to classify
> the public activities of house-to-house canvassing and hand
> distribution as such a part of the sect's religious activity as to
> be immune from any supervision by licensing and freed from
> any fees in payment thereof. It is another thing to hold that

if the acts are performed by *minors,* they are subject to state regulations. It therefore follows that all such "religious activity" is immune from regulation only when practiced by adults. The effect of the Court's decision is to make age rather than the nature of the activity the determinative feature.

Justice Jackson's "separate" opinion was cited.[28] To this it may be observed simply that the Court presumably would follow *Murdock* if, rather than a child labor law, the Massachusetts statute required children to obtain licenses.

Justice Jackson joined in another "separate" opinion in a similar case the following March.[29] A municipal ordinance of a small South Carolina town imposed a license tax on book agents which a local Witness refused to pay. He peddled the usual tracts, devoting full time to it. His entire income consisted of the proceeds of his pro- selyting activities. Justice Douglas, writing for the Court, took the position that there was no substantial difference between this case and the *Opelika* and *Murdock* cases. He made the same point, that, "preachers of the more orthodox faiths are not engaged in com- mercial undertakings because they are dependent on their calling for a living," that, "freedom of religion is not merely reserved for those with a long purse."

Justices Roberts, Frankfurter, and Jackson thought the decision extended the rule announced in the *Opelika* and *Murdock* cases. "Follett [the witness] is not made to pay a tax for the exercise of that which the First Amendment has relieved from taxation. He is made to pay for that for which all others similarly situated must pay—an excise for the occupation of street vending." They declared that, "in effect the decision grants not free exercise of re- ligion, . . . but, on the other hand, requires that the exercise of religion be subsidized."

The subsidy argument was met in Justice Murphy's concurring opinion. "It is suggested," he wrote, "that we have opened the door to exemption of wealthy religious institutions like Trinity Church in New York City, from the payment of taxes on property investments from which support is derived for religious activities. . . . I am neither disturbed nor impressed by these allegations. . . . There is an obvious difference between taxing commercial property and investments undertaken for profit, whatever use is made of the income, and laying a tax directly on an activity that is essentially religious in purpose and character. . . ."[30] It is something of an over- simplification, but in many of its aspects, the nub of the issue here again was whether to characterize the Witness as a preacher or a book agent—were his activities primarily religious in character or were they commercial.

Professor Kurland has called attention to the fact that although the opinion of Jackson, Roberts, and Frankfurter made the point that to relieve the Witness of paying the tax is to relieve him from "the contribution to the cost of government which everyone else will have to pay," it did not take up the question whether this does not violate the separation clause. Kurland's explanation is that the Justices failed to recognize the inseparable nature of the free exercise and establishment clauses.[31] It would appear here that the two clauses may, in some situations, be in conflict, a point recognized by some of the Justices when the Court developed more awareness of the complexity of these problems and a more sophisticated treatment of them.

Prior to the first flag salute case, the Supreme Court had dismissed several appeals from state court decisions upholding salute requirements of school children. The Court could detect no "substantial federal question."[32] In fact, as Justice Frankfurter pointed out in his dissenting opinion in the second flag case, the Court had actually affirmed a similar decision in another case before *Gobitis*.[33]

On June 3, 1940, it handed down its decision, holding valid a requirement of a Pennsylvania school board that all children in public schools must salute the flag and pledge allegiance to it. The Gobitis children had refused on religious grounds and had been expelled. Mr. Justice Frankfurter wrote the opinion for the Court, with Chief Justice Stone the lone dissenter. Some three years later *Gobitis* was overruled in *West Virginia State Board of Education* v. *Barnette*.[34] Between the two decisions, Chief Justice Hughes had retired and Justice Stone had taken his place. McReynolds had retired. The two vacancies were filled by Justices Jackson and Byrnes. Byrnes in turn resigned in 1942 and was replaced by Justice Rutledge. Thus there were two new members of the Court when the *Barnette* case came before it. But since there was but one dissent in *Gobitis* and a six-judge majority in *Barnette*, it is obvious that three Justices had changed their votes. The three were Justices Murphy, Black, and Douglas.

The latter three Justices concurred in *Barnette* with an explanatory opinion by Black and Douglas. "Reluctance," they wrote, "to make the Federal Constitution a rigid bar against state regulation of conduct thought inimical to the public welfare was the controlling influence which moved us to consent to the Gobitis decision. Long reflection convinced us that although the principle is sound, its application in the particular case was wrong" [citing the second decision in *Opelika,* which overruled the first one]. "Neither our domestic tranquility in peace," they continued, "nor our martial effort in war depend on compelling little children to participate in a ceremony which ends in nothing for them but a fear of spiritual condemnation. . . . The ceremonial, when enforced against conscientious objectors, more likely to defeat than to serve its high purpose, is a handy implement for disguised religious persecution. As such, it is inconsistent with our Constitution's plan and purpose."

These three Justices had, in fact, already announced their change of heart in their dissent in the first *Opelika* case. They there wrote:

> The opinion of the Court sanctions a device which in our opinion suppresses or tends to suppress the free exercise of a religion practiced by a minority group. This is but another step in the direction which Minersville School Dist. v. Gobitis, 310 US 586 . . . took against the same religious minority and is a logical extension of the principles upon which that decision rested. Since we joined in the opinion in the Gobitis Case, we think this is an appropriate occasion to state that we now believe that it was also wrongly decided. Certainly our democratic form of government functioning under the historic Bill of Rights has a high responsibility to accommodate itself to the religious views of minorities however unpopular and unorthodox those views may be. The First Amendment does not put the right freely to exercise religion in a subordinate position. We fear, however, that the opinions in these and in the Gobitis Case do exactly that.[35]

Justice Jackson, in the *Barnette* case, wrote one of the Court's great opinions of all time. "The case is made difficult," he observed, "not because the principles of its decision are obscure but because the flag involved is our own. Nevertheless, we apply the limitations of the Constitution with no fear that freedom to be intellectually and spiritually diverse or even contrary will disintegrate the social organization. To believe that patriotism will not flourish if patriotic ceremonies are voluntary and spontaneous instead of a compulsory routine is to make an unflattering estimate of the appeal of our institutions to free minds." It should not require a war between an open and a closed society to recognize the profound truth of Jackson's solemn admonition: "Those who begin coercive elimination of dissent soon find themselves exterminating dissenters. Compulsory unification of opinion achieves only the unanimity of the graveyard."[36]

Justice Jackson concluded with an eloquent paragraph, repeatedly quoted in subsequent opinions: "If there is any fixed star in our constitutional constellation, it is that no official, high or petty, can prescribe what shall be orthodox in politics, nationalism, religion, or other matters of opinion, or force citizens to confess by word or act their faith therein."[37]

Quite naturally, all this Witness litigation attracted widespread attention. After the first *Opelika* case upholding the tax ordinance against them, the Court came in for extensive criticism from liberal sources both lay and professional. Raymond Moley in *Newsweek*[38] declared, "The decision of the Supreme Court upholding the imposition of fees on Jehovah's Witnesses for the privilege of distributing religious tracts is . . . shocking in its implications. For to whittle away the freedom of one religion is to attack the freedom of all religion. To suppress one liberty is to threaten all liberty." *Time,*[39] heading its news story "Ominous Decision," quoted similar opinions from various newspapers' editorials.

Comment in the law journals was also highly critical. Here are some samples: ". . . [A]n unlimited power of revocation would seem to make the ordinance clearly unconstitutional. . . ."[40] "It would seem that the decision is wrong . . . since the power to revoke a license appears as great a threat of censorship as the power to deny one in the first place."[41] "It is feared that the principal case . . . will offer an excellent opportunity to those who seek the suppression of this unpopular minority."[42] In fact the writer anticipated the precise analogy subsequently used by Mr. Justice Douglas in the *Murdock* case. "Jehovah's Witnesses are no more peddlers than the ordinary minister who preaches a sermon from the pulpit and passes a collection plate."[43] Critical of the Court's treatment of the activities of the Witnesses as "commercial" the *Fordham Law Review* asked, "when is 'money earned?' . . . . In the instant case the majority appears content with a finding that money was *collected*."[44] (Emphasis original.) The *Yale Law Journal* expressed the thrust of most comment, namely, that the decision was, "a serious threat to civil liberties."[45]

The *Gobitis* flag case had aroused similar expressions of concern as to the future of religious freedom in the country. "If individual liberties are something more than the by-product of a democratic process, if in fact they have an intrinsic value worthy of protection, it is difficult to justify a decision which subordinates a fundamental liberty to a legislative program of questionable worth," declared the *Michigan Law Review.*[46] The *New York University Law Review* expressed a similar view: "The Court's acceptance of so vaguely defined an interest as 'national unity' and its refusal to scrutinize the legislative judgment is open to criticism."[47] Writing a year and a half after the decision, William A. Fennell observed: "The unfortunate effects of the decision during the past year are now a matter of public record."[48] He then discussed a New Hampshire case in which, after two children had been suspended from school for refusing to salute the flag, and their parents, unable to send them to a private school, were instructing them at home, the children were committed to the State Industrial School as delinquents. Fortunately for this troubled family, the Supreme Court of the state reversed this decision on the grounds of statutory interpretation. It could not attribute to the legislature an intent "to authorize the breaking up of family life for no other reason than because some of its members have conscientious religious scruples not shared by the majority of the community. . . ."[49] A similar case in New York arrived at the same result.[50]

When the Court reversed the first *Opelika* case, the liberal press was exultant. "The outright about-face," wrote Irving Dilliard in the *New Republic*,[51] "of the United States Supreme Court on the constitutionality of city ordinances under which members of the Jehovah's Witnesses sect were convicted for distributing religious literature without a license is one of the most notable acts in the entire span of 154 years of Supreme Court history."

The *New York Times*, in its editorial for May 4, 1943, commented as follows:

> The vote of the Supreme Court's latest member, Justice Rutledge, was decisive in two opinions rendered yesterday, one of which reversed a position taken last June, and both of which taken together, reaffirmed the right of Jehovah's Witnesses to agitate for their unusual creed. . . . It is a gross under-statement to say that Jehovah's Witnesses are not popular in this country. Their beliefs are their own concern, but their methods of urging them upon other people are annoying. . . . Yet, if we permit extremists of an unpleasant sort to be deprived of their rights, it is hard to tell where the line can be drawn and who is to be deemed secure. We think the rights of all Americans are a little safer because Jehovah's Witnesses have had their second day in court.

The *Washington Post*[52] declared, "Monday's action by the Court is of tremendous historical importance." The *St. Louis Post-Dispatch*[53] expressed the view that, "the first two of President Roosevelt's four freedoms—freedom of speech and freedom of religion—have been staunchly bulwarked in the United States by the Supreme Court by the

reversal of its sorely mistaken *Opelika* decision of last June 8th. . . .
Justice Rutledge has tipped the scales on the side of the cherished
freedoms of the Bill of Rights." Even the *Chicago Tribune*,[54] a newspaper not often belligerent in support of the Bill of Rights, applauded the decision. The reason, however, was apparent—the shoe
had been on a different foot or the other axe had been ground. "The
Tribune greets this opinion with special satisfaction because the
Court has carried forward the trend to which this newspaper contributed much of the original impetus." It then referred to its victory in a libel suit brought against it by the city of Chicago,[55] and the
Minnesota free press case[56] in which the Supreme Court held invalid
an injunction against the publication of a newspaper as "previous
restraint," contrary to the First Amendment.

With the resignation of Justice Byrnes, it was recognized in many
quarters that a shift in the Court's point of view on such controversial
issues by a sharply divided Court was quite possible. The *Christian
Century* for January 13, 1943, had editorialized: "The man whom
President Roosevelt appoints to the Supreme Bench may well have it
within his single power to answer that question. The greater the importance, therefore, that the choice be made with great care and
passed on by the Senate with full consideration of all that is at stake."
In its January 27 issue, the magazine expressed satisfaction with Rutledge's nomination by the President. "The new Justice should prove
to be a stalwart champion of religious liberty and civil rights. . . . The
Christian Century has tried to emphasize the interest which the
churches have in securing a Justice who, in the present evenly divided state of the Supreme Court, can be depended upon to uphold
freedom of conscience and speech. President Roosevelt appears to
have chosen just such a man." No editor ever made a more accurate
prediction.

Justice Rutledge's performance in the Jehovah's Witnesses cases
was in fact surprising to no one who had followed his work on the
Court of Appeals. Less than a year before he took his seat on the
High Court, he had dissented in a case involving much the same
issues as in *Opelika*. Several Witnesses had been convicted of selling
tracts on the streets of the District of Columbia without a license or
paying a tax. Each had been fined five dollars (what the license in
question would have cost) and sentenced to one day in jail. The
license law was upheld by two members of a three-judge court.[57]

In his dissent Judge Rutledge indicated that the statutes should
not be applicable to appellant's "selling" their pamphlets. With them
it was a religion, not a business. (The same issue, over and over

again.) But, if applicable, he thought the law unconstitutional. Referring to the *Gobitis* flag case, he wrote:

> Jehovah's Witnesses have had to choose between their consciences and public education for their children. In my judgment, they should not have to give up also the right to disseminate their religious views in an orderly manner on the public streets, exercise it at the whim of public officials [the law vested discretion without express limitations in the licensing officials], or be taxed for doing so without their licenses.

Although it had not always been true of previous, nor, for that matter, of succeeding Justices, it was not to be assumed that Rutledge would change his attitude or his constitutional philosophy once he found himself in a position to make it more effective. When appointed, it was altogether predictable what his position would be in this series of cases with the possible exception of the Massachusetts child labor case.

After the 1943 favorable decisions, the Witnesses took great pride in themselves as "molders of constitutional law." They referred to May 3rd and June 14th of 1943 as "Field Days" by winning 12 out of 13 cases, leading ones, of course, being *Opelika, Murdock* and *Barnette.* "As a result, beginning in the summer of the year 1943, there was a marked decline in the number of cases brought against Jehovah's Witnesses. Simultaneously, there was a tremendous increase in the number of prosecutions that were dismissed."[58] Charles A. Beard pleased them greatly when he wrote, "whatever may be said about the Witnesses, they have the courage of martyrs. And they have money to hire lawyers and fight cases through the courts. As a result in recent days, they have made more contributions to the development of the constitutional law of religious liberty than any other cult or group."[59] And this remains largely true today.

The "Wall"

The New Jersey school bus case,[60] decided in 1947, was one of the most controversial cases in which Justice Rutledge took part and wrote an opinion. The state legislature had enacted a law authorizing local school boards to make rules and enter into agreements for the transportation of children to schools and back home. Pursuant to this statute a township board provided for reimbursement of parents for transportation costs in buses of the public transportation system. It included reimbursement to parents who sent their children to public schools and to Catholic parochial schools. Transportation to private schools operated for profit was expressly excluded. The parochial schools, of course, gave religious as well as secular instruction. A taxpayer challenged the power of the school board to reimburse from public funds parents of Catholic school children.

Although a number of cases had reached the Supreme Court involving the free practice of religion clause of the First Amendment, this was the first to raise questions concerning the meaning and scope of the provision forbidding any "law respecting an establishment of religion." The principal issue was whether this law was one which violated the establishment clause, as applicable to the states through the Fourteenth Amendment, by being in substance a law aiding religion. A secondary point raised was whether the law offended the due process of law clause of the Fourteenth Amendment as taking money from some people by taxation to help others carry out their personal desires and purposes.

The Court upheld the state law by a five to four vote of the Justices. In his majority opinion, Black quickly disposed of the due process argument. "The fact that a state law, passed to satisfy a public need, coincides with the personal desires of the individuals most directly affected," he wrote, "is certainly an inadequate reason for us to say that a legislature has erroneously appraised the public need." He declared that legislation intended to facilitate opportunity for children to get a secular education serves a public purpose. So also does legislation to enable children to avoid the "risk of traffic" and other hazards incident to walking or "hitchhiking" to school. Moreover, subsidies to individuals, whether parents of school children, farmers or home owners, to further a public purpose, are valid. A case closely in point, decided in 1930, had upheld a Louisiana law challenged under the due process clause (but not the First Amendment), which provided for the use of tax funds for the purpose of buying school books for children attending private and parochial schools. In an opinion written by Chief Justice Hughes, such expenditures were held to be for a "public purpose" and valid under the Fourteenth Amendment.[61]

The case under the establishment clause, however, was not a "horse [so] quickly curried."[62] There were no judicial guideposts. There were, however, the writings of Jefferson and Madison, which, more than any other force, were responsible for the First Amendment. Particularly, there was Madison's famous "Memorial and Remonstrance," which brought about the termination in Virginia of taxation to support religion, and Jefferson's "Bill for Religious Freedom" enacted shortly thereafter, in 1786. Then, of course, there was the history of religious intolerance with its bloody record of torture, persecution, and execution of individuals, and even wars between nations.

Champions of the "Wall of Separation" believed it necessary for the purity of religion and the integrity of the state although some would emphasize the one more than the other. Roger Williams, a deeply devout man, was one of the first to declare for separation, and for this he was banished from Massachusetts. The great danger, for him, was the corruption of religion. One of the things he regarded as intolerable was a uniform and compulsory prayer which he characterized as "spiritual rape."[63] This view was shared by Madison. "Experience shows," he wrote, "religion corrupted by establishments."[64] He also emphasized, of course, the corrupting effect of religion on the state. "What influence in fact," he asked, "have ecclesiastical establishments had on Civil Society? In some instances they have been seen to erect a spiritual tyranny on the ruins of Civil authority; in many instances they have been seen upholding the thrones of political tyranny; in no instance have they been seen as guardians of the liberties of the people."[65]

It was on such a note that Justice Black began his discussion. "A large proportion of the early settlers of this country came here from Europe to escape the bondage of laws which compelled them to support and attend government-favored churches." He then continued:

> With the power of government supporting them, at various times and places, Catholics had persecuted Protestants, Protestants had persecuted Catholics, Protestant sects had persecuted other Protestant sects, Catholics of one shade of belief had persecuted Catholics of another shade of belief, and all of these had from time to time persecuted Jews. In efforts to force loyalty to whatever religious group happened to be on top and in league with the government of a particular time and place, men and women had been fined, cast in jail, cruelly tortured and killed. . . . These practices of the old world were transplanted to and began to thrive in the soil of the New America.[66]

After reviewing the history of the separation struggle leading to the First Amendment, Black began a catalogue of the things neither state nor federal government can do. Neither government "can set up a church. Neither can pass laws which aid one religion, aid all religions, or prefer one religion over another. . . . No tax in any amount, large or small, can be levied to support any religious activities or institutions, whatever they may be called, or whatever form they may adopt to teach or practice religion."[67]

As to what New Jersey had done, he found that it was not a law prohibited by the establishment clause although it might approach "the verge" of the state's constitutional power. It was true that children were "helped to get to church schools." Perhaps some children might not be sent to church schools if free transportation had been limited to public schools. But, Black argued, the same result might ensue if policemen paid by the city did not protect children from traffic hazards on their way to parochial schools or if the city cut off from them such general public services as fire protection and sewage disposal. But the First Amendment was not intended to prevent the state from furnishing such services. It "requires the state to be neutral in its relations with groups of religious believers and non-believers; it does not require the state to be their adversary." And then the final conclusion: "The State contributes no money to the schools. It does not support them. Its legislation, as applied, does no more than provide a general program to help parents get their children, regardless of their religion, safely and expeditiously to and from accredited Schools."[68]

To many readers, Black's opinion makes little sense. By the time he finishes with what a state may *not* do, there seems no way in which the decision can be supported. This was Irving Brant's reaction. "When I started to read the Everson case," he wrote to Rutledge, "I flipped the leaves and missed the break in it, therefore thought it was a unanimous decision."

> As I read along through Hugo's opinion, I got a real lift; it showed such a complete understanding of the principles which governed the writing of the First Amendment. At one point, I got out the manuscript of one of the chapters of the [*i.e.,* Brant's] unpublished volume on Madison and read parallel sections to Hazeldean [Mrs. Brant], to show how even the wording was almost duplicated. Then, by gosh, on a point negatived by his own prior reasoning, he jumped over and affirmed the decision.[69]

Justice Jackson, in the beginning of his dissenting opinion also pointed up the apparent inconsistency between what he called "the undertones of the [majority] opinion advocating complete and uncompromising separation of Church from State" and the conclusion upholding the New Jersey law. It was, he thought, another case of Byron's Julia who, "whispering, 'I will ne'er consent',—consented."[70]

He also thought that the law made the character of the school rather than the needs of the children determine whether the parents could be reimbursed. Payments could be made for transportation to public schools and Catholic schools but not to private schools operated for profit. Moreover, under the provisions made by the local board, transportation to any religious school other than Catholic was excluded. Thus, if "all children of the state were objects of impartial solicitude," there was no sound reason for discrimination.

But it was Justice Rutledge's classic dissent, reviewing the history of the struggle for the separation of government and religion, which brings conviction, in Justice Jackson's words, that the Court's decision gave "the clock's hands a backward turn." With scholarly care he reviewed the Virginia fight for religious freedom. Although reliance on Madison and Jefferson has been recently belittled by some critics,[71] Rutledge made a convincing case that the great instruments of the Virginia experience "became the warp and woof of our constitutional tradition" and that Madison was indeed the architect of the federal "Wall." "By contrast with the Virginia history, the congressional debates on consideration of the Amendment reveal only sparse discussion, reflecting the fact that the essential issues had been settled."[72]

In view of the events leading up to the amendment and its history, it was clear to Rutledge that any appropriation from public funds to aid or support any religious exercise was forbidden. Not even "three pence" contribution, as Madison had declared. Did the New Jersey law furnish aid or support for religion by the taxing power? "Certainly it does," he insisted, "if the test remains undiluted as Jefferson and Madison made it, that money taken by taxation from one is not to be used or given to support another's religious training or belief, or indeed one's own." But the majority appeared to take the position that the collateral "aid" to religious instruction was not what the law contemplated as "support" to religion. To this, Rutledge answered: "But Madison and Jefferson were concerned with aid and support in fact, not as a legal conclusion 'entangled in precedents.'" He thought New Jersey's action was exactly the type of evil at which they struck. "Under the test they framed it cannot be said that the cost of transportation is no part of the cost of education or of the religious instruction given." And he added, significantly, "that it is a substantial and necessary element is shown most plainly by the continuing and increasing demand for the state to assume it."[73]

It was also obvious to Rutledge that where transportation was required to get children to school, its cost is as much a part of the expense of education as the cost of school books, school lunches, athletic equipment or any other item of the total financial burden. There was, of course, no denial that the Catholic schools gave both religious and nonreligious instruction. The very purpose of their existence was the combination of the religious and the secular. But "this very admixture is what was disestablished when the First Amendment forbade 'an establishment of religion.' " Would the Constitution permit the state to defray the cost of transportation of children to Sunday School, week day special religious classes at the church or parish house, or to meetings of young people's religious societies, such as the Y.M.C.A., the Y.W.C.A., or the Y.M.H.A., even though some non-religious subjects might be discussed? The argument that defraying transportation costs was not "support" was as flimsy to Rutledge as the same argument would be if applied to the payment of tuition, teachers' salaries or the cost of construction of a school building. He could find no substantial difference except "between more dollars and less." If all that is necessary to evade the force of the amendment is to find that the appropriation is for a "public purpose," that it is "public welfare legislation," then, indeed the state could build school buildings for religious groups, equip them, pay teachers' salaries and pupils' tuition. The trouble with the "public purpose" argument was, he thought, that it ignored the religious factor, the vital element in the case.

The Justice recognized the hardship upon those who are taxed to pay for the education of other people's children but have an added cost for the education of their own. But this is because they are not content with what the state can constitutionally furnish in the field of education, namely, purely secular instruction. And if the state were to include religious training in any faith but their own, they would be the first to protest. Thus Rutledge concluded his opinion:

> Two great drives are constantly in motion to abridge, in the name of education, the complete division of religion and civil authority which our forefathers made. One is to introduce religious education and observances into the public schools. The other, to obtain public funds for the aid and support of various private religious schools. . . . In my opinion both avenues were closed by the Constitution. Neither should be opened by this Court. The matter is not one of quantity, to be measured by the amount of money expended. Now as in Madison's day it is one of principle, to keep separate the separate spheres as the First Amendment drew them; to prevent the first experiment upon our liberties; and to keep the question from becoming entangled in corrosive precedents.[74]

Certainly recent history in the country confirms the fact that the "two great drives" are still very much in motion "to abridge the division of religious and civil authority which our forefathers made."

At several places in his dissent, Rutledge emphasized the point that the relatively small amount of tax aid to religious schools which was involved was not significant. This apparently inspired the editorial writer for the *Washington Post*, as follows:[75]

> Justice Black's argument favoring this small encroachment upon a constitutional principle reminds us of the young woman who tried to excuse transgression of the moral law by saying that her illegitimate child was "only a small one." It is the principle that is vital, as Justice Rutledge made clear in his powerful dissent, and not the amount of the assistance given. Taxes are wholly public. The religious function is wholly private. The two cannot be intermingled in our opinion without grave damage to both.

And the *New York Times* observed, prophetically, that the vigor with which four Justices dissented in this case suggests that "this is only the beginning of a grave judicial controversy."

The controversy was resumed the very next year in the *McCollum* "release-time" case[76] in which the Court held invalid under the establishment clause, the practice in the Illinois public school system which excused students, whose parents so elected, from school classes in order to take religious instruction on the school premises. Others were required to continue their secular studies. Justice Black again wrote the opinion of the Court. Justice Reed alone dissented.

The situation had developed from the adoption by the school board of Champaign, Illinois of a plan for religious instruction originated by the Champaign Council on Religious Education which included representatives of Protestants, Catholics and Jews. When the program was inaugurated, each parent received a "Parents' Request Card" with instructions to furnish the information desired. These cards were in the following form:

> Please permit ——— in Grade —— at ——— School to attend a class in Religious Education one period a week under the auspices of the Champaign Council of Religious Education.
>
> (Check which)
>
> ( ) Interdenominational
> ( ) Protestant
> ( ) Roman Catholic
> ( ) Jewish
>
> Date ————————.

The mother of the McCollum boy refused to let him participate. She had been reared as a Freethinker and would have no part of the traditional, organized religions. When she learned that her son had been given a place at a desk in the hall during "release-time" and was the butt of jeers and sneers by conforming pupils, Vashti McCollum started her lawsuit.

Although the sponsoring organization which also supplied the religious instructors, was interfaith, it in fact failed to provide instruction in all three faiths for every school, with the result that in several instances Catholic and Jewish pupils were sent to Protestant classes. Many church groups expressed disapproval of the program, particularly Unitarian and Jewish. Indeed, some Baptists, presumably following in the tradition of Roger Williams, reputedly the founder of the first American Baptist Church in Rhode Island after leaving Massachusetts, vigorously opposed the practice although others supported it. Notwithstanding Jewish participation, a brief amicus curiae (friend of the court) was filed on behalf of the Synagogue Council of America. The brief protested the use of the public schools and facilities on the grounds that it amounted to financial aid to sectarian religious instruction, that it favored one religion over another and thus discriminated, and that it in fact influenced and enforced religious instruction upon children contrary to their own and their parents' wishes.

Four years later the Court backtracked, upholding a release time New York law which required the children who were excused for religious training to leave the school premises to obtain it.[77] The off-premises factor was thought to distinguish the situation from the Illinois case. Justices Black, Frankfurter and Jackson wrote separate dissents in this case. Justice Douglas wrote for the Court, joined by Chief Justice Vinson, Justices Reed and Burton as well as Justices Minton and Clark who had taken the seats vacated by the deaths of Rutledge and Murphy. One could safely guess that the decision would have been otherwise had they lived.

And then there was the prayer case, in which Black once again writes for the Court, Justices Frankfurter and White taking no part, Justice Stewart, the lone dissenter.[78] A government agency had composed a prayer for school children to recite. But although the Court did not characterize it as "spiritual rape," it thought that "it is no part of the business of government to compose official prayers. . . ."

Justice Black reviewed the clash of opinions over the prayers of the Church of England and the history of the Book of Common Prayer: "The controversies over the Book and what should be its content," wrote Black, "repeatedly threatened to disrupt the peace of that country as the accepted forms of prayer in the established church changed with the views of the particular ruler that happened to be in control at the time."

> . . . . It is an unfortunate fact of history that when some of the very groups which had most strenuously opposed the established Church of England found themselves sufficiently in control of colonial governments in this country to write their own prayers into law, they passed laws making their own religion the official religion of their respective colonies. . . . By the time of the adoption of the Constitution, our history shows that there was a widespread awareness among many Americans of the dangers of a union of Church and State. These people knew, some of them from bitter personal experience, that one of the greatest dangers to the freedom of the individual to worship in his own way lay in the Government's placing its official stamp of approval upon one particular kind of prayer. . . . The First Amendment was added to the Constitution to stand as a guarantee that neither the power nor the prestige of the Federal Government would be used to control, support or influence the kinds of prayer the American people can say.[79]

Justice Stewart found that Black's historical review of the quarrels over the Book of Common Prayer in England and the history of the early establishment and later rejection of an official church in our own states threw no light for him on the issue in the case. He simply could not understand how it could be a violation of the Constitution to permit school children who wished to do so to recite the twenty-two word prayer. He thought it neither interfered with the free practice of anyone's religion nor established an official religion. On the contrary, according to Stewart, to deny the wish of the children to join in the prayer was "to deny them the opportunity to share in the spiritual heritage of the Nation."

Justice Douglas had voted with the majority in the New Jersey school bus case and had written the opinion for the Court in the New York release time case. But in the prayer case, he was not content merely to join in the decision. He apparently felt constrained to write a concurring opinion even though the prayer involved was only a "little one." It may or may not be significant that in Justice Black's opinion, no mention is made of the New Jersey case except, altogether collaterally, in a footnote. But Douglas felt it necessary to repent in public and, belatedly, join in Rutledge's dissent in that case. And so he wrote: "Mr. Justice Rutledge stated in dissent what I think is durable First Amendment philosophy," and thereupon quoted the following passage:

> The reasons underlying the Amendment's policy have not vanished with time or diminished in force. Now as when it was adopted the price of religious freedom is double. It is that the church and religion shall live both within and upon that freedom. There cannot be freedom of religion, safeguarded by the state, and intervention by the church or its agencies in the state's domain or dependency on its largesse. Madison's Remonstrance, Par. 6, 8. The great condition of religious liberty is that it be maintained free from sustenance, as also from other interferences, by the state. For when it comes to rest upon that secular foundation it vanishes with the resting. Id., Par. 7, 8. Public money devoted to payment of religious costs, educational or other, brings the quest for more. It brings, too, the struggle of sect against sect for the larger share or for any. Here one by numbers alone will benefit most, there another. That is precisely the history of societies which have had an established religion and dissident groups. Id., Par. 8, 11. It is the very thing Jefferson and Madison experienced and sought to guard against, whether in its blunt or in its more screened forms. Id. The end of such strife cannot be other than to destroy the cherished liberty. The dominating group will achieve the dominate benefit; or all will embroil the state in their dissensions. Id., Par. 11.[80]

Justice Rutledge's post-*Everson* mail was especially heavy—more so, indeed than about any other case in which he participated. Most of it was extremely favorable. This was true not only from personal friends but from strangers, as well, in all walks of life. Not untypical was a brief note from Max Lerner, then writing for New York's *P.M.* and who had never met the Justice. Lerner wrote as follows:

Dear Mr. Justice Rutledge

I want to tell you how exciting I found your dissent in the *Everson* case. I count it as one of the great opinions of recent years, and it puts you in the company of the choice spirits in the great tradition of the Court.

An article in the magazine *America* by R. F. Drinan, S.J., later Dean of the Law School of Boston College, summarized the comments of the leading law journals on the case. "The *Everson* case," he wrote, "in which a New Jersey statute authorizing funds for bus

"SUPREME COURT?"

transportation of children going to parochial schools was held constitutional, elicited some twenty comments, more than did any case decided by any court in the nation in recent years."

The overwhelming majority of these comments specifically support the *dissent* of Justice Rutledge, in which he held that any State aid to a religious organization, however incidental, is forbidden by the First Amendment. Discrimination against religious institutions in the gratuitous distribution of public funds is *commanded* by the Constitution, according to the *Michigan Law Review*. The commentator in the *Harvard Law Review* questions the validity of the "child-benefit" theory (*i.e.,* the *child* in a sectarian school gets the benefit of incidental aid, not the *school*) and insists that all state aid to sectarian institutions should be barred. . . . New York University's *Law Review* gives a qualified approval to the decision but observes that further extensions of the doctrine might very well be disastrous so far as separation of Church and State is concerned.[81]

Among the professional critics of the Court and its decisions, few have exceeded the late Professor T. R. Powell of the Harvard Law School in perspicuity or perspicacity. In discussing the *Everson* case in the *Harvard Educational Review,* he wrote:

Public assistance to private worship within ecclesiastical walls seems clearly to be support of such worship even though the money goes to carry communicants and not for heat and light and pay of priests and parsons. How is it different to go to rooms with desks and blackboards instead of to transept, nave and choir? The majority do not tell us. Quite possibly they may have been influenced by the facts that parochial schools save public expense and that Catholic citizens are taxed to support public schools and their appurtenances. They might differentiate free rides to private churches because there are no public churches. No one can be compelled to go to church. Children may be compelled to go to school, but they may not be compelled to go to public school. Thus a public ride to the school of their choice helps them to do a duty laid down by law. So might the majority reason. The reasoning would be acceptable if the only question were whether the expenditure is for a public or for a private purpose. It is far less acceptable when to the public purpose of education is added the private purpose of indoctrination in denominational dogma. Then the state is spending public funds to aid access to private preaching of a sectarian creed. To add to the audience is *pro tanto* to promote the preaching.[82]

Editorial, critical and popular opinion appeared highly divided after the *McCollum* and *Regents'* Prayer cases. For example, a Tennessee newspaper, heading its editorial, "Court Rules Against God," declared that "American citizens who fear and worship God should be deeply disturbed by the United States Supreme Court's far-fetched ruling, in a Champaign, Ill. case, that a voluntary Bible study plan in public schools is unconstitutional. . . . It was an arbitrary ruling in keeping with the so-called 'liberalism' with which society is currently afflicted."[83]

On the other hand, a Missouri newspaper, anticipating the Court's ruling thought the public school no place to teach sectarian beliefs. Denominational teaching is the responsibility of pastors and parents. The places for it are the church, the Sunday school, and the home.[84] Similar approving editorials appeared in the *Washington Post*, the *Evening Star* (Washington, D. C.), and a number of other city newspapers, including, surprisingly, the *Chicago Tribune*.[85]

Professor E. S. Corwin, late of Princeton, took a different view. In an article in Fordham University's magazine *Thought,* he severely criticized the case. His summary of the argument against the decision follows:

> In the first place the justification for the Court's intervention was most insubstantial. In the second place the decision is based, as Justice Reed rightly contends, on "a figure of speech," the concept of "a wall of separation between Church and State." Thirdly, leaving this figure of speech to one side, the decision is seen to stem from an unhistorical conception of what is meant by "an establishment of religion" in the First Amendment. The historical record shows clearly that the core idea of "an establishment of religion" comprises the idea of *preference*; and that any act of public authority favorable to religion in general cannot, without a falsification of history, be brought under the ban of that phrase. Undoubtedly, the Court has the right to make history, as it has often done in the past; but it has no right to *remake* it. In the fourth place, the prohibition of the establishment of religion by Congress is not convertible into a similar prohibition on the States, under the authorization of the Fourteenth Amendment, unless the term "establishment of religion" be given an application which carries with it invasion of somebody's freedom of

religion, that is, of "liberty." Finally, the decision is accompanied by opinions and by a mandate which together have created great uncertainty in the minds of governing bodies of all public educational institutions. And of course, as is always the case, the Court's intervention is purely negative. It is incapable of solving the complex problems with which forty-six states and 2,200 communities have been struggling by means of the "released time" expedient. With the utmost insouciance the Court overturns or casts under the shadow of unconstitutionality the "conscientious attempt" of hundreds of people to deal with what they consider to be a pressing problem in a way that they considered to be fair and just to all.[86]

After the prayer cases, an extensive sampling of conflicting views went something like this:[87]

"The Congress should at once submit an amendment to the Constitution which establishes the right to religious devotion in all govermental agencies—national, state or local."—*Former President Herbert Hoover.*

"I realize, of course, that the Declaration of Independence antedates the Constitution, but the fact remains that the Declaration was our certificate of national birth. It specifically asserts that we as individuals possess certain rights as an endowment from our common creator—a religious concept."—*Former President Dwight D. Eisenhower.*

"I am shocked and frightened that the Supreme Court has declared unconstitutional a simple and voluntary declaration of belief in God by public school children. The decision strikes at the very heart of the Godly tradition in which America's children have for so long been raised."—*Cardinal Spellman of New York.*

"The recitation of prayers in the public schools, which is tantamount to the teaching of prayer, is not in conformity with the spirit of the American concept of the separation of church and state. All the religious groups in this country will best advance their respective faiths by adherence to this principle."—*New York Board of Rabbis.*

"This is another step toward the secularization of the United States. Followed to its logical conclusion, we will have to take the chaplains out of the armed forces, prayers cannot be said in Congress, and the President cannot put his hand on the Bible when he takes the oath of office. The framers of our Constitution meant we were to have freedom of religion not freedom from religion."—*Evangelist Billy Graham.*

"I am surprised that the Court has extended to an obviously non-sectarian prayer the prohibition against 'the establishment of religion' which was clearly intended by our forefathers to bar official status to any particular denomination or sect."—*Bishop James A. Pike, of the California Protestant Episcopal diocese.*

"All parties agreed that the prayer was religious in nature. This being so, it ran contrary to the First Amendment—which is well grounded in history and has served to save the United States from religious strife."—*Representative Emanuel Celler, D., N. Y.*

"I believe it is no loss to religion but may be a gain in clarifying matters. Prayer that is essentially a ceremonial classroom function has not much religious value."—*Dr. Sterling M. McMurrin, United States Commissioner of Education.*

"It is important that people not be misled by distorted statements about the decision. The Supreme Court has nowhere in its decision denied belief in God, prayer, religious songs, Bible reading, or any other religious belief or practice."—*Rabbi Albert M. Lewis, Los Angeles, West Coast president of the American Jewish Congress.*

"We hear a good deal of talk about the rights of minorities in a democratic society—and this is as it should be. But we have come to the point where we must give some attention to the rights of majorities as well and very few are prepared to raise their voices in this cause. As in the present situation concerning prayer in school, the long-standing traditions of the Republic are under continual assault."—*The Pilot, Roman Catholic weekly, Boston.*

"We are not excited about the decision, either way. The decision denies no one his opportunity to pray in the manner his conscience dictates. If our religious faith is weakened by lack of a public school prayer, it is already on the road to extinction."—*Detroit News.*

"Wisely, the founders of this country saw that the power to embrace or sponsor any particular religious form or religious group likely would be abused. . . . Monday's decision has not dealt a blow to religion. . . . On the contrary, it has fortified constitutional guarantees that our Government must leave each individual free to worship in his own way."—*Atlanta Constitution.*

"The United States Supreme Court has extended the logic of the constitutional prohibition of the 'establishment of religion' straight out of the realm of common sense. . . . This decision interprets the Constitution with a rigidity which is ridiculous."—*Raleigh (N. C.) News and Observer.*

"I think that it is important for us, if we're going to maintain our constitutional principle, that we support Supreme Court decisions even when we may not agree with them. In addition, we have in this case a very easy remedy, and that is to pray ourselves."— *President Kennedy.*

"The decision came as no surprise to me. It is just one in line with the philosophy this group of men sitting over there have been handing down for a long time. . . . There are many instances where the Court has overstepped its bounds."—[the late] *Representative Francis E. Walter, D., Pa., Chairman House Committee on Un-American Activities.*

"I disagree with the Supreme Court's decision. . . . Having said this, I must also express my concern about some of the reaction to the Supreme Court's decision. It should not be used as an excuse for another massive assault upon the institutions of the Court. Right or wrong, the Supreme Court is a vital part of our Republic, and it does not serve any point of view in this controversy to heap abuse upon its members or to undermine its status."—*Senator Kenneth B. Keating, R., N. Y.*

"Can it be that we, too, are ready to embrace the foul concept of atheism. . . . Is this not in fact the first step on the road to prompting atheistic and agnostic beliefs? . . . Somebody is tampering with America's soul. I leave to you who that somebody is."— *Senator Robert C. Byrd, D., W. Va.*

"For some years now the members of the Supreme Court have persisted in reading alien meanings into the Constitution of the United States. . . . They have sought, in effect, to change our form of government. But never in the wildest of their excesses . . . have they gone as far as they did on yesterday."—*Senator Herman Talmadge, D., Ga.*

"We do not impugn the sincerity of most of those who favor the Supreme Court decision, many of whom are themselves devoted to religion. But they are in serious error if they think nonsectarian prayer to God, not forced on anyone, is a violation of rights. Rather it is the Supreme Court which is guilty of violating the 'free exercise' of religion guaranteed by the Constitution."—*San Francisco Examiner.*

"If we accept the ruling with respect, and calm, we will not stumble to the conclusion that a serious blow has been struck to the very core of religious teaching. If we seek ways to live with the decree against official prayer, to understand it, we certainly can reach an accommodation less troublesome than some see possible in these first hours when striking headlines leave many in a state of disbelief. The court's intent—and eventually, we trust, its great achievement—is to strengthen the foundation of religious heritage by limiting secular intrusions that could become a mischievous and enervating force. If it does not work this way, changes can be made."—*The New York Herald Tribune.*

"It is naive to see in this decision the hand of communism. A Communist state does have a state religion—communism—one of whose tenets is atheism. The whole power of the state is behind it. The net result of the court's decision, by contrast, is to leave us free. We can be sure that In God We Trust will remain stamped upon our coins, as it has upon the hearts of most of us."—*The Hartford Courant.*

"The Court has correctly interpreted the Constitution in this instance. Those religious leaders of various faiths who disagree will, we believe, ultimately come to the same conclusion. Separation of church and state is the best guarantee they have that they and their followers will always be permitted to worship God according to the dictates of their own conscience."—*The Chicago Sun-Times.*

"This is America, and in America loyal citizens accept decisions whether they like them or not, until they can change them legally, just as they changed the Eighteenth Amendment. If they cannot change them legally they accept them. This is the strength of America.

"After all, prayer has not been outlawed in the United States, nor has religion been outlawed—save in the public schools, and attempts to compare the Supreme Court ruling and lack of religion in Soviet Russia are wide of the mark."—*The Cleveland Plain Dealer.*

"Brief reflection might well induce critics to some second-thought questions. What if the prayer were not as 'neutral' as it is? What if one denomination, numerically large enough to wield political control, had dictated it? What of the freedom of conscience guaranteed free-thinkers and atheists and nonconformists as much as to Christians and Jews? . . .

"The court has upheld the glorious purpose of the First Amendment. For this Protestants, Catholics, Jews and non-conformists alike should be grateful. Prayer and religious exercises are not for a Government to encourage or discourage; they are for the church, the home, the heart."—*The Louisville Courier-Journal.*

In his recent penetrating study of church and state, Professor Kurland has suggested that it was no accident that the free practice clause and the establishment clause were included in the same amendment. Keeping the government out of religion and religion out of government was necessary to make individual religious freedom a reality.[88] He further thought that the two clauses should be "read together as creating a doctrine more akin to the reading of the equal protection than to the due process clause of the Fourteenth Amendment, *i.e.*, they must be read to mean that religion may not be used as a basis for classification for purposes of governmental action, whether that action be conferring of rights and privileges or the imposition of duties or obligations."[89] As one reviewer put it, Kurland emphasizes that the separation and freedom aspects of the First Amendment are unitary and inseparable and that the former forbids all that the latter does not require. "Government may accord a benefit or exemption to a religious institution or activity only as a part of a larger classification not identified by religion and not otherwise vulnerable to successful attack under the equal protection clause."[90]

The author makes a plausible case that Black "came close" to accepting this interpretation in the school bus case. It is true that the Justice did "read together" the two clauses. But he seemed to regard the "free practice" provision as a limitation on the "establishment" prohibition rather than the latter as a guarantee of the former. Thus, he wrote:

> New Jersey cannot consistently with the "establishment of religion" clause of the First Amendment contribute tax-raised funds to the support of an institution which teaches the tenets and faith of any church. On the other hand, other language of the amendment commands that New Jersey cannot hamper its citizens in the free exercise of their own religion. Consequently, it cannot exclude individual Catholics . . . or the members of any other faith, because of their faith or lack of it, from receiving the benefits of public welfare legislation. . . . [W]e must be careful, in protecting the citizens of New Jersey against state-established churches, to be sure that we do not inadvertently prohibit New Jersey from extending its general state law benefits to all its citizens without regard to their religious belief.[91]

The complexity of the two religious provisions of the amendment thus appears from the fact that although they may complement each other, they also quite clearly protect different interests. As Justice Black pointed out in the case of the New York school prayer, "Although these two clauses may in certain instances overlap, they forbid two quite different kinds of governmental encroachment upon religious freedom."[92]   The Sunday law cases are in point here.   A recent case involved a Maryland law under which several employees of a discount house were prosecuted for selling a few trifling articles on Sunday.   They defended on the grounds that the statute violated both clauses.   The Supreme Court held that they had no standing to raise the question of individual religious freedom.   They were certainly not practicing religion by selling toys on Sunday.   They could, however, raise the establishment issue.   A divided Court thereupon found a justification for the law as one of rest and relaxation rather than one, the operative effect of which was "to use the State's coercive power to aid religion."[93]   Nor is the result different if the complainant is an Orthodox Jewish merchant, placed at an economic disadvantage in that he has but five days, as against his competitor's six in which to do business. It offends neither the establishment nor the free practice clause.   It merely makes his religious practice "more expensive."[94] This is an "indirect burden" which the Court thought didn't count "unless the state may accomplish its purpose by means which do not impose such a burden."[95] It might have been suggested that the day of rest, relaxation and family get-together-ness could as well have been legislatively designated as say, Wednesday rather than, as in Massachusetts, the "Lord's Day," and thus impose no burden on any known religious group.

Justices Brennan and Stewart dissented from the decision as to the free practice clause but concurred as to the establishment clause. The effect of these laws, wrote Brennan, is that no one may at one and the same time be an Orthodox Jew and compete effectively with his Sunday-observing fellow tradesmen.   "This clog," he continued, "upon the exercise of religion, this state-imposed burden on Orthodox Judaism, has exactly the same economic effect as a tax levied upon the sale of religious literature."[96]   And as put by Justice Stewart, "Pennsylvania has passed a law which compels an Orthodox Jew to choose between his religious faith and his economic survival.   That is a cruel choice."   A choice, he thought, which "no State can constitutionally demand."   Stewart felt strongly about it.   For him, it was not "something that can be swept under the rug and forgotten in the interest of enforced Sunday togetherness."

In 1956, a study made at the University of Chicago disclosed that twelve states and the District of Columbia have laws requiring Bible reading in the public schools; ten states do not permit it, while twenty-six states permit it by statute or judicial decision.[97] Professor Dierenfield in his 1962 study of religion in the public schools, found, for the country as a whole, 41.74% of the public school systems in the United States conduct Bible reading.   The distribution by region was as follows: the East, mostly New York and New England, 67.56%; South, including the eastern seaboard, 76.84%; Midwest, 18.26%; West, 11.03%. Home room devotional services were held in most schools in the East (68.33%) and South (60.-53%), but in relatively few in the Midwest (6.40%) and West (2.41%).[98]

In the New York prayer dispute, the "Regents prayer" represented an attempt to provide a "nonsectarian" prayer: "Almighty God, we acknowledge our dependence on Thee and we beg Thy blessings upon us, our parents, our teachers and our Country." Theologically, it was probably as good as any such prayer could be so far as it concerned Catholics, Protestants, Jews and perhaps some other faiths. The effect on nonbelievers need not be considered here. In any event, however "nonsectarian" the Regents prayer might have been, it is clear that there is still no such thing as a nonsectarian Bible. Protestants use the King James version or the new Standard Revision based on it and the Catholics have the Douay version. Scholars of both faiths are coming closer to agreement on a translation but have as yet not attained it. The Jews, of course, recognize only the Old Testament and most congregations use the Jewish Publication Society's version. It is undoubtedly true that substantially all public schools which have Bible reading exercises use a Protestant version thereof.

On June 17, 1963, the Supreme Court handed down its decision in two Bible reading cases, holding laws of both Pennsylvania and Maryland unconstitutional as in conflict with the "establishment" clause of the First Amendment.[99] Only Justice Stewart dissented.

The Pennsylvania law required at least ten verses from the Bible to be read, without comment, at the opening of each public school on each school day. Provision was made for the teacher to excuse any student from attending such reading on written request from his parents. The Maryland case arose under a rule adopted by the School Board of Baltimore pursuant to a state statute which provided for opening school exercises at which a chapter from the Bible should be read without comment or the "use of the Lord's Prayer." Justice Clark, writing for the Court declared that the Court had "rejected unequivocally the contention that the establishment clause forbids only governmental preference of one religion over another." This would appear to be a blow at Professor Kurland's thesis, plausible as it is, that the establishment and free exercise clauses together merely forbid discrimination among faiths. Clark quoted Rutledge's dissent in _Everson_ that the Constitution does not deny "the value or the necessity for religious training, teaching or observance. Rather it secures their free exercise. But to that end it does deny that the state can undertake or sustain them in any form or degree. For this reason the sphere of religious activity, as distinguished from the secular intellectual liberties, has been given the two-fold protection and, as the state cannot forbid, neither can it perform or aid in performing the religious function."[100]

Justice Clark also relied upon a 1961 case in which the Court held that a state may not constitutionally require an applicant for a commission of Notary Public to swear or affirm his belief in God: "[N]either a state nor the Federal Government can constitutionally force a person 'to profess a belief or disbelief in any religion. Neither can constitutionally pass laws or impose requirements which aid all religions as against non-believers, and neither can aid those religions based on a belief in the existence of God as against those religions founded on different beliefs."

The test for constitutionality in this troubled area, Justice Clark thought, was to inquire of the purpose and primary effect of the law. To conform to the establishment clause there must be a secular legislative purpose and a primary effect that neither advances nor inhibits religion. He denied that the exclusion of the exercises involved in these cases amounted to the establishment of a "religion of secularism." There was no hostility toward religion involved. There was no preference or advantage or aid to those who believe in no religion over believers. He did not believe that the concept of "neutrality" which denies to the state the power to require religious exercises even with the consent of the majority, interferes with the majority's right freely to practice its religion. The majority has no right to the use of governmental machinery to practice its religious beliefs.[101]

Justice Brennan concurred—in forty pages. "The importance of the issue," he wrote, "and the deep conviction with which views on both sides are held seem to me to justify detailing at some length my reasons for joining the Court's judgment and opinion." Like all the other Justices, he attempted to interpret the "establishment" clause and the "free exercise" clause as reflecting a consistent policy with respect to the relations between the state, the religious establishments and the individual. He noted the difference between the power of government to regulate or prohibit conduct induced by religious motives such as the Mormon cases and the Jehovah Witnesses violation of the Massachusetts child labor law on the one hand, and the power to compel behavior offensive to religious principles. He explained the case where students at a state university were required to participate in military training on the grounds that they were not compelled to attend a state university. If they chose to do so, they could be required to conform to a program reflecting a legitimate governmental interest.[102] The second flag salute case was a good example of limitations on the power to coerce conduct against religious principles. The distinction between the two cases, Justice Brennan thought, was important. The one dealt with the voluntary attendance at college of young adults, the other involved compelled attendance of young children at elementary and secondary schools. The distinction warranted a "difference in constitutional results."

Brennan carefully reviewed the history of Bible reading and prayers in the schools, public and private, from early colonial times including cases under state statutes and constitutions before the ruling that the First Amendment was applicable to the states via the Fourteenth. The conclusion which he reached—and could hardly escape reaching—was that these exercises had always been designed to be and are still intended as religious. Although there may, as claimed, be collateral secular benefits, educational and moral, they are insufficient to take the practices out of the prohibition of the establishment clause. Somewhat inconsistent, perhaps, with his discussion of the distinction between prohibition and compulsion of conduct contrary to religious belief, he brushed aside the argument that provision for excusing offended pupils absolved the religious exercises from unconstitutional contamination. It had no relevance to the establishment question since the practices were religious in character, designed to achieve religious aims through use of public school facilities during school hours. Presumably the vice would still be present if the parents of every pupil had requested in writing the reading of a specific chapter and the recitation of a particular prayer.

The Justice finally met the "foot-in-the-door" argument that the invalidation of the practices in these cases would compel the Court to rule out "every vestige, however slight, of cooperation or accommodation between religion and government." It would require nothing of the kind. Because religious exercises in the public schools are forbidden does not mean that the national anthem must be expurgated and the legend removed from the silver dollar. "[T]he line we must draw," wrote the Justice, "between the permissible and the impermissible is one which accords with history and faithfully reflects the understanding of the Founding Fathers." Justice Brennan then sought to formulate a generalization which deserves careful thought and consideration whenever the establishment clause is under discussion. Forbidden by that clause are "those involvements of religious with secular institutions which (a) serve the essentially religious activities of religious institutions; (b) employ the organs of government for essentially religious purposes; or (c) use essentially religious means to serve governmental ends, where secular means would suffice."

Justices Goldberg and Harlan in a concurring opinion written by the former, also were at pains to emphasize the point that the decision does not mean that "all incidents of government which import of the religious are therefore and without more banned by the strictures of the Establishment Clause." They even went so far as to predict that the Court would recognize the propriety of providing military chaplains and of "teaching *about* religion, as distinguished from the teaching *of* religion, in the public schools."

Justice Stewart dissented. He did not think the records in these cases furnished enough information to warrant decision on the merits of the constitutional issue. To him, the vital point was coercion, direct or indirect, by rule, regulation or administration. He would remand the cases for further hearing and evidence on the point.

All in all, the opinions of the Justices in their recognition of religion, as a part of American life, should tend to reassure the citizens that, as James Reston expressed it in the *New York Times,* "the country is not going to hell with the blessing of the Supreme Court."[103]

The *Times* in its lead editorial after the Regents' prayer case,[104] after pointing out what the Court did *not* decide, observed that "what Justice Black and six other members of the Court did object to was that the State of New York, in formulating and using a school prayer, took a position on a religious matter." This, it may be said, is precisely what the Court did in the Lord's Prayer and Bible reading cases. The states of Pennsylvania and Maryland had taken a position on a religious matter. Even though joining in the prayer or even listening to it was voluntary, it can hardly be denied that the state takes a position as much so as when it includes a course of study in the curriculum, even though it is elective.

On the last day of the October 1962 term, on June 17th, 1963, the Court decided a unique case under the religious clauses of the First Amendment. The state of South Carolina had refused unemployment compensation to a Seventh Day Adventist who refused, from religious convictions to work on Saturday which, for her was the Sabbath. She was not "available" for work within the state

"LEAVING RELIGION TO PRIVATE INITIATIVE
IS UNAMERICAN"

law.[105] Justice Brennan, in the majority opinion, held that the state law clearly imposed a burden on the free exercise of the woman's religion. Religious practices can be impaired directly, as by criminal sanctions and indirectly as in this case. A person in this worker's position must choose between adherence to her religious beliefs and thereby forfeiting the benefits to which she otherwise was entitled or committing what her religious faith regarded as a sin. The Justice rejected the claimed distinction between a "privilege" and a "right" as irrelevant to the issue inasmuch as denial of either could offend the free practice provision. Nor could he find any overriding state interest to mitigate the vice of the law. He rejected the state's argument that a different ruling would open the door to fraudulent claims by unscrupulous claimants on the ground, not particularly convincing, that there was nothing in the record of the instant case to suggest fraud. It is generally recognized that fraud, involving as it does a state of mind, is frequently difficult to prove.

The lack of a compelling state interest was thought to distinguish this case from the Sunday closing cases in which the Court had found "a strong state interest in providing one uniform day of rest for all workers." That purely secular objective could be achieved only by declaring Sunday to be a day of rest. To exempt Sabbatarians would be administratively inexpedient. The Justice insisted that the present case involved the application of a principle announced fifteen years ago in the New Jersey school bus case. No state may constitutionally "exclude individual Catholics, Lutherans, Mohammedans, Baptists, Jews, Methodists, Non-believers, Presbyterians, or members of any other faith, *because of their faith, or lack of it,* from receiving the benefits of public welfare legislation."[106] [Emphasis in original.]

Justice Douglas wrote a concurring opinion. He first called attention to the scruples of some of the well-known religious faiths. The Moslems must go to a mosque on Friday and pray five times each day. The scruples of the Sikh require him to carry a real or symbolic sword. The Jehovah Witness must be a proselyter. The Quaker must refrain from swearing, although he may affirm. The scruples of the Buddhist require that he not eat flesh or fish. Douglas referred to the cases upholding the Sunday closing laws which held that a majority of the community could impose their particular scruples on a minority whose religious scruples were thereby offended —cases in which the Justice had dissented. "That ruling of the Court," he wrote, "travels part of the distance that South Carolina asks us to go now. She asks us to hold that when it comes to a day of rest a Sabbatarian must conform with the scruples of the majority in order to obtain unemployment benefits." He then went on to write:

> The result turns not on the degree of injury, which may indeed be non-existent by ordinary standards. The harm is the interference with the individual's scruples or conscience— an important area of privacy which the First Amendment fences off from government. The interference here is as plain as it is in Soviet Russia, where a churchgoer is given a second-class citizenship, resulting in harm though perhaps not in measurable damages.
>
> This case is resolvable not in terms of what an individual can demand of government, but solely in terms of what government may not do to an individual in violation of his religious scruples. The fact that government cannot exact from me a surrender of one iota of my religious scruples does not, of course, mean that I can demand of government a sum of money, the better to exercise them. For the Free Exercise Clause is written in terms of what the government cannot do to the individual, not in terms of what the individual can exact from the government.[107]

Justice Stewart also concurred in the result of the case but took occasion to expound his views of the religious clauses and his dissatisfaction with the Court's disposition of many of the cases arising thereunder. He had dissented in the decision that the Sunday blue laws did not interfere with the free practice of religion. He insisted that the decision in this case substantially overruled those cases. The "burden" on religious practices for Jewish merchants was much greater than that involved in denial of compensation for twenty-two weeks at most. The blue laws carried criminal penalties but the economic hardship was far worse. Justice Brennan, in the case of an Orthodox Jewish storekeeper, had observed that if he could not stay open on Sunday, he would lose his capital investment.[108]

But Stewart raised a far more important question. He declared that the result in this case, which he approved, was in collision with the Court's interpretation of the establishment clause. It was "aid" or "support" for a religion. "South Carolina," he wrote, "would deny unemployment benefits to a mother unavailable for work on Saturdays because she was unable to get a babysitter [citing a South Carolina case]."

Thus, we do not have before us a situation where a State provides unemployment compensation generally, and singles out for disqualification only those persons who are unavailable for work on religious grounds. This is not, in short, a scheme which operates so as to discriminate against religion as such. But the Court nevertheless holds that the State must prefer a religious over a secular ground for being unavailable for work —that state financial support of the appellant's religion is constitutionally required to carry out "the governmental obligation of neutrality in the face of religious differences . . ."[109]

The Court, Stewart thought, was under a duty to face up to the dilemma created by the conflict between the free practice clause and the establishment clause, as interpreted in the school bus, the prayer and the blue law cases.

Justice Brennan, in the Bible-reading cases, decided on the same day as the South Carolina unemployment compensation case, also dealt with the problem of conflict between the two clauses. He referred to government employment of chaplains in prisons and the armed services only to distinguish them from the scripture-reading and prayer cases on the ground that the prison inmates and service personnel are required to be where they are and, unless the government made provision therefor, would be denied devotional opportunities of their choice. He thought, too, that the fact that the school cases involved young children was especially important. The "conflict" between the two religious clauses did not bother Justice Brennan as much as they did Justice Stewart. In fact, his opinion in the Bible-reading case was a long and labored effort to reconcile previous cases under the religious clauses.

It is, of course, not surprising that the Justices differ on the application of principles to which all subscribe. This is of the essence of judicial interpretation of the many generalities in the Constitution: "Due process of law," "unreasonable searches and seizures," "cruel or unusual punishment," "with respect to the establishment of religion." As Professor Kurland says anyone maintaining that the answer in a particular case is clear is either "deluded or deluding."[110]

There is, indeed, ambiguity and conflict in the historical evidence as to the position Jefferson took or would take on certain specific questions. There is, for example, his Report, As Rector, to the President and Directors of the Literary Fund at the University of Virginia, quoted by Justice Reed in his dissent in the Illinois release time case. There were several items of business reported including resolutions pertaining to the building of a library, ratification of certain accounts of the bursar and other financial matters. The report then called attention to the fact that "the want of instruction in the various creeds of religious faith existing among our citizens presents . . . a chasm in a general institution of the useful sciences." He then continued as follows: "A remedy, however, has been suggested of promising aspect, which, while it excludes the public authorities from the domain of religious freedom, will give to the sectarian schools of divinity the full benefit the public provisions made for instruction in the other branches of science." He then went on: "It has, therefore, been in contemplation, and suggested by some pious individuals, who perceive the advantages of associating other studies with those of religion, to establish their religious schools on the confines of the University, so as to give to their students ready and convenient access and attendance on the scientific lectures of the University. . . . But always understanding that these schools shall be independent of the University and of each other." It seems that the suggestion was adopted by the University and included in its statutes, presumably with Jefferson's approval, so that the students would be "free, and expected to attend religious worship at the establishment of their respective sects, in the morning, and in time to meet their school in the University at its stated hour."[111] It should be added that Madison was a member of the Board of Visitors which approved Jefferson's report.

Nevertheless, as Justice Brennan observed in his concurring opinion in the Bible-reading cases:

> It may be that Jefferson and Madison would have held such exercises to be permissible. . . . But I doubt that their view, even if perfectly clear one way or the other, would supply a dispositive answer to the question presented by these cases. A more fruitful inquiry . . . is whether the practices here challenged threatened those consequences which the Framers deeply feared; whether, in short, they tend to promote that type of interdependence between religion and state which the First Amendment was designed to prevent . . . A too literal quest for the advice of the Founding Fathers upon the issues of these cases seems to me futile and misdirected for several reasons: First, on our precise problem, the historical record is at least ambiguous, and statements can readily be found to support either side of the proposition. . . . Second, the structure of American education has greatly changed since the First Amendment was adopted. . . . Third, our

religious composition makes us a vastly more diverse people than our forefathers. . . . Whatever Jefferson or Madison would have thought of Bible reading or recital of the Lord's Prayer in what few public schools existed in their day, our use of the history of their time must limit itself to broad purposes, not specific practices.[112]

Of the "two great drives" referred to by Justice Rutledge, it may be that the firm stand taken by the Court and its near unanimity in the Regents' prayer case and the Bible reading cases have blocked at least temporarily the religion-in-the-public-schools program. But the same cannot be said for the campaign to obtain state aid for religious institutions. Since *Everson* that program has flourished luxuriantly. An opinion of the General Counsel of the Department of Health, Education and Welfare in 1961 classified a long list of government activities and programs under which institutions with religious affiliations receive federal funds through grants or loans. A few examples are the following:

School lunches, "nutritious midday meals to children attending schools of high school grade and less;" special milk program for "children in nonprofit schools of high school grade and under;" funds under the National Defense Education Act to enable nonprofit institutions of higher learning to make "low-interest loans to needy students;" grants "to strengthen science, mathematics and modern foreign language instruction in secondary schools;" testing students in private elementary schools; training of secondary school counsellors; grants for research in more effective utilization of Television, Radio and Related Media; grants for research on mental diseases; grants to Divinity Schools for instruction on mental health; research relating to "social security matters;" the allocation of surplus property, personal and real, for educational and public health purposes "at a public benefit discount which can be as much as 100% of the appraised fair value;" summer institutes for higher education in fields relating to atomic energy; training of all types for the rehabilitation of war veterans.

This is not a "three pence" movement. It involves millions. But the amount is not important. It is only money. What is serious is that the "Wall" appears to be crumbling away and may collapse utterly unless repairs are soon forthcoming.

CHAPTER IV

". . . ABRIDGING THE FREEDOM OF SPEECH, OR OF THE PRESS. . . ."

That Preferred Position

A controversial constitutional issue of the first magnitude, and one that is still largely beclouded, is the so-called "preferred position" of First Amendment freedoms—speech, press, religion and assembly. Another related and equally unsettled question is to what extent are the provisions of the first eight amendments applicable as restrictions upon state action by virtue of the adoption of the Fourteenth Amendment in 1868. The First Amendment's restrictions, literally, are addressed to Congress and the other seven are understood as so limited. But, as early as 1925, the Court recognized in the *Gitlow* case[1] that the Fourteenth Amendment, providing that no state may deprive any person of life, liberty or property without "due process of law," limited state legislative bodies to the same extent as Congress with respect to restrictions on speech, press and association. Indeed, several of the Justices, including Rutledge, have been convinced that all the limitations of the first eight of the Bill of Rights on Congressional action are incorporated in the Fourteenth Amendment as applicable to the states. Here, however, we shall consider only the specific guarantees of freedom of speech and press, now concededly applicable to state action.

In a long series of cases involving state legislative incursions on economic liberty, the Court evolved a formula that the due process clause prohibits state restrictions on individual freedom only if they are capricious, arbitrary and without foundation in reason. To promote public health, safety, morals and welfare, the state must have power to impose restrictions on the activities of individuals which reasonably relate to these legitimate objectives of legislation. It must have a reasonable latitude for action to cure or mitigate

97

social and economic evils.   Thus, laws requiring sanitary facilities
in factories, fire escapes and other safety devices in industrial establishments, workmen's compensation, hours of labor and minimum
wage laws, and the like, have been held to meet the constitutional
standard.

But the test has not always been crystal clear.   Largely, however, due to the influence of Justice Holmes, it has come to be accepted in appropriate cases, as one which requires that the law be
upheld as constitutional unless the Justices are persuaded that no
legislature could find the restriction a reasonable means to attain a
legitimate objective.   It is not a question whether the Justices themselves think the law desirable.   They are not to substitute their
judgment as to social policy for that of the legislature whether
national or state.   If the Court finds that the legislative judgment
is within the area in which reasonable men might differ, the law
is to be upheld.   Traditionally the Court has applied a balancing
technique—the effect of the restrictions on personal liberty against
the advantages to society as a whole including the likelihood that
the means employed would be effective.   After this process, the
Court applies the objective standard to determine whether the law
is arbitrary or whether there are reasonable grounds to support it.
As (then) Professor Frankfurter described it in referring to Justice
Holmes, "He has ever been keenly conscious of the delicacy involved
in reviewing other men's judgment, not as to its wisdom but as to
their right to entertain the reasonableness of its wisdom."[2]

To be sure, the Court and particular Justices have not always
scrupulously observed this precaution.   Again, what may appear to
one or more Justices as beyond the area of reasonable judgment,
may, to others, seem within that tolerance.   In fact, one of Holmes'
most lucid expositions of his formula was in a dissenting opinion
involving the constitutionality of a New York law limiting hours
of labor.[3]   "This case," he wrote, "is decided upon an economic
theory which a large part of the country does not entertain."

> If it were a question of whether I agreed with that theory,
> I should desire to study it further and long before making
> . up my mind.   But I do not conceive that to be my duty, be-
> cause I strongly believe that my agreement or disagreement has
> nothing to do with the right of a majority to embody their
> opinions in law.

After referring to several cases in which state restrictive laws
had been upheld by the Court, he continued:

Some of these laws embody convictions or prejudices which judges are likely to share. Some may not. But a Constitution is not intended to embody a particular economic theory, whether of paternalism and the organic relation of the citizen to the state, or of *laissez faire*. It is made for people of fundamentally differing views, and the accident of our finding certain opinions natural and familiar, or novel, and even shocking, ought not to conclude our judgment upon the question whether statutes embodying them conflict with the Constitution of the United States.[4]

It is well known that Holmes' position on the particular issue involved in this case has long since become accepted by all schools of constitutional thought. It is also largely true that his philosophy as to the objectivity of the test in an economic context has become orthodoxy. It puts a heavy burden on anyone who attacks the law to persuade a majority of the Justices that it reflects a legislative judgment outside and beyond what a lawmaking body could regard as a reasonable means of dealing with an admitted social or economic problem. In other words, there is a strong presumption of constitutionality of an Act of Congress, of an enactment of a state legislature, or a municipal ordinance, in dealing with such matters.

This formula was evolved during the first third of the century and related largely to legislative regulations of business and industry. It is usually supposed that Chief Justice Stone first suggested that the constitutional test for the validity of legislation might be quite different in situations which involve the more specific personal freedoms guaranteed in the First Amendment. Stone's first cautious mention of this distinction was in a footnote to an opinion involving restrictions on interstate commerce[5] and later relied upon in his dissent in one of the earlier Jehovah Witnesses cases.[6]

The phrase "preferred position" of First Amendment rights has been used by the Court from time to time to suggest the important difference involved. Justice Douglas, for example, spoke for the majority in one of the later Jehovah Witnesses cases.[7] "Freedom of press, freedom of speech, freedom of religion, are in a preferred position," he wrote. Justice Jackson in the second flag salute case[8] used language substantially the equivalent and even Justice Roberts in an opinion in which Justice Frankfurter joined[9] declared, "mere legislative preferences or beliefs respecting matters of public convenience may well support regulation directed at other personal activities, but be insufficient to justify such as diminishes the exercise of rights so vital to the maintenance of democratic institutions." The case involved the right to distribute hand bills on the street.

But just what is here implied? It is still not altogether clear. Certainly the heavy presumption of constitutionality involved in the objective test of reasonableness would appear to be significantly modified. But to what extent? Is there a presumption of invalidity of laws which abridge freedom of speech or of the press, or which pertain to an establishment of religion or the free exercise thereof? Certainly it can be said that whatever the label means as a technical doctrine, the Court is to scrutinize encroachments on First Amendment freedoms far more closely than limitations on freedom to make money. Free enterprise in the dissemination of ideas has far wider scope than free enterprise in business.

Mr. Justice Frankfurter was the most vigorous opponent of the preferred position doctrine of any member of the Court during Justice Rutledge's tenure and thereafter. He has made it clear in repeated opinions, majority, concurring and minority, that his philosophy of "judicial self-restraint" applies equally to the Court's function in reviewing legislation, federal or state, whether it involves property interests or those including speech, press, religion or the right of assembly. In the second flag salute case he said, in a dissenting opinion: "I think I appreciate fully the objections to the law before us. But to deny that it presents a question upon which men might reasonably differ appears to me to be intolerance." In an obvious reference to the preferred position argument he said in the same opinion:

> There is no warrant in the constitutional basis of this Court's authority for attributing different roles to it depending upon the nature of the challenge to the legislation. Our power does not vary according to the particular provision of the Bill of Rights which is invoked. The right not to have property taken without just compensation has, so far as the scope of judicial power is concerned, the same constitutional dignity as the right to be protected against unreasonable searches and seizures, and the latter has no less claim than freedom of the press or freedom of speech or religious freedom.[10]

Justice Frankfurter has always been a great admirer of Justices Holmes and Brandeis and appeared to feel a profound obligation to carry out their constitutional philosophy. Unquestionably those two Justices felt much as Justice Frankfurter feels concerning the responsibility of the Court to respect the judgment of other governmental agencies. "Judicial self-restraint" was a cardinal virtue in their hierarchy of judicial values. As Brandeis was wont to put it, "the most important thing we do is not doing." On the other hand, although Holmes and Brandeis did not create the label, they may be said to have given birth to something like the "preferred position" doctrine.

There seems to be considerable ambiguity with respect to the origin of the "clear and present danger" formula and what function its authors had in mind for it. As will appear, Justice Frankfurter does not regard it as a standard for testing the constitutionality of legislation restricting freedom of speech or the press, and he has contended that Holmes himself never so regarded it. There are some grounds to substantiate this interpretation. The phrase was first used by Holmes in a case involving the prosecution under the original Espionage Act of a man named Schenck, the general secretary of the Socialist Party, who had participated in printing and mailing leaflets attacking the draft law. The leaflet went to a number of men who had been called to duty by their draft boards, urging them to assert their opposition to the draft. Justice Holmes wrote the opinion for a unanimous Court upholding the conviction against constitutional attack.

> It seems to be admitted that if an actual obstruction of the recruiting service were proved, liability for words that produced that effect might be enforced. . . . If the act (speaking, or circulating a paper), its tendency and the intent with which it is done, are the same, we perceive no ground for saying that success alone warrants making the act a crime.[11]

Holmes also wrote majority opinions in two other cases involving violations of the Espionage Act, one of them involving Eugene V. Debs, prosecuted for a speech made at a Socialist convention. It would be most difficult for rational men to find that any of these cases involved speech so incendiary as to constitute a serious threat to recruitment. These applications of the clear and present danger test were largely, as Professor Pritchett has phrased it, "a rationalization for sending men to jail because of their speech."[12]

One of the most puzzling aspects of the cases in which Holmes and Brandeis discussed this formula was in their references to the "intent" of the speaker. In his eloquent dissent in the *Abrams* case[13], another Espionage Act conviction for distributing anti-war leaflets, Holmes added to the confusion further. "It is only the present danger of immediate evil or an intent to bring it about that warrants Congress in setting a limit to the expression of opinion. . . . Now nobody can suppose that the surreptitious publishing of a silly leaflet by an unknown man, without more, would present any immediate danger that its opinions would hinder the success of the government arms or have any appreciable tendency to do so." He then added: "Publishing those opinions for the very purpose of obstructing, however, might indicate a greater danger and at any rate would have the quality of an attempt. So I assume that the second leaflet if published for the purposes alleged . . . might be punishable."[14] It would thus appear that his dissent was based largely on the grounds of absence of the necessary "intent." However, this may be explained on the ground that such an intention was required by the statute and that since the government had failed to meet the burden of proving the statutory offense, the conviction was erroneous.

Justice Brandeis' concurring opinion in a conviction under a California criminal syndicalism statute[15] is frequently referred to as the classic exposition of the clear and present danger test for constitutional validity under the First Amendment. In that case he wrote:

> Fear of serious injury cannot alone justify suppression of free speech and assembly. Men feared witches and burned women. It is the function of speech to free men from the bondage of irrational fears. To justify suppression of free speech there must be reasonable ground to fear that serious evil will result if free speech is practiced. There must be reasonable ground to believe that the danger apprehended is imminent. There must be reasonable ground to believe that the evil to be prevented is a serious one. . . . In order to support a finding of clear and present danger it must be shown either that immediate serious violence was to be expected or was advocated, or that the past conduct furnished reason to believe that such advocacy was then contemplated.[16]

This would seem to suggest that either the danger of "immediate serious violence" or the advocacy of such violence would satisfy the test. But in the very same paragraph Brandeis went on to say that "even advocacy of violation [lawbreaking], however reprehensible morally, is not a justification for denying free speech where the advocacy falls short of incitement and there is nothing to indicate that the advocacy would be immediately acted on." Again Brandeis in the same case interpreted the rule in the following language: "That the necessity which is essential to a valid restriction does not exist unless speech would produce, or is intended to produce, a clear and imminent danger of some substantive evil which the state constitutionally may seek to prevent has been settled."

It may be that the intention of the speaker is a factor, as Professor Freund has suggested[17] to be considered, but only, it would seem, as to its bearing on the seriousness of the danger. It would seem highly improbable that either Holmes or Brandeis actually meant that the mere intention of a speaker alone could justify suppression in the absence of any reason whatever to believe that anyone would take his speech seriously. On the other hand, it is a plausible argument that mere speech alone, however intemperate, could not justify criminal penalties in the absence of an intention on the part of the speaker to bring about an evil which the state may constitutionally prohibit.

It is also true that Holmes, in the *Schenck* case, used language, subsequently quoted by Brandeis, which in no way involved the intention of the speaker as an alternative which alone would satisfy the test of clear and present danger: "The question in every case is whether the words used are used in such circumstances and are of such a nature as to create a clear and present danger that they will bring about the substantive evils that Congress has a right to prevent." This leaves no room for substituting the mere "intent" of the speaker for the reality of serious and immediate danger which is precisely what Judge Medina did, as will be seen, in the trial of the Communist leaders after the late war.

In spite of the ambiguity and occasional inconsistency of early dicta, it is clear that Holmes never used such language as that quoted above when only economic interests were at stake. Nor, on the other hand, did he ever employ the language of his dissent in the *Lochner* (hours of labor) case when freedom of speech was the issue. It seems to follow that his attitude toward restriction on speech and press were altogether different from his tolerance in other cases.

The overtones of language and logic suggest strongly that under the clear and present danger doctrine or the "preferred position" principle, the normal presumption of constitutionality of legislative restrictions is dissipated when freedom of speech, press, religion or association is involved. If the danger is "clear," it must be made so to appear; not that its absence should be demonstrated.

Indeed, other Justices have thus interpreted the Holmes basic attitude toward First Amendment freedoms. In a case involving an Arkansas law requiring the National Association for the Advancement of Colored People to make public its membership list, Mr. Justice Stewart said:

Decision in this case must finally turn, therefore, on whether the cities as instrumentalities of the State have demonstrated so cogent an interest in obtaining and making public the membership lists of these organizations as to justify the substantial abridgment of associational freedom which such disclosures will effect. Where there is a significant encroachment upon personal liberty, the State may prevail *only upon showing* a subordinating interest which is compelling.[18] (Emphasis added.)

As recently as 1961 in the Connecticut birth control case[19] Justice Harlan, in his powerful dissent from the Court's refusal to pass on the constitutional issue, quoted from the Oklahoma case invalidating a statute providing for compulsory sterilization of habitual criminals. "Where, as here," he said, "we are dealing with what must be considered 'a basic liberty,' . . . there are limits to . . . which the presumption of constitutionality can be pressed." And later, in the same opinion:

Since, as it appears to me, the statute marks an abridgment of important fundamental liberties protected by the Fourteenth Amendment, it will not do to urge in justification of that abridgment simply that the statute is rationally related to the effectuation of a proper state purpose [*i.e.,* preventing or discouraging meritricious relations between unmarried persons]. A closer scrutiny and stronger justification than that are required.[20]

This opinion may be regarded as particularly important since the case did not involve a First Amendment right and Justice Harlan does not accept the doctrine that all provisions of the Bill of Rights are "incorporated" in the Fourteenth and thus applicable to the states. He regards that amendment as an independent guarantee of the "basic" or "fundamental," liberties of which the relations of a man and wife in the privacy of their home is, to him, one. He thus, in effect, asserts a "preferred position" for a constitutional right other than those protected by the First Amendment.

In the Smith Act case involving Dennis and other Communist leaders[21] Chief Justice Vinson, writing for the Court, referring to several free speech cases, wrote: "He [Holmes] and Justice Brandeis dissented. . . . The basis of these dissents was that, because of the protection which the First Amendment gives to speech, the evidence in each case was insufficient to show that the defendants had created the requisite danger under Schenck." Again, in the same case, in discussing the "reasonableness" test applied by the majority in the *Gitlow* case: "Justice Holmes and Brandeis refused to accept this approach, but insisted that wherever speech was the evidence of violation [of a criminal statute], it was necessary to show that the speech created the 'clear and present danger' of the substantive evil which the legislature had a right to prevent."[22] The Chief Justice then proceeded to discuss what he regarded as the meaning of the phrase "clear and present danger."

> Obviously, the words cannot mean that before the Government may act, it must wait until the putsch is about to be executed, the plans have been laid and the signal is awaited. If Government is aware that a group aiming at its overthrow is attempting to indoctrinate its members and to commit them to a course whereby they will strike when the leaders feel the circumstances permit, action by the Government is required. The argument that there is no need for Government to concern itself, for Government is strong, it possesses ample powers to put down a rebellion, it may defeat the revolution with ease, needs no answer. For that is not the question. Certainly an attempt to overthrow the Government by force, even though doomed from the outset because of inadequate numbers or power of the revolutionists, is a sufficient evil for Congress to prevent. The damages which such attempts create both physically and politically to a nation make it impossible to measure the validity in terms of the probability of success, or the immediacy of a successful attempt. In the instant case the trial judge charged the jury that they could not convict unless they found that petitioners intended to overthrow the Government "as speedily as circumstances would permit." This does not mean, and could not properly mean, that they would not strike until there was certainty of success. What was meant was that the revolutionists would strike when they thought the time was ripe. We must therefore reject the contention that success or probability of success is the criterion.[23]

It would appear that the Chief Justice was thus purporting to follow in the footsteps of Holmes and Brandeis by applying their standard to the then current problems. Was the "conspiracy" of the Communist Party to advocate the overthrow of the government by force a clear and present danger to the national security? His application, however, was patently a distortion of the formula. The intent of an ineffective minority—"miserable merchants of unwanted ideas," to use Justice Douglas' phrase[24]—to overthrow the government "as speedily as circumstances would permit" can hardly be characterized as a "present" danger if language is to have its normal meaning. By affirming the conviction of the defendants in the *Dennis* case, the Court lent approval to Judge Medina's instruction that the jury could find the accused guilty provided they *intended* "to overthrow the government by force and violence as speedily as circumstances would permit." Douglas, in his dissent, pointed out the irrational and dangerous quality of such an interpretation of clear and present danger. "The crime," he said, "then would depend not on what is taught but on who the teacher is. . . . Once we start down that road we enter territory dangerous to the liberties of every citizen."

Justice Frankfurter, notwithstanding his devotion to the Holmes-Brandeis tradition, clearly repudiated the clear and present danger test in the top Communists case: "We are to set aside the judgment of those whose duty it is to legislate only if there is no reasonable basis for it." This, of course, is the objective standard of reasonableness applicable to due process issues, as such, when economic and similar restrictions are imposed by legislation on individual action. He proceeded further to expound his ideas of the Court's function in speech cases:

> In reviewing statutes which restrict freedoms protected by the First Amendment, we have emphasized the close relation which those freedoms bear to the maintenance of a free society. [Citation.] Some members of the Court—and at times a majority—have done more. They have suggested that our function in reviewing statutes restricting freedom of expression differs sharply from our normal duty in sitting in judgment on legislation. . . . It has been suggested, with the casualness of a footnote, that such legislation is not presumptively valid, [citation] and it has been weightily reiterated that freedom of speech has a "preferred position" among constitutional safeguards. [Citation.]

> The precise meaning intended to be conveyed by these phrases need not now be pursued. It is enough to note that they have recurred in the Court's opinions, and their cumulative force has, not without justification, engendered belief that there is a constitutional principle, expressed by those attractive but imprecise words, prohibiting restriction upon utterance unless it creates a situation of "imminent" peril against which legislation may guard. It is on this body of the Court's pronouncements that the defendants' argument here is based.

In all fairness, the argument cannot be met by reinterpreting the Court's frequent use of "clear" and "present" to mean an entertainable "probability." In giving this meaning to the phrase "clear and present danger," the Court of Appeals, was fastidiously confining the rhetoric of opinions to the exact scope of what was decided by them. We have greater responsibility for having given constitutional support, over repeated protests, to uncritical libertarian generalities.[25]

Frankfurter then reviewed a large number of the Court's decisions, not attempting "the ungrateful task" of trying to reconcile them. He agreed with some, but not others. But he reiterated what he had repeatedly maintained: "Free speech cases are not an exception to the principle that we are not legislators, that direct policy-making is not our province. How best to reconcile competing interests is the business of legislatures, and the balance they strike is a judgment not to be displaced by ours, but to be respected unless outside the pale of fair judgment."[26]

Thus to repudiate the clear and present danger formula as a test for constitutionality is one thing. To accept it even in diluted form and to deny that it has any effect on the normal presumption of the validity of legislation is less understandable. The usual procedural assumptions are to the contrary. If the restriction is unconstitutional in the absence of a clear and immediate danger, it would appear that the existence of such justifying circumstances should be shown. Moreover, acceptance of the doctrine would appear to eliminate all "balancing" factors against speech except the danger itself, which must appear to be "clear" (not vague), "immediate" (not remote), and "relatively serious" (not trivial). Nevertheless, it must be admitted that there is truth in Professor's Mendelson's conclusion that "since the departure of Mr. Justice Holmes, 'clear and present danger' has suggested all things to all Justices."[27]

Justice Frankfurter's position is puzzling to many students of the Court and its work. Some question seriously the extent to which he is following in Holmes' footsteps and carrying on the Holmes tradition. Professor Kalven has pointed up several of the anomalies involved.[28] To some of us he has grasped one aspect of Holmes' philosophy to the exclusion of others. His deep insight into human problems, his superb scholarship and his devotion to the Court make all the more difficult his passion for a one-sided Holmes which carries a principle so far as to amount almost to abnegation of judicial responsibility. From those who knew and worked with him, we know how much he must have suffered in aligning himself with the defenders of intoler-

ance and reaction. His confession in the second flag salute case gives
some hint. The complete explanation of his judicial career and appraisal of his contribution to constitutional government must, of
course, await the perspective of time and the mature judgment of
history.

An extreme position, as to the Bill of Rights, perhaps more so
than Frankfurter's "judicial self restraint," is that taken by the late
Judge Learned Hand near the end of his long and distinguished
career. In his Holmes lecture at the Harvard Law School he appeared to take the view that judicial review of legislation should be
confined to those critical situations involving the allocation of power
between the federal government and the states and perhaps, between departments of the federal government itself. He is willing for
the Court to determine whether other officials of the government
have acted within the general authority vouchsafed to them by the
Constitution, but not to review the substantive validity of such action.[29] As to the limitations of the Bill of Rights on both federal
and state governments, they were little more than pious admonitions
to the legislative bodies as to which they have the responsibility for
final interpretation. The judiciary is not to function as a "third legislative chamber."[30]

Again in recent years there has been considerable discussion of
a supposed principle of judicial review characterized as "neutralism."
The chief spokesman for this point of view is Professor Wechsler of
Columbia Law School. It is not easy to determine just what he means
by the principle of "neutralism." There are those who think that it
somehow involves judicial integrity in one way or another.[31] Others
see it in an almost uncompromising adherence to *stare decisis*.[32] If
he has in mind that the Justices should approach a constitutional issue in a particular case without any presuppositions as to the outcome before reading the record and the briefs and before hearing
the arguments, most of us would agree that insofar as this is possible
it would be highly desirable. If he suggests that the Justices should
decide controversial issues without regard to their personal scale of
values as to social and political issues, probably most of us would
regard it as highly unrealistic even if desirable. But if he means what
he says in the following recapitulation of his thesis, this reader is not
at all sure that he knows what the author is talking about, doubts
which appear to be shared by others, including Wechsler's colleague,
Professor Golding:[33]

> The demand of neutrality is that a value and its measure be
> determined by a general analysis that gives no weight to acci-

dents of application, finding a scope that is acceptable whatever interest, group, or person may assert the claim. So too,
when there is conflict among values having constitutional protection, calling for their ordering or their accommodation, I
argue that the principle of resolution must be neutral in a
comparable sense (both in the definition of the individual competing values and in the approach that it entails to value competition).[34]

Whatever the philosophical or constitutional basis of Wechsler's
neutralism, it appears that its tendency, as intended by its author, is
to reduce the power of the Court in our system of government
and to accord more scope to the legislative prerogative, without distinction between those issues which affect the very existence of civilized mankind and those which merely go to the methods of organiz-
ing the economy in which he hopes to exist.

Hand's views about judicial review appear to have derived from
the notion that it is incompatible with democracy. Must the nation
be ruled by a small group of platonic wise men? It is easy, however,
to put this matter out of focus.

There is truth in the charge that judicial review of the substantive
behavior of elected officials is what my colleague Bickel calls "anti-
majoritarian." On the other hand it does not imply, as Judge Hand
thought, that we are governed by that "bevy of Platonic Guardians."
It does mean that judges, removed from the pressures of every day
politics, guided by a document originating from the "people," mark
certain limits of what elected officials can do in the process of governing us, and of how they may do it. In this, they are performing a
function, happily described by Bickel as serving "not only what we
conceive from time to time to be our immediate material needs but
also certain enduring values." And this, he added, "in part is what is
meant by government under law." Men who sit in legislatures and
general assemblies, vulnerable to pressure groups as they exist in our
pluralistic society, are more likely, as experience has repeatedly demonstrated, to take the short rather than the long view.[35]

We are not "ruled" by nine men—old or young—nor by one man,
as some would characterize 5-4 decisions. Dean Rostow has made a
strong case that judicial review is altogether consistent with democratic political philosophy.[36] It is not necessary that all questions be
decided by referendum or in town meeting. Even though judges interpret it, it is the people's Constitution and the people can always
change it. Democracy is a difficult way to run a country and this is a
big country. The responsibilities of democratic man are many and

heavy and often present dilemmas of considerable magnitude, as the late Edmond Cahn has pointed out.[37] Perhaps the biggest problem of any democratic government is to protect the individual citizen from itself. It is the problem of how a government polices itself. When it comes to the Bill of Rights, one point seems clear. Whether an itinerate preacher has a right to distribute religious tracts in the street or a labor leader to make a speech without permission of the town policeman should not be a matter of majority vote. The history of this and other nations is conclusive that the liberties of minorities, and especially the minority of one, are best protected by the courts.

Dean Rostow seems to find a somewhat modified view in Hand's Holmes Lecture at the Harvard Law School on the Bill of Rights but he finds slight comfort in it. The Judge conceded that the Court may hold legislation unconstitutional if "it appears that the statutes are not honest choices between values and sacrifices honestly appraised."[38] As to First Amendment freedoms and due process of law, the legislative judgment stands unless the Court finds that it did not reflect an impartial balance of conflicting values. As to this, the Dean pointedly observed that he had "never before heard it suggested that the decisions of a political and partisan body like the Congress of the United States could be impeached if a court concludes that the Congressmen were not 'impartial.' "[39]

It is true that our ideas of due process of law, jury trial and other members of "that bright constellation" came from England and no court there passes judgment on Acts of Parliament. But it is also true that many of the evils against which the Bill of Rights was intended to afford protection were transplanted here, in colonial days, from the mother country. As the late Judge Charles E. Clark has observed, "our governmental institutions might well have developed differently, might perhaps have followed the English model restricting courts as policy makers; but actually they took quite a different course and we are unreal and unwise now to fight it."

> . . . Lawyers and judges are all too prone to cover up their thought processes by the fiction that it is the law which commands, and it seems to me that these remarks, indeed, the great, if inconclusive, debate on neutral principles, tend to befog and bemuse the problem. Better it is, in my view, to face the hard reality of the importance of human judgment. For then we can more clearly do the things which we as citizens should do. The first is constant and intelligent criticism of judicial activity. . . . And the second is a constant and active concern for the selec-

tion of judges with a sophisticated knowledge of their attributes as human beings.[40]

Similar sentiments were suggested by Justice Douglas in his dissenting opinion in the recent *Perez* denaturalization case,[41] in which Justice Frankfurter, with four fellow Justices, upheld the Act of Congress which forfeited the citizenship of a native-born American who voted in a foreign election. "The philosophy of the opinion that sustains this statute," Douglas declares, "is foreign to our constitutional system. It gives supremacy to the Legislature in a way that is incompatible with the scheme of our written Constitution. A decision such as this could be expected in England where there is no written constitution, and where the House of Commons has the final say. But with all deference, this philosophy has no place here. By proclaiming it we forsake much of our constitutional heritage and move closer to the British scheme. That may be better than ours or it may be worse. Certainly it is not ours."[42]

It is submitted that the positions both of Judge Hand and Professor Wechsler are largely academic. It would appear that Wechsler's theory of "neutralism" is fuzzy, not understood, and in any event has little pragmatic value. As to Judge Hand's position, the Supreme Court's decisions make it clear that, at least to some extent, it will review legislation involving alleged violations of the Bill of Rights. All mature constitutional scholars agree to this. As my colleague Professor Pollak has written, "Hand's premise is simply an anachronism. Because Hand was a great judge for a long period of our national history, because he wrote with a strength and cadence which matched his Olympian mien, because, in short, he became in his own lifetime a myth-judge who spoke with oracular power, Hand could cloak his premise in golden raimant. But even he could not invest it with real authority."[43]

Something similar might be said of another great judge who had distinguished himself as a member of the New York Court of Appeals before appointment to the Supreme Court. It fell to the lot of Justice Cardozo to pronounce what has turned out to be a roadblock to the contention that the Fourteenth Amendment incorporated, as against the states, all guarantees of liberty contained in the Bill of Rights. In *Palko* v. *Connecticut*[44] the issue was one of double jeopardy contrary to the Fifth Amendment. Cardozo's opinion rejected the notion that the due process of law clause applicable to the states under the Fourteenth Amendment included the protections of the Fifth. The guarantees of speech, press and religion were applicable to the states, not so much because First Amendment freedoms were "incorporated" in the Fourteenth, but because they were "implicit in the concept of ordered liberty." But protection against repeated trials for the same offense was not "so rooted in the traditions and conscience of our people as to be ranked as fundamental."

Justice Frankfurter, perhaps, has been for a generation, the chief spokesman for the Cardozo interpretation of this Due Process issue. The debate continues. But Cardozo's *Palko* position has, for years, been a dominant influence. Like Hand, his stature as one of the nation's great jurists, still throws a mantle of authority, if not validity, to his opinions, couched, as they were, in eloquent prose.

The doctrines of "incorporation," "preferred position," "judicial self-restraint" and "neutralism," all raise in one way or another the issue of what standards, tests and presumptions are appropriate in judicial review and the extent to which the Bill of Rights is applicable as limitations on state power. While it is true that the "preferred position" doctrine is not as clear as could be desired, it does have some workable applicability, at least in fixing the attitude of the Court in the vital matter of adjudicating conflicts between the real or supposed interests of government, state or federal, and the liberties of the individual citizen. In its relationship to freedom of expression, Professor Pritchett has explained the significance of the preferred position doctrine as "to exalt the clear-and-present-danger test, instead of minimizing it, as Frankfurter does. It supplies a foundation, a justification, which the test otherwise lacks. It induces in a judge a mental set favorable to civil liberties claims."[45]

In his tirade in the *Kovacs* sound truck case[46] against the "mischievous" phrase, Frankfurter purported to construct the chronology of the evolution of "talk about 'preferred position'." He then declared that, "the ideas now governing the constitutional protection of freedom of speech derive essentially from the opinion of Mr. Justice Holmes." In summarizing Holmes' philosophy, he continued:

> Mr. Justice Holmes seldom felt justified in opposing his own opinion to economic views which the legislature embodied in law. But since he also realized that the progress of civilization is to a considerable extent the displacement of error which once held sway as official truth by beliefs which in turn have yielded to other beliefs, for him the right to search for truth was of a different order than some transient economic dogma. And without freedom of expression, thought becomes checked and atrophied. Therefore, in considering what interests are so fundamental as to be enshrined in the Due Process Clause,

those liberties of the individual which history has attested as the indispensable conditions of an open as against a closed society, come to this Court with a momentum for respect lacking when appeal is made to liberties which derive merely from shifting economic arrangements.[47]

The objection, Frankfurter thought, to describing this line of thought by the phrase "preferred position" was that it "expresses a complicated process of constitutional adjudication by a deceptive formula." If, indeed, the phrase is deceptive, it may be thought that little more clarification derives from the proposition that freedom of speech, press and religion "come to this Court with a momentum for respect lacking when appeal is made to liberties which derive merely from shifting economic arrangements." The following statement of the principle in 1948 by Justice Rutledge is neither over-simplified nor over-obfuscated:

As the Court has declared repeatedly, that judgment [legislative] does not bear the same weight and is not entitled to the same presumption of validity, when the legislation on its face or in specific application restricts the rights of conscience, expression and assembly protected by the Amendment, as are given to other regulations having no such tendency. The presumption rather is against the legislative intrusion into these domains. . . . Hence doubtful intrusions cannot be allowed to stand consistently with the Amendment's command and purpose nor, therefore, can the usual presumptions of constitutional validity, deriving from the weight of legislative opinion in other matters more largely within the legislative province and special competence, obtain.[48]

Rutledge did not, in terms, endorse the theory that the First Amendment guarantee of freedom of speech and press was "absolute," whatever that may mean.[49] He subscribed to the Holmesian philosophy of the market place of ideas and the Holmes' limitation as he understood it. But his idea of "clear and present danger" was far different from that of some of his brethren. In any event, Rutledge would have no part of Frankfurter's fanciful notion that the formula was a figment of Holmes' literary imagination.

For Rutledge, communication of ideas was indeed to be free; "incitement" might be different. But it was hard to fool Rutledge by a word or a phrase. He was familiar with ideas and, with Holmes, he knew that every idea is an incitement. "The only difference between an expression of opinion and an incitement in the narrower sense is the speaker's enthusiasm for the result."[50] Danger is not "clear and present" unless it constituted "incitement in the narrower sense."

But even "enthusiasm for the result" should not be enough. "Speech," as a practical matter, should be indistinguishable from "action" in order to be classed as a "danger," clear and present. As Holmes put it in the *Schenck* case, "words that may have all the effect of force" or Douglas more recently, "speech so brigaded with illegal action as to be an inseparable part of it."[51] A man crying "fire" in a crowded theatre; the captain in charge of a squad of soldiers giving the order, "fire"; the officer, miles behind the line, ordering an advance; the fanatic in front of a racist mob yelling "lynch him." It is said that the words must "trigger" the action. More accurately, perhaps, insofar as words can be accurate, the "words" must be a part of the "action." They cannot be disassociated from it. Not that action will be forthcoming "as soon as circumstances will permit," but "presently," "immediately," "now!" Of course, even such an interpretation may call for judgment. The "immediacy" cannot be computed by an I.B.M. machine. To quote Holmes once again, however, the life of the law has been "experience" rather than "logic," and there are three thousand years of history, with all the tragic manifestations of human behavior and responses to forensic stimuli to aid the judge in evaluating the danger.

Perhaps Rutledge would not go so far. And, by his opinion in the *Schenck* case, we may assume that Holmes, too, might stop short. But the logical end of such an analysis comes, it would seem, to this: if nothing happens, as an instantaneous result of the speech, it is protected by the First Amendment. Conceivably there might be a rare exception, as for example, an immediate retraction, or the instant interposition of a superior force to prevent "action." It can be argued that Jefferson's idea of freedom of speech did, indeed, go this far. As Rutledge suggested, perhaps he was the inventor of the equivalent of "clear and present danger" in its purest form. "[I]t is time enough for the rightful purposes of civil government, for its officers to interfere when principles break out into overt acts against peace and good order."[52]

This, of course, comes close, indeed very close to the position that the words, "Congress shall make no law . . . abridging the freedom of speech" are to be taken quite literally. A lesser interpretation, it can be argued, leads into a quagmire of "balancing" factors too difficult to evaluate when what it involves is "the matrix, the indispensable condition of nearly every other form of freedom." A calculated guess is that, if the issue had been squarely presented, Rutledge would have gone all the way with the maximum spread of the First Amendment protection for speech. But it is hard to put it into "words" or any kind of a formula. It is an incredibly difficult psychological problem and the nuances of semantics makes it no less so. Madison recognizes the two-fold aspect of the problem in *The Federalist*:[53] "The use of words is to express ideas. Perspicuity, therefore requires not only that the ideas be distinctly formed, but that they should be expressed by words distinctly and exclusively appropriated to them. But no language is so copious as to supply words and phrases for every complex idea, or so correct as not to include many equivocally denoting different ideas."

My colleague Professor Emerson in his thoughtful article on the First Amendment has declared that the "essence of a system of free expression lies in the distinction between expression and action." "The whole theory," he says, "rests upon the general proposition that expression must be free and unrestrained, that the state may not seek to achieve other social objectives through control of expression, and that the attainment of such objectives must be secured through regulation of action. The dynamics of the system require that this line be carefully drawn and strictly adhered to. The acceptance of this general position was the fundamental decision made in adopting the First Amendment, and this balance of values and methods must be recognized in any interpretation of that constitutional guarantee."[54]

The Matrix

"There is danger that, if the Court does not temper its doctrinaire logic with a little practical wisdom, it will convert the constitutional Bill of Rights into a suicide pact." Thus Justice Jackson concluded his dissenting opinion in the *Terminiello* case.[55] Terminiello was a suspended Catholic priest who had made a Fascist harangue before a large audience in a Chicago auditorium outside of which was a turbulent, angry mob protesting the meeting and the speakers. The meeting had been called by another rabble-rouser named Gerald L. K. Smith. Throughout the meeting the crowd outside was attempting to break through the doors, throwing rocks, ice picks and other objects through the windows. In spite of the efforts of a cordon of police the disturbance continued. In this atmosphere, the priest in his long and intemperate speech made remark after remark such as the following:

". . . Now, I am going to whisper my greetings to you, Fellow Christians. I will interpret it. I said, 'Fellow *Christians*,' and I suppose there are *some of the scum got in by mistake*, so I want to tell a story about *the scum*:

"... And nothing I could say tonight could begin to express the contempt I have for the *slimy scum* that got in by mistake.

"... The subject I want to talk to you tonight about is the attempt *that is going on right outside this hall tonight,* the attempt that is going on to *destroy America by revolution.* ...

"My friends, it is no longer true that it can't happen here. It is happening here, and it only depends upon you, good people, who are here tonight, depends upon all of us together, as Mr. Smith said. The tide is changing, and if you and I turn and run from that tide, we will all be drowned in this tidal wave of Communism which is going over the world.

"... I am not going to talk to you about the menace of Communism, which is already accomplished, in Russia, where from eight to fifteen million people were murdered in cold blood by their own countrymen, and millions more through Eastern Europe at the close of the war are being murdered by these murderous Russians, hurt, being raped and sent into slavery. *That is what they want for you, that howling mob outside.*

. . .

"First of all, we had Queen Eleanor. Mr. Smith said, 'Queen Eleanor is now one of the world's communists. She is one who said this—imagine, coming from the spouse of the former President of the United States for twelve long years—this is what she said: 'The war is but a step in the revolution. The war is but one step in the revolution, and we know who started the war.'

"Then we have Henry Adolph Wallace, the sixty million job magician. You know we only need fifty-four million jobs in America and everybody would be working. He wants sixty million jobs, because some of the bureaucrats want two jobs apiece. Here he is, what he says about revolution: 'We are in for a profound revolution. Those of us who realize the inevitableness of the revolution, and are anxious that it be *gradual and bloodless* instead of *somewhat bloody. Of course, if necessary, we will have it more bloody.*'

"And then Chief Justice Stone had this to say: 'A way has been found for the effective suppression of speech and press and religion, despite constitutional guarantee,'—from the Chief Justice, from the Chief Justice of the United States.

". . . Didn't you ever read the Morgenthau plan for the starvation of little babies and pregnant women in Germany? . . .

"Now, let me say, I am going to talk about—I almost said, about the Jews. Of course, I would not want to say that. However, I am going to talk about some Jews. I hope that—I am a Christian minister. We must take a Christian attitude. I don't want you to go from this hall with hatred in your heart for any person, for no person. . . .

"Now, this danger which we face—let us call them Zionist Jews if you will, let's call them atheistic, communistic Jews or Zionist Jews, then let us not fear to condemn them. . . ." (Emphasis as in opinions.)

Terminiello was arrested under a city ordinance forbidding breaches of the peace. The trial judge instructed the jury that the ordinance made criminal any misbehavior which "stirs the public to anger, invites dispute, brings about a condition of unrest, or creates a disturbance." The prisoner was convicted and the conviction upheld by the state supreme court. As applied in this case, five Justices of the Supreme Court of the United States held the ordinance unconstitutional. Writing for himself and Justices Rutledge, Black, Murphy and Reed, Douglas argued that "a function of free speech under our system of government is to invite dispute." "It may indeed best serve its high purpose," he continued, "when it induces a condition of unrest, creates dissatisfaction with conditions as they are, or even stirs people to anger." He then went on to say:

> Speech is often provocative and challenging. It may strike at prejudices and preconceptions and have profound unsettling effects as it presses for acceptance of an idea. That is why freedom of speech, though not absolute, . . . is nevertheless protected against censorship or punishment unless shown likely to produce a clear and present danger of a serious substantive evil that rises far above public inconvenience, annoyance, or unrest.[56]

Cases like this, of course, constitute the hard test of the principle of free expression. There is no need for it unless it means freedom for the speech that is hated. There are few ideas, indeed, that are hated by all. But there also are few that are not hated by some. In this dilemma, a line must be drawn before freedom of speech becomes a "suicide pact." Four Justices believed that the near riot of hundreds of angry people in the *Terminiello* case was enough to justify the verdict of guilty even though the charge to the jury was too broad and could have misled the jury into a conviction for a much less inciting and infuriating speech. On the other hand, four Justices could not believe that the relatively insignificant membership in the Communist Party in 1951 constituted a "clear and present danger" to the national security such as to lend constitutional sanction to the Smith Act as applied in the trial and conviction of Dennis and the other Communist leaders a few years after the *Terminiello* case. More than one Justice, on occasion, has failed to heed Justice Brandeis' warning in the California syndicalism case: "The fact that speech is likely to result in some violence or in destruction of property is not enough. There must be the probability of serious injury to the State." And it seems that too often the Justices forget what Holmes once reminded us that the history of civil liberties has been largely in efforts to protect the rights of "not very nice people."

A highly complicated free speech issue arose in *Thomas* v. *Collins*.[57] This case involved the conviction for contempt of court of the president of the United Automobile, Aircraft and Agricultural Implements Workers, who was also the vice-president of the Congress of Industrial Organizations. The state of Texas had enacted a law requiring all labor union organizers operating in the state to apply for an organizer's card before soliciting members. The application should indicate his full name, his union affiliations, and a description of his credentials, a copy of which was to be attached. Thereupon he was to receive a card incorporating such data, signed by the Secretary of State and attested by his seal of office. The law required the organizer to carry such card at all times while soliciting members and exhibit it when requested by a person being solicited.

Thomas, the union official, went to Houston solely to make a speech before a group of employees of an oil company whom union members were seeking to organize. The meeting was given wide publicity and before Thomas spoke he was served with a restraining order which had been issued, without notice or hearing, in Austin, Texas, prohibiting him from soliciting members without the required card. In violation of this order Thomas went to the meeting, made his speech, and issued a general invitation to persons present, not members of the labor union, to join the local union involved, and support the labor movement throughout the country. At the conclusion of his written speech, he further said, "Pat O'Sullivan, I want you to join the Oil Workers Union. I have some application cards here, and I would like to have you sign one."

He was convicted of contempt, fined one hundred dollars and sentenced to three days in jail, whereupon he applied to the state supreme court for a writ of habeas corpus which was granted. Thomas was released on bond. Subsequently, however, the state court, after hearing, sustained the commitment. The case was argued twice in the Supreme Court of the United States and decided in January 1945. The state supreme court was reversed. The statute was unconstitutional. It was held to violate the First Amendment as an invalid restraint upon free expression in penalizing the mere asking of a worker to join a union without having procured the card.

On behalf of the state, it was argued that no issue of free speech or free assembly was involved. The statute was directed at business practices, like the selling of insurance, dealing in stocks and other securities, acting as a commission merchant and similar activities. It merely recognized the fact that, "something more" is done by a labor organizer than talking. "He acts for an alleged principal and collects money for the principal, or if he does not actually collect fees and dues in person, he makes it possible for his principal to collect them." The statute required registration and nothing more. The Secretary of State had no discretion. His powers were purely ministerial. The whole procedure was one solely for previous identification.

"The case confronts us again," Rutledge wrote in the opinion for the Court, "with the duty our system places on this Court to say where the individual's freedom ends and the state's power begins. Choice on that border, now as always delicate, is perhaps more so where the usual presumption supporting legislation is balanced by the preferred place given in our scheme to the great, the indispensable democratic freedoms secured by the First Amendment. [Citing Cases.] That priority gives these liberties a sanctity and a sanction not permitting dubious intrusions." As a result, he said, "any attempt to restrict those liberties must be justified by clear public interest, threatened not doubtfully or remotely, but by clear and present danger."

> The rational connection between the remedy provided and the evil to be curbed, which in other contexts might support legislation against attacks on due process grounds, will not suffice. These rights rest on firmer foundation. Accordingly, whatever occasion would restrain orderly discussion and persuasion, at appropriate time and place, must have clear support in public danger, actual or impending.[58]

Rutledge conceded, of course, that the state may regulate labor unions to protect the public interest. They had no special immunity. But members of labor organizations, like anyone else, are protected in the exercise of the right to free speech. The statute in this case was a restriction upon the rights of a labor leader to speak to workers in what he regarded as their best interests and the right of such workers to hear what he had to say. The right to speak is equated with the right to listen and hear.

In Justice Roberts' dissenting opinion, joined by the Chief Justice and Justices Reed and Frankfurter, it was argued that Thomas had not been enjoined from making a speech nor from advocating union affiliation. He had been enjoined from soliciting membership without first obtaining a card. But Rutledge could not understand how Thomas could "laud unionism" and yet not imply an invitation to join in the circumstances of this case. He thought that the workers at the meeting would readily understand that the president of the U.A.W. and vice-president of the C.I.O., addressing an organization meeting, was not urging merely a philosophic attachment to abstract principles of unionism, disconnected from the business immediately at hand. "The feat would be incredible for a national leader, addressing such a meeting, lauding unions and their principles, urging adherence to union philosophy, not also and thereby to suggest attachment to the union by becoming a member."

He pointed out that the assembly was altogether peaceable and had a lawful purpose. The statements for which Thomas was held in contempt were not in themselves unlawful, nor had they any tendency to incite to unlawful action or any other immediate danger to the public welfare. There was nothing in the word "solicit" at a labor organization meeting to compare with the word "fire" in a crowded theater. There was nothing wrong, nor could it be made wrong, in persuading workers to action by joining the union. The Bill of Rights was not solely for persons in intellectual pursuits. "It extends to more than abstract discussion, unrelated to action. The First Amendment is a charter for government, not for an institution of learning." Rutledge concluded his opinion by declaring that the exercise of the rights of free speech and free assembly could not be made a crime nor could this be accomplished by the device of requiring previous registration as a condition for exercising them and making such condition the foundation for restraining in advance their exercise and for imposing a penalty for violating such an order. "So long as no more is involved than exercise of the rights of free speech and free assembly, it is immune to such a restriction. . . . We think a requirement that one must register before he undertakes to make a public speech to enlist support for a lawful movement is quite incompatible with the requirements of the First Amendment."[59]

Justice Jackson in his concurring opinion emphasized the difference between the power of the state to regulate business activities and to restrict freedom of speech and assembly. He agreed with Justice Rutledge that the case "falls in the category of a public speech, rather than that of practicing a vocation as solicitor." The extensive power over the pursuit of a calling as distinguished from speech-making is the result of the different effects which the two have on the interests which the state has power to protect. When one seeks to obtain money from the public through the practice of a calling, the state has a legitimate interest in protecting it against fraud, irresponsibility and incompetence by a system of licensing or other reasonable device.

> But it cannot be the duty, because it is not the right, of the state to protect the public against false doctrine. The very purpose of the First Amendment is to foreclose public authority from assuming a guardianship of the public mind through regulating the press, speech, and religion. In this field every person must be his own watchman for truth, because the forefathers did not trust any government to separate the true from the false for us.[60]

This was by no means an easy case for the Court and the result, as a whole, left much to be desired. After the numerous conferences, months of consideration, two oral arguments and the many drafted and redrafted opinions, the Justices were far apart on the merits and the reasoning. The *Washington Post* for January 14, 1945, summarized the net results as follows:

> Whatever one may think of the decision of the Supreme Court in the R.J. Thomas case, it certainly will not enhance public confidence in that august tribunal. In the first place, Justice Rutledge was apparently the only man on the court wholly in agreement with his own opinion for the majority. . . . That great diversity of viewpoints, to say nothing of the narrowness of the majority, unavoidedly intensifies confusion as to what the law is.
> More serious, in our opinion, is the paucity of common understanding between the majority and minority groups as to what the case involved. Justices Rutledge and Jackson wrote strong and convincing opinions upholding the right of free speech. The dissenters asserted that the issue was not freedom of speech, but whether the Texas Legislature may require a

paid solicitor to register himself. If the conflicting opinions were not read consecutively, one would scarcely realize that both grew out of one set of facts.

Yet the facts were not in dispute. . . .

The newspaper was mistaken as to the lack of agreement with Rutledge on the part of the other Justices constituting the majority. Justice Douglas wrote a brief concurring opinion to deny the relevance of two Labor Board cases. He expressly stated, however, that he joined in the Rutledge opinion. Justices Black and Murphy joined in the Douglas opinion and therefore in Rutledge's. Moreover, Rutledge's opinion was designated as "of the Court." The "preferred position" doctrine thus had the approval of the "Court" in this case.

In the middle forties the use of loud speakers on sound trucks became an increasingly popular means of harassing the public. Cities began to enact ordinances prohibiting or controlling the use of such sound amplification devices. Two cases reaching the Supreme Court again split the Justices several ways and resulted in ambiguous decisions leaving the matter in a confused state where it largely remains to this day. Although both cases reached the Court at the same time, one was decided in June, 1948, the other, for some reason, carried over into the next term of Court and was decided in January, 1949.

The city of Lockport, New York, had passed a penal ordinance prohibiting the use of sound trucks except with the permission of the Chief of Police. A Jehovah Witness, without such permission, set up his loud speaking apparatus on the street near a public park with the microphone through which he delivered his sermons, in the park itself. In *Saia v. New York*, this Witness was arrested and convicted of violating the ordinance.

Justice Douglas wrote the opinion for the Court holding the law unconstitutional as in violation of the freedom of speech provision of the First Amendment, made applicable to the states through the Fourteenth. The ordinance was unconstitutional on its face as a previous restraint on free speech because it left the matter of permission to the arbitrary discretion of the Chief of Police. No standards were prescribed to control him with respect to the volume of sound, the hours or places of use, the content of the broadcast or any other matter.[61] In three previous cases,[62] the Court had struck down ordinances requiring licenses to distribute Jehovah Witnesses religious tracts, to distribute any kind of literature, and to hold a public meeting on the streets or public parks. "Unless we are to retreat from the firm positions we have taken in the past," the Douglas opinion went, "we must give freedom of speech in this case the same preferred treatment that we gave freedom of religion in the *Cantwell* case, freedom of the press in the *Griffin* case, and freedom of speech and assembly in the *Hague* case."

Justices Black, Murphy, Rutledge and Chief Justice Vinson joined in the Douglas opinion. Justice Frankfurter wrote a dissenting opinion with which Justices Reed and Burton concurred. They held it was not beyond the power of the state, in this manner to protect the public against "aural aggression" and "intrusion into cherished privacy." Justice Jackson dissented on his own. He thought the Court's decision endangered rather than protected the right of free speech by making it ridiculous and obnoxious. It was "astonishing news" to him that the Constitution prohibited a city from policing its streets and parks in this manner. Jackson insisted that the accused had been arrested for setting up his "system of microphone, wires and sound truck without a permit," and not for making a speech or preaching a sermon.

In his opinion for the Court, Douglas concluded with these words: "Courts must balance the various community interests in passing on the constitutionality of local regulations of the character involved here. But in that process they should be mindful to keep the freedoms of the First Amendment in a preferred position." With the balancing technique as a judicial device, Jackson disagreed entirely. "It is for the local communities to balance their own interests—that is politics—and what courts should keep out of. Our only function is to apply constitutional limitations." To which Douglas might have replied that if the community interests got too far out of balance, constitutional limits have been exceeded.

At one point in his opinion Douglas remarked that the sound truck had become an accepted method of political campaigning. "Must a candidate for governor or the Congress depend on the whim of the Chief of Police in order to use his sound truck for campaigning," he asked. "Must he prove to the satisfaction of that official that his noise will not be too annoying to people?" To which Justice Jackson replied that "even political candidates ought not to be allowed irresponsibly to set up sound equipment in all sorts of public places, and few would regard it as tactful campaigning to thrust themselves upon picnicking families who do not want to hear their message." He then added the following sentence: "I think the Court is overconcerned about danger to political candidacies and I would deal with that problem when, and if, it arises."[63]

Whether so intended or not, at least one seasoned observer interpreted this as a "dig" at what Jackson apparently thought were Douglas' political aspirations. "It is hard," he wrote, "to read about 'danger to political candidacies' without recalling the continuing political activity in behalf of Justice Douglas for the Democratic nomination next month [July, 1948]. In fact, at the very moment the Jackson comment was handed down in Washington an organization known as the William O. Douglas for President Club, with headquarters in Chicago, was circulating through the mail letters and brochures in support of Douglas. . . ."[64]

The Christian Science Monitor "ruefully" agreed with the decision, quoting Walt Whitman's "conscious, good-humored exaggeration" ["I sound my barbaric yawp over the roofs of the world."], and continued: "Too many political candidates whose voices penetrate the American home from cruising sound trucks turn Whitman's boast into raucous reality. People who cherish their freedom not to listen to what they don't want to hear, should remember to protest. If the protest is loud enough, politicians will listen."[65]

It will be remembered that in the Illinois release time case, the Court held that public owned property could not be used for religious purposes. But since the children left the school house to go elsewhere for religious instruction, the New York release time law did not violate the establishment clause.[66] The result of this sound truck case, however, is that the state must permit a preacher to use public property to give his religious harangue. Why should it make the difference that this use of public property turned not on the free practice of religion but on the free speech principle, when the basic issue appears to be the same. Justice Jackson declared that he could not understand how the Court could "read the Constitution one day to forbid and the next day to compel use of public tax-supported property to help a religious sect spread its faith." A plausible explanation and distinction might well be that children are required to go to school and thus the choice is between going to some part of the premises where religious instruction is being given or become conspicuous for nonconformance. But there is no such problem in connection with the preacher in the park.

Six months later, the decision came down involving a similar but not identical ordinance of the city of Trenton, New Jersey. It was entitled "An Ordinance to Prohibit the Making of Unnecessary Noise." It provided:

> That it shall be unlawful for any person, firm or corporation, either as principal, agent or employee, to play, use or operate

for advertising purposes, or for any other purposes whatsoever, on or upon the public streets, alleys or thoroughfares in the City of Trenton, any device known as a sound truck, loud speaker or sound amplifier, or radio or phonograph with a loud speaker or sound amplifier, or any other instrument known as calliope or any other instrument of any kind or character which emits therefrom loud and raucous noises and is attached to and upon any vehicle operated or standing upon said streets or public places aforementioned.

A man named Kovacs was arrested and convicted for playing recorded music and making a speech on a pending labor dispute over loud speakers mounted on a truck. His conviction was upheld by the state supreme court. The case was decided by the Supreme Court of the United States on January 31, 1949, affirming the conviction against the charge that the Trenton ordinance, like that of the Lockport law, was unconstitutional under the First Amendment. The Court divided five to four, and although there were five separate opinions, there was no majority opinion. Justice Reed wrote for himself, the Chief Justice and Justice Burton. Justices Frankfurter and Jackson concurred in separate opinions. Justice Black dissented in an opinion in which Justices Douglas and Rutledge joined. Justice Rutledge wrote a separate dissenting opinion while Justice Murphy dissented without opinion and without joining in the other dissents.[67]

Justice Reed circulated a draft opinion as early as October, 1948. He argued that it was unnecessary to determine whether the ordinance and the New Jersey court's interpretation of it prohibited all sound trucks on the streets or only those which emitted "loud and raucous noises." He thought a state or city had the power to prohibit all kinds of such amplifying devices. A few days later, a revised draft limited the scope of the city ordinance as to prohibit only "loud and raucous noises" and, as thus interpreted, valid.

Justice Black maintained that the ordinance, properly interpreted did prohibit all sound trucks and that if it was limited, as Reed suggested in his revised draft, then Kovacs had been convicted of an offense that was neither charged nor proven. He also insisted that to uphold the Trenton law would in substance overrule the *Saia* case.

Justice Jackson concurred in upholding the ordinance, as he said, for the reasons which led him to dissent in the *Saia* case. He thought there was no violation of the Fourteenth Amendment by infringement of free speech in the absence of any censorship of the contents of the broadcast. "Freedom of speech for Kovacs does not, in my view, include freedom to use sound amplifiers to drown out the natural speech of others." He also agreed with Justice Black that the decision would be a repudiation of *Saia* for which, of course, he was gratified.

It will be remembered that Chief Justice Vinson had voted with the majority in the *Saia* case which held the Lockport ordinance unconstitutional. He switched his vote in *Kovacs* to uphold the Trenton law. Presumably he was able to distinguish the two on the grounds that in the latter, not all sound trucks were prohibited, but only those emitting "loud and raucous noises." It may be significant that Reed had changed the tenor of his position on this point. In the first draft of his opinion which he circulated, he thought it unnecessary to decide whether the ordinance was limited in its scope or whether it excluded from the streets all sound amplifying devices. His final opinion accepted the state court's narrower interpretation. He could be reasonably sure that Frankfurter, Jackson, and Burton would vote against the validity of the ordinance under either interpretation. If his strategy was to attract Vinson to this view by affording a basis for distinguishing the two cases, it was successful.

The situation thus appeared to be something like this: A majority of five Justices voted to uphold the law, but only Justices Burton and Vinson joined in Reed's opinion based on the interpretation of the city law that restricted the crime to the omission of "loud and raucous noises" from sound trucks. The other two (Frankfurter and Jackson) went further. The ordinance was constitutional even if it prohibited all sound trucks emitting any kind of noise.

Justice Rutledge in his dissent emphasized the anomaly of the Court's position as suggested by Justice Black. He pointed out that only a minority of the Justices took the view that the Trenton ordinance merely forbade amplifying instruments which emitted "loud and raucous noises." "Yet a different majority," he continued, "one including that minority and two other Justices sustain the ordinance and its application. In effect Kovacs stands convicted, but of what it is impossible to tell, because the majority upholding the conviction do not agree upon what constituted the crime." "How," he continued, "on such a hashing of different views of the thing forbidden, Kovacs could have known with what he was charged or could have prepared a defense, I am unable to see. How anyone can do either in the future, under this decision, I am equally at loss to say."

Rutledge had no doubt of the power of the state to regulate the use of sound trucks, by appropriately drawn legislation, to protect the interest of the public in the use of the streets and to prevent public nuisances. But he could not concede that the First Amendment limited its protection of speech to the natural range of the human voice as it existed in 1790 any more than he could believe that the power over interstate commerce was limited to navigation by sailboats and overland travel by horses and oxen, the principal modes of carrying on commerce in 1789. "The Constitution was not drawn with any such limited vision of time, space and mechanics."

Justice Frankfurter, as earlier noted, in his dissent paid special attention to the doctrine of the "preferred position" of the First Amendment freedoms. In referring to Rutledge's opinion in *Thomas v. Collins* which contained perhaps the strongest endorsement of that doctrine, he stated in a preliminary draft of his opinion that the Rutledge opinion in that case was "not the opinion of the Court." In his final published opinion he changed this statement to read that "it was the opinion of only four members of the Court, since Mr. Justice Jackson, in a separate concurring opinion, referred to the opinion of Mr. Justice Rutledge only to say that he agreed that the case fell into 'the category of a public speech, rather than that of practicing a vocation as solicitor'." This is all true, but it is also true that the Rutledge opinion was the "opinion of the Court."

An "opinion of the Court," so designated in the official reports, is one which has been authorized as such by a majority of the Justices. This authorization is given by a formal vote at the last conference held before decision day. Thus, in the *Thomas* case, Justice Jackson presumably cast his vote to authorize Justice Rutledge to designate his opinion as the "opinion of the Court." This, however, does not necessarily mean that he agreed with everything stated in the opinion, although it necessarily means that he was willing for it to reflect a solidarity of the Court's position.

In his repudiation of the "preferred position," Frankfurter quoted language from a number of cases which he relied upon as supporting the doctrine. He declared that "the claim that any legislation is presumptively unconstitutional which touches the field of the First Amendment and the Fourteenth Amendment, insofar as the latter's concept of 'liberty' contains what is specifically protected by the First, has never commended itself to a majority of this Court."[68] To this Rutledge replied simply, "I think my brother Frankfurter demonstrates the conclusion opposite to that which he draws, namely, that the First Amendment guarantees of the freedoms of speech, press, assembly and religion occupy a preferred position not only in the Bill of Rights but also in the repeated decisions of this Court."[69]

Criminal statutes run afoul of the Fourteenth Amendment as such if they are so vague in defining the prohibited act that those who are law-abiding cannot reasonably know what constitutes the crime and persons accused thereof are unable to prepare an adequate defense. In 1947, a statute of the state of Utah made criminal any conspiracy "to commit any act injurious to . . . public morals. . . ." One Musser and others were convicted of violation of this statute and their convictions upheld by the state supreme court. In these proceedings, it appeared that the accused had relied, somewhat uncertainly, on the First as well as the Fourteenth Amendments.

Writing for the Court, Mr. Justice Jackson conceded that the law under which appellants were convicted was "no narrowly drawn statute." He went on:

> We do not presume to give an interpretation as to what it may include. Standing by itself, it would seem to be warrant for conviction for agreement to do almost any act which a judge and jury might find at the moment contrary to his or its notions of what was good for health, morals, trade, commerce, justice or order. In some States the phrase "injurious to public morals" would be likely to punish acts which it would not punish in others because of the varying policies on such matters as use of cigarettes or liquor and the permissibility of gambling. This led to the inquiry as to whether the statute attempts to cover so much that it effectively covers nothing. Statutes defining crimes may fail of their purpose if they do not provide some reasonable standards of guilt.[70]

By a six to three decision, the Court held that the state court had not passed upon the meaning of the statute, that its interpretation would be binding on the Supreme Court since it was a matter of state law, and before the Court could pass on any constitutional issues, the case should have the benefit of the state court's ideas as to what the statute meant, and the ultimate federal questions which might be involved. Accordingly the judgment was vacated and the case remanded to give the courts of Utah an opportunity to make its disposition of the matters in issue. Justice Rutledge dissented in an opinion concurred in by Justices Murphy and Douglas.

The actual charge against appellants was that they had conspired "to advocate, promote, encourage, urge, teach, counsel, advise *and* practice polygamous or plural marriages and to advocate, promote, encourage, urge, counsel, advise *and* practice the cohabiting of one male person with more than one woman and in furtherance and pursuance of said conspiracy and to effect the object thereof, did commit the following acts: . . . ."

Eleven overt acts were charged but only three were submitted to the jury, (1) that for some ten years the accused had published and distributed monthly pamphlets called "Truth," (2) that they bought a house in Salt Lake City to carry on their activities, and (3) that they attempted to convert one Helen Smith to believe in and to live in polygamy. In affirming the convictions, the Utah court appeared to rely only on the overt acts (2) and (3). In the Supreme Court, the appellants contended that their freedom of speech and religion had been violated. They admitted that they could be punished for the actual practice of polygamy but insisted that they were constitutionally protected in expressing their belief and in advocating it.

To Rutledge, "a deeper vice" infected the convictions than the apparant invalidity for vagueness, "even if further construction by the Utah courts might possibly remove that ground for reversal." He conceded that a direct and personalized incitement to commit a crime could be proscribed by the state as a criminal offense. But this, he thought, was quite different from an agreement to advocate and urge the practice of polygamy. He pointed out that although the accused had been charged with a conspiracy to advocate *and* practice polygamy, the Utah courts had treated it as though the charge was only to *advocate* the practice of polygamy. He emphasized that the advocacy was "at least in part conducted in religious meetings where, although pressure may also have been applied to individuals, considerable general discussion of the religious duty to enter into plural marriages was carried on." The state court, however, made no distinction between the "specific incitations and the more generalized discussions." The trial had proceeded on the theory that the statute applied to the latter as well as the former. There was, thus, a situation similar to that in the *Kovacs* case discussed above and it was impossible to determine which, if not perhaps both grounds, were the basis of the convictions. Insofar as the statute made "the more generalized discussion" a crime, it contravened the First Amendment. He thus thought the sweep of the statute too broad. The Constitution required that it be limited more narrowly. He set forth his philosophy of free speech in clear and cogent language.

It is axiomatic that a democratic state may not deny its citizens the right to criticize existing laws and to urge that they be changed. And yet, in order to succeed in an effort to legalize polygamy it is obviously necessary to convince a substantial number of people that such conduct is desirable. But conviction that the practice is desirable has a natural tendency to induce the practice itself. Thus, depending on where the circular reasoning is started, the advocacy of polygamy may either be unlawful as inducing a violation of law, or be constitutionally

protected as essential to the proper functioning of the democratic process.

In the abstract, the problem could be solved in various ways.
At one extreme it could be said that society can best protect
itself by prohibiting only the substantive evil and relying on a
completely free interchange of ideas as the best safeguard against
demoralizing propaganda. Or we might permit advocacy of law-
breaking, but only so long as the advocacy falls short of incitement. But the other extreme position, that the state may prevent any conduct which induces people to violate the law, or
any advocacy of unlawful activity, cannot be squared with the
First Amendment. At the very least, as we have indicated, under
the clear-and-present-danger rule, the second alternative stated
marks the limit of the state's power as restricted by the
Amendment.[71]

Rutledge found that the state had, in effect, adopted the third
alternative on the theory that the agreement to advocate polygamy
could be made a crime and was, in this case, unlawful. He would
have reversed the Utah court rather than vacate the judgment and remand it for further proceedings, as the majority ordered.

On remand to the state supreme court, that court did, indeed,
hold the statute unconstitutional for vagueness. It held that there
was nothing in the language of the statute or any other act of the
legislature or in the common law of the state which would indicate
any limitation in the words used. The law was in violation of the
Fourteenth Amendment. The lower court was reversed and the convictions set aside. The court explained that the question of vagueness
had not been raised in briefs or previous arguments before it.[72]

Among the most baffling issues of freedom of speech or press are
those in which the conflicting interest is one of a fair trial for persons
accused of crime. A responsible press! An impartial jury! The
"climate" of opinion! These are all factors involved in this conflict.
Unfortunately not all newspapers and their reporters and editors are
responsible. Unfortunately, jurors, or many of them, are not immune
to the influences of vacillating public opinion, including community
prejudices, bigotries and politically inspired notions of "justice" in
particular situations. Indeed, it may even be thought that judges, too,
on occasion, are sensitive to popular reaction to crime.

These interests came into head-on collision in a Florida case involving convictions for contempt of court. The *Miami Herald* had
published two editorials and a cartoon indicating, in no ambiguous
terms, that Florida courts were not serving the public interest by

being too lenient toward persons accused of crime. The Herald Publishing Company and its associate editor were found guilty of contempt by interfering with the orderly administration of justice.

The case was argued in the Supreme Court of the United States on November 5, 1945, and decided the following June. In the meantime, Chief Justice Stone had died. His successor, Chief Justice Vinson, did not assume his duties until after the decision had been handed down but would not have participated in any event because he had not heard the arguments. Justice Jackson was absent from the bench during this term. Although the seven-judge Court unanimously reversed the state court's judgment, the Justices circulated ten opinions, and revisions, three each by Frankfurter, Reed and Rutledge; one by Murphy.[73]

The newspaper's allegedly contemptuous publications referred to three criminal cases. One involved eight indictments for rape, all of which were quashed. The other two consisted of actions against two "clubs," presumably for bookmaking or other gambling enterprises. Both actions were dismissed. The editorial comments were published while at least the rape cases were still pending. Pertinent parts are as follows:

> November 2, 1944:
>
> It is beyond question that American courts are of, by and for the people.
>
> Every accused person has a right to his day in court. But when judicial instance and interpretative procedure recognize and accept, even go out to find, every possible technicality of the law to protect the defendant, to block, thwart, hinder, embarrass and nullify prosecution, then the people's rights are jeopardized and the basic reason for courts stultified.
>
> The seeming ease and pat facility with which the criminally charged have been given technical safeguard have set people wondering whether their courts are being subverted into refuges for lawbreakers.
>
> This week the people, through their grand jury, brought into court eight indictments for rape. Judge Paul D. Barns agreed with the defense that the indictments were not properly drawn. Back they went to the grand jury for representation to the court.
>
> . . . . A padlock action against the Brook Club was initiated last spring before Judge George E. Holt, who granted a temporary injunction.

After five months, the case appeared Tuesday out of the blue sky before Judge Marshall C. Wiseheart at the time State Attorney Stanley Milledge was engaged with the grand jury.

Speedy decision was asked by defense counsel despite months of stalling. The State Attorney had to choose between the grand jury and Judge Wiseheart's court.

The judge dismissed the injunction against the club and its operators. The defense got delay when it wanted and prompt decision from the court when it profited it.

On Oct. 10 Judge Holt had before him a suit by the state to abate a nuisance (bookmaking) at the Tepee Club.

Five affidavits of persons who allegedly visited the premises for the purpose of placing bets were introduced by the state over the objection of the defendants.

Judge Holt ruled them out, explaining in denying the injunction against the Tepee Club:

"The defendant cannot cross-examine an affidavit. The court cannot determine who is testifying and whether belief can be placed upon such testimony. . . . The fact that such affidavits were taken before the State Attorney does not give them any additional weight or value."

November 7, 1944:

Here is an example of why people wonder about the law's delays and obstructing technicalities operating to the disadvantage of the state—which is the people—in prosecutions.

After stalling along for months, the defense in the padlock case against the Brook Club appeared before Judge Marshall C. Wiseheart for a decision. The State Attorney was working with the grand jury. The court knocked out the injunction. There was speed, dispatch, immediate attention and action for those charged with violation of the law. So fast that the people didn't get in a peep.

Accompanying the first editorial was a cartoon which caricatured the court as a robed, compliant figure, turning over a document marked "Defendant dismissed" to a grotesque criminal type, while on the other side of the bench a futile figure labeled "Public Interest" vainly protested.

Justice Reed in his majority opinion accepted the doctrine of the first *Bridges* case[74] that the "clear and present danger" test was the criterion to be applied in cases of this sort. The "substantive evil" to be avoided was the danger of "disorderly and unfair administra-

"BUT JUDGE!"

This cartoon by Enright is a part of the public record of Pennekamp v. Florida.

tion of justice." The threat to the impartial and orderly administration of justice must be a grave and immediate danger. He thus, in substance, accepted the "preferred position" of First Amendment freedoms.

The state supreme court had declared that "the vice in both the editorials was the distorted, inaccurate statement of the facts and with that statement were scrambled false insinuations that amounted to unwarranted charges of partisanship and unfairness on the part of the judges." "The record was available in all these cases," the court said, "and it does not reveal a breath of suspicion on which to predicate partisanship and unfairness on the part of the judges. It is shown rather that they acted in good faith and handled each case to the very best advantage possible. . . . A newspaper may criticize, harass, irritate, or vent its spleen against a person who holds the office of judge in the same manner that it does a member of the Legislature and other elective officers, but it may not publish scurrilous or libelous criticisms of a presiding judge as such or his judgments for the purpose of discrediting the court in the eyes of the public."

Justice Reed conceded that the full truth in regard to these cases had not been published, and that the editorials did not state objectively the attitude of the judges. Nevertheless, he declared that the court was not willing to say under the circumstances of this case that these editorials were a clear and present danger to the fair administration of justice in Florida.

Justice Frankfurter concurred on the grounds, largely, that the cases on which the newspaper made adverse comments were not in fact "pending." He pointed out that the word "pending" was an ambiguous term. It was not a technical question but was to be determined by the substantial realities of the specific situation. "The decisive consideration," he declared, "is whether the judge or jury is, or presently will be, pondering a decision that comment seeks to affect. Forbidden comment is such as will or may throw psychological weight into scales which the court is immediately balancing. . . . In the situation before us, the scales had come to rest. The petitioners offended the trial court by criticising what the court had already put in the scales, not by attempting themselves to insert weights. The petitioners here could not have disturbed the trial court in its sense of fairness but only in its sense of perspective." In one of the earlier drafts of Frankfurter's opinion, instead of a "sense of perspective," it was only the judge's "sense of humor" that would be "disturbed" by the editorials.

It may be doubted that Frankfurter's analysis of the situation was an accurate one. It is true that the state court's decision as to the validity of the indictments in the rape cases had necessarily been made before the newspaper comment was published. But the cases were returned to the grand jury which reindicted the accused the following day. The court would again have to pass upon the adequacy of the indictments. It would thus appear that the "perspective" was a short one.

In the course of his opinion, Frankfurter again went into a rambling discussion of the "clear and present danger" formula: "It does an ill-service to the author [Justice Holmes] of the most quoted judicial phrases regarding freedom of speech, to make him the victim of a tendency which he fought all his life, whereby phrases are made to do service for critical analysis by being turned into dogma. . . . 'Clear and present danger' was never used by Mr. Justice Holmes to express a technical legal doctrine or to convey a formula for adjudicating cases. It was a literary phrase not to be distorted by being taken from its context." In effect, Frankfurter repudiated the clear and present danger doctrine in this context, as he did in others. The question was not, he thought, whether there was an immediate threat of a grave danger that the judicial process would be subverted, but "whether the State court went beyond the allowable limits of judgment in holding that conduct which has been punished as a contempt was reasonably calculated to endanger a State's duty to administer impartial justice in a pending controversy." In fact, this test had been applied in a previous case in which Justice Holmes had dissented,[75] but disapproved and repudiated by the Court even before the *Bridges* case.[76]

Justice Rutledge in a brief concurring opinion pointed out that if every newspaper which published critical comments about judges without justifiable grounds or which gave inaccurate accounts of trials or misstatements of what was done, could be punished for contempt, there would be few newspapers which would escape. Therefore "any standard which would require strict accuracy in reporting legal events factually or in commenting upon them in the press would be an impossible one. Unless the courts and judges are to be put above criticism no such rule can obtain. There must be some room for misstatement of fact, as well as for misjudgment, if the press and others are to function as critical agencies in our democracy concerning courts as for all other instruments of government." He thought that in large part the editorials came within the scope of fair comment although some exceeded that boundary. But he was confident that they tended in no way to block or obstruct the proper functioning of the judicial process. As Reed pointed out in his opinion, if newspaper criticism exceeds the bounds of fair comment, it is subject to a civil action on the part of the defamed judge for libel. But it would be an unusual and extraordinary extension of criminal libel if the newspaper in every such case were to be subject, as well, to punishment for contempt of court.

It was the practice in Rutledge's office for his law clerk to go through the record and prepare a statement of the case and the issues involved before the Justices' conference. Often the clerk would express his own opinion on the merits and it was not infrequent that it would be contrary to the position eventually taken by the Justice. It appears that Rutledge would take the clerk's analysis with him to the conference and make brief notes on the back of the pages as to the initial reaction of the other Justices. In the *Miami Herald* case, it will be remembered that Chief Justice Stone was living at the time of the oral arguments, February 8, 1946. The conference was held the following Saturday, as was customary. It appears from Rutledge's sketchy notes that all the Justices except Frankfurter were in favor of reversing the contempt convictions from the beginning. Stone indicated that, were it not for the *Bridges* case, he thought the state could punish factually untrue statements and biased comment thereon. And this may have suggested the tenor of Rutledge's dissent. But the Chief Justice conceded that if the Fourteenth Amendment "takes over the 1st," then *Bridges* controls. He would reverse on the authority of that case. Like Reed, he thought this was an easier case for reversal. Frankfurter's reaction appeared to have been different. The *Bridges* case was not controlling. Frankfurter would "wait to see what is written," presumably to decide how to vote and whether to write an opinion, again presenting his position on the issues involved. He had done so in a twenty page forceful dissent in the *Bridges* case in which the Chief Justice had joined. Although Stone bowed to the authority of *Bridges,* Frankfurter was still dissenting from the basis for decision in that case.

About a year after the Florida case the Court faced a similar problem involving a contempt conviction of three newspaper men in Corpus Christi, Texas. There had been pending an action by a landlord to recover the possession of a building in the city for arrears in rent. The question was whether the lease had been forfeited by reason of nonpayment. The lessee at the time was in the armed services and his affairs were being handled by an agent. At the close of the testimony the judge instructed the jury to return a verdict for the lessor. The jury balked and returned a verdict for the absent soldier. This happened a second time. After the judge had again refused to accept the verdict, the jury reluctantly returned a third verdict, as instructed, noting that it acted under coercion of the court and against its conscience. The lessee's attorney moved for a new trial.

During these proceedings and before the judge ruled on a new trial, the allegedly contemptuous publications were made in the newspapers with which the accused were connected. In fact, the judge in the case was a layman, legal qualifications not being required by Texas law for the particular court. The editorials complained of were couched in harsh language and in fact represented inaccurate reporting in that they failed to reveal the precise issue before the judge. For example, they said that the tenant had tendered a rental check, without disclosing that the check was post-dated and thus, in the opinion of the judge, not a valid tender.

The editorials went on to complain that the judge had failed to hear both sides of the case, that his action was "high handed," a "travesty on justice" and that public opinion was "outraged." The judge's ruling had properly "brought down the wrath of public opinion upon his head" since a serviceman "seems to be getting a raw deal."

Reminiscent of Justice Rutledge's concurrence in the Florida case, Justice Douglas, writing for the Court, in reversing the conviction said:

> . . . [T]he news articles were by any standard an unfair report of what transpired. But inaccuracies in reporting are commonplace. Certainly a reporter could not be laid by the heels for contempt because he missed the essential point in a trial or failed to summarize the issues to accord with the views of the judge who sat on the case.[77]

Notwithstanding the inaccuracies of reporting and the intemperance of the editorial comment, the Court failed to find a clear and present danger to the proper administration of justice.

> It [the language] might well have a tendency to lower the standing of the judge in the public eye. But it is hard to see on these facts how it could obstruct the course of justice in the case before the court. The only demand was for a hearing. [The judge had directed a verdict for the landlord without hearing the witnesses for the defense.] There was no demand that the judge reverse his decision—or else.

Justice Frankfurter wrote a dissenting opinion in which he was joined by Chief Justice Vinson who, according to Rutledge's conference notes, thought the case distinguishable from the *Bridges* case. Justice Jackson also wrote a dissenting opinion in which he emphasized that the legal proceeding which was the subject of the editorials was a private lawsuit between individuals involving no issue of great public importance. He also pointed out that one of the convicted individuals, the publisher, had a complete monopoly on newspaper publicity in that locality.

Again, Frankfurter addressed himself to what he regarded was the distortion of the "clear and present danger" formula and the meaning which its author intended it to carry. After quoting Justice Holmes that "a judge of the United States is expected to be a man of ordinary firmness of character," he thought that it was "pertinent to observe that that was said by an Olympian who was so remote from the common currents of life that he did not read newspapers." Frankfurter thought that if, under the circumstances of this case, a Texas court was not justified in finding a "clear and present danger" of the substantive evil that Texas had a right to prevent, the phrase was merely one for "covering up a novel, iron constitutional doctrine." It is not clear here whether Frankfurter is trying to pay lip service to the Holmes' formula, or whether he is again attempting to characterize it as a mere figure of speech.

Deep-rooted in such cases is a problem of the greatest magnitude for a democratic society. As Mr. Justice Cardozo wrote in the Connecticut double jeopardy case,[78] referring to freedom of speech, "Of that freedom one may say that it is the matrix, the indispensable condition of nearly every other form of freedom." But again, as Justice Frankfurter has emphasized in several of his concurring and dissenting opinions, it is capable of subverting and destroying another freedom perhaps as vital—freedom of an individual accused of crime from a trial in the atmosphere of the lynching mob. "Trial by newspaper" may be as fatal to a fair hearing as one held in secret where the prosecutor acts also as judge.

The nation, in the waning days of 1963, was subjected to an appalling example of undue publicity concerning the events following the assassination of President Kennedy and the proposal to afford to the public a television view of the trial of Ruby who shot the alleged assassin, and thus do what Justice Douglas once said the courts were not designed to do, viz. "provide the public with recreation." The entire disgraceful situation which developed after the Dallas tragedy was perhaps as much the fault of the local police as of the news media. The handling of the situation called forth a

letter to the *New York Times* for December 1st by seven Harvard
Law School professors who were concerned with the administration
of the criminal law, in part, as follows:

> From Friday, November 22, through Sunday the shocking
> manner in which our processes of criminal justice are often ad-
> ministered was exhibited to ourselves and to the world.
>
> . . . .
>
> Precisely because the President's assassination was the ulti-
> mate in defiance of law it called for the ultimate in vindication
> of law. The law enforcement agencies, in permitting virtually
> unlimited access to the news media, made this impossible. Not
> only would it have been virtually impossible to impanel a
> jury which had not formed its own views on those facts which
> might come before it, but much of the information released,
> such as statements by Mrs. Oswald, might have been legally in-
> admissible at trial.
>
> It is ironic that the very publicity which had already made
> it virtually impossible for Oswald to be tried and convicted by a
> jury meeting existing constitutional standards of impartiality
> should, in the end, have made such trial unnecessary.
>
> For the fact is that justice is incompatible with the notion
> that police, prosecutors, attorneys, reporters and cameramen
> should have an unlimited right to conduct *ex parte* public
> trials in the press and on television.
>
> As long as we adhere to that notion, and as long as our
> legislatures and courts are unwilling to protect the processes of
> justice, we must recognize that the lamentable behavior of the
> Dallas law enforcement agencies and of the communications
> media reflect a flaw in ourselves as a society.

Perhaps the Supreme Court has weighted the scales too heavily
in favor of the press and its criticism of the courts. On the other
hand, the English courts may have shifted the weight too much on
the other side. It has been said that: "If they had lived in England, the majority of American newspaper editors and crime reporters would probably be sent to jail for contempt."[79] As an example, a case against the editor of the *New Statesman* was cited.[80] He
had been convicted of contempt of court for his comment on "a
man bites dog" case in which a newspaper had brought a libel
suit against Dr. Marie Stopes, an ardent advocate of birth control.
She declared that the newspaper had suddenly refused to carry her
advertisement because of the influence of the Roman Catholic Church.

She lost. The *News Statesman,* in an editorial, said: "The serious point in this case, however, is that an individual owing to such views as those of Dr. Stopes cannot apparently hope for a fair hearing in a court presided over by Mr. Justice Avory—and there are so many Avorys."

"If men, including judges and journalists, were angels," wrote Justice Frankfurter in the *Florida* case, "there would be no problems of contempt of court. Angelic judges would be undisturbed by extraneous influences and angelic journalists would not seek to influence them." But unfortunately there are few angels on the bench or in newspaper offices and the problem is ever with us.

Inasmuch as the doctrine of judicial review is firmly established, notwithstanding occasional distinguished skeptics, many informed citizens may be puzzled at the Court's reluctance to decide important constitutional questions. In the first place, there are limits to its judicial powers and, as Justice Frankfurter has observed from the bench, the Court in any event "decides constitutional questions last." The Constitution restricts the jurisdiction of the Supreme Court to cases and controversies.[81] Thus the Court may not give advisory opinions either to other branches of the government or to individuals. Nor is it authorized to decide moot cases or fictitious issues.

Aside from these constitutional limitations, the Court, as previously noted, has evolved over the years certain self-imposed restrictions on the exercise of its jurisdiction. This is especially true where constitutional questions are involved. The intricacy of the relationship in our federal system between the national and the various state governments has made the Court particularly sensitive in reviewing action by the states, whether through their legislatures, courts or executive departments. Much the same is true in situations involving constitutional questions where the Congress or the executive establishment of the federal government is involved. Various doctrines of "justiciability," "ripeness," and "standing" of litigants to raise the issue have been developed as deterrents on review by the Court. Another avenue of escape from constitutional adjudication is the doctrine that if it is possible on any plausible grounds to dispose of litigation on the basis of state, as distinguished from federal law, the Court will do so. It might accurately be said that the Supreme Court will not decide a constitutional question if it can avoid it by any rational theory.

Questions of this sort frequently arise in connection with litigation in which declaratory relief is sought. Early in the century a mode of litigation was evolved by Congress and state legislatures known as the declaratory judgment procedure. It was intended to enable litigants, where real controversies were involved, to secure resolution at a minimum of expense, inconvenience and time. This procedure is frequently used to challenge the constitutionality of criminal or other statutes involving some kind of a penalty. If, for example, a citizen believes that a criminal statute impairs his constitutionally protected rights, he may, under appropriate conditions, obtain a decision on the issue without exposing himself to the criminal sanctions of the statute. In other words, he is not required to violate the law and subject himself to the risk of punishment in the event that he and his lawyers are mistaken as to the constitutional issue and the courts uphold the law as valid.

From time to time, individuals have attempted to achieve this end by praying for an injunction against the enforcement of a law believed by them to be unconstitutional. Quite understandably, however, courts have been reluctant to enjoin the enforcement of criminal laws. Here, in a sense, the shoe is on the other foot. If, after an injunction is issued, the highest court of the state or federal government reverses the trial court and holds the law to be constitutional, the public will have been deprived of the protection of this legislation during the months or years of litigation to obtain a final judgment. When the declaratory judgment legislation was enacted, it was not uncommon for the litigant to seek both injunctive and declaratory relief on constitutional issues. This was the situation in a case involving the validity of what was popularly known as the Hatch Act.

This law enacted by Congress in 1940 was designed to restrict the political activities of government employees. One section of the act forbade, with certain exceptions, officers and employees in the executive branch from taking "any active part in political management or in political campaigns." It applied to industrial as well as administrative personnel. A penalty of dismissal from employment was provided for violation. One federal employee named Poole, a skilled worker in the United States Mint in Philadelphia, various other individual employees and the United Public Workers of America, a labor union purporting to represent all of its members, sought an injunction against the members of the Civil Service Commission from enforcing the act and for a declaratory judgment that the law was unconstitutional, among other reasons, because it violated the First Amendment guarantee of freedom of speech.

None of the employees except Poole had actually violated the provisions of the law. They declared that they desired to participate in political campaigns, but that they were threatened with dismissal if they did so. Poole had indeed violated the act. He had been a ward committeeman for the Democratic Party and had worked on election day at the polls. The Civil Service Commission had adopted a proposed order of dismissal, subject to his right to a hearing.

The chronology of this case in the Supreme Court is interesting. The appeal was allowed on October 26, 1944. Justice Roberts resigned on July 31, 1945, and his successor, Justice Burton, took his oath and seat the following October. After several continuations during which Chief Justice Stone died and Vinson took his place, the case was finally reargued on October 17, 1946, and decided in February, 1947.[82] Only seven Justices participated in the final decision. Justice Jackson had been absent from the bench for most of the period while the case was pending and Justice Murphy disqualified himself, presumably, because, as Attorney General at the time of the enactment of the Hatch Act he had written a long memorandum to the President indicating that although he did not like parts of the law, he then thought it constitutional. He did not recommend a veto. The final result was that the Court upheld the act by a vote of four to three. Justice Reed wrote the plurality opinion, joined only by Burton and the Chief Justice. Frankfurter concurred in a separate opinion. Black dissented. Douglas and Rutledge, in separate opinions, dissented in part.

The first conference was held on the 8th of December, 1945. It appears that Justice Black felt strongly, as his subsequent dissent disclosed, that all the individual employees had made out a case for a declaratory judgment and that on the merits of the controversy, the Hatch Act was unconstitutional. Justices Douglas and Rutledge indicated agreement, as did Justice Murphy although he suggested that he might eventually disqualify himself, as he did. Chief Justice Stone thought the law constitutional and, as Rutledge's notes disclose, that "Holmes was right." This apparently was an allusion to Holmes' opinion in an earlier Massachusetts case in which a police officer had been dismissed for political activities. In upholding the city of New Bedford's right to remove the officer, Holmes' disposed of the case with the epigram: "The petitioner may have a constitutional right to talk politics, but he has no constitutional right to be a policeman."[83] Justices Burton, Reed and Frankfurter expressed agreement with the Chief Justice. This suggested that, even if Murphy participated, the Court would divide four to four in which case the decision of the lower court in favor of the government would prevail as the law of the case. The Hatch Act would be upheld.

There was, however, another problem which must first be met. The appeal was allowed by the Supreme Court on October 26, 1944.

An Act of Congress governing appeals required the docketing of cases within sixty days after the order allowing the appeal. This case was not docketed until February 12th. A week later Chief Justice Stone circulated a typewritten memorandum suggesting that the case could be dismissed because it had not been docketed within the sixty days after the order allowing the appeal as required by the Act of Congress. If four Justices agreed, he favored this course. But four of the seven Justices who were participating in the case declined to go along with the suggestion. A couple of months later, the Chief Justice tried again. This time he sent around a brief *Per Curiam* with a memorandum explaining that if the case were decided it would be by a four to three vote and again emphasizing his reluctance to have the Court decide a constitutional question by less than a majority of the full bench.

In this opinion the Chief Justice proposed to dismiss the case on the grounds that neither Poole nor any of the other employees had presented a "justiciable" controversy which required adjudication by the Court under the federal Declaratory Judgment Act. Apparently he was unable to obtain the concurrence of three other members of the Court for dismissal either on these grounds or on the grounds that the Court had lost jurisdiction because the appeal had not been docketed within the sixty-day statutory period. In the final disposition of the case the Court held that only Poole had actually presented a case requiring decision.

In Justice Reed's opinion he regarded the allegations of the other employees that they *desired* to engage in political activities as presenting an insufficient case of "definite rights" upon the one side and "definite prejudicial interferences" upon the other. "A hypothetical threat is not enough." To be sure there was a high degree of probability that the performance of political activities in which these employees desired to engage would result in action against them similar to that against Poole. But this was not such an immediate threat as to satisfy the requirement of a real, as distinguished from an "abstract" controversy under the Declaratory Judgment Act. As to Poole, the situation was different. He had engaged in the forbidden political behavior and the Civil Service Commission had initiated action which, if the law was constitutional, inevitably would result in his final dismissal from government employment. Moreover, since Poole admitted that he had violated the rule against political activity and that removal from office was therefore mandatory under the act, there was no question as to the exhaustion of administrative remedies. The act provided no administrative or statutory review from the order of the Civil Service Commission. Justice Frankfurter thought the case should have been dismissed on the grounds first suggested by the Chief Justice, viz., that the Court had lost jurisdiction by the tardy docketing. But, "under the compulsion of the Court's assumption of jurisdiction," he concurred in Justice Reed's opinion.

Justice Reed began his argument on the merits with the declaration that "of course," First Amendment rights "are not absolutes." He then emphasized that it was only partisan political activity that was forbidden, *i.e.*, active participation in political management and political campaigns. Expressions, public or private, on public affairs, personalities and matters of public interest were unrestricted by law so long as the government employee did not "direct his activities toward party success." He declared that the question of regulation of the political activities of governmental employees was a matter primarily for Congress and courts would interfere "only when such regulation passes beyond the generally existing conception of governmental power." Consequently when Congress concluded that the political activities of civil servants threatened the integrity and competency of the service, it could enact such legislation as that involved in the Hatch Act. Actually, Reed never came to grips with the First Amendment problem involved in this case.

Justice Douglas in his partial dissent, conceded that partisan political activities of civil servants in the administrative category might be restricted. "The philosophy is to develop a civil service which can and will serve loyally and equally well any political party which comes into power." These are the officers who contribute to the making of policy for administrative action and partisanship should play no part in this process. But, he pointed out, Poole was an industrial worker "as remote from contact with the public or from policy-making or from the functioning of the administrative process as a charwoman. . . . He is in a position not essentially different from one who works in the machine shop of a railroad or a steamship which the Government runs, or who rolls aluminum in a manufacturing plant which the Government owns and operates." Therefore, Douglas thought the statute had not been sufficiently narrowly drawn. No showing had been made as to industrial workers which justified their political sterilization "as distinguished from selective measures aimed at the coercive practices on which the spoils system feeds."[84]

Justice Reed referred briefly to this point but again made no effort to answer it on its merits.

Congress has determined that the presence of government employees, whether industrial or administrative, in the ranks of political party workers is bad. Whatever differences there may be between administrative employees of the government and industrial workers in its employ are differences of detail so far as the constitutional power under review is concerned. Whether there are such differences and what weight to attach to them are all matters of detail for Congress.[85]

This appears to answer nothing.

Nor did Reed's opinion attempt to meet the powerful argument of Justice Black's dissent. "Forcing public employees to contribute money and influence can well be proscribed in the interest of 'clean politics' and public administration," Black wrote.

> But I think the Constitution prohibits legislation which prevents millions of citizens from contributing their arguments, complaints, and suggestions to the political debates which are the essence of democracy; prevents them from engaging in organizational activity to urge others to vote and take an interest in political affairs; bars them from performing the interested citizen's duty of insuring that his and his fellow citizen's votes are counted.[86]

There is nothing about federal employees as a class, Black concluded, which justified depriving them or society of the benefits of their participation in public affairs. They pay taxes like everyone else. They come from the same homes, communities, schools, churches and colleges as other citizens. They fight in the same wars. It might be that some high-placed employees attempt to coerce their subordinates or use their power to coerce other citizens. But employees in private business and industry have the same opportunity and some no doubt seize it. And yet, who would defend a law which suppressed the political freedom of all employees of private employers or even of "employers who borrow money or draw subsidies from the Government?" Black thought that the law reduced the constitutionally protected liberty of government employees to less than a shadow of its substance. He agreed with Douglas that the sweep of the statute was too broad although he did not dwell on the distinction between administrative and industrial employees. He deemed it unnecessary to muzzle millions of citizens because some of them, if not deterred by legislation, might corrupt the political process. If some public employees, because of their influential positions might coerce their subordinates or other citizens, laws could be drawn to punish them. It was unnecessary, to borrow a phrase from Justice Frankfurter, to burn down the house to roast the pig. But the event was otherwise.

Justice Rutledge dissented as to Poole for the reasons stated by Justice Black.

One of the latest freedom of expression opinions written by Justice Rutledge also involved a labor organization, the Congress of Industrial Relations, and its then president Phillip Murray.[87] Both were prosecuted in a federal court under the Labor Management Act of 1947 (the Taft-Hartley law) making it "unlawful . . . for any corporation, or any labor organization to make a contribution or expenditure" in connection with any election of federal officers. It also made it an offense for any officer of a labor organization to consent to such a contribution or expenditure.

The indictment charged that the *C.I.O. News,* a weekly periodical, had carried a front page statement by Murray urging all members of the C.I.O. to vote for a particular candidate for Congress in Maryland. The statement said that it was made in the belief that the law prohibiting its publication was unconstitutional as abridging freedom of speech, press and assemblage as guaranteed by the Bill of Rights. The lower court granted a motion to dismiss on the ground of unconstitutionality. The Supreme Court affirmed this ruling but the Justices split wide open on the reasons. And their differences are important.

The case again indicates how far the Court will sometimes go in order to avoid a question of constitutionality. Justice Reed, writing the opinion of the Court by what many regard as a tortured interpretation of the statute, managed in some way to find that the Congressional prohibition did not include the type of political "expenditure" which was here involved. He appeared to think the law was not intended to apply to a newspaper published in the regular course of union activity, as distinguished from a special publication directed at a particular election, even though financed from the general funds in the union treasury. It is almost impossible for the rational mind to comprehend the thought processes which led to this conclusion or how the cited excerpts from the legislative record support it. Actually some of what Reed relied upon as "informed congressional discussion" appeared to contradict his conclusion. Indeed, Justice Jackson must have had misgivings of this sort to have prompted a three sentence, unpublished, concurring opinion in which he disavowed reliance on "informed congressional discussion," adding, acidly, that he did not know how to distinguish "informed" from "uninformed" discussions by members of Congress. One can readily guess why the Justice, on second thought, decided to withhold the opinion. The case was thus disposed of without reaching the constitutional issue.

Justice Frankfurter joined in the Reed opinion but added a concurring one of his own. Here again, the reasoned path to the result is not one of the more lucid opinions by a Supreme Court Justice. He quoted generalizations from authorities respected by everyone. The trouble comes, as is so often the case, in proceeding from the general to the particular. He relied upon Justice Brandeis, dissenting in the *Tennessee Valley Authority* case[88] who pointed out that "the Court developed, for its own governance in the cases confessedly within its jurisdiction, a series of rules under which it has avoided passing upon a large part of all the constitutional questions pressed upon it for decision." Again he quoted from a source described as an "authoritative commentator," to the effect that "it is only with the light afforded by a real contest that opinions on questions of the highest importance can safely be rendered."[89] He even invoked the authority of Chief Justice Marshall, the architect of judicial review of legislation, that constitutional questions should be decided by the Court only when "indispensably necessary."

Now all constitutional critics are in agreement with these general principles. But, to quote Justice Holmes against Justice Frankfurter, "general principles do not decide concrete cases." In the opinion of the district court, the position of the government had been described as one which conceded that the law abridged "rights guaranteed under the First Amendment" but that Congress had the power to do so if it thought such abridgment necessary to insure the integrity of elections. Of course, the logical fallacy here is obvious and, on appeal, the government contended that no such foolish argument had been made. But apparently Frankfurter thought the trial judge *might* have been misled. He also complained that the defendants had failed to urge a construction of the Taft-Hartley law (as the Reed opinion purported to do) which would restrict its scope so as to exclude the publication in question. Accordingly, the Justice concluded that the question of the powers of Congress to enact this law had come before them "not so shaped by the record and by proceedings below as to bring those powers before this Court as cleanly and as sharply as judicial judgment upon an exercise of congressional power requires."

Just what the point of Frankfurter's concurrence was does not leap to the mind's eye. He finally decided to "join in the Court's opinion" because his brethren found the case "calls for adjudication." And why not? The Court avoided a constitutional decision which apparently is what the Justice thought the district court might have done. But why send the case back to be tried all over again in the hope that the trial judge would come to the same conclusion that a majority of the Supreme Court had reached? This was not a case arising in a state court. It was an all-federal judicial affair involving an Act of Congress. The relationship between an inferior federal court and the Supreme Court could hardly be regarded as so "delicate" as to require a remand and new trial. Frankfurter's performance in this case is particularly puzzling in view of the fact that six weeks before the decision was handed down, he had written a memorandum for the conference to demonstrate that the Court did have appellate jurisdiction to pass on a matter of statutory construction even though it had not been raised in the court below when the question involved was the unconstitutionality of an Act of Congress.

Rutledge's opinion, in which Black, Douglas and Murphy joined was neither ambiguous nor difficult to follow. If the Taft-Hartley law covered the costs of any political publication by a labor union, it certainly covered the "expenditures" in this case. He agreed entirely with the policy against deciding questions of constitutionality unnecessarily, but he did not believe that such a policy justified the Court in abdicating its function by emasculating a statute. He thought the statute clearly applied to the indictment, and, in such application, it was invalid.

The opinion is devastating in its attack on the Court's interpretation of congressional intent. Repeatedly citing excerpts from the Senate discussion and from the President's veto message, Rutledge demonstrated that this was exactly the type of situation which was intended to come within the prohibition of the law. President Truman had declared that the act "would prevent the ordinary union newspaper from commenting favorably or unfavorably upon candidates or issues in national elections," which was the precise case before the Court. And "in the debate preliminary to the overriding of the veto, none of the legislators in change of the measure gave any indication that they differed from the President's interpretation."

On the constitutional issue, Rutledge began by restating, in vigorous terms, the preferred position argument for First Amendment rights. The presumption of validity of legislation in other areas disappears altogether here. "The presumption rather is against the legislative intrusion into these domains." He rejected the government's argument that constitutional power to regulate elections[90] should be "balanced" against the First Amendment guarantees and that such balancing results in the usual presumptive validity to the legislation in question. He pointed out that the statute was not "narrowly drawn" to meet the precise evil sought to be curbed. Moreover, the prohibited conduct was not defined with sufficient specificity to escape the vice of vagueness. "Blurred signposts to criminality will not suffice. . . ." Nor did he accept the government's contention that labor exerted too great an influence by creating "bloc" political power. "The expression of bloc sentiment is and always has been an integral part of our democratic electoral and legislative process." Rutledge thought a fair interpretation of the statute, in the light of "informed congressional discussion" as found in the *Congressional Record,* could lead to the conclusion that the source of the funds used was the crux of the offense. Dues paid by a political minority should not be used against their will. But the effect of the statute "is not merely one of minority protection. It is also one of majority prohibition." It not only prevents the union from spending funds obtained from dues-paying members for a political end which a few of them do not desire. It prohibits the union from making expenditures desired by the majority.

As it thus turned out, the result of this litigation shed little light on the extent to which Congress might go in regulating the activities of labor unions in the political field. As the *Washington Post* editorialized the next day:[91]

> Seldom has the Supreme Court placed a statute under scrutiny and then left more confusion as to its meaning than in the case of Section 304 of the Taft-Hartley Act restricting expenditures by labor unions and corporations for political purposes. The action of the court in dismissing the case against the CIO for supporting a candidate for Congress through its newspaper was unanimous. But members of the court arrived at the conclusion by three different routes, and the clash of views could scarcely have been sharper if the Rutledge-Black-Douglas-Murphy opinion had been a dissent.

Indeed, from an ideological point of view, it was precisely that.

Freedom of expression, the brightest star in our constitutional constellation, has on many occasions shone with great luster, but at times seems to have been in utter eclipse. The Court, with an especial responsibility to keep it constantly in view, has, on too many occasions, lost sight of it completely—in some instances, perhaps blinded by its brilliance. Again to quote Professor Emerson, "conditions in modern democratic society demand that a deliberate, affirmative, and even aggressive effort be made to support the system of free expression. The natural balance of forces in society today tends to be weighted against individual expression. Only through a positive approach, in which law and judicial institutions play a leading role, can an effective system be maintained."[92] Sensitivity to the gravity of this problem and the heavy responsibility of the judiciary led Justice Rutledge to face squarely these cases with the courage and insight which consistently distinguished his service on the highest court of the land.

CHAPTER V

"... TO BE SECURE IN THEIR PERSONS, HOUSES ...."

TO the men who founded this nation the idea that "a man's house is his castle" was no mere figure of speech. One of the many just causes of complaint by the colonists and one largely responsible for the Fourth Amendment protection against unreasonable searches and seizures, was the practice of British courts to issue the notorious "writs of assistance." These writs enabled the King's customs officers to go ransacking at large through homes and warehouses on fishing expeditions for contraband. Smuggling during colonial days was costing the royal treasury large sums and the ruthless writ was a catchall device to meet it.

As early as 1886 in *Boyd* v. *United States*[1] Justice Bradley pointed out the close relationship between the Fourth Amendment and the provision against self-incrimination of the Fifth. The seizure or compulsory production of a citizen's private papers to be used against him is the equivalent of compelling him to be a witness against himself. In the course of his opinion the Justice took occasion to go into the history of the Fourth Amendment. He quoted James Otis of Massachusetts that this writ was "the worst instrument of arbitrary power, the most destructive of English liberty, and the fundamental principles of law, that ever was found in an English law book." The liberty of the citizens was placed in "the hands of every petty officer."

The occasion was a court argument in the Boston Town House in 1761 between a representative of the crown on the one hand and Otis and Oxenbridge Thatcher on the other. An authentic account was prepared by John Adams who was present at the argument.[2] Otis went on to point out that "not more than one instance can be found of it in all our law-books; and that was in the zenith of arbitrary power, viz., in the reign of Charles II when Star-Chamber powers were pushed to extremity by some ignorant clerk of the Exchequer." Adams states that the one precedent of issuing general warrants in the time of Charles

151

II was by Chief Justice Scroggs, for which he was afterwards impeached by the House of Commons.[3]

In view of their bitter experiences with these general writs giving officers blanket authority, it is understandable that the framers of the Bill of Rights took care in the Fourth Amendment to prohibit such outrages in the future by the national government. There were not only to be no "unreasonable searches and seizures" but magistrates were forbidden to issue warrants except upon "probable cause" and the warrant must particularly describe "the place to be searched and the person or things to be seized." There was to be no more random housebreaking.

Justice Frankfurter in a recent dissenting opinion[4] pointed out that the Fourth Amendment was modeled after the similar provision in the Massachusetts Constitution of 1780 which also required probable cause under oath before a warrant would issue and that the warrant be "accompanied with a special designation of the persons or objects of search, arrest or seizure." "It is significant," the opinion continued, "that the constitution of every State contains a clause like that of the Fourth Amendment and often in its precise wording."

> Nor are these constitutional provisions historic survivals. . . . It tells volumes that in 1938, New York, not content with statutory protection, put the safeguard into its constitution. If one thing on this subject can be said with confidence it is that the protection afforded by the Fourth Amendment against search and seizure by the police, except under the closest judicial safeguards, is not an outworn bit of Eighteenth Century romantic rationalism but an indispensable need for a democratic society.[5]

As a general proposition, no search is reasonable unless made pursuant to the authority of a warrant or as incident to a lawful arrest. Peace officers may on occasion break and enter a building without a warrant for the purpose of arresting a suspected felon. If the circumstances justify the arrest, documents or other articles thought to be connected with the crime may be seized as incident to the arrest. But the extent of such a search has been defined only in general and often inconsistent terms by the Supreme Court. The officer is not limited to articles in plain sight or on the person of the prisoner but, on the other hand, he is not authorized to search a house from attic to cellar. The limits are somewhere between, but a policeman's or lawyer's guess is about as good as a Supreme Court Justice's.

In the much cited case of *United States* v. *Rabinowitz,* decided a year after Rutledge's death,[6] the Court upheld a search and seizure as "incident" to a lawful arrest under the following circumstances. Federal officers had sufficient information to constitute "probable cause," that is reasonable grounds, to think that the accused was engaged in traffic in forged postage stamps. They obtained a warrant for his arrest but no search warrant was issued. When they arrested him in his place of business, they searched his desk, safe and file cabinets and seized over five hundred forged stamps. In finding the search "reasonable," the Court pointed out a number of factors bearing on the issue. It was "incident" to a lawful arrest, the place searched was not a home but a business room to which the public was invited, the room was small and under the complete control of the person arrested, the search did not extend beyond the premises used for unlawful purposes, and the possession of forged stamps itself was a crime just as it is a crime knowingly to possess burglar's tools or counterfeit money.

Justices Frankfurter and Jackson dissented sharply. The search, they thought, was unlawful since it was practical for the officers to have obtained a search warrant either at the time of the issuance of the warrant for arrest or, for that matter, thereafter. This had been the rule laid down by the Court less than two years before[7] and now overruled. The two Justices pointed to the origin of the exception that a search may be "reasonable" when made as "incident" to a lawful arrest. Its basic roots lie in necessity, they declared.

> What is necessity? Why is a search of the arrested person permitted? For two reasons: first, in order to protect the arresting officer and to deprive the prisoner of potential means of escape [Citing cases], and secondly, to avoid destruction of evidence by the arrested person. [Citing cases.] From this it follows that officers may search and seize not only the things physically on the person arrested, but those within his immediate physical control. What a farce it makes of the whole Fourth Amendment to say that because for many legal purposes everything in a man's house is under his control therefore his house—his rooms —may be searched.[8]

They also pointed out that the lawfulness of the search of a motor vehicle is likewise "rooted in necessity" because of the impracticability of securing a warrant.

It is clear, however, aside from the extent of the search allowable as incident to an arrest, that the arresting officer must have a search warrant or, if it is impracticable to obtain one, he must have "probable cause" to make the arrest. This means by the common-law rule that the crime must have been committed in his presence or he must have reasonable grounds to believe that the arrested person has committed a felony. And such cause must exist before the arrest—not afterwards, as a result of the search. As Justice Jackson remarked: "[T]he Government is obliged to justify the arrest by the search and at the same time to justify the search by the arrest. This will not do."[9]

And even if officers have "probable cause" for entering and making an arrest without warrants, they may not ordinarily force an entry, if the suspect is in the house, without first giving notice of their authority and purpose in demanding admission. Justice Brennan, recently quoted from an early seventeenth century English opinion. "In all cases where the King is party, the sheriff (if the doors be not open) may break the party's house, either to arrest him, or to do other execution of the K[ing]'s process, if otherwise he cannot enter. *But before he breaks it, he ought to signify the cause of his coming, and to make request to open doors*" (Justice Brennan's emphasis).[10] The occasion for the reference was a case in which officers had knocked on the door and when the householder opened it on an attached chain and asked what they wanted, the officers put their hands inside the door, ripped off the chain and entered. The Supreme Court held the ensuing search unlawful. An exception to the requirement, of course, is where it is obvious that the householder knows what the officers are there for. In a 1963 case from California, the Court by a five to four decision added another exception, viz., when entry by stealth is necessary to prevent escape or destruction of evidence—an exception likely to destroy the rule itself.[11]

One of the last cases in which Justice Rutledge participated was *Wolf* v. *Colorado*.[12] His dissenting views here were noteworthy for several reasons, not the least of which is their complete vindication in an epoch-making case, twelve years after his death. The *Wolf* case involved the use of illegally obtained evidence in a criminal trial in a state court. In 1914, the Court had held in *Weeks* v. *United States*[13] that evidence obtained in violation of the search and seizure provision of the Fourth Amendment could not be used in a criminal trial in a federal court. The accused had been convicted of using the mails in connection with a lottery. The opinion was by Mr. Justice Day, in the course of which he wrote:

> The tendency of those who execute the criminal laws of the country to obtain conviction by means of unlawful seizures and enforced confessions, the latter often obtained after subjecting accused persons to unwarranted practices destructive of rights secured by the Federal Constitution, should find no sanction in the judgments of the courts, which are charged at all times with

the support of the Constitution, and to which people of all conditions have a right to appeal for the maintenance of such fundamental rights.

It should be noted that Justice Day echoed Justice Bradley in the *Boyd* case, by linking "unlawful seizures" (the Fourth Amendment) with "enforced confessions" (the Fifth) which was later to be reechoed by Justices Clark and Black in a 1961 case.

In *Wolf*, a physician had been convicted of abortion in the state courts of Colorado. The police had entered his office without a warrant and without his consent. They obtained from his records the names of patients who were subsequently used as witnesses against him. The Court held that there was a distinction between the Constitutional provision against search and seizures and the exclusionary rule of evidence as applied in *Weeks*. The former was applicable to the states by the Fourteenth Amendment, guaranteeing due process of law; the latter was not so applicable. The states were free to adopt different rules of admissibility of evidence.

Mr. Justice Frankfurter wrote for the Court as follows:

> The security of one's privacy against arbitrary intrusion by the police—which is at the core of the Fourth Amendment—is basic to a free society. It is therefore implicit in "the concept of ordered liberty" and as such enforceable against the States through the Due Process Clause. The knock at the door, whether by day or by night, as a prelude to a search, without authority of law but solely on the authority of the police, did not need the commentary of recent history to be condemned as inconsistent with the conception of human rights enshrined in the history and the basic constitutional documents of English-speaking peoples.
>
> Accordingly, we have no hesitation in saying that were a State affirmatively to sanction such police incursion into privacy it would run counter to the guaranty of the Fourteenth Amendment. But the ways of enforcing such a basic right raise questions of a different order.

He then held that the fruits of such an unconstitional breaking, entry and seizure may be used in state criminal courts to convict the victim of such unconstitutional procedure.

Thus, Justice Frankfurter, to quote a figure of speech used by him in another case,[14] appeared to have marched the king's men up the hill, turned them around, and then marched them down again. For purposes of the practical business of law enforcement, he ended up exactly where he started. For whatever value it had, he tabulated the states which had voluntarily followed the *Weeks* doctrine and those which had not. "As of today," he wrote, "30 States reject the Weeks doctrine, 17 States are in agreement with it." That was in 1949. In an appendix to his opinion in the *Elkins* case,[15] Justice Stewart listed 26 states which in 1960, as a matter of local law, excluded evidence obtained in violation of the federal Constitution.

Justices Douglas, Murphy and Rutledge dissented, but Black, curiously enough, concurred in a short opinion which added little or nothing to support the Court's decision. Rutledge's notes taken at the conference indicate Black's first reaction was to reverse Wolf's conviction. He later expressed doubt but finally supported the majority. Justice Murphy pointed out the inadequacy of the common-law relief afforded the victims of police lawlessness. Many states disallow punitive damages in a tort action for trespass in the absence of malice. "If the officer searches with care, he can avoid all but nominal damages—a penny, or a dollar." That an action for damages against an offending police officer is not effective to protect the citizen's constitutional right to privacy under the Fourth Amendment has been repeatedly demonstrated. Murphy also thought that questions of due process of law should not be determined by taking a poll of the practices in the various states.

Rutledge's dissent was gentle but penetrating.

> . . . [O]ne should not reject a piecemeal wisdom merely because it hobbles toward the truth with backward glances. Accordingly, although I think that all "the specific guarantees of the Bill of Rights should be carried over intact into the first section of the Fourteenth Amendment" [citing *Adamson* v. *California*, 332 U.S. 46, dissenting opinion], I welcome the fact that the Court in its slower progress toward this goal, today finds the substance of the Fourth Amendment "to be implicit in the concept of ordered liberty, and thus, through the Fourteenth Amendment, . . . valid as against the states."

He thereupon rejected "the Court's simultaneous conclusion that the mandate embodied in the Fourth Amendment, although binding on the states, does not carry with it the one sanction . . . failure to observe which means that 'the protection of the Fourth Amendment' . . . might as well be stricken from the Constitution. [Citing *Weeks* v. *United States*.] For I agree with my brother Murphy's demonstration that the Amendment without the sanction is a dead letter."[16] For Rutledge, the necessary implication of the Amendment was to for-

"ALL I GOT TO SAY IS THIS IS ONE HELL OF A TIME TO LOSE A SEARCH WARRANT"

bid the use of evidence so obtained against him "in any criminal proceeding involving the victim of the unconstitutional search." It was
compounding the original wrong and unworthy of civilized government, whether federal or state. "Compliance with the Bill of Rights
betokens more than lip service." He believed with Holmes that the use
of evidence obtained in violation of those constitutional mandates
"reduces the Fourth Amendment to a form of words."

Less than three years later, Justice Frankfurter, writing for the
Court in another sensational case,[17] reversed a conviction by the
California courts of an accused charged with selling narcotics. State
officers had entered the home of the suspect and forced their way into
the bedroom occupied by himself and his wife. When they questioned
the petitioner about some capsules lying on a bedside table, he grabbed
them, put them in his mouth and swallowed them. After an attempt to
extract the capsules by force, the police took the petitioner to a hospital where an emetic was forced into his stomach over his protests.
He vomited the two capsules which were found to contain morphine
and which were used in evidence against him.

This was too much for Frankfurter to stomach.

> This is conduct that shocks the conscience. Illegally breaking
> into the privacy of the petitioner, the struggle to open his mouth
> and remove what was there, the forcible extraction of his
> stomach's contents—this course of proceedings by agents of gov-
> ernment to obtain evidence is bound to offend even hardened
> sensibilities. They are methods too close to the rack and the
> screw to permit of constitutional differentiation.

But the case turned on the Fourteenth Amendment as such, not on
the Fourteenth Amendment as incorporating the Fourth. Justices
Black and Douglas concurred on the basis of the self-incriminating
clause of the Fifth Amendment as incorporated under the Fourteenth.
"I think," wrote Black, "a person is compelled to be a witness against
himself not only when he is compelled to testify, but also when as here,
incriminating evidence is forcibly taken from him by a contrivance of
modern science."

Justice Frankfurter, dissenting, also found a violation of due process, as such in another California case[18] in which police had had a
key made to fit the door of the suspect's house, entered it, and installed
a secret microphone in the bedroom of the accused and his wife. He
did not, however, make any departure from his position in the *Wolf*
case with respect to Fourth Amendment sanctions. He thought the
performance of the law enforcement officers here so "repulsive" as to

violate the canons of decency prescribed by "due process." Perhaps as much as any other case, this case tends to support Justice Black's skepticism of a principle so general that it permits opposite conclusions by such eminently wise and humane Justices as Jackson who wrote for the majority in upholding the conviction, and Frankfurter, eloquent in dissent.

Further confusion was added in 1957 when the Court upheld a conviction in a criminal case in which evidence of intoxication of a truck driver was admitted. The police had instructed a physician to take a blood test by use of a hypodermic needle while the accused was unconscious after a traffic accident. A majority of the Court was able to distinguish the case from the stomach pumping situation. Chief Justice Warren, Justices Black and Douglas dissented.[19]

The complete vindication of Rutledge's *Wolf* dissent came in 1961 when on the last day of the term, the Court handed down its decision in *Mapp* v. *Ohio*.[20] Mr. Justice Clark, in reversing the Ohio Supreme Court, wrote a devastating opinion for the Court, Justices Black and Douglas concurring in separate opinions and Mr. Justice Harlan, with whom Justices Frankfurter and Whittaker joined, dissenting.

The facts in *Mapp* were indeed shocking. Three police officers of Cleveland, Ohio, had information that a suspect, wanted for questioning in connection with a recent bombing, was hiding in a house in which the Mapp woman lived with a daughter by a former marriage. They also suspected that some "policy paraphernalia" was concealed there. The officers went to the house, knocked on the door and demanded entrance. Miss Mapp, after telephoning her attorney, refused to admit them without a warrant. Later, a half dozen officers arrived and broke through one of the doors. When the householder asked for a warrant, an officer waved before her some kind of paper which she immediately grabbed and concealed in her bosom. As stated by Justice Clark in his opinion, "a struggle ensued in which the officers recovered the piece of paper and as a result of which they handcuffed appellant because she had been 'belligerent' in resisting their official rescue of the 'warrant' from her person." After some further "roughing up," Miss Mapp, "in handcuffs, was forcibly taken upstairs to her bedroom where the officers searched a chest of drawers, a closet and some suitcases." They then went through the rest of the house including the basement. In the course of this widespread search, they found the materials for which she was subsequently prosecuted and convicted for having in her possession. The materials seized had nothing to do with the "bombing" or the "policy paraphernalia." Miss Mapp was convicted of having in her possession obscene literature. No search warrant had ever been issued.

In the course of his opinion, Justice Clark again referred to the close connection between the Fourth and Fifth Amendments as running "almost into each other." He reviewed developments subsequent to *Wolf*. He then held that the Fourth Amendment right of privacy was equally enforceable against the states by the same sanction of exclusion as against the federal government.

"Moreover," continued Clark, "our holding that the exclusionary rule is an essential part of both the Fourth and Fourteenth Amendments is not only the logical dictate of prior cases, but it also makes very good sense."

> There is no war between the Constitution and common sense. Presently, a federal prosecutor may make no use of evidence illegally seized, but a State's attorney across the street may, although he supposedly is operating under the enforceable prohibitions of the same Amendment. Thus the State, by admitting evidence unlawfully seized, serves to encourage disobedience to the Federal Constitution which it is bound to uphold. . . . In non-exclusionary states, federal officers, being human, were. . . invited to and did, as our cases indicate, step across the street to the State's attorney with their unconstitutionally seized evidence.[21]

Inasmuch as Justice Clark had himself been a law enforcement officer, albeit at the highest level, many lawyers and others were surprised at his forthright position in connection with search and seizure. But as Professor Allen has pointed out, although the Justice had from time to time displayed a sympathetic attitude toward the problems of police and prosecutors, he was not a member of the Court when the *Wolf* case was decided and, in fact, had actually stated his disapproval of the decision in that case. "Clearly, Mr. Justice Clark meant what he said."[22]

Only a year before the *Mapp* case, the Court, over the protest of four Justices, outlawed the rule that federal prosecutors could avail themselves of evidence illegally seized by state officers operating entirely on their own account. Theretofore, although federal officers were prohibited from conducting illegal raids and seizures, the fruits of such lawlessness by state officials could be handed to them "on a silver platter."

Justice Stewart, writing for the Court admitted an awareness on its part, that the *Wolf* decision, refusing to apply the exclusionary rule to state prosecutions, "operated to undermine the logical foundation of the *Weeks* admissibility rule which applied the exclusionary rule" to federal prosecutions. "To the victim," he said, "it matters not whether his constitutional right has been invaded by a federal agent or by a state officer."[23] He summarized the considerations of "reason and experience" calling for the rejection of evidence illegally seized by state agents and turned over to federal authorities. "But," he continued, "there is another consideration—the imperative of judicial integrity," quoting from Holmes, thirty-odd years before in a wire-tapping case,[24] that "no distinction can be taken between the Government as prosecutor and the Government as judge." Justice Stewart also made a pointed argument on the effect of the old rule on federalism. By admitting evidence in federal criminal courts illegally seized by police officers in states which excluded such evidence, the national government frustrates state policy "in a particularly inappropriate and ironic way." It serves to defeat the state's effort to assure obedience to the federal Constitution.

Five years earlier in 1956, a method was formulated to prevent federal officials from stepping "across the street" to hand over evidence which *they* had illegally seized, to state agents "on a silver platter." This was accomplished by the use of an injunction against a federal agent which prohibited him from turning over to state prosecutors evidence which he had obtained in an invalid search. The order also enjoined him from testifying in the state court.[25] In other words before 1956, state and federal agents "cooperated" to their mutual satisfaction in successfully violating the constitutional rights of citizens suspected of criminal offenses.

Nevertheless, a number of states still accepted such evidence obtained by their own officers. The New York Constitution, as Justice Frankfurter has pointed out, contains a provision identical with the Fourth Amendment and a statute repeats the same language. Apparently the people wanted to be "secure in their persons, houses, papers and effects." But New York courts, until *Mapp,* rejected the exclusionary rule. In a case in which a plain-clothes man obtained a key to a hotel room from the clerk and, without a warrant, conducted a search, a judge at Special Sessions complained indignantly: "The case at bar is merely a mild example of how the liberties of New Yorkers are destroyed by the police and the courts. The rule of evidence subordinates the courts to the lawlessness of the police."[26]

Mr. Justice Black, in his concurring opinion in the *Mapp* case relied heavily on the *Boyd* case wherein the Court decreed that it was unable to perceive that the seizure of a man's private books and papers to be used in evidence against him was substantially different from compelling him to be a witness against himself. He had not accepted this doctrine in *Wolf* in which he wrote his brief concurring

opinion. He did, however, in *Mapp*. "It was upon this ground," he
wrote, "that Mr. Justice Rutledge largely relied in his dissenting opinion in the Wolf case. And, although I rejected the argument at that
time, its force has, for me at least, become compelling with the more
thorough understanding of the problem brought on by recent cases."
He then referred to the two California cases discussed earlier and
pointed out the confusion which had resulted therefrom. "Finally, today, we clear up that uncertainty."

In his lengthy *Mapp* dissent, Justice Harlan with whom Justices
Frankfurter and Whittaker concurred, relied upon "judicial restraint,"
and *stare decisis*. He concluded with the ominous statement that "our
voice becomes only a voice of power, not of reason. Justice Douglas,
concurring with the majority, declared that in his opinion the *Wolf*
case, supporting a double standard for law enforcement officers could
hardly be called the voice of reason. It led to "working arrangements"
between federal and state authorities and, in many ways, reduced the
administration of justice to "shabby business."

Associate Justice Roger Traynor of the Supreme Court of California has discussed some of the problems created for the fifty states
by the *Mapp* decision. Justice Traynor himself had undergone a
change of view as to the conflicting policies involved in the issue. He
had written the opinion for his court in 1942 rejecting the exclusionary
rule as a matter of state law.[27] After the *Wolf* case held that states
were free to accept or reject it as a rule of evidence, the *California Law
Review* commented adversely.

> The decision makes it plain that the federal law of search
> and seizure is not to be applied to the states in its entirety but is
> to be classified into (1) constitutional rules and (2) federal rules
> of "procedure" or "evidence" such as the exclusionary rule. Only
> the constitutional rules bind the states. However, if the exclu-
> sionary rule is the only effective means of enforcing the guaran-
> tee, the Court has proclaimed an illusory right.[28]

The article then examined the situation in California and concluded that "it seems clear that present protection is insufficient to
secure respect for the right." In 1955 after what Justice Traynor
called his "education in the biokinetics of law enforcement agencies,"
he wrote the opinion for his Court, reversing the earlier case, and establishing the rule in California that evidence obtained in violation of
constitutional rights of the accused may not be used against him.[29]
In his opinion excluding the tainted evidence, the judge explained:

We have been compelled to reach that conclusion because other remedies have completely failed to secure compliance with the constitutional provisions on the part of police officers with the attendant result that the courts under the old rule have been constantly required to participate in, and in effect condone, the lawless activities of law enforcement officers.[30]

Traynor further explained his thinking as something like this. Excluding vital evidence of guilt would mean, in Judge Cardozo's words, that "the criminal is to go free because the constable has blundered."[31] But as illegally obtained evidence was offered by enforcement authorities in case after case, almost as a routine procedure, Traynor's misgivings grew. "It was," he wrote in 1962, "one thing to condone an occasional constable's blunder, to accept his illegally obtained evidence so that the guilty would not go free. It was quite another to condone a steady course of illegal police procedures that deliberately and flagrantly violated the Constitution of the United States as well as the state Constitution."[32] Under the rule of *Mapp*, as Justice Clark conceded, "the criminal goes free, if he must." He then added pointedly, "but it is the law that sets him free." Under the nonexclusionary rule, the criminal goes to prison, but it is the lawlessness of the police that sends him there.

There is no doubt, however, that in striking at the nasty problem of police lawlessness in various states, the Supreme Court has created other problems for them. Justice Traynor has summed up some of them.

There is no bill of particulars as to what constitutes lawful arrest or reasonable search incident to lawful arrest. Silence rings the large question of how much sweep there can be to a search. We will have to find out what constitutes probable cause for arrest and probable cause for a warrant. We will have to find out what it is that makes a search or seizure unreasonable. And now that the erstwhile rule of evidence is transfigured as constitutional doctrine, now that it has emerged from the wings to the *mise en scene* of the fourth amendment, what will become of its unsettled relations with the fifth amendment, which has not yet so boldly advanced as the fourth from the wings of the fourteenth amendment? To call but a partial roll of the myriad questions is to seize how spare is the rule of *Mapp* and to understand how wide must be our search for the clues to its orderly evolution. We will come upon enduring answers only if we first come to some understanding of the nature and scope of the right to privacy that the fourth amendment protects. Such understanding will take time, but it is not impossible to achieve.[33]

One of the most serious issues raised by the *Mapp* decision is that of retroactivity. Will it "open wide the prison gates?" There are hundreds, yes, thousands of inmates of prisons throughout the states whose convictions were brought about by unconstitutionally obtained evidence or at least, against whom, illegally obtained evidence was admitted. Most, no doubt, are guilty. Some undoubtedly would have been convicted by properly admissible evidence. In many situations it would be impossible to establish the "unreasonable" character of the "search and seizure" if for no other reason, because the record will fail to disclose the necessary facts. Defense counsel could well have thought it futile to raise the point under the prevailing rule of admissibility.

Nevertheless, there is a serious matter here. Are these prisoners, at whose trial evidence obtained by violation of the law of the land was used, now unconstitutionally detained?[34] The California Supreme Court, after reversing itself, did indeed, apply its rule retroactively to cases which had been tried before the decision but with appeals still pending. However, it declined to open the Pandora's Box for prisoners of longer standing. This distinction was legally feasible since at the time the only change in the California law was one of procedure. *Mapp* had not yet been decided. Although prisoners had been erroneously convicted because the judge made a mistaken ruling on a question of the law of evidence, the convictions were not void and thus subject to collateral attack, years thereafter. The situation now is quite different. Prisoners were not only convicted erroneously, but perhaps unconstitutionally. It is a plausible argument that their convictions were void and that they are unconstitutionally imprisoned.

The New York Court of Appeals has also applied the *Mapp* rule retroactively to appeals pending at the time of the decision.[35] As so retroactively applied, no insoluble questions arise as to the "unreasonableness" of the search. If the record does not disclose sufficient facts for the appellate court to pass final judgment, the case can be remanded to the lower court and retried. This is what happened in the New York case. The record which reached the highest New York court indicated that the search was unconstitutional unless there was "probable cause" to believe that criminal activities were occurring on the premises searched. "Of course," the court said, "when this case was tried, the People were not required to prove that the police had probable cause to arrest defendant. . . . It may well be that at the time of the entry the officers had probable cause which would have justified their making an arrest. . . .[36] The Supreme Court of New Jersey handled a similar case in the same way.[37]

Pre-*Mapp* convictions with an appeal still pending thus presented only a relatively small number of cases. Retroactive application to cases in which final judgments have been rendered, perhaps many years before, is quite a different matter.[38] In 1956, the Supreme Court held that indigent persons convicted in state courts are constitutionally entitled to a transcript of the record furnished by the state to enable them to appeal to a higher court if such appeals are available under state law. The Fourteenth Amendment required as much. Two years later the Court applied the rule to the case of a prisoner who had been convicted of murder in the state courts of Washington some twenty odd years before. He was indigent and had requested a free copy of the transcript of the record at his trial to enable him to appeal. It was denied. The Supreme Court held it a denial of his constitutional rights.[39]

But the situation here is somewhat different and may be distinguished. Again to quote Justice Traynor of the California court, "unlike the denial of the right to counsel, the knowing use of perjured testimony or suppression of evidence, the use of an involuntary confession, or . . . the denial of an opportunity to present a defense, the use of illegally seized evidence carries with it no risk of convicting an innocent person. The purpose of the exclusionary rule is not to prevent the conviction of the innocent, but to deter unconstitutional methods of law enforcement."[40] Several state cases have declined to apply the *Mapp* rule retroactively as to cases in which final decisions had been rendered prior to *Mapp* and the issue of the validity of the search had not been raised in the original proceedings.[41] On the other hand, a federal Court of Appeals has held that where the prisoner in his pre-*Mapp* trial *did* raise the issue, the *Mapp* rule could not be the basis for attacking the decision because of the doctrine of *res judicata, i.e.,* the matter has been decided.[42] Obviously this is an unsatisfactory state of affairs which the Supreme Court should soon clear up.

Justice Harlan, late in 1963, complained that "in the current swift pace of constitutional change" the Court should "deal definitively" with the problem of the retroactive application of the rule of the *Mapp* and other cases which reversed previous rulings on important constitutional questions. Like Justice Traynor, he did not regard the decision requiring free transcripts of the trial for indigents an adequate basis for a rule of general application. Nor was the answer to be found in the fiction that the law had always been what the last case in such a situation had held.[43]

Another matter to be settled is with respect to the phrase "persons, houses, papers, and effects." Just what is included? The Supreme Court has purported to hold that "house" may include a business office, store, hotel room, apartment, automobile or occupied taxicab but not a public jail or cell or room therein.[44] In that case a man named Lanza was convicted of contempt for refusing to answer questions put to him by a state legislative committee. He claimed immunity from punishment because the basis for questions asked him was a transcript of an electronically intercepted conversation between him and his brother in a room in a jail where the latter was imprisoned at the time. The talk had been recorded surreptitiously by state officials and a copy thereof turned over to the committee. Justice Stewart, writing for the Court declared: "For the reasons which follow, we hold that this constitutional claim is not valid, and we accordingly affirm the judgment before us." Justices Frankfurter and White took no part in the decision while the Chief Justice and Justices Black and Douglas dissented.

The "reasons which follow" were set forth briefly. First, the opinion conceded "as settled that the Fourteenth Amendment gives to the people like protection against the conduct of the officials of any State" as the Fourth gives against officials of the federal government. It also declared that "there can be no doubt" that "surreptitious electronic eavesdropping under certain circumstances may amount to an unreasonable search or seizure." But the notion that a jail is the equivalent of a man's "house," the Court thought, was "at best a novel argument." In any event, the Court declared that "to hold that the petitioner could not constitutionally be convicted for refusing to answer such [pertinent] questions simply because they related to a conversation which had been unlawfully overheard by other state officials would . . . be a completely unprecedented step."

Curiously enough, the opinion then proceeds to declare that the "ultimate disposition of this case, however, does not demand consideration of whether such a step might ever be constitutionally required" because two of the questions asked and to which answers were refused were in no way related to the intercepted conversation. There was in no way involved a federal issue under the Constitution.

But the Court's long practice has been, as previously indicated, to avoid constitutional questions if there are other adequate grounds for decision. The departure into this "exercise in futility" drew strong objections from the dissenters. Justice Brennan expressed his views as follows:

> I must protest the Court's gratuitous exposition of several grave constitutional issues confessedly not before us for decision

in the case. The tenor of the Court's wholly unnecessary comments is sufficiently ominous to justify the strongest emphasis
that of the abbreviated Court of seven who participate in the decision, fewer than five will even intimate views that the constitutional protections against invasions of privacy do not operate
for the benefit of persons—whether inmates or visitors—inside
a jail, or that the petitioner lacks standing to challenge secret
electronic interception of his conversations because he has
not a sufficient possessory interest in the premises, or that the
Fourth Amendment cannot be applied to protect against testi-
monial compulsion imposed solely as a result of an unconstitutional search or seizure.[45]

In this "brief" sentence, Justice Brennan was far more sharply
critical of a brother Justice for unnecessarily discussing constitutional issues than was Justice Black in an earlier case which attracted considerable journalistic attention.[46] However, not a line of
newsprint or editorial comment has been found on Brennan's opinion.
Perhaps it is no longer news that Supreme Court Justices are not only
justified but are obligated to point up what they regard as error in their
colleagues' opinions with which they disagree. As the Chief Justice set
forth in his Memorandum opinion in the *Lanza* case, "these expressions of dicta are in a form which can only lead to misunderstanding
and confusion in future cases." He went on to say that such dicta,
"when written into our decisions, have an unfortunate way of turning
up in digests and decisions of lower courts. . . ." As if to underscore
what the Chief Justice thus wrote, headnote 3 in the *Supreme Court
Reporter,* Advance Sheet, reporting the case under the West Publishing Company's key number—"*Searches and Seizures,* Key 7 (10)"—is as
follows: "Public jail is not equivalent of 'house,' within fourth amendment protection, or place where he can claim constitutional immunity
from search or seizure of his person, papers, or effects. U.S.C.A.
Const. Amend. 4."

The lawyer or judge in a hurried search for authority could plausibly conclude from this that the Court had held the Fourth Amendment did not protect a prisoner in jail against eavesdropping. If he
should so cite the case in his brief or opinion, he would be in error;
if he were sufficiently careful to read the opinion, he would be dis-
appointed and exasperated at the waste of his time.

It would appear that Justice Harlan who was one of the majority of
four also recognized as mere dicta the entire constitutional discussion
and wanted to make sure that his vote would not be misunderstood.
It will be remembered that he was a dissenter in the *Mapp* case. He

did not believe that the Fourteenth Amendment afforded the same protection against state governments as the Fourth does against the national government. This he reiterated in *Lanza*. Thus, his concurring opinion: "I do not understand anything in the Court's opinion to suggest either that the Fourteenth Amendment 'incorporates' the provisions of the Fourth, or that the 'liberty' assured by the Fourteenth Amendment is, with respect to 'privacy,' necessarily coextensive with the protections afforded by the Fourth. On that premise, I join the Court's opinion.[47]

It will be noted that the questions complained of were based upon conversations, knowledge of which had been obtained by an eavesdropping operation by electronic devices. Today this is a highly developed science. Resonator radio transmitters no larger than a silver quarter can be secreted under a bed and will transmit conversations for several blocks. Wire tapping too is a refined art almost impossible to detect. The usual case of search and seizure produces "papers and effects" in the nature of tangible objects sought to be used in evidence. But in a case decided in 1963, the Court held that statements and conversations overheard during an illegal search come within the exclusionary ban. Justice Brennan again writing for the Court developed the argument thus:

> The exclusionary rule has traditionally barred from trial physical, tangible materials obtained either during or as a direct result of, an unlawful invasion. . . . Similarly, testimony as to matters observed during an unlawful invasion has been excluded in order to enforce the basic constitutional policies. [Citation.] Thus, verbal evidence which derives so immediately from an unlawful entry and an unauthorized arrest as the officers' action in the present case is no less the "fruit" of official illegality than the more common, tangible fruits of the unwarranted intrusion. [Citation.] Nor do the policies underlying the exclusionary rule invite any logical distinction between physical and verbal evidence.[48]

The actual decision in the *Mapp* case is with respect to evidence obtained by a violation of the Fourth Amendment prohibiting unreasonable search and seizure. What are its implications for the use of evidence obtained illegally but not unconstitutionally? Evidence obtained by wire tapping presents such a case. Wire tapping is not unconstitutional, but it is forbidden by an Act of Congress. Evidence obtained thereby, either by state or federal officers, may not be used in criminal trials in the federal courts,[49] but the Court held in 1952, that it could be admitted in state criminal trials if, under state rules of evidence it was admissible. It has been suggested that the *Mapp* case may indicate the end of this practice as well, not because the constitutional rights of the accused have been violated but because Congress has extended to him this statutory protection which, under the supremacy clause of the Constitution, should prevail over state law.[50]

Although most commentators approve the adoption of the exclusionary rule, in all fairness, it should be noted that the opposite view has had its champions, on the merits, among the greatest legal scholars. There were some who considered the doctrine of the *Weeks* case "heretical" and "sentimental." "The doctrine of *Weeks* v. *United States*," wrote Professor Wigmore in his monumental work on Evidence, "also exemplifies a trait of our Anglo-American judiciary peculiar to the mechanical and unnatural type of justice. The natural way to do justice here would be to enforce the healthy principle of the fourth amendment directly, i.e., by sending for the high-handed, overzealous marshal who had searched without a warrant, imposing a thirty-day imprisonment for contempt of the Constitution and then proceeding to affirm the sentence of the convicted criminal. But the proposed indirect and unnatural methods are as follows:" He then ironically described the exclusionary rule in his classic words to Titus and Flavius, quoted by Justice Stewart in his "silver platter" opinion:

> Titus, you have been found guilty of conducting a lottery: Flavius, you have confessedly violated the Constitution. Titus ought to suffer imprisonment for crime, and Flavius for contempt. But no: We shall let you *both* go free. We shall not punish Flavius directly, but shall do so by reversing Titus' conviction. This is our way of teaching people like Titus to behave, and incidentally of securing respect for the Constitution. Our way of upholding the Constitution is not to strike at the man who breaks it, but to let off somebody else who broke something else.[51]

Just as it is generally thought that the admission of illegally seized evidence encourages lawlessness on the part of police, it is also assumed that the exclusionary rule tends to deter, although the empirical evidence is inconclusive on the latter point.[52] Indeed, it is not conclusive on either point but such evidence as there is certainly supports the first proposition.

An extended study of police behavior in Philadelphia when evidence obtained by unconstitutional means was admissible in state criminal trials revealed a wide gap between the law of arrest and search on the one hand and police practice on the other. After presentation of various patterns of police action and specific cases of law violation, two conclusions emerged: " (1) the police in Philadelphia are in many cases arresting without sufficient information, and (2) even when they do have the information required by law for a legal arrest, it has often been gained by illegal means, notably the illegal search." It was further observed by the investigators: "The amount of illegality discovered is perhaps startling in view of the facts that chiefly formal arrests were studied, which generally are far more commendable than the informal types, and that the bulk of information gathered was derived from police sources, which probably present police practice in its most favorable light."[53] This study was financed by an annual grant for studies in Law Enforcement and Individual Liberty, provided by Jacob Kossman of the Philadelphia Bar, in memory of Justice Rutledge.[54]

Perhaps Justice Traynor's observations, as an appellate judge with many years' experience, is enough to convince most persons that police lawlessness was greatly encouraged by the non-exclusionary rule. Justice Jackson's remarks in a 1949 case[55] tends to confirm Traynor's experience. "Only occasional and more flagrant abuses," he wrote, "come to the attention of the courts, and then only those where the search and seizure yields incriminating evidence and the defendant is at least sufficiently compromised to be indicted."

> If the officers raid a home, an office, or stop and search an automobile but find nothing incriminating, this invasion of the personal liberty of the innocent too often finds no practical redress. There may be, and I am convinced that there are, many unlawful searches of homes and automobiles of innocent people which turn up nothing incriminating, in which no arrest is made, about which courts do nothing, and about which we never hear.

As pointed out by Barth,[56] the victims are frequently in no position to make resistance. They usually are poor and ignorant, sometimes without counsel. If they do complain it is unlikely to carry much weight. "Trial courts are often not disposed to scrutinize police methods with much severity so long as they are persuaded of a defendant's guilt." They are unwilling to let the criminal go free merely "because the constable blundered."

Many state officials and some others are apprehensive of the exclusionary rule on law enforcement. They fear that the police will be handicapped. And so they will. They are now required to act within

constitutional limits or their efforts will be altogether futile. However, the arguments as to the actual ill effects of the exclusionary rule
have probably been exaggerated. Professor Allen has summed it up in
a thoughtful article, as follows:

> That the *Mapp* decision will produce both immediate and
> long-range consequences of considerable importance seems very
> likely. An effort to catalogue all the possible results of the case
> would constitute a highly speculative enterprise, indeed. One
> statement can be made with reasonable confidence, however:
> The decision in *Mapp* does not spell disaster for American law
> enforcement at the state and local levels. Nothing in previous
> experience suggests that the presence or absence of the exclu-
> sionary rule is the factor crucial to the effectiveness of the
> criminal law.[57]

He might have added that the Federal Bureau of Investigation and
other agents of the national government have lived with the exclusionary rule for fifty years without noticeable impairment of their
effectiveness.

Here, as in other problems of democracy, there is no doubt that
what is needed is a more efficient and effective education in the
principles under which this nation was brought into being and under
which it will survive only if it adheres thereto. Unfortunately, the evidence accumulates that the American people are losing contact with
what they started with.

In an address before the American Bar Association in Chicago recently, Justice Brennan referred to the apparent failure of many
Americans, especially the young generation, to understand the value
and importance of their constitutional liberties. He referred to a recent study made at Purdue University of high school students. More
than a third of those polled, for example, did not object to third degree
methods used by police. The Justice believed that public understanding is essential to assure official observance of individual rights. "As
the power of Government expands," he is reported to have said, "so
the opportunities for official abuse of that power multiply. If those
who wield the power are not sensitive to the guarantees of individual
liberty, the likelihood of official lawlessness cannot help but increase."[58]

Justice Rutledge was altogether sensitive to this fact. He understood it well—in fact much better than some of his brethren. Shortly
after his death, Professor Rockwell wrote:

To Rutledge, the vast expansion of governmental power in social and economic matters required correspondingly greater protection of civil liberties. The impact of the massive political community on individuality must be cushioned by comprehensive safeguards of personal liberty if the promises of democratic life are to remain meaningful. Big government can remain healthy only if civil liberties are rigorously protected. Thus he contributed as forcefully as anyone to the recent trend of the Court in practicing judicial self restraint where economic and social legislation is involved. But when fundamental democratic values are at stake, he asserted in *Thomas* v. *Collins,* this "presents a question this Court cannot escape answering independently, whatever the legislative judgment." To him the protection of personal liberty was the most vital responsibility of the Court.[59]

CHAPTER VI

"... WITHOUT DUE PROCESS OF LAW ...."

Loyal Citizens and Enemy Belligerents

THE Constitution of the United States is a document providing a framework for government in time of war as in peace. The document vests in the Congress and the Executive, as Commander in Chief, the power to wage war, and war power of the government, in the words of Chief Justice Hughes, is the "power to wage war successfully." This, then, is the authority, and with it the responsibility of two branches of the government. But what of the third?

The Supreme Court has the authority, and with it the responsibility, to interpret and apply the Constitution with its limitations on the acts of the other two departments whether the nation is at war or peace. But war is war and the Supreme Court most certainly was not intended as a tribunal to decree defeat. This, of course, solves nothing. It merely suggests the incredible problems presented to the Court in a war for survival.

There are wide differences of intelligent and responsible opinion as to the performance of the Court and its several Justices, not all of whom were consistent, in decisions dealing with crucial problems of the late war. Most positions taken by Rutledge were strictly in line with his character and philosophy. As to others, opinion is divided. On one point, however, there is no question. He was sincere; he was conscientious; he spared nothing of himself for his work. Perhaps no one on his or any other Court suffered more in coming to decision. He gave all, and he had much to give. Here are some of the problems which pushed Wiley Rutledge along the path to his premature grave.

Early in the war, General DeWitt, military commander in the west coast area promulgated a curfew restriction pursuant to an Executive Order issued by the President. Shortly thereafter, Congress ratified and confirmed the President's order, the result of which was to make a violation of military orders a misdemeanor. The curfew required all persons of Japanese ancestry to be within their places of residence from 8 p.m. to 6 a.m. Hirabayashi, an American citizen of Japanese ancestry, was convicted of violation. The Court upheld his conviction against the charge of unconstitutionality of the Executive Order and the Act of Congress. The national government, under the constitutional authority to wage war, could impose such restrictions as "an emergency war measure."[1] Justices Douglas, Murphy and Rutledge wrote concurring opinions. There was no dissent.

Chief Justice Stone, in a careful opinion, reviewed the situation following the attack on Pearl Harbor and the effective espionage which made it successful as revealed by the President's Commission in its report of January 23, 1942. There were, he noted, 112,000 persons of Japanese ancestry in the three west coast states, many of whom were claimed by Japan as citizens of that country. Although undoubtedly many of these people were loyal to the United States, he could not "reject as unfounded the judgment of the military authorities and of Congress that there were disloyal members of that population, whose number and strength could not be precisely and quickly ascertained." "We cannot say," he went on, "that the war-making branches of the Government did not have ground for believing that in a critical hour such persons could not readily be isolated and separately dealt with. . . ."

Justice Douglas in his concurring opinion agreed with this reasoning, as did Justice Murphy, but pointed out that he believed that any one affected was entitled in a later and appropriate proceeding to an opportunity to prove his loyalty. He also thought it important to point out that the problem was one of loyalty not assimilation. "Loyalty is a matter of mind and of heart, not of race. . . . Detention for reasonable cause is one thing. Detention on account of ancestry is another."

The Rutledge papers indicate that this problem troubled Douglas considerably. At some point during the circulation of draft opinions, he scribbled a note to Rutledge: "I wish you would turn over in your mind this weekend whether I should stick with my concurring opinion . . . if the C. J. takes out all of the stuff in his opinion on assimilation and mistreatment." Both Justices used the term in their final opinions. There is no trace or record of Rutledge's reply.

At one point, the Chief Justice addressed a "Memorandum for the Court" stating that he was revising his opinion to include a paragraph making the point that the case presented no occasion for determining whether circumstances and conditions which might arise after violation of the curfew would afford a basis for a judicial inquiry as to any person's loyalty and whether the courts could provide a procedure for determining the loyalty of individual members of the group of citizens of Japanese ancestry.

This clearly was an attempt to mollify Douglas by implying that the question of an opportunity for subsequent clearance, although not before the Court in this case, was not foreclosed. But in the Chief Justice's final published opinion all this was left out. Only the first sentence of the paragraph was included. It was innocuous: "We need not now attempt to define the ultimate boundaries of the war power." Mason in his book on Stone gives an explanation. The Chief, it seems, was having trouble with some of the other Justices who apparently wanted the opinion to suggest that all avenues of legal relief were foreclosed. One was irreconcilably opposed, we are told, to Douglas' invitation to Japanese to bring a thousand habeas corpus suits. Stone refused to discourage Douglas on the point but wrote him that if such a suggestion were to be included in the Court's opinion he would "lose most of my adherents."[2]

Justice Murphy originally planned to dissent. In fact at one point he wrote and circulated an opinion in the course of which he said:

> Undoubtedly we must wage war to win, and do it with all our might. But the might of America lies in something else, something that is unique—the consecrated purpose of free men of all faiths, all creeds, of all extractions, to preserve our free institutions. It will avail little to win the war on the battlefield and lose it at home. We do not win the war, on the contrary we lose it, if in the process of achieving military victory we destroy the Constitution and the best traditions of our country.

He went on to say:

> It is also true that the Fifth Amendment, unlike the Fourteenth, contains no guarantee of equal protection of the laws. . . . It by no means follows, however, that there may not be discrimination of such an injurious character in the application of the laws as to amount to a denial of due process as that term is used in the Fifth Amendment. I think that point is reached where we have one law for the majority of our citizens and another for those of a particular racial heritage.

In his final concurring opinion, Murphy included the foregoing paragraph with a modification of the last sentence, as follows: "I think that point is *dangerously approached* when we have one law for the majority of our citizens and another for those of a particular racial heritage." [Emphasis added.]

Rutledge, in his brief concurrence, merely entered his caveat to any intimation that the discretion of the military in regard to control over civilian citizens was beyond judicial review, at least short of the suspension of the writ of habeas corpus. However, an earlier typewritten opinion, apparently written when Murphy was planning to dissent, expressed his views more fully. "I have strong sympathy," he wrote, "with Mr. Justice Murphy's views. Next to totalitarian power, sheer racial discrimination goes to the heart of Nazi-Fascist policy we now fight." Nevertheless, he could not say that there was no reasonable grounds for the curfew order. "Obeying that was a small sacrifice for any citizen to pay for preservation of his heritage." He thought the "emergency existing when the action taken, and now questioned here, justified what was done."

A year and a half after the *Hirabayashi* case, the Court was faced with the problem of the validity of a military order, issued under the same presidential and congressional authority, which excluded the Japanese from the war area on the Pacific coast. Korematsu, whose home was in that area, had been convicted of violating this order. The Court affirmed in an unusual division of the Justices, Frankfurter writing a concurring opinion, Roberts, Murphy and Jackson writing separate dissents. Justice Black, writing for the majority, relied on the same line of reasoning as that employed by the Chief Justice in *Hirabayashi*. Although pressed by petitioner's counsel, he declined to pass on the validity of the entire relocation and detention program.[3] Frankfurter's concurring opinion emphasized the point that, in upholding the restriction, the Court did not necessarily approve the action of the Congress and the Executive. "That is their business, not ours."

Justice Roberts could not divorce the exclusion order from another military promulgation which prohibited all Japanese, whether citizen or alien, from leaving the particular area other than to report to an Assembly Center. Thus he described the predicament of the petitioner: "He was forbidden, by Military Order, to leave the zone in which he lived; he was forbidden, by Military Order, after a date fixed, to be found within that zone unless he were in an Assembly Center located in that Zone." In Roberts' quite rational view, this meant "that an Assembly Center was an euphemism for a prison. . . . The two conflicting orders, one which commanded him to stay, the other which commanded him to go, were nothing but a cleverly devised trap to accomplish the real purpose of the military authority, which was to lock him up in a concentration camp."[4]

Justice Murphy thought the exclusion on a plea of military necessity in the absence of martial law ought not to be approved. "Such exclusion goes over 'the very brink of constitutional power' and falls into the ugly abyss of racism." The exclusion order, he thought, had no reasonable relation to the removal of the dangers of invasion, sabotage and espionage. Although he appeared to have agreed in the *Hirabayashi* case that the military authorities could reasonably find it impractical to deal individually with the question of loyalty of 112,000 persons, he took a different view in this case.

Justice Jackson objected to the decision as based on *Hirabayashi* as authority. It was entirely an inadequate basis. He referred to Stone's guarded language in that case. The "mild measures" upheld in *Hirabayashi* he thought were quite different from the "very harsh ones" involved in the instant case. "Because we said that these citizens could be made to stay in their homes during the hours of dark, it is said we must require them to leave home entirely." Curiously enough, he thought the order unconstitutional even though he conceded that he could not say, on the evidence, that the orders were not "reasonably expedient military precautions," an argument presumably accepted by him in *Hirabayashi*. "The limitation under which courts always will labor," he wrote, "in examining the necessity for a military order are illustrated in this case. How does the Court know that these orders have a reasonable basis in necessity? No evidence whatever on that subject has been taken by this or any other court. There is sharp controversy as to the credibility of the DeWitt report. So the Court, having no real evidence before it, has no choice but to accept General DeWitt's own unsworn, self-serving statement, untested by any cross-examination, that what he did was reasonable." Then he added, ominously, "and thus it will always be when courts try to look into the reasonableness of a military order."[5]

On this position, Frankfurter in his concurrence commented:

> To recognize that military orders are "reasonably expedient military precautions" in time of war and yet to deny them constitutional legitimacy makes of the Constitution an instrument for dialectic subtleties not reasonably to be attributed to the hard-headed Framers, of whom a majority had had actual participation in war.[6]

Douglas circulated a printed dissenting opinion on December 1, eighteen days before the decision was handed down. If nothing more than evacuation was involved, he thought that *Hirabayashi* would be controlling. But more was involved. "Removal to an Assembly Center had become merely the first stage in a trip to a Relocation Center." Detention there was indefinite and he found no authority in the Act of Congress to support it. This opinion was never published. It may have been influenced by Roberts' opinion concerning the "two conflicting orders." There is no available evidence as to what caused Douglas to change his mind.

Critics have been puzzled about Rutledge's concurrence in these two cases. His position, at least in retrospect, appears somewhat out of his judicial character, particularly in view of his positive position in the case of the Japanese general, Yamashita. It may be, however, that there is less discrepancy between his attitude in these cases and his general philosophy than at first appears. After all, *Yamashita* involved issues of due process of law between a man and the gallows after the war was concluded. Rutledge's position there was perfectly consistent with his unalterable views in domestic criminal cases involving capital offenses. In the Japanese exclusion cases, much less invasion of human rights was involved—and a war was very much on. Rutledge was no conceptual fanatic. He was, in many ways, a constitutional pragmatist, as, for example, in the Massachusetts' child labor case. He recognized the responsibility of the military authorities to protect the nation against invasion and sabotage, and he was deeply sensitive to the fallibility of human judgment, particularly when under great stress. The record shows the intellectual and emotional travail of a Justice who was painfully aware of his own responsibility. There is reason to believe that his position in these cases troubled him to the day of his death.

Another case in this group gave Rutledge, as well as the other Justices, less trouble. A Japanese woman named Endo, a detainee in a War Relocation camp, had sought release in a proceeding for a writ of habeas corpus. It had been denied, although it was admitted that she was a citizen, loyal to the United States and had received leave clearance. On the same day that the Court decided the *Korematsu* case, the judgment denying her release was reversed. In an opinion by Mr. Justice Douglas, the Court, avoiding discussion of constititional issues, found no authority for her detention in the Act of Congress. "When the power to detain is derived from the power to protect the war effort against espionage and sabotage, detention which has no relationship to that objective is unauthorized." There was no dissent, although Justices Murphy and Roberts wrote concurring opinions, the latter believing that the Court should have based its decision on constitutional grounds.[7]

Before Yamashita's surrender Dean Rostow wrote: "All in all, the internment of the West Coast Japanese is the worst blow our liberties have sustained in many years. . . . Unless repudiated, they may encourage devastating and unforeseen social and political conflicts."[8] He also wrote an article in *Harper's Magazine* about "our worst wartime mistake; treatment of Japanese Americans on the West Coast."[9] The Dean made these points: (1) The Supreme Court decision converted a piece of wartime folly into national policy, enlarging the power of the military in relation to civil authority. (2) The principle of these decisions (quoting Justice Jackson) was about like a loaded weapon ready for the hand of any authority that can bring forward a plausible claim of an urgent need. (3) The precautions taken on the East Coast and in Hawaii were quite different: persons were placed in custody on the basis of individual suspicion. (4) The evidence supports one conclusion only: the dominant element in the development of our relocation policy was race prejudice, not a military estimate of a military problem. (5) The Court should not declare such a problem beyond the reach of judicial review. Perhaps the last point made by the Dean was the most important, from the long view—which is usually the most important so far as the judiciary is concerned. The elective branches of the government—the legislative and the executive—may ordinarily be expected to take the short view in the sense that they are subject to the pressures of the moment more than the judiciary. When the judges and justices yield to the same pressures, they fall short of the function in the American system of checks and balances which they are expected to perform.

Nine months before *Endo* and *Korematsu* were decided by the Supreme Court, the *Washington Post* had sounded a solemn warning.[10] It pointed out that the *Endo* case would not test the validity of the detention in the Tule Lake camp of Japanese who had *not* received loyalty clearance. "Their disloyalty," the *Post* editorial commented, "has been administratively determined without jury trial—a most dangerous precedent in these times when certain members of Congress are prone to hurl charges of disloyalty with great recklessness." With how much greater recklessness such charges were to be hurled in the years to come the newspaper's editors could hardly have anticipated.

The *Post* had in fact been concerned after the *Hirabayashi* decision. Although not critical of the Court, it thought that "the outright deprivation of civil rights which we have visited upon these helpless, and for the most part, no doubt, innocent people, may leave an ugly blot upon the pages of our history."[11] The *New York Herald Tribune* followed a somewhat similar line of thought.[12]

> The American people must admit the practical wisdom of this decision in the present emergency. But they cannot forget that it was written for a war emergency as a concession to the imperative demands of a specific and extraordinary situation. Distinctions based on ancestry are still "odious to a free people."

After *Korematsu* liberal opinion both in lay magazines and legal periodicals was generally critical. "We find the weak handling of racial issues by the United States Supreme Court deeply disturbing," editorialized the *Nation*.[13] "We fear that these Japanese cases are the edge of the wedge by which racial discrimination makes its first unmistakable appearance in American Constitutional Law." The *Christian Century* thought that the "future stability of the republic requires that long before a generation has passed the doctrines which Justice Murphy and Justice Jackson enunciated in their dissenting opinions shall become the law of the land."[14]

Perhaps Rutledge's most spectacular dissent was in the *Yamashita* case in 1946. The "Tiger of Malaya," in charge of all Japanese armies in the Philippines, General Yamashita, surrendered to the American Forces on September 3, 1945. On September 25, he was served with a charge prepared by the Judge Advocate General's Department of the Army with violations of the law of war. He was later tried by a military commission, convicted and sentenced to death. Thereafter, he petitioned for a writ of certiorari to review an order of the Supreme Court of the Philippines which had denied his application for a writ of habeas corpus. He also applied to the Supreme Court of the United States for leave to file a petition for writs of habeas corpus and prohibition (to enjoin execution of the sentence). In an opinion delivered by Chief Justice Stone, the writs were denied, leaving Yamashita's conviction by the military commission to stand. Justices Rutledge and Murphy dissented in separate opinions.[15]

The Court, relying on a previous case,[16] held that on application for habeas corpus from the decision of a military commission, the guilt or innocence of the petitioner was not in issue. The Court would not review the merits of the case. "We consider here only the lawful power of the commission to try the petitioner for the offense charged. In the present cases it must be recognized throughout that the military tribunals which Congress has sanctioned by the Articles of War are not courts whose rules and judgments are made subject to review by this Court." The Chief Justice then held that General Styer's order for the appointment of the commission, having been authorized by General MacArthur, Commander of the United States Army in the Pacific, was valid. The commission had jurisdiction. The fact that hostilities had ceased did not terminate its authority.

The charge was that petitioner as commander of the armed forces of Japan had unlawfully disregarded and failed to discharge his duty to control the operations of members of his command, permitting them to commit brutal atrocities and other high crimes against the people of the United States and its allies, particularly inhabitants of the

Philippines, thereby violating the laws of war. After referring to the Fourth Hague Convention, the Chief Justice continued:

> [I]t is urged that the charge does not allege that petitioner has either committed or directed the commission of such acts, and consequently that no violation is charged as against him. But this overlooks the fact that the gist of the charge is an unlawful breach of duty . . . to control the operations of members of his command. . . . That this was the precise issue to be tried was made clear by the statement of the prosecution at the opening of the trial.[17]

The Convention plainly imposed on petitioner, he contended, who, at the time specified, was Military Governor of the Philippines, as well as Commander of the Japanese Forces, "an affirmative duty to take such measures as were within his power and appropriate in the circumstances to protect prisoners of war and the civilian population." He further held, however, that various depositions by persons not present and hearsay evidence were not prohibited in a trial of an army combatant; that such types of evidence were inadmissible only in trials of our own army personnel. He thought that the Geneva Convention, requiring the same procedure in trials of a prisoner of war as in the case of persons belonging to the armed forces of the detaining power, was not applicable. In some curious way, he came to the conclusion that such provisions of the Geneva Treaty were applicable "only to judicial proceedings directed against a prisoner of war for offenses committed while a prisoner of war."[18]

> Mr. Justice Rutledge began his dissent with these words:
>
> Not with ease does one find his views at odds with the Court's in a matter of this character and gravity. Only the most deeply felt convictions could force one to differ. That reason alone leads me to do so now, against strong considerations for withholding dissent.
>
> More is at stake than General Yamashita's fate. There could be no possible sympathy for him if he is guilty of the atrocities for which his death is sought. But there can be and should be justice administered according to law.[19]

In Rutledge's view, the decision could be upheld only on the ground that an enemy belligerent in Yamashita's position was altogether beyond the reach of constitutional protection. He thought, in the first place, that the military commission was not validly constituted as a result of the directive and the accompanying detailed rules describing the procedure and rules of evidence to be followed.

> A more complete abrogation of customary safeguards relating to the proof . . . hardly could have been made. So far as the admissibility and probative value of evidence was concerned, the directive made the commission a law unto itself.

> It acted accordingly. . . . Every conceivable kind of statement, rumor, report, at first, second, third or further hand, written, printed or oral, and one "propaganda" film were allowed to come in, most of this relating to atrocities committed by troops under petitioner's command throughout the several thousand islands of the Philippine Archipelago during the period of active hostilities covered by the American forces' return to, and recapture of the Philippines.[20]

Yamashita had surrendered on September 3, was served with charges on September 25, and was arraigned on October 8. The trial itself began three weeks later and lasted until December 7. It is one of those little ironies of history that he was condemned to death on the fourth anniversary of the attack on Pearl Harbor. On the first day of the trial, the prosecution filed a supplemental bill of particulars containing an additional fifty-nine specific charges of atrocities by Japanese troops over a wide area of the islands. On November 8, the Chief Counsel for the defense was asked when he would be prepared to proceed on the supplemental bill. The prosecutor himself stated: "Frankly, sir, it took the War Crime Commission some three months to investigate these matters, and I cannot conceive of the Defense undertaking a similar investigation with any less period of time." On November 20, the prosecution had finished its case on the additional fifty-nine charges. The senior defense counsel stated that his staff had been "working day and night" but had been unable to prepare an adequate defense. He asked for a reasonable continuance which the Commission denied. "Obviously," Rutledge wrote, "the burden placed upon the defense in the short time allowed for preparation of the original bill, was not only 'tremendous'." [But,]

> In view of all the facts, it was an impossible one, even though the time allowed was a week longer than asked. But the grosser vice was later when the burden was more than doubled by service of the supplemental bill on the eve of the trial, a procedure which . . . was wholly arbitrary, cutting off the last vestige of adequate chance to prepare defense and imposing a burden the

most able counsel could not bear. This sort of thing has no place in our system of justice, civil or military.[21]

Rutledge then demonstrated, after tracing the history of United States military tribunals from the time of the Mexican War, that the Articles of War prohibited the use of depositions in capital cases except for the defense. He also demonstrated that these rules applied to proceedings "before any military court or commission." He rejected the Court's holding that the Geneva Convention did not apply. He could not accept the view that the treaty applied only to offenses committed by a prisoner of war and not to those committed by an enemy combatant. He found suggested no such limitation in any provision thereof. He construed the Convention to be strictly applicable, and continued:

> Policy supports this view. For such a construction is required for the security of our own soldiers, taken prisoner, as much as for that of prisoners we take. And the opposite one leaves prisoners of war open to any form of trial and punishment for offenses against the laws of war their captors may wish to use, while safeguarding them, to the extent of the treaty limitations, in cases of disciplinary offense. This, in many instances, would be to make the treaty strain at a gnat and swallow the camel.[22]

Rutledge concluded his opinion by holding that the Fifth Amendment of the Constitution had been violated in this trial.

> Wholly apart from the violation of the Articles of War and of the Geneva Convention, I am completely unable to accept or to understand the Court's ruling concerning the applicability of the due process clause of the Fifth Amendment to this case. Not heretofore has it been held that any human being is beyond its universally protecting spread in the guaranty of a fair trial in the most fundamental sense. That door is dangerous to open. I will have no part in opening it. For once it is ajar, even for enemy belligerents, it can be pushed back wider for others, perhaps ultimately for all.[23]

His final words were a quotation from Tom Paine: "He that would make his own liberty secure must guard even his enemy from oppression; for if he violates this duty, he establishes a precedent that will reach to himself."

"This case . . . poses a problem that cannot be lightly brushed aside or given momentary consideration. It involves something more than the guilt of a fallen enemy commander under the law of war or the jurisdiction of a military commission. This nation's very honor, as well as its hopes for the future, is at stake." Thus, Justice Murphy began his dissent in the case of General Homma, who like Yamashita, had been condemned to death by a military commission. The majority had, indeed, brushed the matter aside in a one paragraph *Per Curiam,* on the authority of *Yamashita's* case.[24]

Justice Rutledge joined in Murphy's opinion and wrote a brief dissent in which the latter joined. "For the first time," he wrote, "the Court . . . permits trial for a capital offense under a binding procedure which allows forced confessions to be received in evidence; makes proof in prior trials of groups for mass offenses prima facie evidence that the accused likewise is guilty of that offense; and requires that findings and judgment in such mass trial 'be given full faith and credit' in any subsequent trial of an individual person charged as a member of the group." He thought this shameful procedure vitiated the entire proceeding.

There is a good deal of evidence on the differences the Justices had during the consideration of the *Yamashita* and *Homma* cases. The Chief Justice circulated several opinions, changing and altering them to meet the criticisms and objections not only of the dissenters, but of the majority. He had his greatest troubles with the latter in trying to meet Rutledge's Fifth Amendment argument, particularly after the circulation of one of Rutledge's draft dissents. This problem became so acute that the Chief Justice in his final opinion eliminated all discussion of the Fifth Amendment save for one sentence. After referring to his holding that the proceedings of the Military Commission were not reviewable by the courts on the merits he said: "From this viewpoint it is unnecessary to consider what, in other situations, the Fifth Amendment might require, and as to that no intimation one way or the other is to be implied."

The draft of one of Stone's opinions, circulated on January 28, contained an attempt to answer Rutledge's Fifth Amendment argument. But three days later he circulated a "Memorandum for the Court," which, after a few minor emendations, directed the omission of everything in the text of the opinion down to a certain page. On Rutledge's copy of this memo, he wrote at this point: "The Big Backup." The material omitted under this direction included the proposed answer to Rutledge's "due process" argument. It was unconvincing, apparently, even to those Justices who agreed with the decision.

In that part of his opinion which he omitted the Chief Justice argued that the due process clause did not apply to trials by military tribunals, and thus there was nothing unconstitutional about the admission of hearsay evidence and other material to which the prisoner's counsel had objected. The common law rules of evidence were the product of jury trial and thus inapplicable to this case. He cited a similar rule in deportation proceedings in which hearsay evidence was admissible. "The law of war," he wrote, "the Articles of War and the Constitution thus left the military commission, which is a body of military officers, not untrained jurors, free to receive and consider any evidence of probative value, regardless of rules of exclusion, and subject only to review by the military reviewing authorities." He also denied that defense counsel was not allowed adequate time for preparation.

On the whole, this part of the opinion was pretty thin and would have been an easy target for rebuttal. The argument that the common law rules of evidence are inapplicable to military trials was clearly irrelevant. The objection was not that rules of admissibility, as such, were violated but that they were violated to the extent and in such a manner as to amount to a denial of due process of law in violation of the Fifth Amendment. As to the refusal to allow additional time for preparation by the defense, the position taken by the Chief Justice is unconvincing on the facts as presented by Justice Rutledge in his dissent. It is little wonder that to hold his supporters, this part was omitted.

My ex-colleague and former law clerk for Justice Black, John P. Frank, in his recent book, *The Marble Palace,* included a letter to him from Justice Rutledge detailing the troubles and the problems of the Justices in the ordeal of decision-making in the *Yamashita* case. What Frank did not publish, because he never received it, was the original draft of Rutledge's letter to him. With a few minor deletions, the letter is as follows:

> Some day perhaps I can tell you the whole story of this fight, which began just before Christmas. It was a battle royal all the way, first to get a hearing; then after the hearing, to get the very minimum time for writing; and finally to get any time at all for revision. These facts tell a story themselves.

> So far as my own part was concerned, I think I can say to you, in view of your former connection with and knowledge of the Court's ways of doing things, as well as your capacity for keeping things to yourself, that after the hearings were concluded I knew or thought that the decision would be handed down two weeks later in any event, whether we were ready or not. The Chief Justice took the full first week and one day of the second week before submitting his opinion, although about half

of it was sent to me on Monday night of the second week. . . .
I did not start writing until I received his full opinion Tuesday
morning. I wrote from then until six minutes of twelve on Saturday. Of course everything else had to be put aside and that
explains why I did not participate in the cert. list of that week.
[Consideration by the Justices of petitions for writs of certiorari
to review decisions of lower federal courts and of state courts.]
I was up one night until five o'clock, and on Friday night before
the conference on Saturday, Edna [Edna Lingreen, secretary],
Richard [Richard Wolfson, law clerk] and I stayed here until
after midnight. Then I went home and worked the rest of the
night, not taking off my clothes, and coming back the next
morning without either breakfast or shaving, to spend the next
two hours driving here at my desk with all my might. . . .
Murphy of course had started writing earlier, in advance of the
Chief's submission.

While I did not want to send things down in such shape
and with such haste, I notified the conference that my opinion
would be circulated that afternoon. They were then driving to get the case down on Monday morning, but of
course they hadn't seen what I had written. Up until that
time there had been not only the greatest pressure to get the
things down that Monday, but the suggestion had been made
that the majority would put down its opinion and give the
dissenting members leave to file theirs later. I would have
none of that. I did not dare note dissent in these cases without giving full reasons for doing so. . . .

The real hero of this whole story is the printer. He got
the last installment of my stuff after noon on Saturday and
he had copies for circulation back here by 3:30. Since I was
not participating in the certs., I came out of conference and
looked over the draft, then ordered it circulated. When conference was concluded I announced that the opinion had been
distributed and would be found in their offices on their return
and that I was ready for things to go that Monday.

The Chief Justice then said that if the dissenting opinions
presented nothing that needed answering the case would go
down, but that if there was anything in them that needed
response he for one did not propose to be rushed into handing
the opinions down without time to answer. Then too . . .
he said to me that if anything he might write in response to
mine required answer he thought I should have time. Again
the suggestion was made to announce the judgment with

opinions to follow later. Again Murphy and I fought that and blocked it. I went home that night and caught up partly on my sleep, though I went over the opinions again to do what revising I could.

The next day of course was Sunday. I heard nothing from the Chief Justice until six o'clock. It turned out that he had been working all day, except to take time out to go to the Red Mass in the morning, in answer to our drive on Fifth Amendment due process. He had not mentioned that in the original draft. So when he called in the evening, he said, "Rutledge, I've written an addition to our opinion today and I am without a chauffeur. Have you any suggestion concerning how I can get this to you?"

I answered, "Yes, Chief Justice, I am going downtown for dinner and I'll drop by for it in about an hour." We went by for it as promised, went on to dinner and got back home about nine o'clock. [Dean] Mason Ladd, who was returning to Iowa a day or two later, was with us. I took time out to go back to my study and glance the thing through. On that hurried reading I concluded that I need not add more than a brief paragraph in response. . . . Then I decided, almost subconsciously, that I'd better get away from those distractions around the house, get down here and pin down on what the Chief had written to make sure I wasn't overlooking anything. Things here were quiet and I could work. It wasn't fifteen minutes until I saw that I had a night's job to do.

Some day maybe I can show you the draft of what he wrote. Then you will fully understand why the opinion does nothing more than brush due process aside. I knew that the majority was not in agreement about it. I decided to take out my brief treatment of due process, put it in a separate section, and ram it home. I also decided to state flatly that the Chief Justice had misstated the facts of record in several respects concerning this angle. So I stayed here until five o'clock Monday morning revamping my opinion. I left it in the safe for Edna to type first thing that morning. She did and I circulated. Ten o'clock came and we went to conference. [Two hours before the Court would assemble to deliver opinions.]

I can't tell you all that went on in that hour and a half. The two ends of the table were in direct and irreconcilable clash. It was obvious from the beginning that the cases could not go down with a unanimous opinion for those who were the Court. The threat of course was that there would be several. This was worse than none at all. . . . And that is also why the opinion says no more about due process. It couldn't say any more without a blowout and a wide-open split. The fact is, and I say it deliberately, that in this respect the opinion is the most aggravated instance of run-around in the history of the Court so far as I have knowledge of its decisions and opinions.

. . . . Of course when the Chief Justice ran into the snag on his constitutional treatment he had to revamp and the revamping brought what you have read. It was as deliberate as anything ever done by this Court. It was the only thing that could be done and at the same time to keep all of them together. I leave you to surmise the reasons for this.

To one who knows the inside of what went on, this makes the case even more rank than it is on its merits. I had all I could do to keep my tone within some bounds of restraint, but I knew I dared not do otherwise. So much for this phase of the case. It comes down, as I said in the dissent, to a total abrogation of constitutional or other restraint upon the military in dealing with enemy belligerents. This is true even more in the Homma case, which went down, so far as the majority is concerned, with the simple word "Denied," and a citation to the Yamashita case. Although I joined Murphy, I am not sure he didn't speak with too much vehemence for the most effective force.

And of course there is nothing in the outcome of either case which gives the press occasion to crow. If we dissenters have accomplished nothing else, I think maybe we have had a part in bringing that about and, if so, perhaps our efforts are not altogether in vain. These trials cannot be glorified now and the time will come when they will be generally condemned. American justice just isn't done this way, whoever the accused may be, except that is in a time of war fever. It wouldn't even be done in war because the fear of retaliation, if nothing else, would prevent it. Nor do I think it could be done after a formal declaration of peace. So we are now in one of those interludes of lawlessness which is worse than either war or peace. . . .

I stated above that I had not yet seen a gloating comment about either of these cases. I have seen a few very forthright editorial comments about the Yamashita case, although there was a notable editorial silence for two or three days after it came down and they didn't dare speak until they had seen what might be said against these performances. When they did see it, some did what the Court did, namely, ignored the real significance of what had been done and brushed it all aside with the statement that it was military business, with which the courts have nothing to do.

Since Monday, when Homma's case went down, there has been a similar silence or attenuated statement in the news of what had taken place. I have seen no editorial comment about Homma's case and the only news items I have seen have been brief statements that the action of the Commission had been sustained on the same basis as was used in *Yamashita's* case. Today, however, Gene Gressman brought into the office at noon a copy of the Star containing a blast on the first page under the headline "Keenan blasts Murphy and Rutledge." He says there will be no "judicial lynchings." That, as you will note from Murphy's opinion was his phrase.

By his blast he has stirred up attention for what otherwise would have gone altogether unnoticed, namely, that in Homma's case the directive issued to govern the trial authorized the use of mass trials and the imputation of evidence received in them to individuals having membership in the group. Of course we could not say that this had been done in Homma's case because his application was filed here and actually had been determined before his sentence had been imposed. As you may recall, the announcement here and the announcement of the Commission's action came the same day. Nevertheless, even though they did not use these types of evidence or the forced confessions which also were authorized, the directive permits it. In other words, the stage had been set for repetition of the mass trials and purges which were so common in Germany and Russia prior to the war. I hope the protest may be able to prevent the use of that type of evidence in any case, but that is about all I can hope for in the present state of things, so far as further trials of enemy belligerents may be concerned.

The "Keenan" to which Rutledge referred in this letter was Joseph B. Keenan, Chief of the Army's International Prosecution Section. He was quoted by the newspapers as characterizing Murphy's dissent as "offensive to say the least." He was, understandably, nettled by the prediction of a "succession of judicial lynchings." He was confident that no such thing would occur. As if to reassure the American people by utterly refuting Justice Murphy, he declared that "General McArthur has been emphatic in his instructions that every care be exercised to see that these trials are fair and that due precautions are taken to insure adequate opportunity for fair presentation of defense."25

Newsweek for December 10, 1945, had commented as follows on the Commission's *Yamashita* hearing:

> . . . Its rules of evidence . . . permitted almost anything, even the prosecution's introduction of third-hand hearsay evidence—a break with Anglo-Saxon justice that scandalized trial observers. When it closed its case, the prosecution had produced hundreds of thousands of Japanese military documents captured in the Philippines. But not one directly implicated Yamashita in the war crimes for which he was held responsible.

Newsweek later reported,26 "Twelve correspondents who covered the Manila trial, were asked: 'If you had been a member of the Court would you have voted a death sentence?' Result: A unanimous 'No'."

In spite of Rutledge's hope that the press had nothing to "crow" about, there was some crowing in high press circles after the Court's decision. The *New York Herald Tribune* seemed quite complacent: "There were many who fretted and scoffed when a request for Supreme Court intervention was permitted in the Yamashita case. . . . The delay was justified on the ground that democratic principle guarantees the full process of justice even to our enemies."27 Even more satisfied, the *New York Times* in its editorial February 5, 1946, declared that "General Yamashita received a fair trial. . . . The Yamashita case sets a precedent. We believe it is a good one." Surprisingly, the *St. Louis Post-Dispatch* was similarly gratified.

> The case of Yamashita is an illustration of full and determined justice which Japan must heed. Probably no man so hated and despised by conquerors has had such a day in court, and in the highest court that the conquerors could provide. Perhaps it will seem strange to the Japanese that a conquering power would grant a detested war criminal the right of appeal, and the benefit of every legal protection.28

Even the majority of the Supreme Court did not go to this extent to soothe American citizens who may have been distressed with the decision or to remind the Japanese of the generosity of their conquerors.

The *Washington Post,* however, found much less to "crow" about. "The disquieting thing," it said soberly, "is that it gives the military *carte blanche* to go ahead with proceedings of the kind that brought Yamashita's conviction with no guarantee that justice is being done." After quoting from Rutledge's opinion that hearsay, propaganda and other improper evidence had been admitted, the newspaper continued:

> The majority does not refute this statement, but holds simply that the Commission's rulings on evidence and on the mode of conducting the trial are "not reviewable by the courts." . . . . We shall not make progress in establishing a regime of law and justice in the world by ignoring the basic elements of fair play—not even in the trial of war criminals.[29]

Most scholarly discussion of the case tended to agree with Rutledge that "any person" should include a Japanese general captured in war. "If war criminals are to be 'tried' rather than summarily condemned by political decision, is it not more consistent with the notion of supremacy of the 'law of the land' to conduct the trials in accordance with at least minimum requirements of fair procedure?" asked the *Michigan Law Review.*[30] "Do the rights guaranteed by the due process clause belong only to the victor?" queried the *Marquette Law Review.* "If they do, in what way does this differ from the theory that 'might is right'."[31] In a careful article, Professor Davis, after the Supreme Court's decision, wrote:

> The following observation of Mr. Justice Rutledge seems well supported: "The Court does not declare expressly that petitioner as an enemy belligerent has no constitutional rights, a ruling I could understand but not accept. Neither does it affirm that he has some, if but little, constitutional protection. Nor does the Court defend what was done. I think the effect of what it does is, in substance, to deny him all such safeguards. And this is the great issue in this cause."[32]

John Frank confirms this judgment in his book, *The Marble Palace.*[33]

> There are occasions when necessity results in ambiguity that approaches unintelligibility. A classic instance is the case of General Yamashita, the Japanese General in the Philippines. . . . If General Yamashita was entitled to a trial with due process of law, he did not have it. Any Ameri-

can judge would be outraged if a pickpocket charged with taking twenty cents were thus tried in an American court. . . . The resulting opinion by Chief Justice Stone has never been regarded as marking one of the better days in the Court's history. The Court recognized the question of whether the General was entitled to due process. It held that the General might be executed. But the Court never did say what it thought about the constitutional question.

Professor Gancoe in his careful review of the *Yamashita* case, called attention to that part of the opinion of the Chief Justice in which he dismissed, as irrelevant, any discussion of a due process of law problem under the Fifth Amendment to the Constitution. "It was to this portion of the Court's decision," he wrote, "that Justice Rutledge gave a masterful dissent." He concluded his article with the ominous words:

> The Court has spoken. Yamashita is dead, and we shed no tears. The issue, however, is not dead. It is of momentous importance, not only to the legal profession but to the people of the United States as a whole, whether certain guarantees which are a fundamental part of our constitutional system can be swept away by saying, "These are matters for the political branches of the government."[34]

Frank Reel, an attorney for Yamashita, has recorded brilliantly his version of the case in a book published by the University of Chicago Press.[35] In reply, Courtney Whitney, Brigadier General of the Army, Government Section, wrote a "Memorandum for the Record" dated November 22, 1949. "The book," he declared, "is essentially an attack upon our American system of jurisprudence— indeed, it might better be said upon our American system—in the refusal of the author, a practicing attorney, to accept the judgment of the United States Supreme Court, acting through a majority thereof, on issues both argued before that tribunal and discussed in the book.

Instead, in an almost hysterical endeavor to propagate the minority viewpoint, subscribed to by only two of the eight participating Justices, by re-pleading anew his identical views pled and lost before the trial commission and the highest forums of civil appeal and military review, the author but shows himself unable to accept the ethical base establishing in our country the primacy of majority decision.

The General then purported to set forth what the Supreme Court had held, among other things, that "the regulation governing the procedure to be followed by the Commission . . . was not in conflict with the Articles of War as alleged, nor did it deprive Yamashita of due process of law provided by the Fifth Amendment to the Constitution. . . ." Of course, the statement as to the Constitution is completely inaccurate. This is precisely what the Court took pains to explain that it was *not* deciding, which is the whole point of Rutledge's dissent. Neither the trials of these Japanese war criminals nor General Whitney's defense of them adds to the luster of military justice.

As might be expected, Rutledge received extensive gratuitous correspondence about his opinion. It is unlikely that he preserved all or even most of it. But assuming that what he retained is representative of the bulk, most of it was favorable. The experience of most public figures who receive communications from unknown correspondents find that it is critical. People who agree with the position taken seldom bother to write. In many instances those who oppose vigorously express their hostility. In this case most of the correspondence came from Rutledge's friends who approved of his opinion. Many of them were lawyers.

There is no doubt that some who disapproved felt strongly. One telegram from California thanked God "for six sane men against two Jap coddlers in the Supreme Court." A post card inquired, "Why don't you two hand in your resignations after you pulled that boner on Gen. Homma after what that dirty, cruel, murderer did to our poor boys and those poor Philippinos." The writer then concluded, "Now get out and stay out." Several such letters were from parents of members of the Armed Forces. One concluded that "it is obvious that neither you or Murphy ever wore the uniform of a soldier."

For a man with the sensitivity and sympathy for humanity such as Justice Rutledge, these messages must have cut deeply. However, he was prepared for them and repeatedly answered his correspondents that both he and Justice Murphy expected far more abuse than they received. The Justice did not answer his violent critics. Indeed, a number were anonymous and could not be answered. He did, however, take scrupulous care to answer both friends and strangers who wrote sympathetically.

He was obviously cheered by the expression of approval, particularly by the nonjudicial personnel of the Court and its staff. Some messages he apparently received while still sitting in the case. He preserved a penciled note from C. E. Cropley, Clerk of

Court: "Though you do not subscribe to the new law made in the heat of today—your contribution to the classics of American philosophy will be recognized in a cooler tomorrow, and I hope, not too late." From his faithful secretary, Miss Edna Lingreen, the note read, "You did a superb job! Everbody says so. I wouldn't have missed it for anything. (The C.J. didn't look very happy)." She added, "Even the page boy (Robert) said, 'Boy, the Judge gave a perfect opinion! Wasn't that neat?' "

That the Justice was pleased with approval from such quarters was indicated by a note he sent to his secretary a few days later. "Robert, the Robber, said to me this morning: 'Justice, you shorely spoke a fine piece Monday. I didn't know you could *preach* like that!' He also spoke to me saying that I sure could preach the Gospel. He admires our courage and he is a fine man. I wonder if people of color also have an unconscious sympathy with the brown people of the Orient."

A number of his letters of approval came from professors and scholars, former associates while he was himself a member of the law teaching profession. From a distinguished professor of the Harvard Law School he received a letter the first paragraph of which was as follows:

> The number of the Supreme Court Reporter containing the *Application of Yamashita* reached the School on Monday, and yesterday every member of the Faculty who met me asked me what I thought about the case. There is quite lively disagreement, particularly on matters of procedure. Morgan and I think your opinion hits the nail on the head. Personally, I feel deeply ashamed of what we have done in this trial. The only bright spot is the vigorous and sincere defense, which seems up to the best traditions of our bar. But the ablest advocacy is a sounding brass and tinkling cymbal when a court ducks and dodges on constitutional and statutory interpretation as did your majority in this matter. To me, the opinion of the Chief Justice is a painful example of the kind of thing which makes the common citizen distrust lawyers.

Professor Hans J. Morganthau of the University of Chicago wrote a congratulatory note on "the courage and wisdom of your dissenting opinion." Senator Milligan of Colorado characterized the dissent as "magnificent." Congressman Pettengill of Indiana thought "the reasons and ideals of constitutional liberty which led you to

your conclusion represent to me the loftiest conception of justice."
Several approving letters came from members and former members of
the Armed Forces, men who did "wear the uniform of their country."
A letter from a federal judge of the Circuit Court of Appeals wrote
that "the sweep of your ideas, the moving phrases, and the profound
concern for justice as voiced in your opinion have recurred in my
mind from day to day. It is fortunate indeed for our country and
for civilization that this voice of conscience of yours was heard in
the midst of confusion and clamor."

One letter obviously from an unknown person, and Rutledge's
reply throw light on the character of both. The note was postmarked
from a small village of rural Kansas. It is as follows:

> Mr. Rutledge: Been reading what the paper has to say
> about Yamashita. Now over the radio this morning I heard
> someone say that Yamashita ought to apologize to people for
> what he has done. Mr. Rutledge, he was a soldier or at least
> that is what I suppose, from what I hear.
>
> I would like a copy of some of the proceedings of his trial,
> if you will send them to me.
>
> I also notice Mr. Rutledge, that you and Mr. Murphy
> seemed to disagree with the majority. Have sometimes done
> that myself.
>
> Sincerely,

To this "Mr. Rutledge" replied within the week:

> I was interested to receive your letter yesterday and to
> note your interest in the Yamashita case. While the number
> of copies of the opinions that are now available is limited,
> I am enclosing a copy in accordance with your request. You
> will note that this pamphlet contains both the opinion of
> the Court and the two dissents, one written by Justice Mur-
> phy and one by myself.
>
> Since it is not customary for members of the Court to
> comment on decisions after they have been rendered, except
> officially in the course of some later opinion, I will say only
> that the circumstances presented by this case were such that
> I felt compelled to dissent and to state at length the reasons
> why I should do so.
>
> With every good wish, I am,
>
> Sincerely yours,

The only Japanese civilian to be executed as a war criminal pursuant to a sentence of the International Military Tribunal, Far East, was the former prime minister, Hirota. In the early 30's he had been foreign minister, becoming prime minister in 1936. His government fell the following year. He again became foreign minister and served until 1938 when he resigned and retired to private life. He had no direct contact with the Pacific War.

For an understanding of the performance of the Justices in the case of Hirota and others who joined in his motion for leave to file a petition for the writ of habeas corpus, it is necessary to recall some of the lesser German war criminal cases. These included a number of convictions of officers and civilians who sought review in the Supreme Court after trials by United States military tribunals mostly in Nürnberg and Dachau. These included the case of General Milch, sentenced to life imprisonment for slave labor, crimes against humanity, etc., the "medical cases" involving Karl Brandt, Hitler's personal physician, the medical director of the Buchenwald concentration camp and a dozen others, the *Stroop* case in which the defendants had been convicted of the murder of American aviators grounded on German soil, and the famous *Malmedy* cases in which American prisoners of war had been murdered during the Battle of the Bulge. All in all, there were approximately a hundred cases in which German war criminals sought leave to file petitions for the writ of habeas corpus.

Until Hirota's case, all petitions had been summarily denied usually by an evenly divided vote of the Justices. Rutledge, Murphy, Douglas and Black consistently dissented, maintaining that hearings should be ordered and arguments held on the issue of the Court's jurisdiction. Four Justices adhered to the position that it was clear that the Supreme Court had no original jurisdiction in habeas corpus. Justice Jackson had declined to participate in all of these cases because of his activities as chief prosecutor in the international military proceedings in Nürnberg and his identification in other respects with the trials of war criminals. Only in the *Stroop* cases were the petitions denied by a unanimous Court. The practice of summary dismissal without hearings, it appears, was first adopted by the Court in Milch's case. Rutledge objected vigorously to this departure from the usual rule, namely, that the votes of four Justices were sufficient to insure oral argument. *A fortiori* this rule should be followed when the Justices were evenly divided.

In *Hirota,* Jackson departed from his previous practice, and took part in the decision to hear arguments by joining the dissenters.

In so doing, he stated his reasons in an opinion of historic importance. "If I add my vote," he wrote, "to those who favor denying these applications for want of jurisdiction, it is irrevocable."

> The Japanese will be executed and their partisans will forever point to the dissents of four members of the Court to support their accusation that the United States gave them less than justice. This stain, whether deserved or not, would be impressed upon the record of the United States in Oriental memory for all time to come. If, however, I vote with those who would grant temporary relief, it may be that fuller argument and hearing will convert one or more of the Justices on the one side or the other from the views that have equally divided them in the German cases.[36]

As it turned out, "fuller argument" did, indeed, so convert two members of the Court from their former doubts. Whether Rutledge's doubts were resolved, as we shall see, will never be known.

Thus did Jackson deviate from his previously consistent policy. The Rutledge papers disclose an interesting basis for speculation as to the factors which persuaded Jackson to do so. My colleague, Professor Louis Pollak who was Rutledge's law clerk at the time, had submitted the usual initial memorandum in which he accurately pointed out that the decision would probably turn on the issues, (1) whether the tribunal which convicted Hirota was "international" and (2) if so, whether an American court had jurisdiction to review the decision. He felt that arguments should be heard on the first issue. If it were decided that the tribunal was international in character, the second issue would be presented. In such an event he supposed that Jackson would "be forced to state his position which would mean a 5 to 4 denial of jurisdiction." Pollak added that "perhaps it would be just as well to force that issue to decision, even if it be adverse."

This may explain the preparation by Rutledge of his unpublished dissenting opinion on the issue whether hearings should be set. "For me," he wrote, "the applications set forth serious challenges to the validity of the tribunal's constitution and jurisdiction. . . . The questions presented raise doubts so serious that in conscience I cannot join my brethren in summary denial." Whether the circulation of this opinion among the Justices was intended to persuade Jackson to break a tie vote we do not know. In any event, Jackson's participation by voting with the dissenters eliminated any occasion for the publication of the opinion. Oral arguments were held and the Court declined to disturb convictions of Hirota and the other petitioners by a majority of six, Black and Douglas voting with Burton, Frankfurter, Reed and the Chief Justice. Douglas noted that he would release a concurring opinion at a later time. Murphy dissented without opinion while Rutledge reserved his vote, to be announced at some indefinite future time. He died some nine months later without announcement of his position. With the cases disposed of by a clear and substantial majority, Jackson refrained from voting. Military officials acted with customary punctuality. Two days after the Court refused to act, Hirota, ex-Premier Togo, and five others were hanged.

In its brief *Per Curiam* opinion, the majority held that the tribunal which tried the accused was international in character over which the Court had no appellant jurisdiction.[37] The implication of the decision, of course, was that no civilian court of any of the allied powers could review the decisions of the tribunal and that the convicted prisoners were without appellate relief. Hirota's was the first appeal to the Supreme Court by either German or Japanese war criminals convicted by an international court. The original Nürnberg prisoners made no effort to obtain review either from the Supreme Court or from British, French, or Russian courts.[38]

Douglas filed his concurring opinion on June 27, 1949. Although the tribunal which tried and convicted Hirota was "international," he pointed out that it was an American officer who held these prisoners and the Court's process could reach him wherever he might be. "To that extent at least the Constitution follows the flag." General MacArthur "is an American citizen who is performing functions for our government. It is our Constitution which he supports and defends. . . . I assume that we have no authority to review the judgment of an international tribunal. But if, as a result of unlawful action, one of our Generals holds a prisoner in his custody, the writ of habeas corpus can effect a release from that custody." In other words, he seemed to be saying that General MacArthur could not divest himself of constitutional limitations on his activities merely because he acted for nations which imposed no such limitations. Nevertheless, Douglas concurred in the decision of the majority. The tribunal which convicted Hirota and his fellow prisoners did so, he thought, as an exercise of naked power. "For the capture and control of those who were responsible for the Pearl Harbor incident was a political question on which the President as Commander-in-Chief, and as spokesman for the nation in foreign affairs, had the final say."[39]

Although the ultimate result so far as petitioners were concerned, was not changed by Jackson's participation, his decision to vote with the dissenters to summary denial was undoubtedly a wise one. As the *Washington Post* editorialized,[40] "It would have been tragic if an evenly divided Court had declined to hear an issue of this sort. Men would have gone to the gallows under circumstances casting serious doubt upon the validity of their condemnation." The same newspaper was less pleased with the final disposition of the case. A month later under the title "Injustice in Tokyo," it felt that it was now even more evident "that the good name of justice, let alone of the United States, has been compromised by the war criminal cases in Tokyo."[41] The *Post* had been troubled by the *Yamashita* decision. Its worries, like those of Rutledge, were now compounded.

Juries—Grand and Petit

One of the most unusual cases ever to come before the Supreme Court involved the "one-man grand jury" contrivance of the law of Michigan. What happened in this case, briefly, was as follows: A man named Oliver, in response to a subpoena, appeared before a judge as a witness. The judge was investigating gambling and corruption in government, acting under a Michigan law as a grand jury. The questioning was conducted in secret. The witness was not permitted to have counsel or friends present and the public was excluded. At a certain stage of the questioning, the judge-grand jury told the witness that neither he nor his judicial advisors who were present believed his story. It seems that in addition to what the judge regarded as inconsistent and evasive in Oliver's testimony, at least one other witness also examined in secret, had given testimony which the judge thought confirmed his belief that Oliver had perjured himself. The judge-grand jury then turned himself into a prosecutor-judge-petit jury, charged the witness with contempt, convicted him and sentenced him to sixty days in jail.

This one-man grand jury law was enacted by the Michigan legislature in response to a recommendation of the state bar association. Actually the bar association had recommended that justices of the peace be vested with inquisitorial powers comparable to those traditionally conferred upon coroners. The law, however, vested these powers in police judges and trial judges as well. It also authorized the appointment by the judge-grand jury of detectives, prosecutors, and other staff members and provided for punishment for contempt in the event the judge believed a witness to be evasive or untruthful.

This procedure, of course, was a considerable innovation and departure from the normal practice of the traditional twelve to twenty-three member grand jury. As Justice Black, in his opinion for the Court pointed out:

> Grand juries investigate, and the usual end of their investigation is either a report, a "no-bill" or an indictment. They do not try and they do not convict. They render no judgment. When their work is finished by the return of an indictment, it cannot be used as evidence against the person indicted. Nor may he be fined or sentenced to jail until he has been tried and convicted after having been afforded the procedural safeguards required by due process of law. . . . Witnesses who refuse to testify before grand juries are tried on contempt charges before judges sitting in open court.[42]

It was quite evident that the Michigan procedure was a travesty on both grand jury and criminal court procedure. Oliver brought a habeas corpus proceeding to obtain his release from prison. The Supreme Court of Michigan denied relief. The Supreme Court of the United States dealt with the case as one involving the right of a defendant in a case of criminal contempt and it judged the powers of the judge-grand jury, not as a grand jury but by the constitutional standards applicable to a criminal trial. By these standards, the prisoner had been denied due process of law—the one-man grand jury was unconstitutional.

Justice Black found several aspects of the judge-grand jury's performance to have violated the Fourteenth Amendment. In the first place the secrecy of the proceedings alone was fatal. There is no place in this country for criminal trials *in camera*. Since the abolition of the Court of the Star Chamber in 1641, there has been no such place in Anglo-American traditions. Americans did not need the examples of such trials in Hitler's Germany or in Stalin's Russia to warn them of the dangers of this form of tyranny. They saw to it in the Sixth Amendment that the national government which they were creating could resort to no such methods. "In all criminal prosecutions, the accused shall enjoy the right to a speedy and public trial." And Black pointed out that forty-one of the (then) forty-eight states had prohibitions of secret trials in their constitutions, two other states had statutes to that effect and still a third had apparently done so by judicial decision. "The knowledge that every criminal trial is subject to contemporaneous review in the forum of public opinion," the Justice wrote, "is an effective restraint on possible abuse of judicial power."

Of course, a "public trial" does not necessarily mean that every member of the public is entitled to be present at every stage of the proceedings. Young children, for example, may properly be excluded from trials involving testimony concerning episodes so unfit for them to hear that they can find access to them only on television programs. But Justice Black declared that he had found no American case, in which every one except the judge's staff was excluded throughout the trial.

Again, the procedure was invalid because Oliver never had his "day in court," in the sense that he did not have reasonable notice of the charge against him, an opportunity to be heard in his defense, the right to be faced with hostile witnesses and an opportunity to cross-examine them, the chance to offer witnesses in his defense, and the assistance of counsel.

Justice Black distinguished and explained the type of summary conviction of contempt committed within the personal view of the judge, as for example in the *Terry* case.[43] Mrs. Terry had so misbehaved in the courtroom that the judge ordered the marshal to remove her. While attempting to obey the judge's order, the marshal was assaulted and beaten over the head with a gun by Terry who immediately fled from the courtroom. Shortly thereafter, in Terry's absence, the judge held him guilty of contempt and sentenced him forthwith, without notice or hearing. This ruling was upheld by the Supreme Court as one of a "class of contempts which, being committed in the face of the court, imply a purpose to destroy or impair its authority, to obstruct the transaction of its business, or to insult or intimidate those charged with the duty of administering the law."[44] The judge who sentenced Terry was Justice Stephen J. Field of the Supreme Court while sitting on circuit in California, as Justices did in those days. Terry was subsequently shot to death by a United States marshal, acting as body guard for the Justice, when Terry sought to kill Field at a railroad restaurant in Lathrop, California, about a year after the contempt episode.[45]

It is obvious that the trial court must maintain some semblance of order in the courtroom. Any overt behavior which interferes with the work at hand must be dealt with summarily. But the Supreme Court has made quite clear the limitations on this type of procedure. As Justice Black explained in the *Oliver* case:

That the holding in the Terry case is not to be considered as an unlimited abandonment of the basic due process procedural safeguards, even in contempt cases, was spelled out with emphatic language in Cooke v. United States, 267 US 517, 69 LEd 767, 45 SCt 390, a contempt case arising in a federal district court. There it was pointed out that for a court to exercise the extraordinary but narrowly limited power to punish for contempt without adequate notice and opportunity to be heard, the court-disturbing misconduct must not only occur in the court's immediate presence, but that the judge must have personal knowledge of it acquired by his own observation of the contemptuous conduct. This Court said that knowledge acquired from the testimony of others, or even from the confession of the accused, would not justify conviction without a trial in which there was an opportunity for defense. Furthermore, the Court explained the Terry rule as reaching only such conduct as created "an open threat to the orderly procedure of the court and such a flagrant defiance of the person and presence of the judge before the public" that, if "not instantly suppressed and punished, demoralization of the court's authority will follow."[46]

The *Oliver* and *Cooke* cases would appear to uphold the right to notice and hearing in contempt cases within the broadest limits. Only when there is "demoralization of the court's authority" by "flagrant defiance" can there be an exception. Unfortunately, at least two subsequent cases throw serious doubt on the durability of this principle.

A year or so after the *Oliver* case, a lawyer was summarily adjudged guilty of contempt of a Texas court while participating in a case in which he represented a claimant seeking compensation under the Texas Workmen's Compensation Act for injuries to a foot sustained while he was in the course of employment.[47] While making his opening argument to the jury, an incident occurred as follows. (Mr. Fisher was the lawyer found guilty of contempt. Mr. Cox was opposing counsel.)

"Opening argument to Jury of Plaintiff's Attorney, Joe J. Fisher:

"Now, bear in mind, gentlemen, that this is what we call a specific injury. A general injury is an injury to the entire body. This is what is known as a specific injury, and it is confined to the left foot. We have specific injuries where you have injuries to the eye, to your hand, and to your foot; this is an injury to the foot, to the left foot; and the law states the amount of maximum compensation which a person can receive for such an injury, that is, one hundred and twenty-five weeks. That is the most compensation Anderson Godfrey could receive, would be one hundred and twenty-five weeks, because his injury is confined to his left foot. That is all we are asking. Now, that means one hundred and twenty-five weeks times the average weekly compensation rate.

"By Mr. Cox: Your Honor please—

"By the Court: Wait a minute.

"By Mr. Cox: The jury is not concerned with the computation; it has only one series of issues. That is not before the jury.

"By the Court: That has all been agreed upon.

"By Mr. Fisher: I think it is material, Your Honor, to tell the jury what the average weekly compensation is of this claimant so they can tell where he is.

"By the Court: They are not interested in dollars and cents.

"By Mr. Fisher: They are interested to this extent—

"By the Court: Don't argue with me. Go ahead. I will give you your exception to it.

"By Mr. Fisher: Note our exception.

"By the Court: All right.

"[By Mr. Fisher:] This negro, as I stated, can only recover one hundred and twenty-five weeks compensation, at whatever compensation the rate will figure under the law.

"By Mr. Cox: I am objecting to that discussion, Your Honor, as to what the plaintiff can recover.

"By the Court: Gentlemen! Mr. Fisher, you know the rule, and I have sustained his objection.

"By Mr. Fisher: I am asking—

"By the Court: Don't argue with me. Gentlemen, don't give any consideration to the statement of Mr. Fisher.

"By Mr. Fisher: Note our exception. I think I have a right to explain whether it is a specific injury or general injury.

"By the Court: I will declare a mistrial if you mess with me two minutes and a half, and fine you besides.

"By Mr. Fisher: That is all right. We take exception to the conduct of the Court.

"By the Court: That is all right; I will fine you $25.00.

"By Mr. Fisher: If that will give you any satisfaction.

"By the Court: That is $50.00; that is $25.00 more. Mr. Sheriff come get it. Pay the clerk $50.00.

"By Mr. Fisher: You mean for trying to represent my client?

"By the Court: No, sir; for contempt of Court. Don't argue with me.

"By Mr. Fisher: I am making no effort to commit contempt, but merely trying to represent the plaintiff and stating in the argument—

"By the Court: Don't tell me. Mr. Sheriff, take him out of the courtroom. Go on out of the courtroom. I fine you three days in jail.

"By Mr. Fisher: If that will give you any satisfaction; you know you have all the advantage by you being on the bench.

"By the Court: That will be a hundred dollar fine and three days in jail. Take him out.

"By Mr. Fisher: I demand a right to state my position before the audience.

"By the Court: Don't let him stand there. Take him out."

The attorney brought an action for his release on a writ of habeas corpus. His conviction was affirmed by the Supreme Court of Texas and upheld in the Supreme Court of the United States. Justice Reed, in an opinion for the Court denied that the prisoner had been deprived of his liberty without due process of law, as claimed. He thought that such "mildly provocative language" from the bench was insufficient to afford constitutional protection for an attorney who had shown contempt for the judge as appeared in the case.

Justices Murphy and Rutledge dissented. Murphy thought the judge had acted in an irresponsible manner and Rutledge felt forced to conclude that the judge's behavior indicated that he had acted in the heat of temper and not with that calm control which the fair administration of judicial office commands under the circumstances. "Whatever the provocation, there can be no due process in trial in the absence of calm judgment and action, untinged with anger, from the bench."[48]

The first Smith Act trial, involving a number of high-ranking officers of the Communist Party, began January 17th, 1949, and ended on October 14th, 1949, after nine months of harrowing experiences for all participants and especially for Judge Medina whose phenomenal patience must have been close to the breaking point on more than one occasion. After the entry of the verdict convicting the accused of conspiracy to advocate the overthrow of the government by force, the trial judge addressed the defendant's lawyers, saying, "Now I turn to some unfinished business." He then read from a contempt certificate according to which the lawyers, without a hearing, then and there stood convicted of criminal contempts. Sentences of from thirty days to six months imprisonment were imposed. The several specifications amounted to a charge of a conspiracy to obstruct justice by the various contemptuous acts enumerated.[49]

On appeal to the Second Circuit Court of Appeals, the ruling of Judge Medina was affirmed by a vote of two to one and the Supreme Court declined to review the case over the protests of Justices Black and Douglas.[50] Judge Charles E. Clark's dissent in the Court of Appeals was noteworthy. He felt strongly that there was no justification for denying the lawyers a hearing on all charges. The trial was over when they were held guilty of contempt. It was unnecessary for the judge to exercise summary authority. With admirable skill and finesse he had successfully completed the trial. Moreover, the charge that the attorneys had evolved a "plan" to make "concerted" efforts to disrupt the trial by creating "disorder and confusion" was such that it could hardly have taken place entirely in open court. It is altogether improbable that the "plan" was agreed upon in the presence of the judge. The Federal Rules of Criminal Procedure then in force provided for summary punishment for contempt only when the judge certifies "that he saw or heard the conduct constituting contempt and that it was committed in the actual presence of the Court." In all other cases, there must be notice and hearing and if "the contempt charged involves disrespect to or criticism of a judge, that judge is disqualified from presiding" unless the defendants consent thereto.[51]

Justices Frankfurter and Jackson dissented in the *Oliver* case on the grounds that the issue of a public trial, emphasized in the Court's opinion, was never raised in the Michigan courts nor passed on by the state's highest tribunal. Relying on the principle constantly stressed by him, Justice Frankfurter thought it more consonant with the delicate relations between the United States and the courts of the states, "that the courts of the States be given the fullest opportunity, by proper presentation of the issues, to make such a finding of unconstitutionality."[52] The case, in his opinion, should have been returned to the state supreme court to enable it to pass on the point. The Justice also pointed out that this was an "attempt of a State having the seventh largest population in the Union to curb or mitigate the commission of crimes by effective prosecution." It is not altogether clear what point Frankfurter was making but there appears to be an overtone of caution in considering the constitutionality of serious state experiments in dealing with the problem of criminality. If so, Rutledge directed an answer to the argument in his opinion in which he expressed full agreement with Justice Black's views but felt that there was more which needed to be said.

It is to be noted that at no place in Justice Black's opinion is there any suggestion that the procedural safeguards of the Sixth Amendment are applicable to the case by "incorporation" in the Fourteenth Amendment. Of course, he was writing the opinion of the Court and, with Frankfurter and Jackson dissenting, he wanted as large a majority as possible. In any event, it was left to Rutledge to add the incorporation argument in his concurring opinion which he did in one of the most persuasive pleas for that doctrine that has ever been made. Only extensive quotations from the text can convey the full power of his argument and the depth of feeling behind it.

> The case demonstrates how far this Court departed from our constitutional plan when, after the Fourteenth Amendment's adoption, it permitted selective departure by the states from the scheme of ordered personal liberty established by the Bill of Rights. In the guise of permitting the states to experiment with improving the administration of justice, the Court left them free to substitute, "in spite of the absolutism of continental governments," their "ideas and processes of civil justice" in place of the time-tried "principles and institutions of common law" perpetuated for us in the Bill of Rights. Only by an exercise of this freedom has Michigan been enabled to adopt and apply her scheme as was done in this case. . . .

> So long as they stand, so long as the Bill of Rights is regarded here as a strait jacket of Eighteenth Century procedures rather than a basic charter of personal liberty, like experimentations may be expected from the states. And the only check against their effectiveness will be the agreement of a majority of this Court that the experiment violated fundamental notions of justice in civilized society.

> I do not conceive that the Bill of Rights, apart from the due process clause of the Fifth Amendment, incorporates all such ideas. But as far as its provisions go, I know of no better substitutes. A few may be inconvenient. But restrictions upon authority for securing personal liberty, as well as fairness in trial to deprive one of it, are always inconvenient—to the au-

thority so restricted. And in times like these I do not think substitutions imported from other systems, including continental ones, offer promise on the whole of more improvement than harm, either for the cause of perfecting the administration of justice or for that of securing and perpetuating individual freedom, which is the main end of our society as it is of our Constitution.

One cannot attribute the collapse of liberty in Europe and elsewhere during recent years solely to the "ideas and processes of civil justice" prevailing in the nations which have suffered that loss. Neither can one deny the significance of the contrast between their success in maintaining systems of ordered liberty and that of other nations which in the main have adhered more closely to the scheme of personal freedoms the Bill of Rights secures. This experience demonstrates, I think, that it is both wiser and safer to put up with whatever inconveniences that charter creates than to run the risk of losing its hard-won guaranties by dubious, if also more convenient substitutions imported from alien traditions.

The states have survived with the nation through great vicissitudes, for the greater part of our history, without wide departures or numerous ones from the plan of the Bill of Rights. They accepted that plan for the nation when they ratified those amendments. They accepted it for themselves, in my opinion, when they ratified the Fourteenth Amendment. [Citation.] It was good enough for our fathers. I think it should be good enough for this Court and for the states.

Room enough there is beyond the specific limitations of the Bill of Rights for the states to experiment toward improving the administration of justice. Within those limitations there should be no laboratory excursions, unless or until the people have authorized them by the constitutionally provided method. This is no time to experiment with established liberties.[53]

Justice Rutledge's feelings about the judge-grand jury law of Michigan were further forcibly reflected in "a letter to a friend." A couple of weeks after the decision, he received a congratulatory letter from Dean Henry M. Bates of the University of Michigan Law School who, for many years, had taught Constitutional Law at that institution. "The opinion [Rutledge's]," the Dean wrote, "is incisive, vigorous, and makes, in an astonishingly brief space, a fine demonstration of the importance of protecting our so-called Bill of Rights."

And then he added, "The one-man grand jury in this state has been dangerous." Rutledge's reply included the following paragraph:

> It is really shocking to me that a case like *Oliver* could arise within the United States, but even more so that it could come from the great state of Michigan. One gets the feeling at times that shouting in dissent or even whispering becomes, if not entirely useless, then boresome to the country. But, whether fortunately or unfortunately, in the face of such an over-all deprivation of right I could not keep silent in this instance, and of course I could say some things that the writer of the opinion for the Court was not free to include.

The New York "blue ribbon" jury had smoother constitutional sailing than the Michigan "one-man" grand jury, although it survived by the margin of one Justice's vote. This device of law enforcement officials was something as follows: The administration of general legislation pertaining to petit juries produced a general jury panel of 60,000 from a population of 1,800,000 in New York County at that time. To qualify, a person had to be literate, of sound mind and character, never convicted of a serious crime, and between the ages of 21 and 70. Exempt from service were clergymen, doctors, lawyers, dentists, pharmacists, embalmers, optometrists, firemen, policemen, editors and other journalists and members of the armed services.

Sifting procedures, however, caused a shrinkage of the general panel of 60,000 to the special or "blue ribbon" panel of approximately 3,000. Either the prosecution or the defense could request a jury from this panel in a criminal case. The trial judge had discretion to grant or deny the request. In *Fay* v. *New York*[54] the request of the prosecution for such a jury was granted. The accused were two officers of labor unions charged with extortion from contractors who employed members of the unions, Hod Carriers and Operating Engineers. They were found guilty. Justice Jackson, writing for the Court, held that the special jury did not deprive the accused of due process of law or the equal protection of the law by its method of selection. He found no discrimination on the basis of occupation. It was not proven by the evidence that laborers and service employees were "systematically, intentionally and deliberately" excluded, nor that women were so excluded, nor was it established that such juries were more prone to convict than those drawn from the general panel. The standards applicable for inclusion on the "blue ribbon" panel being intelligence, citizenship and understanding of the English language, a lack of proportional representation of any economic class did not indicate a violation of due process or equal protection. There must be a clear showing of discrimination. The state's right to apply intelligence and citizenship tests seemed clear to the majority. Moreover, no one has a constitutional right to have friends on the jury.

Although the Judicial Council of New York had on a number of occasions recommended that "special" juries be abolished, the Court could find no constitutional reasons for doing so. To the Council's findings that, over a two year period, "blue ribbon" juries did in fact convict in double the number of convictions by ordinary juries, the Court answered that it was not shown that these convictions were unwarranted.

The data adduced in the case on women jurors was interesting. Approximately 7,000 women were on the general panel of 60,000 but only 30 on the special panel of 3,000. Jackson pointed out that for nearly a half century after the enactment of the Fourteenth Amendment, only men sat on juries. Washington was the first state to permit women jurors and that was as late as 1911. In 1945, the Department of Labor reported that seventeen states did not permit women on juries. Even of these two (male) appellants had "standing" to complain that women were systematically excluded or discriminated against, it would be of no avail. Justice Jackson could find no constitutional requirement to set aside verdicts of juries "unleavened by feminine influence."

Justice Murphy wrote a dissent joined by Justices Rutledge and Black. They took the view that the equal protection clause "prohibits a state from convicting any person by use of a jury which is not impartially drawn from a cross section of the community." They believed that the following statistics demonstrated that the "blue ribbon" jury was not so constituted:

	Percentage of total experienced labor forces in Manhattan	Percentage of representation on "blue ribbon" panel
Professional and semi-professional......	12.1	18.8
Proprietors, managers and officials......	9.3	43
Clerical, sales and kindred workers......	21.3	38
Craftsmen, foremen and kindred workers	7.7	0.2
Operatives and kindred workers........	17	0
Service workers.......................	27.6	0
Laborers.............................	4.9	0
Farmers..............................	0.1	0

Although the discrimination was "subtle and sophisticated," the proof, they thought, was adequate to demonstrate that this panel,

like every discriminatorily selected "blue ribbon" panel, suffers from
a constitutional infirmity—denial of equal protection. Murphy continued:

> There is no constitutional right to a jury drawn from a
> group of uneducated and unintelligent persons. Nor is there
> any right to a jury chosen solely from those at the lower end
> of the economic and social scale. But there is a constitutional
> right to a jury drawn from a group which represents a cross-
> section of the community. And a cross-section of the community
> includes persons with varying degrees of training and intelli-
> gence and with varying economic and social positions. Under
> our Constitution, the jury is not to be made the representative
> of the most intelligent, the most wealthy or the most success-
> ful, nor of the least intelligent, the least wealthy or the least
> successful. It is a democratic institution, representative of all
> qualified classes of people.

Crime and Punishment

"I shot a cop," Malinski was reported to have told his girl friend,
his brother-in-law and an old criminal side-kick. In a later confession
to the police, he implicated Rudish. Both were tried, convicted and
sentenced to death in the state courts of New York. The Supreme
Court reversed the conviction of Malinski on the ground that the
police coerced a confession from him. The Justices divided five to
four. But the Court affirmed the conviction of Rudish, concluding that
his conviction was in no way dependent on Malinski's confession.
Both prisoners had been tried together but their cases had been submitted to the jury separately. Justice Douglas wrote for the Court.
Justice Frankfurter wrote a separate, concurring opinion. Justices
Rutledge and Murphy dissented from the affirmance of Rudish's conviction while Chief Justice Stone supported by Justices Roberts, Reed
and Jackson thought that both convictions should be affirmed. All in
all there were thirty-seven pages of opinions.

A policeman named Fox had been shot and killed by robbers while
escorting a manager of a theatre to a bank depository at night in
Coney Island. It was late when the pedestrians approached a parked
automobile near the corner of an intersection. There were only a
few persons on the street. The door of the car on the sidewalk side
was open. As the two passed, a man jumped out, knocked the manager down and shot the officer. He then picked up the bag of money,
got back into the automobile and drove off. The wounded police
officer fired a half dozen shots as he lay on the sidewalk. None of the

three robbers was identified. The few witnesses were able to testify only to the speed of the automobile, the number of persons in it and the sound of the officer's revolver shots.

Malinski was picked up by the police a year and a half later while on his way to work. They did not arraign and book him but instead took him to the Bossert Hotel in Brooklyn. He arrived about eight A.M. The police immediately stripped and kept him naked for three hours. They then gave him his shoes, socks, underwear and a blanket. He remained that way until six o'clock in the evening. Taking off a suspect's clothes is supposed to be standard police practice, to look for bullet wounds—among other things. "Why this talk about being undressed? Of course they had a right to undress him to look for bullet scars, and keep the clothes off him. That was quite proper procedure. That is some more psychology—let him sit around with a blanket on him, humilitate him there for a while; let him sit in the corner; let him think he was going to get a shellacking." One officer testified that Malinski was still stripped at three A.M. the following morning.

It was claimed that the prisoner confessed about five or six in the afternoon of the first day but, if so, no transcript was made. A further confession was made in writing four days later. He claimed that he was beaten by the police the first day, but this was denied by them. He complained of illness and asked to see a doctor. This was denied. He also asked to see a rabbi and an assistant district attorney whom he named, and a lawyer. He was refused. In his address to the jury the prosecuting attorney explained that they weren't going to let Malinski contact "a smart mouthpiece" who would "sue out writs;" that when you were trying a murder case, especially that of a police officer, you don't give the accused "a pat on the back and ask him if he wants anything;" that the officer in charge was a veteran in the department of seventeen years and was not going to let "this jerk from the East Side tell him his business."

All day long, the officers and detectives were questioning him. It went on and off for nineteen hours until three or four o'clock the following morning. Malinski testified that when he would fall asleep, the police would wake him up for further questioning. This continued for several days by relays of police and detectives. On the third day he was taken to the scene of the crime in Coney Island, an assistant district attorney and a stenographer accompanying and questioning him all the way. Back in the hotel, the questioning continued until two o'clock in the morning. Ten or twelve detectives were still with him on the fourth day when he was taken to the police station and questioned some more for several hours. At about two A.M. or a little later the next morning Malinski confessed in writing.

Although there was considerable evidence of Malinski's guilt other than his confession, notably the testimony of the three witnesses who swore that he admitted to them that he had "shot a cop," five Justices felt reversal was required because of the circumstances of the oral confession after ten hours of continuous questioning. They concluded that the evidence made it clear that this confession, at least, was the product of fear. As Justice Rutledge put it in his opinion, the first day's proceedings weaved into a "pattern typical of 'third degree' method." Since the judgment of conviction rested in part on a coerced conviction, it required reversal.[55]

It was the second and written confession which implicated Rudish and although the majority did not actually make a finding, it conceded, for purposes of the latter's appeal that it, too, was coerced. The jury had been instructed that that confession was admitted and should be considered only against Malinski. Moreover, the judge, with the approval of counsel for Rudish, substituted "X" for Rudish and told the jury it should not speculate on the identity of "X." In sustaining the jury's finding and affirming the judgment against Rudish, the New York Court of Appeals stated that it in no way relied upon this or any other Malinski confession to the police.

Justice Rutledge was not so easily satisfied as to the *Rudish* case. He found the final written confession as coerced as the first oral one. In fact he thought "the entire procedure, from the time Malinski was taken into custody until his written confession nearly five days later, was a single and continuous process of coercion. . . ." He was convinced that it was naive to think that the identity of Rudish had been kept from the jury. Under the circumstances of the case, including the fact that the two prisoners were tried together, he thought the device of substituting "X" for Rudish's name probably served to emphasize his identity rather than conceal it. He was equally confident that due process of law forbade the conviction of one person based on a confession wrung from another by coercion. "A conviction supported only by such a confession could be but a variation of trial by ordeal."

Justice Frankfurter's separate opinion is in fact a concurrence in the Court's judgment in both cases. It consists, however, of a long discussion of the Justice's views of the due process clause of the Fourteenth Amendment and its effect on the administration of criminal justice. Congress could, of course, employ criminal sanctions to make effective and carry into execution, powers granted to it. Otherwise the entire field of criminal justice was left to the states by the original Constitution except that they were forbidden to pass Bills of Attainder, that is, the enactment of laws pronouncing an individual guilty of an offense and providing punishment without the usual judicial process. Nor did the Bill of Rights impose restrictions upon the states. The adoption of the Fourteenth Amendment in 1868 with its due process and other clauses made important changes. But unlike the limitations of the Bill of Rights on the power of Congress to impose criminal penalties, the due process clause was a general limitation and imposed no specific restrictions on the states.

The thrust of Frankfurter's opinion was to fortify the decision in *Palko* v. *Connecticut*[56] which had held that due process did not "incorporate" the double jeopardy prohibition of the Fifth Amendment and make it applicable to the states. The Bill of Rights, he argued, was prepared by eighteenth century statesmen to protect the individual against historic grievances. Some of these are not regarded as vital to a free society, *e.g.*, the requirement that criminal prosecution must be initiated by a grand jury. Others are so "fundamental" that they are necessarily implied in the comprehensive concept of "due process of law." The phrase "expresses a demand for civilized standards of law." It must have a meaning of its own, because the Fifth Amendment itself has a due process provision as applied to the federal government. It may not deprive a person of life, liberty or property "without due process of law." And so the Justice continued:

The Due Process Clause of the Fourteenth Amendment thus has potency different from and independent of the specific provisions contained in the Bill of Rights. Apart from all other considerations, how could it be otherwise without charging Madison and his great contemporaries in the framing and adoption of the Bill of Rights with writing into it a meaningless clause? The Fifth Amendment specifically prohibits prosecution of an "infamous crime" except by indictment; it forbids double jeopardy and self-incrimination, as well as deprivation of "life, liberty, or property, without due process of law." Not to attribute to due process of law an independent function but to consider it a shorthand statement of other specific clauses in the same Amendment is to charge those who secured the adoption of this Amendment with meretricious redundancy by indifference to a phrase—"due process of law"—which was one of the great instruments in the very arsenal of constitutional freedom which the Bill of Rights was to protect and strengthen. Of course the Due Process Clause of the Fourteenth Amendment has the same meaning. To suppose that "due process of law" meant one thing in the Fifth Amendment and another in the Fourteenth is too frivolous to require elaborate rejection.[57]

It is probably true that grand jury indictment as distinguished from a charge of crime by information filed by a prosecuting officer does not, today, appeal to most of us as a necessary incident of a civilized society. Nor does there appear to be anything sacred about the number "twelve" for a jury. Nevertheless, it is pretty clear that Madison and the others regarded them as important and there is evidence that they were so regarded in 1868. The redundancy argument, too, loses force when it is remembered that neither Justice Black nor anyone else has ever contended that due process of law was *limited* to the incorporation of the guarantees of the Bill of Rights, as Frankfurter conceded in his concurring opinion in a subsequent case.[58] Professor Crosskey quotes Justice Curtis in 1855[59] that the "due process of law" clause of the Fifth Amendment comprehended the other detailed requirements and prohibitions upon process contained in Amendments Four to Eight.[60]

Moreover, there is substantial historical evidence that the privileges and immunities clause of the Fourteenth Amendment was intended to make applicable to the states the same prohibitions as the Bill of Rights made applicable to the federal government. That clause provides that no state may abridge the privileges and immunities of the citizens of the United States. These "privileges and immunities" were intended, according to a member of Congress who was one of the draftsmen of the Amendment, to refer to the first eight Amendments of the Constitution. "These eight articles," he said, "I have shown never were limitations upon the power of the States, until made so by the fourteenth amendment."[61] And Justice Bradley, dissenting in the famous *Slaughter House* cases,[62] after mentioning freedom of speech, religion, assembly, freedom from searches and seizures, stated flatly that these and others specified in the Constitution, "or in the early amendments" thereto, were among the privileges of citizens of the United States.

During the Court's consideration of the *Malinski* case, Justice Black circulated a memo in which he said that one day he would write an opinion challenging what he regarded as Justice Frankfurter's "natural law" theory derived, presumably from Cardozo's opinion and the Court's decision in the *Palko* case. A case coming to the Court from California in 1947 offered the occasion. The state had amended its Penal Code in 1934 to provide that although a defendant in a criminal action cannot be compelled to take the stand and be a witness against himself, "the failure of the defendant to explain or to deny by

Conf. 1/18/47:

C.J. affirms,

Black: Thinks self-increm
applies to states, But
not sure this
violates it. Pass.

Reed: affirm, no
viol. of self-increm,
if applies,

F.F. affirm,

W.O.D. Reverse

F.M. Reverse,

R.H.J. affirm,

W.R. Reverse,

H.H.B affirm,

**RUTLEDGE'S CONFERENCE NOTES ON
ADAMSON v. CALIFORNIA**

his testimony any evidence or facts in the case against him may be commented upon by counsel." The appellant had been tried for murder, convicted and sentenced to death. The Supreme Court of California affirmed the conviction holding that the statute was constitutional.

That the Fifth Amendment protection against self-incrimination was not incorporated in the Fourteenth Amendment and thus applicable to criminal trials had been specifically decided as early as 1908.[63] Nevertheless, Justice Black's remarkable opinion in the *Adamson* case[64] carried Rutledge, Douglas and Murphy and, together with the Appendix, constitutes the most persuasive defense of the theory that the basic protections of individual liberty of the Bill of Rights are equally applicable to state as to federal actions. Rutledge's conference notes indicated that Black at first was undecided as to what position he would take on the case. It was not that he was uncertain as to the effect of the Fifth Amendment on state action; he was temporarily undecided as to whether there had in fact been self-incrimination. The tentative votes at this first conference were: the Chief Justice (Vinson), Justices Reed, Frankfurter, Jackson and Burton for affirming the conviction; Justices Douglas, Murphy and Rutledge for reversal; Justice Black, "pass."

Black did not think that the supreme law of the land should depend upon the Court's view of "civilization" at the given moment. Such an interpretation, he declared, would enable the Court to ignore the Bill of Rights and substitute its own judgment as to what state legislatures could and could not do. This power had been used in the past primarily to preserve the economic status quo, but far less often and "grudgingly" to protect individual civil rights as included in the Bill of Rights.

The argument as to how far, if at all, the Fourteenth Amendment "incorporates" the first eight Amendments continues, not only among the Justices but among scholars and commentators. It must be admitted that there is evidence to support both sides and there is considerable literature on the subject.[65]

"This case became a cause célèbre the moment it began." So began Justice Rutledge's dissent in the *United Mine Workers* case of 1947.[66] He thought, with Holmes that "great cases like hard cases make bad law." "For great cases," Holmes continued, "are called great, not by reason of their real importance in shaping the law of the future but because of some accident of immediate and overwhelming interest which appeals to the feelings and distorts the judgment."

Nothing could better describe the *Mine Workers'* case. John L. Lewis was anything but a popular character except among members of his union. The government had been forced to seize and operate the mines for a considerable period during the war. Many regarded Lewis as unpatriotic and un-American and, of course, he was the whipping boy of the professional anti-labor group. Today, it is almost commonplace for governors of states, superintendents of schools, and school boards to challenge the validity of Supreme Court decisions and, indeed, to defy direct orders of the courts. Only recently at the 1963 meeting of the American Bar Association, a Justice of the Supreme Court thought it necessary to warn the bar and the nation that democracy cannot exist long when prominent officials refuse to obey court decisions. But in 1947 it was news, because it was most unusual for otherwise responsible persons in public life or respectable organizations to behave in such manner.

The United States Government had taken possession of most of the nation's bituminous coal mines in May, 1946, pursuant to the War Labor Disputes Act which authorized seizure and operation of facilities necessary to the war effort. Such authority under the act terminated six months after the ending of hostilities. The President of the United Mine Workers entered into an agreement governing terms and conditions of employment for the period of government possession. In October of that year a dispute arose between the parties to this agreement. Lewis claimed that either party could give ten days' notice of a desire to negotiate another agreement and the other party was obligated to attend and negotiate in good faith, and fifteen days after the beginning of the conference either party could give notice of termination of the old agreement. The government disputed this contention but did enter negotiations. "Hostilities," at this time had not officially terminated and, indeed, were not so terminated until the following December when the President, by proclamation, declared them ended.

Fifteen days after the negotiating conference began, Lewis gave notice of termination of the agreement under which the miners were working. At the request of the government, a federal court issued a temporary order restraining the union from striking and Lewis from encouraging a strike. Two days later, pursuant to their "no contract, no work" policy, the miners walked out on strike. Over defendants' objection that the court had no jurisdiction to issue the injunction because the Norris-LaGuardia Act prohibited it, Lewis and the unions were held in both civil and criminal contempt, the former fined $10,000, the union $3,500,000. Roughly and generally, civil contempt has for its purpose to compel compliance with a court order while criminal contempt is to punish the defendant for noncompliance or other contumacious behavior.

The case was argued before the Supreme Court on January 14, 1947. The strike had long since been called off. The trial judge had extended the temporary restraining order on November 27, 1946 and heard arguments on his jurisdiction to issue the injunction. On November 29, he overruled defendants' motion to discharge and vacate it and held that he had power to enjoin the defendants from striking and that the prohibition of the Norris-LaGuardia Act against injunctions in labor disputes did not apply. Exactly what happened thereafter to induce Lewis to terminate the strike is not a matter of public knowledge, but presumably it was on advice of his lawyers. Drew Pearson, in his Washington Merry-Go-Round for December 6, 1946, gives the following account:

> When John L. Lewis' lawyers, Welly K. Hopkins and Joe Padway, came out of Supreme Court a week ago, newsmen reported them looking dejected and unhappy. Before they could be interviewed, Attorney General Tom Clark came to the rescue of his legal adversaries and whisked them away in his own limousine. Speculation has been rife ever since as to what happened inside the Chief Justice's chambers to make the two labor lawyers look so crestfallen.
>
> It is now possible to tell the inside story on that conference.
>
> The meeting with Chief Justice Vinson was for the purpose of seeing whether the Supreme Court would take immediate jurisdiction of the Miners' injunction dispute and to fix a time for argument. The Chief Justice listened carefully, said nothing, while labor lawyers Hopkins and Padway asked for a 25-day delay. They claimed they needed that time to prepare their case.
>
> To this Attorney General Clark flatly objected. In his slow but friendly Texas drawl, he pointed out that the Nation faced an emergency.
>
> . . . .
>
> Accordingly, he asked the Chief Justice to set Monday, December 16, as the date for argument, thus giving the miners nine days to prepare their case.
>
> "Would you like to know what I think?" asked square-jawed Chief Justice Vinson, who hitherto had said little.
>
> Both sides indicated they would like to have his views.
>
> "I had in mind," he continued, "setting argument for next Thursday."
>
> His words fell like a bombshell on Miner Lawyers Hopkins and Padway. This would have given them from December 7

to December 12, or five days, to prepare their case—as against nine days proposed by the Attorney General.

That ended the private conference in the Chief Justice's chambers, following which Hopkins and Padway rushed back to United Mine Workers Headquarters. Two hours later John L. Lewis called off his strike.

Three days before the oral arguments in the Supreme Court, Rutledge received a copy of an "Extra Bituminous Edition" of *The Miner.* This was a paper published in Wilkes-Barre, Pennsylvania, and while not an official organ of the United Mine Workers it was avowedly devoted to their interests. It described itself as "A Constructively Progressive Rank and File Paper, Serving in the Interest of Industrial Peace and Prosperity—Devoted to Community Progress." As found among his papers, a note in the Justice's handwriting was clipped to it: "Received 1/11/47. Filed without reading 1/11/47. W.R." In addition to the cartoon by Howards, the paper contained a front page editorial which read, in part, as follows:

On January 14, Attorney General Tom Clark's case against the United Mine Workers of America comes subject to judicial review by the nine Justices of the United States Supreme Court, uttermost bastion for the definition of constitutional law in the land.

. . . .

It has always been considered a cardinal principle in the code of American journalism to refrain from indulgence in editorial excursions, which might even in the remotest sense be construed as impingement upon the sovereign sanctity of judicial processes while a case of law is pending for disposition. This principle was so completely disregarded, so malignantly and venally breached and abused by over ninety percent of the press and radio, with impunity, and without censure by the court involved, that it can no longer be held to apply, in this particular instance, to an objectively fairminded editorial effort in behalf of the aggrieved parties.

. . . .

While it is true, that the nation was facing a dire emergency by a continued stoppage in the bituminous coal mining industry, it is an obvious contradiction and a flagrant inconsistency to contend that the crisis, which was then imminent, was occasioned by a violation of, interference with, or even by a distant threat to the sovereign power and functions of the peo-

"MURKY OVERCAST"

Cartoon by Howards reproduced by permission of The Miner.

ple of the United States on the part of the United Mine Workers of America.

. . . .

The threat to the national economy, and to the safety and well-being of the country last November, was created by governmental officials, who though representatives and servants of the people, caused a curtailment in the production of bituminous coal, by seeking, in violation of the sovereign interests of the citizens of the United States, to coerce 400,000 American citizens into submitting to involuntary servitude, under terms and conditions injurious to their health, safety and security. The remedy—the Constitution of the United States—was available then, as it is now, and within easy reach of any constituted authority, truly desirous of invoking the real sovereign powers of the nation.

The editorial concluded with a quotation from Justice Davis in the great case of *Ex parte Milligan:*

The Constitution of the United States is a law for rulers and people, equally in war and peace, and covers with the shield of its protection all classes of men, at all times and under all circumstances. Its provisions cannot be suspended during any of the great exigencies of government. Such a doctrine leads to anarchy and despotism.[67]

There turned out, because of the division of the Justices, three questions to be answered in the Supreme Court. The first was whether the federal district court had the power to issue the injunction. On this point Chief Justice Vinson and Justices Reed, Burton, Black and Douglas voted "yes;" the other four, Rutledge, Murphy, Frankfurter and Jackson, "no." The second question was whether the defendants were required to obey an invalid injunction. The Chief Justice and Justices Reed, Jackson, Burton and Frankfurter thought that they were so required. Justices Rutledge and Murphy thought that they were not. Inasmuch as Justices Black and Douglas had taken the position that the injunction was valid, they declined to pass on the question. It was unnecessary. One may wonder why the Court passed on this issue in view of its policy of avoiding all constitutional or, for that matter, any other question not required for the disposition of the case. The plausible and no doubt correct answer is that, this being an important and highly controversial case, the Chief Justice wanted to bolster the decision with as many affirmative votes as possible. Had the Court not taken up the second question the decision would have hung on a bare majority of five to four. As it was, the Chief Justice picked up two additional votes, Justices Jackson and Frankfurter, who believed that the defendants were bound to comply with the Court's order whether valid or not.

The third issue decided by the Court was whether the defendants should be fined for contempt. Justices Rutledge and Murphy, consistent throughout, answered "no." The five Justices, who thought the defendants should have obeyed the injunction even though invalid, answered "yes" with the proviso that a part of the three and a half million dollar fine against the union should be conditional.

Justices Black and Douglas thought all the fines should be conditional. The final holding was that the fine of $10,000 against Lewis was justified. As against the union, $700,000 was to be paid as a

"WHO ME?"

This Pulitzer Prize drawing by Pease reproduced by permission of the Newark News © *1947.*

penalty for criminal contempt. The remaining $2,800,000 was conditional. If the union purged itself by compliance with the injunction within five days after the issuance of the Court's mandate, that amount was to be remitted.

The Chief Justice wrote the opinion of the Court. The prohibition of injunctions in labor disputes contained in the Norris-LaGuardia Act was indeed intended to prevent strikebreaking by the courts, but neither the policy nor the legislative history of the Act, the opinion held, disclosed any intention of Congress that the law should apply to disputes between the Government and its employees. It is true, the Act was applicable to disputes between "employers and employees," but the Court did not construe the general term "employer" as including the sovereign without something to indicate that the term was to be so interpreted. Moreover, Vinson found the public policy of the Act to be an effort to relieve the helplessness of the individual worker to exercise actual liberty of contract in dealing with "owners of property" who have been permitted to "organize in the corporate and other forms of ownership association." The Act provided that its purpose was to contribute to the worker's "full freedom of association, self-organization, and designation of representatives of his own choosing, to negotiate the terms and conditions of his employment, and that he shall be free from the interference, restraint, or coercion of employers of labor, or their agents, in the designation of such representatives . . . for the purpose of collective bargaining. . . ." These considerations, on their face, Vinson declared, obviously "do not apply to the Government as an employer or to the relations between the Government and its employees."[68]

In an opinion remarkable for its incisiveness even for a judicial stylist of Justice Frankfurter's quality, he made a plausible case that although, as he concluded, the Norris-LaGuardia Act did, indeed, deprive the courts of jurisdiction to issue the injunction, either against Lewis or the union, nevertheless both were bound to conform to it and were in contempt of court for failure to do so. The trial court had jurisdiction to decide whether it had jurisdiction and therefore it could preserve existing conditions during the process of decision.

It required extended argument, lengthy briefs, study and reflection preliminary to adequate discussion in conference, before final conclusions could be reached regarding the proper interpretation of the legislation controlling the case. . . . To say that the authority of the court may be flouted during the time necessary to decide is to reject the requirements of the judicial process.[69]

Justice Frankfurter also made a convincing case that "the whole course of legislation indicates that Congress withheld the remedy of injunction." He had no doubt about it. The contention to the contrary was frivolous. Thus the two arguments of his opinion run head into each other. In concurring with the Chief Justice on the issue of the duty to obey an invalid injunction, he found that the question was "substantial," not "frivolous." "It required extended arguments, lengthy briefs, etc."[70] If one reads the arguments separately, each sounds persuasive. But presumably they were supposed to be read together.

Justice Jackson was the fifth Justice to hold that there is a duty to obey an injunction which the trial court or an appellate tribunal subsequently holds invalid. And only Justices Rutledge and Murphy took the opposite view. Of course, Frankfurter himself did not fail to qualify his proposition. It is not every purported ruling of a judge that must be obeyed. It is true, that a defendant may not himself decide whether he is to be brought before the bar of justice, but he must be able to recognize the difference between a bar of justice and a "kangaroo court." It is only in situations crystal clear to the layman and lawyer alike that he may do so. "Only when a court is so obviously traveling outside its orbit as to be merely usurping judicial forms and facilities may an order issued by a court be disobeyed and treated as though it were a letter to a newspaper."

Even so modified, Justice Rutledge could not agree. This was not a situation in which disobedience would destroy the subject matter of the litigation as, for example, where, after the Supreme Court had ordered a stay in proceedings against a prisoner in a state court, the sheriff disobeyed the order by engaging, with others, in a conspiracy to lynch the prisoner.[71] "Lewis and the United Mine Workers necessarily took the risk that the order would be found valid on review and, in that event, that punishment for contempt would apply. They did not take the risk that it would apply in any event, even if the order should be found void as beyond the jurisdiction of the Court to enter." He knew of no controlling case to the contrary.

What bothered Rutledge most was the failure of the trial court to differentiate clearly the civil from the criminal aspects of the case. There was in fact just one procedure. "In any other context than one of contempt," he wrote, "the idea that a criminal prosecution and a civil suit for damages or equitable relief could be hashed together in a single criminal-civil hodgepodge would be shocking to every American lawyer and to most citizens." He did not think the Constitution contemplated that there should be in any case an admixture of civil and criminal proceedings in one. Such an idea was altogether foreign to its spirit.

Rutledge believed that most of the guarantees of the Fifth and Sixth Amendments should apply to proceedings for criminal contempt. "Some at least are applicable" by virtue of the due process clause of the Fifth Amendment. He relied, in part, upon a previous decision of the Court which held that due process of law in the prosecution of contempt, except of that committed in open court, "requires that the accused should be advised of the charges and have a reasonable opportunity to meet them by way of defense or explanation." And the Court went further. "We think this includes the assistance of counsel, if requested, and the right to call witnesses to give testimony, relevant either to the issue of complete exculpation or in extenuation of the offense and in mitigation of the penalty to be imposed."[72]

Not only was the proceeding both civil and criminal, but so were the "fines." Each was imposed as a lump sum with no separation or allocation as to what part constituted damages suffered by the government, what was civil coercion to force defendants into compliance, and what part was penal. Such amounts are neither congealable nor fungible and there are, the Justice pointed out, standards for the assessment of each. Damages to the government may not exceed what is necessary for just compensation. For coercion, the amount should not exceed that required to insure obedience. As a penalty, the Eighth Amendment prohibiting cruel and unusual punishment, is applicable. When these distinct types are all lumped together, it is, he thought, impossible to apply the appropriate basis for measurement as required by law. Justice Murphy, who wrote a dissent of his own, joined in the Rutledge opinion.

As usual, Rutledge's mail was heavy. One woman from Albany wrote on a postcard that it "is decisions like yours that throw disrespect upon our Court and which has made it the laughing stock of the country since F.D.R. packed it to do his bidding." For the most part, however, it was favorable. Former Secretary Ickes, who knew what it was to deal with Lewis and his union, wrote admiringly that "he had a feeling of gratification as a citizen" that the Justice could be depended upon at all times "to see clearly through the issues that are presented to the Supreme Court and go to the heart of them." From Yale, Professor Rodell wrote that he believed the

Rutledge opinion would "go down in history as one of the Court's truly great dissents. Its arguments are as unanswerable as they were pitifully unanswered in the Court's opinion." The opinion, he continued, combined "scholarship of the highest order with statesmanship of the highest order." From Indiana University Law School, Professor Frank wrote that he thought Justice Rutledge's dissent in the United Miner's case was "the best thing," except the *Yamashita* dissent, that the Justice had ever done.

"After the current turmoil subsides a bit, they will be reciting those opening paragraphs in the law schools. They may even find their way into Fourth of July orations. They ought to." So wrote Ernest Kirschten of the *St. Louis Star-Times*. But, he continued quite seriously:

> Of course, it would have been naive not to recognize the pressures which were operating. So the possibility suggested itself that the Court would uphold the contempt citation on the very argument which Justice Frankfurter used. However, it seems to me that the Court ought to be above such expediency—especially since there is no logical answer to your argument on this point. It is sad to think that an American citizen is now liable to punishment for ignoring a restraining order, no matter how invalid. It gives the lower courts an intolerable power—and not alone in labor matters. Surely, this is not necessary to protect the "dignity and majesty of the law," since, as you pointed out, the citizen who ignores a contempt citation under these circumstances always assumes the risk of an adverse determination. Unhappily, I have not been able to say anything like this editorially. Nor is there space in newspaper columns for dissenting opinions. How illuminating it would be if there were!

Editorial comment, in general, tended to confirm Holmes' dictum about "great" cases and "bad" law. There was, of course, nothing surprising about the views of the *Chicago Tribune* which captioned its editorial, "The Lewis Decision is Not Enough." It demanded Congressional legislation outlawing such strikes permanently.[73] The *Washington Post* also approved the decision as "A Blow for Law and Order" although it conceded that the question whether the Norris-LaGuardia Act forbade injunctive relief was a "close one, with some margin for the majority view."[74] Even from his old journalistic friends in St. Louis, Justice Rutledge got scant support. The *Post-Dispatch*, after expressing "respect" for the dissents, concluded that "when all this is said, it remains that, in a time of national crisis the Government had to look to judicial tools to avert a possible catastrophe."[75] And it will be recalled that an editorial writer of the *Star-Times* of that city confessed that he could not write what he believed about the case.

On the other hand, the law reviews, for the most part, appeared to vary from skepticism to criticism of the majority position, particularly on the alternative ground of decision which attracted Justices Frankfurter and Jackson, that the union and Lewis were obliged to obey the order even though invalid. As the *Columbia Law Review* observed, this meant that the person against whom an injunction is issued must decide whether, as the Chief Justice put it, the question of jurisdiction is "frivolous" or "substantial." And he takes the risk that he guesses wrong. But "frivolous" and "substantial" do not have the same content in the minds of different Justices.[76]

The Right to Work

By January, 1949 some sixteen states had outlawed the "closed shop" or "union security" contracts either by statute or by constitutional amendment. Thirteen were in the southern and agricultural midwestern anti-labor block. The other three were Delaware, Nevada and Arizona. The constitutionality of these so-called "right-to-work" laws came before the Court early in the year on appeals from the Supreme Courts of North Carolina, Nebraska and Arizona. The cases involved an Arizona constitutional amendment and statutes of the other two states. Justice Black, writing for the Court, upheld the validity of these laws against a multipointed attack. Justice Murphy was the lone dissenter and he wrote no opinion. Justices Frankfurter and Rutledge wrote separate concurring opinions.[77]

The first complaint was that the laws violated the rights of unions and their members by denying them freedom of speech and assembly. This was pretty far-fetched. As Justice Black put it, "there cannot be wrung from a constitutional right of workers to assemble to discuss improvement of their own working standards, a further constitutional right to drive from remunerative employment all other persons who will not or can not, participate in union assemblies." To the charge that the equal protection clause of the Fourteenth Amendment was violated, Black answered that in identical language the North Carolina and Nebraska law forbade discrimination against union and non-union workers alike.

The unions also claimed that they were denied freedom of contract and thus were deprived of their "liberty" without due process of law. The answer here, too, was clear. Forbidding closed shop contracts between unions and employers was merely an enforcement device to eliminate discrimination against non-union employees. "If the states have constitutional power to ban such discrimination by law, they also have power to ban contracts which if performed would bring about the prohibited discrimination." Justice Black reviewed earlier cases in which the due process clause had been invoked by the Court to invalidate federal and state legislation, including laws prohibiting "yellow dog" contracts, so hated by organized labor. He then pointed out that the Court at least as early as 1934 had steadily rejected this "due process philosophy." No longer are Congress and state legislatures to be held in a strait jacket when they attempt to suppress business and industrial conditions which they regard as offensive to the public welfare.

The language of the Arizona constitutional amendment prohibited employment discrimination against non-union workers but not against union workers. Justice Black thought this unimportant in view of legislation forbidding "yellow dog" contracts. In one of his earlier draft opinions Rutledge dissented in this case. The law of Arizona, he argued, permitted discrimination against union men except by the use of "yellow dog" contracts. Apparently, he changed his mind and agreed with Black that, as a practical matter, discrimination against both union and non-union workers was effectively prohibited.

In this original draft Rutledge also voiced objection to a statement in Frankfurter's draft of his concurring opinion that the Court was a "non-democratic" institution and was "aristocratic" in tenure, not subject to democratic corrective processes. "I cannot agree," Rutledge wrote, "that in performing its highest function under the Constitution, it [the Court] acts either as a non-democratic or as an aristocratic institution. True it is not immediately responsive to popular will or demand. But the protection of the constitutional rights of individuals and of minorities is as much a part of the democratic process in our scheme as is giving rightful play for the working of other departments of government and the popular will." In the end, Frankfurter, while retaining the phrase "non-democratic" in reference to the Court, substituted the word "oligarchic" for "aristocratic" and Rutledge deleted all reference to the matter.

One point Rutledge insisted on in his concurrence. He reserved opinion on the issue whether the states could make it illegal or could enjoin a strike by union workers who refused to work with non-union men and whether the decision in these cases could be so interpreted. "[T]he right to prohibit contracts for union security is one thing. The right to force union members to work with non-union workers is entirely another." Justice Murphy, having dissented in the Arizona case, joined in the Rutledge concurrence in the other two.

In Justice Frankfurter's wide-ranging concurring opinion he invoked the views of the late Justice Brandeis before he became a member of the Court, on the evils of the closed shop. This and other aspects of the opinion drew the wrath of certain newspapers, particularly the *St. Louis Post-Dispatch*.[78] The burden of complaint was not so much the actual decision as in the overtones of the opinions which the editor thought cast a cloud on the merits of the closed shop. If the people of a state decided to outlaw this type of collective agreement, perhaps they had a constitutional right to do so. But in so holding it was unnecessary for the Court to indicate approval of such a policy. After quoting Frankfurter's dictum that "in the day-to-day working of our democracy it is vital that power of the non-democratic organ of our Government be exercised with rigorous self-restraint," the two full-column editorial continued:

> But having said this, Justice Frankfurter proceeds to throw away restraint. He literally studs his opinion with figures designed to show that the argument that a closed shop is needed by the union does not stand up statistically. He presents tables of union membership and employment from 1898 to 1948 and similar tables concerning the membership of the railroad brotherhood since 1919. He quotes "the experience of countries advanced in industrial democracy, such as Great Britain and Sweden, where deeply rooted acceptance of the principles of collective bargaining is not reflected in uncompromising demands for contractually guaranteed security."
>
> Then, as if to sweep the closed shop adherents off their feet, Justice Frankfurter reaches back to 1912 to quote a letter from Louis D. Brandeis to Lincoln Steffens. The Supreme Court Justice-to-be said, 37 years ago: "The American people should not, and will not accept unionism if it involves the closed shop."

On the same editorial page of the newspaper, Marquis Childs in his column praised highly both the Black and Frankfurter opinions. "Every union executive and organizer should read Justice Black's opinion and, equally important, the concurring opinion of Justice Frankfurter. From Justice Frankfurter who has been slurred more than anyone on the court by a smear bund, has come a penetrating analysis of the rights of the individual in relating to the power of mass organization."

This disagreement between editorial writers in the same newspaper was typical of the controversy elsewhere in the country over the decision in these cases.

Unlike the "right to work" cases, most due process problems which came before Justice Rutledge involved procedural issues. If the Court had held invalid laws prohibiting closed shop contracts, it would have been on the ground that such laws violated the due process clause of the Fourteenth Amendment in its substantive aspects by depriving the parties of their freedom of contract. Such decisions had been rendered on a number of occasions during the earlier years of the century. The *Lochner*[79] case dealing with the New York hours-of-labor law and the minimum wage law of the District of Columbia are examples. But *Yamashita, Homma, Hirota*, the one-man grand jury, the "blue ribbon" petit jury and the John L. Lewis —Mine Workers cases all involved procedural due process, the original meaning of the phrase in its constitutional context. Justice Rutledge believed that the first condition for a civilized society called for a system of law in which no person could be punished without the minimum protection of a fair trial. There could be no compromise. The innocent were entitled to no more; the guilty to no less.

CHAPTER VII

"...AND TO HAVE THE
ASSISTANCE OF COUNSEL...."

BY the early English law, in trials for treason or felony, the accused could not be heard by counsel. It was otherwise in the case of misdemeanors. The curious result was that one whose life or liberty was in jeopardy, was not entitled to counsel but if it were a matter of a small fine for a trivial offense, counsel was permitted. Although it is said that the English judges allowed consultation between accused and counsel on matters arising during the trial,[1] it was not until the end of the Seventeenth Century that the prisoner could be represented by counsel at the trial in cases of treason, and not until 1836 in felony trials.[2] At the time of the founding of the nation and the adoption of the Bill of Rights, the problem of the right to counsel and the plight of the prisoner caught in a web of legal technicalities without skill or expertise, was fully realized by both lawyers and knowledgeable laymen. Along with jury trial, the right to face accusers, charge by indictment, compulsory process to obtain witnesses, that "bright constellation" must also include the right to counsel.

An early commentator on the laws of colonial Connecticut declared that "we have never admitted that cruel and illiberal principle of the common law of England that where a man is on trial for his life, he shall be refused counsel, and denied those means of defence which are allowed when the most trifling pittance of property is in question." After referring to the early rule in England that in certain cases the accused could not even call witnesses in his behalf, the author continued: "It seems by the ancient practice, that whenever a person was accused of crime, every expedient was adopted to convict him and every privilege denied him, to prove his innocence."[3]

The term before Rutledge joined the Court, it was decided, what is still a rather hotly contested point of law, viz. that the provision in the Sixth Amendment, guaranteeing the right to counsel is not "incorporated" in the due process clause of the Fourteenth

Amendment and thus applicable to criminal trials in state courts.[4]
The exact wording of the provision in question is "In all criminal
prosecutions, the accused shall enjoy the right . . . to have the Assistance of Counsel for his defense." The Court, in 1938, had made it
clear that this means that an accused in any criminal case in a federal court is entitled to counsel unless he voluntarily waives the
right.[5]

In *Betts* v. *Brady*,[6] the Court was presented with a case in which
a man, convicted of robbery in a state court of Maryland, had requested the trial judge to appoint counsel for him since he had no
money to retain one. The request was denied, the judge explaining
that "it was not the practice in Carroll County to appoint counsel
for indigent defendants, save in prosecutions for murder and rape."

In an opinion by Justice Roberts, it was pointed out that the due
process clause was originally included in the Fifth Amendment as a
limitation only on action by the federal government. Its post-civil
war inclusion in the Fourteenth, as a limitation on state power did
not incorporate all the other guarantees of the Bill of Rights.

> The phrase [due process of law] formulates a concept less
> rigid and more fluid than those envisaged in other specific and
> particular provisions of the Bill of Rights. Its application is
> less a matter of rule. Asserted denial is to be tested by an ap-
> praisal of the totality of facts in a given case. That which, in
> one setting, may constitute a denial of fundamental fairness,
> shocking to a universal sense of justice, may, in other circum-
> stances, and in the light of other considerations, fall short of
> such denial. In the application of such a concept, there is al-
> ways the danger of falling into the habit of formulating the
> guarantee into a set of hard and fast rules. . . .[7]

"The question we are *not* to decide," said Roberts, "is whether
due process of law demands that in every criminal case, whatever the
circumstances, a State must furnish counsel to an indigent defendant.
Is the furnishing of counsel in all cases whatever dictated by natural, inherent and fundamental principles of fairness?" The Court
thought the most relevant data to guide its judgment on this question
would be the constitutional and statutory provisions of the colonies
and states in the early years of the nation. It found "great diversity"
in these as well as in current constitutional and statutory provisions.
The conclusion was: "This material demonstrates that, in the great
majority of the States, it has been the considered judgment of the
people, their representatives and their courts that appointment of

counsel is not a fundamental right, essential to a fair trial." Appointment of counsel for indigents in all criminal cases in state courts, therefore, was not required by the Fourteenth Amendment, although such requirement is imposed upon the federal government by the Sixth.

In the dissenting opinion, in which Justices Douglas and Murphy joined, Justice Black declared his consistent belief that the Fourteenth Amendment "made the Sixth applicable to the states," a view often urged in dissents, but never adopted by a majority of the Court and "not accepted today." Although it is not altogether clear from his opinion, Black appears to take the position that even under the "fundamental right" test approved by the Court, the case should be reversed.

Ten years before the *Betts* case, the Court had decided that due process of law required the appointment of counsel in capital cases, in state criminal courts, if the accused was incapable of defending himself.[8] This was the much discussed *Scottsboro* case, in which eight Negro youths were tried and convicted of the rape of two overall-clad white girls on a freight train. The trial judge appointed "all the members of the bar" as counsel for the boys at the arraignment. This, of course, was an ironically empty gesture. At the trial, an out-of-state lawyer stated that he had been asked to assist any court-appointed counsel. When the judge inquired whether any member of the local bar was prepared to act for defendants, he received a half-hearted affirmative response from a lawyer named Moody. The trial proceeded. Eight (of nine accused) were convicted on the same day, including a thirteen year old.

In his opinion for the Court, Mr. Justice Sutherland emphasized the role of defense counsel in criminal cases and the unhappy plight of even intelligent and educated laymen, lost in a maze of legal technicalities. This, together with his insistence that due process in certain cases required counsel appointed under circumstances which would enable them to render effective assistance, could, as Beaney has pointed out, "be broadened by generous judges into a sweeping rule that counsel must be appointed in virtually all criminal cases if indigents are to have a fair hearing."[9] But the majority in the *Betts* case were not so generous. Nor has there since been such a majority until 1963.

When Rutledge took his seat, therefore, it appeared that in any criminal case in a federal court regardless of the seriousness of the charge, the accused was entitled to counsel if indigent, at the expense of the government, unless he waived his right thereto with knowledge of what he was doing, and an understanding of the consequences of his action. In state courts, he had the same right if the charge against him was a capital offense and if the accused was incapable of defending himself. If the charge was less than a capital offense, accused was entitled to counsel only if a denial thereof would result in a trial so unfair as to be "shocking to a fundamental sense of justice" or, as Justice Cardozo phrased it in the famous *Palko* v. *Connecticut* case, outside the "concept of ordered liberty."

During Justice Rutledge's tenure on the Court, nineteen cases were decided involving the right to counsel. In thirteen cases the right was sustained under the prevailing doctrines. In all but four the Court was divided; in one case, five to four; in five cases, six to three; in two cases, seven to two; and in one, eight to one. Not all of the dissents were on the merits of the "fundamental right" or "conscience-shocking" test, some turning on procedural or other technical grounds. Rutledge voted to uphold the claimed right in every case.

One might suppose that there would be relatively little disagreement among experienced and intelligent judges as to situations which were beyond the limits of civilized tolerance. But Justice Black, writing in 1962, observed that "twenty years' experience in the state and federal courts with the *Betts* v. *Brady* rule has demonstrated its basic failure as a constitutional guide." He thought that it has served not so much to guide but to confuse the state judges as to when an accused was entitled to a lawyer. "[O]ne need only look at the records of the right-to-counsel cases . . .," he wrote, "to understand the capriciousness with which the 'shocking to the universal sense of justice' standard bestows its protection upon persons accused of crime."[10] Several of the cases in which Rutledge participated fully support this charge.

But there were other technicalities to plague the Justices in situations involving the right to counsel. Two companion cases were decided early in 1945. Both involved convictions in Missouri courts of capital offenses. In one case, the prisoner claimed in his petition for a writ of habeas corpus that prior to his conviction and sentence he had requested the assistance of counsel but none had been appointed, that he was incapable of making an adequate defense, and as a result was compelled to plead guilty. The Court held, in an opinion by Justice Douglas, that in such circumstances and assuming that the accused had no funds to employ counsel, refusal by the Court to appoint one constituted a denial of the constitutional right of the accused.[11] The Court relied on the *Scottsboro* case[12] where the Court had said that in capital cases at least, "where the defendant is unable to employ counsel, and is incapable adequately of making his own defense because of ignorance, feeble mindedness, illiteracy or the like, it is the duty of the court, whether requested or not, to assign counsel to him as a necessary requisite of due process of law."[13] Right to counsel in such a case is "fundamental." The other Missouri case was disposed of in the same way and for the same reasons.

The dissent by Justices Frankfurter and Roberts pointed out that, on the record it might well have been that the Missouri court denied relief on the ground that the prisoner had failed to comply with state procedural rules, rather than on the merits of the constitutional issue. The Court, they thought, should assume in such cases that the denial was thus based on adequate grounds of state law and not a denial of a constitutional right. Respect for the state judiciary and the principle of comity required that they be given the benefit of the doubt. It will be seen that this question, whether the prisoner had followed the appropriate state procedure so that the constitutional merits of his case were before the state court, was to cause no end of trouble for the Justices.

It appears that in both these Missouri cases, the prisoners had proceeded *in forma pauperis,* that is by acting on their own without counsel and without funds. In such cases, court fees, costs of printing petitions and briefs are not required. These prisoners had been convicted years before and had already served a substantial part of their sentences of imprisonment. Each year, the Supreme Court must dispose of dozens and sometimes hundreds of such petitions, many submitted in the prisoner's own handwriting. As might be expected, they frequently lack precision and clarity. But, as Justice Douglas pointed out in one of the Missouri cases, "we can hardly demand of a layman and pauper who draws his petition behind prison walls the skill of one trained in the law. If we were to take that course, we would compound the injury caused by the original denial of counsel."[14] A recent article by two distinguished lawyers explains that the Supreme Court in 1921 created a fund from fees paid by lawyers when they are admitted to practice before the Court which is available to defray costs in connection with *in forma pauperis* cases. For the 1959-'60-'61 terms, total payments of $19,545 were paid in indigent cases.[15]

If the accused has counsel of his own, the state may not deny him the right of consultation. The Court has held it a denial of due process for a trial court, over a prisoner's protest, to require him to plead to a charge of serious crime without the aid and advice of his counsel whose presence he had requested. This was in 1945. The charge was burglary to which, after denial of his request, he pleaded guilty. "We need not consider," the opinion declared, "whether the state would have been required to appoint counsel for petitioner on the facts alleged in the petition. [Cases cited]."

> It is enough that petitioner had his own attorney and was not afforded a reasonable opportunity to consult with him. The fact that petitioner pleaded guilty after the denial of his request for time to consult with his counsel, does not deprive him of his constitutional right to counsel.[16]

Similarly, the fact that the accused pleaded guilty did not deprive him of his right to counsel in a case decided two months later where an Indian, charged with burglary, had no counsel and had not been advised of this right or of his right to call witnesses in his behalf. The state court held that the accused had waived his right to counsel by pleading guilty. It conclusively presumed such a waiver. The Supreme Court could not approve such a rule. A defendant's constitutional rights do not depend on whether he pleads guilty or not guilty, if he needs counsel and cannot employ one in a felony case. That the accused needed counsel, Justice Black pointed out, was "strikingly emphasized by the allegation in his habeas corpus petition that the offense for which the state court convicted him was committed on a government Indian reservation 'without and beyond the jurisdiction of the court.' This raises an involved problem of federal jurisdiction, posing a problem that is obviously beyond the capacity of even an intelligent and educated layman, and which clearly demands the counsel of experience and skill."[17] As was customary in such cases, the Chief Justice appointed counsel to argue the prisoner's case before the Supreme Court. Justice Rutledge suggested Edmund Campbell of Washington, D.C. and Bartan H. Kuhns of Omaha, both distinguished members of the bar. Kuhns was named and ably represented his client's cause.

Henry Hawk, another Indian, was convicted of first degree murder by a Nebraska jury and sentenced to life imprisonment in 1932. Nine years later, after repeated frustrating failures, he finally got a hearing by the Supreme Court which held that if he could prove his allegations, he would gain his freedom. This is one of several cases involving the rule that a prisoner convicted in a state court must "exhaust all state remedies" before appealing to the federal courts on a constitutional issue. This, in turn, frequently involves the question whether the state court declined relief because the prisoner had resorted to the wrong state procedure to get the merits of his case before the court.

After his conviction, Hawk had filed a petition for a writ of habeas corpus in the state courts, alleging that he had been forced to stand trial while in the custody of federal guards and while he was serving a federal sentence. This was denied by the supreme court of Nebraska and the Supreme Court of the United States declined to review the decision. He then filed another petition for habeas corpus in the federal district court of Nebraska, this time alleging that he had been deprived of counsel at his trial and that the state had knowingly used perjured testimony against him. This petition, also, was denied on the sole ground that he had not exhausted his remedies under Nebraska law. Although he had attempted to sue out a writ of habeas corpus in the state courts, he had not done so on the grounds now alleged, *i.e.*, denial of the right to counsel. The Supreme Court again declined to review the case. After filing one more application in the state court and two in the federal court in Nebraska, all of which were denied, the persistent Indian applied directly to the Supreme Court for leave to file a petition for habeas corpus. This, too, was denied, on the ground that the prisoner had failed to exhaust remedies in the lower courts of Nebraska, his previous application on denial of counsel grounds having been made in the state supreme court.[18] He then started all over again in the lower state court and finally got to the Supreme Court of the United States.

This was Hawk's story: He claimed that he had been brought to Omaha from the federal penitentiary to stand trial for murder, a capital offense. He was held incommunicado by state officials except for fifteen minutes with two lawyers from the Public Defender's office who, as he insisted, tried to intimidate him into pleading guilty. When he refused, they left, declaring that they would have nothing to do with the trial scheduled for the following day. Then next morning, the prisoner was arraigned, pleaded not guilty and moved for a twenty-four hour continuance to enable him to consult with counsel. This the judge denied and ordered the trial to proceed, which it did. The two Public Defender attorneys then purported to represent Hawk without any consultation whatever concerning his defense.

"These facts, if true," wrote Justice Reed for a unanimous Court, "we think set out a violation of the Fourteenth Amendment." Denial of "effective assistance" of counsel violates due process. The state may not avoid its constitutional obligations by a sham appointment of counsel. "Continuance," Reed went on, "may or may not have been useful to the accused, but the importance of assistance of counsel in a serious criminal charge after arraignment is too large to permit speculation on its effect. We hold that denial of opportunity to consult with counsel on any material step after indictment or similar charge ... violates the Fourteenth Amendment."[19]

So, Hawk was once again to try his luck in the courts of Nebraska.
He did and got nowhere. A year after his illusory victory in Washington, he was back in Lincoln where the state supreme court held that
under the local rules of procedure, the prisoner could not raise the
questions which the Supreme Court said he was entitled to have settled, in a habeas corpus proceeding. He had adopted the wrong state
remedy.[20]

The last possibility was to try a proceeding known as a writ of
error *coram nobis* [before us], a common-law writ originally before the
full King's Bench. In its 1944 opinion the Supreme Court of the
United States had stated that state remedies could not be deemed exhausted in Nebraska until *coram nobis* had been tried. But this also
failed. The state supreme court held that this procedure was a remedy
provided to enable a person convicted to bring into the record significant and relevant facts unknown to the defendant at the time of the
trial through no want of reasonable diligence and which, if introduced
at the trial would have resulted in a different judgment. The court,
however, purported to consider the merits of the case and come to the
conclusion that the prisoner's allegations were unfounded. In any
event, if his defense was not made out to his satisfaction for lack of
time or counsel or for other reasons, he must have known of it at the
time and should have moved for a new trial and, if denied, appealed
to the state supreme court. The Supreme Court of the United
States denied a petition to review and the curtain was lowered on this
litigation on March 27th, 1950. After sixteen efforts to obtain a hearing on the merits, all Hawk got was a thorough course in Nebraska
criminal procedure and some instruction in criminal law.

While the Hawk habeas corpus case was pending in the Supreme
Court, Justice Reed in working on his opinion, for some reason, made
a sample survey of such cases during the fiscal year 1942. In five
federal districts alone, there were 233 applications for habeas corpus
made by prisoners. Undoubtedly most of them, like the *Hawk* case,
were *in forma pauperis*, and prepared by the prisoners themselves
without the aid of counsel. Of the 233 cases, only 9 prisoners were
successful in gaining releases, 6, however, on the ground that their
sentences had expired. Only two were successful because of denial
of constitutional rights. In his dissent in a case decided in March,
1963, Justice Clark cited further statistics from Reports of the Administrative Office of the United States Courts that the number of applications for habeas corpus filed in lower federal courts by state prisoners rose from 127 in 1941 to 1,232 in 1962. In the twelve year period
from 1946 to 1957, only 1.4% were successful.[21] The prisoner's sta-

tistical chances in a habeas corpus suit are obviously pretty slim, frequently for reasons which do not touch the merits of his case.

There is no doubt that the procedure whereby constitutional issues may be raised in state criminal cases and carried to its highest court is solely a matter of state law. As Justice Frankfurter has explained, "an accused may have been denied the assistance of counsel under circumstances which constitute an infringement of the United States Constitution."

> If the State affords no mode for redressing that wrong, he may come to the federal courts for relief. But where a remedy is provided by the State, a defendant must first exhaust it in the manner in which the State prescribes. [Cases cited.] For the relation of the United States and the courts of the United States to the States and the courts of the States is a very delicate matter.[22]

We have seen something of Henry Hawk's troubles over this rule. A Negro named Carter found the Illinois procedure equally baffling although his stamina for prolonged litigation was not so great. Carter had pleaded guilty to an indictment for murder and had been sentenced to imprisonment for ninety-nine years. This was in 1928. In 1945 he brought a petition for his release in the Supreme Court of Illinois on a writ of error claiming that his conviction was a violation of due process by denial of assistance of counsel, the method of his arrest and the unfairness of the trial, generally. His claim was denied by the state supreme court. He had represented himself in this proceeding and had made the usual mistake of resorting to the wrong state remedy, according to Justice Frankfurter who wrote the opinion for the Supreme Court in affirming the state decision. "The only thing before the Illinois Supreme Court," he wrote, "was what is known under Illinois practice as the common law record."

> That record, as certified in this case, included only the indictment, the judgment on a plea of guilty, the minute entry bearing on sentence, and the sentence. And so, the very narrow question now before us is whether the common law record establishes that the defendant's sentence is void because in the proceedings that led to it, he was denied the assistance of counsel.[23]

Frankfurter then concluded that on the "common law record" which was before the state court, there was nothing to show a denial of the prisoner's constitutional rights. In restricting its review to that record, the Illinois Supreme Court followed local practice and such practice constituted "allowable State appellate procedure." Factors which would have a bearing on the fairness of his conviction were not considered by the state court because not a part of the "common law record" although they were in the actual trial record of the case.

Justice Murphy was not so easily satisfied. In his dissent, he characterized the situation in these words:

> Petitioner, an uneducated, bewildered layman, was allegedly held incommunicado for fifteen days and was then called upon to make a vital decision upon the basis of his unintelligent understanding of the indictment—a legalistic, verbose document of five pages which would doubtless mean many things to many learned lawyers in light of the particular facts involved. Petitioner's very life and liberty depended upon his ability to comprehend the variety of crimes covered by the indictment and which one, if any, applied to the facts of his case. He was compelled to weigh the factors involved in a guilty plea against those resulting from the submission of his case to a jury. He was forced to judge the chances of setting up a successful defense. These are all complicated matters that only a man versed in legal lore could hope to comprehend and to decide intelligently. Petitioner obviously was not of that type. Yet at this crucial juncture petitioner lacked the aid and guidance of such a person. In my view, it is a gross miscarriage of justice to condemn a man to death or to life imprisonment in such a manner.

Justices Douglas, Rutledge and Black also dissented. Although the state supreme court ruled that the prisoner could not raise the question of the method of his arrest and the unfairness of his trial on the skeleton "common law record," when it came to the specific claim of denial of counsel, that court in fact gave a different reason. "No duty rests upon the court," it declared, "to provide legal assistance for an accused, unless he states, under his oath, his inability to procure counsel, and expresses a desire to have the court appoint one for him." But the Supreme Court in the *Williams* case[24] had held that in a capital case at least, if the accused is incapable of making his own defense, it is the duty of the trial judge to appoint counsel for him, whether requested or not. It would appear from Justice Murphy's opinion that there was abundance of material in the entire record to indicate that this prisoner was far from capable of adequately looking after his own interest at the trial.

The *Marino* case threw more dramatic light on what was happening in the criminal courts of Illinois and produced some sensational results, although only eight pages of opinions in the Supreme Court. In 1925, Tony Marino, an eighteen year old Italian immigrant was convicted of murder and sentenced to life imprisonment. He had been in this country less than two years and could speak no English. The officer who arrested him served as one of two interpreters at his trial. He had no lawyer, and, as far as the record disclosed, his right to counsel was never explained to him. Although the record indicated that he had signed a waiver of jury trial and that he had entered a plea of guilty, he did not in fact do either and the judge at his trial probably knew it.

Twenty years later, acting as his own lawyer, Marino sought a writ of habeas corpus in a state court which was denied without assignment of any reason. The prisoner then asked for review by the Supreme Court, there being no right or appeal to the state appellate courts under Illinois practice. Ordinarily, as Justice Rutledge pointed out, the Supreme Court would have declined to hear the case by assuming that the denial of the writ by the state court had been on the ground that habeas corpus was not the appropriate remedy in this kind of case. But, strangely enough, the Illinois Attorney General "confessed errors," by conceding facts (not appearing in the "common law record") which plainly constituted, in a capital case, a denial of due process of law. In these circumstances, the Court in a unanimous *Per Curiam* opinion, reversed and vacated the judgment of the state court.[25]

But Rutledge was not content merely to join in the opinion of the Court. He wrote a concurring opinion, joined in by Murphy and Douglas, which had resounding reverberations.

> The trouble with Illinois is not that it offers no procedure. It is that it offers too many, and makes them so intricate and ineffective that in practical effect they amount to none. The possibility of securing effective determination on the merits is substantially foreclosed by the probability, indeed the all but mathematical certainty, that the case will go off on the procedural ruling that the wrong one of several possible remedies has been followed.

The Illinois Attorney General, in his confession of error explained that although ordinarily, habeas corpus was not available if the prisoner did not challenge the jurisdiction of the court which convicted him or allege subsequent events which would void his conviction, the writ would lie in a case such as this one where the trial judge actually knew the existence of facts which violated due process even though they were not a matter of official record. He then conceded that the appellate procedure in Illinois was baffling and confusing.

This was too much for Rutledge. Indignantly he wrote:

> In short, the effect of the state's confession of error in this case is not to clarify, it is rather to confuse further, a situation already so muddled that only one rational conclusion may be drawn. It is that the Illinois procedural labyrinth is made up entirely of blind alleys, each of which is useful only as a means of convincing the federal courts that the state road which the petitioner has taken was the wrong one. If the only state remedy is the possibility that the attorney general will confess error when he determines that a flagrant case will not survive scrutiny by this Court, it is hardly necessary to point out that the federal courts should be open to a petitioner even though he has not made his way through several courts applying for habeas corpus, then writ of error, and finally coram nobis.[26]

He concluded his opinion by declaring that until the state of Illinois afforded a reasonably clear and adequate means for the disposition of cases like *Marino*, the Court should no longer require exhaustion of the present "labyrinth" of inadequate procedural devices before permitting resort to the federal courts in the state.

This disgraceful situation in Illinois was well known to legal scholars. Before the *Marino* case, the *University of Chicago Law Review* had pointed out that "under present procedures, it is nearly impossible to secure adjudication of the merits of alleged constitutional defects in judgments of conviction in Illinois courts; yet petitioners must present their applications for consideration seven to twelve times in order to escape the procedural maze of the state courts and to secure their initial hearings on the truth of their allegations in the federal courts."[27] As examples, among others, the article cited the case of a prisoner named Woods who had been in court nine times without getting a hearing on the merits of his allegations, and another, John Rooney, was able to exhaust his state remedies and thus qualify for a hearing in a federal court only after seven tries.[28]

After the decision in *Marino*, the Attorney General of Illinois filed a motion in the Supreme Court for an order instructing the local state judge to release the prisoner from custody. The judge had taken the position that the Supreme Court's decision had merely authorized a hearing to determine the accuracy of the facts conceded in the confession of error and whether the actual facts constituted a denial of due process of law for want of counsel for the prisoner. The judge, apparently, did not feel bound by the Attorney General's confession of error, in the absence of a ruling to that effect by the Supreme Court. The motion was denied,[29] the hearing was held and the prisoner denied relief in the Illinois court where he was originally indicted. The Supreme Court declined to review.[30] Justices Rutledge, Murphy and Douglas dissented. They thought the Court should review the state courts' decision. Marino made one more try in the state courts, this time challenging the legality of the grand jury which indicted him. He lost,[31] and when the Supreme Court denied the petition for certiorari to review the decision,[32] the prisoner's last chance for freedom was terminated, a quarter of a century after he had been convicted. In fairness to the state courts, it should be noted that on the hearing on the merits following the confession of error, the finding that the prisoner had not been denied his constitutional rights was based upon evidence at substantial variance from the facts conceded by the Attorney General's confession. What the actual facts were, we shall never know.

In his *Marino* opinion, Rutledge pointed out that during the three preceding terms of the Supreme Court, it had been flooded with petitions from Illinois alleging deprivation of constitutional rights, almost all from prisoners. In the 1944 term, of a total of 339 petitions filed *in forma pauperis*, 141 came from Illinois; in the 1945 term 175 out of 393; and in the 1946 term, 322 out of 528. Of the last 322 petitions only two were granted.

The reason for the sudden barrage of petitions for review of alleged denial of constitutional rights from Illinois appears to be that prior to 1943, prison officials did not allow petitions to be mailed from state penitentiaries. Thus, prisoners who were unable to employ counsel could not even get their cases before a court. The Supreme Court of the United States in 1941 declared this practice unconstitutional as a denial of equal protection.[33] After the change in prison rules, petitions galore were filed seeking relief through all the various types of state procedure. The invariable result in the state courts was denial. The reason so few cases were considered for review by the Supreme Court, of course, was its rule that state remedies must be exhausted and the near impossibility of knowing when such was the case, coupled with the presumption that when the state court wrote no opinion, the denial was on the ground that the prisoner had pursued the wrong remedy.[34]

After the Rutledge blast at the Illinois "labyrinth of blind alleys," the Illinois Bar Association took the matter in hand, drafted a rule of court and submitted it to the Supreme Court of Illinois. With a

"JUGGLING WITH HUMAN LIVES"

few changes, it was adopted by that Court and went into effect on September 1, 1948. The provisions of this rule were as follows:

> In all criminal cases wherein the accused upon conviction shall, or may, be punished by imprisonment in the penitentiary, if, at the time of his arraignment, the accused is not represented by counsel, the court shall before receiving, entering, or allowing the change of any plea to an indictment, advise the accused he has a right to be defended by counsel. If he desires counsel, and states under oath he is unable to employ such counsel, the court shall appoint competent counsel to represent him. The court shall not permit waiver of counsel, or a plea of guilty, by any person accused of a crime for which upon conviction, the punishment may be imprisonment in the penitentiary, unless the court finds from proceedings had in open court that the accused understands the nature of the charge against him, and the consequences thereof if found guilty, and understands he has a right to counsel, and understandingly waives such right. The inquiries of the court, and the answers of the defendant to determine whether the accused understands his rights to be represented by counsel, and comprehends the nature of the crime with which he is charged, and the punishment thereof fixed by law, shall be recited in, and become part of the common law record in the case; provided, in no case shall a plea of guilty be received or accepted from a minor under the age of nineteen years, unless represented by counsel.

The Court did not adopt a complementary rule providing for an effective post-conviction procedure for prisoners who claimed that they had been denied their constitutional rights at the trial in which they had been convicted. The following year, however, the bar association successfully appealed to the Illinois legislature which promptly enacted a simple measure to meet this problem amd to provide for costs and counsel fees for prisoners proceeding as paupers.

Illinois, was by no means the only state which had utterly inadequate provisions to meet constitutional problems involved in criminal proceedings which, for lack of counsel or otherwise, were not finally adjudicated therein. Few states had a post-conviction procedure sufficient to insure justice without undue delay. The report of a special committee of the Conference of State Chief Justices recently observed:

> The courts appear to be impaled upon the horns of a dilemma. If a person has been unconstitutionally imprisoned for from

two to ten years while litigation has pursued the even tenor of its way, the situation becomes abhorrent to our sense of justice. On the other hand, if there has been no violation of constitutional right, and if from 90 to 99 per cent of the claims are groundless, the wear and tear on the judicial machinery, resulting from years of litigation in thousands of cases, State and Federal, becomes a matter of serious import to courts and judges, who, after all, are dedicated to the task of clearing their dockets with reasonable expedition. The element of expense is not to be ignored.

In view of this situation, the Commissioners on Uniform State Laws in 1955 adopted a Uniform Post-Conviction Act. The aim of the proposed act is to "clarify and simplify present procedures through consolidating them into a single action and so to eliminate the confusion of cases that now burden the courts, and at the same time provide for the petitioner a more complete protection than he now has in his assertion of valid claims." By 1964, only two states, Maryland and Oregon, had adopted this statute. North Carolina enacted a "Post Conviction Hearing Act" in 1951 but, like the Illinois legislation, it varies considerably in detail from the Uniform Act.

As usual, in cases which attracted wide-spread public attention, Rutledge received a number of letters, some of which he saved. His correspondents after the *Marino* case included a number of prisoners who detected in the news stories about the case, a sympathetic judge in high place. One prisoner asked permission to send the Justice a copy of his petition for a writ of habeas corpus which he had already filed in a federal court. Another, an inmate of a state mental hospital, said that she had been "framed" and wanted the Supreme Court to review her case. She had written to the President about her plight, to the Attorney General and most of the higher officials of New York from the governor down. Rutledge penciled a note to Miss Edna Lingreen that this "petition" should be referred to the clerk of the Court. Another letter came from a drug addict who was in prison for violation of his probation. He asked for advice as to what could be done on his behalf. The Justice replied, pointing out that, as a member of the Judiciary, he was not permitted to practice law and therefore was unable to advise him. Still another letter from California addressed to Rutledge, Murphy and Douglas, declared that that state, too, had its "merry-go-round" of procedure. The writer wanted to know how to get his case to the Supreme Court. A letter from Crystal City, Missouri, claimed that the writer had been denied his constitutional rights by the Pittsburgh Plate Glass Co. He had been "framed, discriminated against and lied on" by the company and the union. Rutledge acknowledged the letter and told him to get a lawyer.

A number of letters, of course, came from responsible sources. Dean Katz of the University of Chicago Law School wrote a congratulatory note on "a masterful presentation of the problem" which had "blown things open in a wholesome way." Illinois, however, had its apologists. "For example," the Dean wrote, "the Chief Justice of the Illinois Supreme Court told a [Chicago] *Tribune* reporter that Illinois citizens are protected by rules and statutes clear and simple enough to guarantee justice to all." Presumably such assurance inspired a *Tribune* editorial,[35] in part as follows:

> The decision of the Roosevelt justices in Washington has attracted wide attention, and this is true particularly of the concurring opinion of Mr. Justice Rutledge speaking for himself and Justices Douglas and Murphy. They took occasion to denounce the methods of Illinois law as applied by the Illinois Supreme Court in matters such as this. The implication was that judicial hearts in Washington are warm and in Springfield cold; that the judicial conscience in Washington is alert and in Springfield calloused; that the judicial mind in Washington is keen and in Springfield dull.

> Surely the opinion of the Roosevelt court comes at a propitious moment for the New Dealers. The language may serve for a few days, at least, to distract attention from the manifold disclosures of corruption in the Roosevelt-New Deal regime. Any diversion, however brief, must be more than welcome even if it is obtained at the expense of honorable men in this state.

> In fact, of course, the Supreme Court of Illinois and its members today, as for many years in the past, have commanded popular respect. As much cannot be said for the Supreme Court in Washington and all its members.

> Mr. Justice Jackson can claim to have invented the Kangaroo court at Nürnburg with its apparatus of *ex posto facto* law. Mr. Justice Murphy is that man who sat with folded hands in the governor's chair in Michigan when the terror was unleashed which still threatens our country's existence. [Presumably this referred to the so-called "sit down" strike]. Mr. Justice Black was a gold-card Kluxer whose appointment, an evil thing in itself, led to vastly greater evil, when the facts regarding Mr. Black's shameful association came to light soon after his appointment was confirmed. Mr. Roosevelt sought to change

the subject by making a provocative speech in Chicago at the dedication of the outer bridge. It was then that Mr. Roosevelt embarked on the policy which eventually drove America into war and brought the world to its present ruin.

There is no need here to rehearse the many criticisms of the Roosevelt Supreme Court to be found in the pages of the law journals these days. Serious students of the law, reviewing the record of this court have found it light-minded, evasive, quarrelsome, inconsistent, exhibitionist. Suffice it to say that it is members of this court who now assume an attitude of moral and intellectual superiority toward the justices who sit on the Supreme bench of Illinois, an honor to their profession and the State.

A few days later, Rutledge received a letter written on Stevens Hotel stationery in the innocent Douglas' handwriting. It referred to the Tribune's editorial charge that the purpose of Rutledge's opinion was to divert attention from "New Deal corruption," concluding "Now, Wiley, what goes on anyway?"

In 1947, the Court unanimously reversed the conviction of a seventeen year old Michigan youth for murder.[36] He had pleaded guilty and was sentenced to life imprisonment. He had no counsel, none was offered by the trial court. The consequences of a plea of guilty were not explained to him, no evidence was offered in his behalf and none of the state's witnesses were cross-examined. The Court found "considerable confusion in the petitioner's mind" as to the effect of the guilty plea. Arraignment, trial, conviction and sentence all occurred on the same day, something of a record for a criminal proceeding in a capital case. He had followed the correct Michigan procedure, by asking for time to file a motion for a new trial and appealing to the state supreme court from a denial.

The Court, however, in a New York case, held that if a prisoner was represented by competent counsel at the time of sentencing, his constitutional rights were not invaded even though he had no counsel at the time of his arraignment, and a plea of guilty and his right to counsel were not explained to him.[37] The accused was a youth of 19, unfamiliar with legal proceedings. He had pleaded guilty to a crime of robbery, sentenced to imprisonment from 15 to 30 years. After serving 14 years of his sentence, he sought release, by the proper New York procedure [coram nobis] which was denied. At the conference held the day following oral argument in this case, all the Justices except Murphy, Rutledge and Jackson [who did not participate], indicated that they would affirm the state court. Chief Justice

Stone thought the accused, Canizio, had been a "bad boy" and that since he could have withdrawn his plea of guilty at any time before sentence, he ought not to be permitted to do so after 14 years. Justice Black thought the fact that the prisoner did in fact have counsel who participated in extended hearings prior to sentencing, during which time the guilty plea could have been withdrawn, no right of counsel had been denied. In his opinion for the Court, Black pointed out that the accused had been charged under three counts and had pleaded guilty under a charge of robbery without arms on condition that he would not be prosecuted under the other two counts, one of which was first degree robbery while armed. Thus, although he could have withdrawn his plea of guilty, his counsel probably thought it unwise to do so, since at the trial, he might be convicted of the more serious offense and receive a much heavier sentence.

Justice Murphy declared the record revealed a "complete travesty of justice." The ordinary layman, and especially "the ignorant, the indigent, the illiterate and the immature" are ill prepared "to combat the arsenal of statutes, decisions, rules of procedure, technicalities of pleading and other legal weapons at the ready disposal of the prosecutor." The right to counsel means nothing unless it means the right to counsel at each and every step of the proceeding.

Justice Rutledge's dissent stressed the rule of New York law which would have permitted the state, in a new trial, to have introduced in evidence the fact that the accused had originally pleaded guilty. This could not be done in a federal court and Rutledge regarded the New York law on the point as a form of self-incrimination. Such a rule made it impossible for the full effects of the prisoner's invalid plea of guilty to be wiped out. The burden of defense would thus have been much greater than if the plea of guilty had never been entered in the first place and would have gone far to destroy the presumption of innocence to which all accused of crime are entitled until lawfully proved guilty. Thus, the belated aid of counsel at the sentencing stage was by no means the equivalent of advice of counsel at the time of arraignment and plea. In view of this situation, Rutledge thought that about the only thing that counsel could do, in the best interest of his client, was to let the guilty plea stand and argue for the minimum sentence. "There was no choice but Hobson's."

Aside from the points made by Murphy and Rutledge, as a practical matter there would seem to be a great deal of difference between having counsel at the time of plea and having counsel at the time of sentence. Plea-bargaining with the prosecutor can be tricky business. This prisoner may have done quite well for himself, perhaps as well as competent counsel could have done. But there is no way to find out and neither the Justices nor anyone else will ever know. As the Court said in another important case, "the right to have the assistance of counsel is too fundamental and absolute to allow courts to indulge in nice calculations as to the amount of prejudice arising from its denial."[38] Furthermore, when a lawyer comes into a case at the sentencing stage, it is too late for him to be thinking about the merits of his client's case and the chances for getting an acquittal. It may also be too late for him to get into the record matters bearing in his client's favor on the severity of the sentence which might have been possible if he had come in on the case at the beginning.

What in substance amounted to an echo over the years from *Canizio* was a 1963 Maryland case of a prisoner charged with a capital offense who had pleaded guilty at his preliminary hearing at which time he had no lawyer. Later, counsel was appointed and at a formal arraignment he entered pleas of not guilty and not guilty by reason of insanity. At his trial, the earlier plea of guilty was introduced against him. He was convicted and sentenced to death. The Supreme Court reversed, holding that the so-called "preliminary hearing" at which the prisoner, without advice of counsel, had pleaded guilty, was a "critical stage" of the proceedings at which he was entitled to counsel.[39] The Court did not mention the *Canizio* case nor Rutledge's opinion therein.

That an accused in a capital case "requires the guiding hand of counsel at every step in the proceedings" was again vividly illustrated in a recent case in which a Negro was sentenced to death in an Alabama court after a verdict of guilty of breaking and entering a dwelling with intent to ravish. The accused had been arraigned without counsel and had pleaded guilty. The state supreme court, although admitting that an accused in a capital case had a right to be represented by counsel, denied relief because it did not appear that he had been prejudiced in any way by lack of counsel.

In reversing the state court, Justice Douglas, writing for a unanimous bench pointed out that the arraignment, at which the accused is charged with crime and enters his plea, is a critical stage in Alabama criminal proceedings. It is then, for example, that the defense of insanity must be pleaded or the opportunity is lost unless the trial judge in his unreviewable discretion allows it at a later stage. Other pleas and motions must be made at that time or be irretrievably lost. When matters so vital are involved and an accused pleads to a capital charge without benefit of counsel, Douglas declared, "we do not stop to determine whether prejudice resulted."[40]

On the same day that the Court handed down its decision in the
much cited *Adamson* case reaffirming the rule that the guarantee in
the Fifth Amendment against self-incrimination in the federal courts
is not incorporated in the due process clause of the Fourteenth
Amendment,[41] it also reaffirmed in another Illinois case the doctrine
of *Betts* v. *Brady* that the right to counsel as contained in the Sixth
Amendment is not in this way applicable to the states. Only if such
denial results in what a majority of the Justices regard as an unfair
trial is there a failure of due process of law.[42] In both cases, Justice
Rutledge had joined in dissent with Justice Murphy. In the Illinois
case,[43] he wrote a separate dissent in which Justices Black, Douglas
and Murphy concurred. In his opinion for the Court, Justice Frankfurter again pointed out the limitations of review on what in Illinois
is known as the "common law record," so abbreviated that little appeared therein except the charge, the arraignment, the pleas and a
statement that the judge advised the accused of his "rights of trial,"
whatever that might mean. Frankfurter feared it would be an "innovation" which would "open wide the prison doors of the land" to
hold that the record of conviction must show an offer of counsel to a
defendant before accepting a plea of guilty. Justice Black, perhaps
lifting himself by his own bootstraps, thought this consideration irrelevant "to a determination that we should decline to enforce the
Bill of Rights." A better answer might have been found in the statistics showing that less than two per cent of the petitions of prisoners
are successful in obtaining their release.

Justice Rutledge cut through the sham in which the case was
enshrouded. He and all the other Justices were thoroughly familiar with
what went on in Illinois criminal trials. They knew the "vague and
formal recital" in the common law record that the accused had been
advised of his "rights of trial" was a mere gloss which covered up the
fact that he had not been advised of his right to counsel. Under
Illinois law and practice, counsel would be appointed only when a
defendant requested it and stated under oath that he could not obtain counsel. The state court had expressly held that the trial judge
was under no duty "to proffer the services of counsel." Rutledge felt
it utterly inconsistent with the constitutional scheme of things for
the Court to "shut its eyes" to such a situation. Judges "owe something more than the negative duty to sit silent and blind while men
go on their way to prison, for all that appears, for want of any hint of
their rights."

In this brief dissent, Rutledge touched upon another aspect of
this problem which had received little if any attention but which,
seventeen years later, was to receive the disposition which he then

advocated. What the Court did in this, and other cases coming up from Illinois, was "to presume" regularity of the criminal proceedings in the face of knowledge of the actual violation of the constitutional rights of the accused. The consequences of such a course of action for those too poor to employ a lawyer and too ignorant to know that they were entitled to one "must be, not merely a denial of the basic right of counsel, but also a denial of the equal protection of the laws in sweeping application." He then went on to say, "poverty or wealth will make all the difference in securing the substance or only the shadow of constitutional protections."[44]

As late as 1953, the equal protection theory in this connection was regarded by Beaney as an "unusual position."[45] Three years later, however, the Supreme Court held that a state was obligated by the Fourteenth Amendment's equal protection provision to furnish a free transcript of the trial record to enable an indigent defendant to appeal from his conviction or "find other means of affording adequate and effective review to indigent defendants."[46] And then, ten years later,[47] the Court relied upon the transcript case to hold it a failure of equal protection to deny counsel to an indigent for an appeal of right from his conviction. There can be no equal justice where the kind of appeal, if any, depends on the amount of money the defendant has. Justice Douglas, for the Court, declared that "the indigent, where the record is unclear or the errors are hidden, has only the right of a meaningless ritual, while the rich man has a meaningful appeal."[48]

Justice Clark dissented in the 1963 case on the ground that the state had met its obligations under the equal protection provision by the requirement that the Court make "an independent investigation of the record" to determine whether the appointment of counsel would be of advantage to the accused or helpful to the appellate court. If it answered these questions in the negative, it need not appoint counsel. Inasmuch as the statistics indicated that an overwhelming per cent of appeals *in forma pauperis* were frivolous, Clark thought "this new fetish for indigency" piled up an "intolerable burden on the State's judicial machinery."[49]

The "new fetish," however, was indulged by the Court in two other cases decided on the same day [March 18, 1963], one again involving the failure of a state to provide a pauper with a free transcript to enable him to appeal.[50] In the other case, the state of Washington had refused a transcript after the trial judge found that an appeal would be frivolous. This time, Justices White, Harlan and Stewart as well as Clark dissented.[51]

Also on the day that the Court handed down its opinion in the *Adamson* and *Foster* cases, it decided the case of a youth named Gayes who sought to invalidate a conviction of robbery for lack of counsel. He was sixteen years old at the time, indigent and alone, without relatives, friends, money or counsel to aid him. He, too, had pleaded guilty. The property he was charged with stealing, or intending to steal, consisted of seventy-five cents worth of cigarettes, two flashlights worth one dollar, and three dollars in cash. He served his sentence but was later charged and convicted of a similar crime, sentenced as a second offender, and, as such, given a longer sentence of imprisonment than if it were his first offense. The prisoner's strategy, of course, was to attack the first conviction and then be in a position to challenge the sentence in the second.[52]

The Court denied relief to this youth in another five to four decision. The brief opinion written by Justice Frankfurter appeared to rely primarily on the ground that Gayes had had an opportunity to attack the first conviction at the trial for his second offense. Just why this should prevent him from trying it later was not explained. In fact, nothing was explained in this opinion. Rutledge, writing for himself and Murphy, Douglas and Black would have no part of it. "I am," he declared, "unwilling to subscribe to such a doctrine of forfeitures concerning constitutional rights, which in the extreme circumstances of this case, seems to me shocking." He pointed out that under New York law, Gayes had followed the proper and apparently the only procedure to obtain relief from his sentence as a second offender. The procedure was a reasonable one. In these circumstances, the decision apparently makes it impossible for a prisoner in the position of this one to obtain relief for the unconstitutional denial of the right to counsel. Moreover, if the only course originally open to him, as Frankfurter seemed to hold, was to raise the issue on the occasion of the second offense trial, it would appear that such limitation should derive from New York law, not from the Supreme Court.

The war time sedition case of Mariana Von Moltke was a "right-to-counsel case" which attracted widespread attention. The woman was indicted for conspiracy to violate the Espionage Act. The specific charge against her was that she and twenty-three others had agreed during World War II, to collect and deliver vital military information to German agents. She at first declined to plead one way or the other and a plea of not guilty was entered. Two weeks later on October 7, 1943, she changed her plea to guilty and waived in writing her right to be represented by counsel. On August 7, 1944 she requested leave again to change her plea to not guilty, on the ground that her guilty plea was made without knowledge of her legal rights and without a thorough understanding of the nature of the offense charged. Her motion was denied by the trial judge who, on the same day, sentenced her to prison for four years.

Since this was a criminal proceeding in a federal court for a serious felony, the accused was entitled to the absolute right of counsel as provided in the Sixth Amendment. Of course, the court may not force counsel upon an intelligent person who, knowingly and understandingly waives the right. This is true whether the case is a non-capital one or whether, as here, the death sentence could be imposed. When the petitioner filed her motion for a writ of habeas corpus after sentence, the federal judge, who was not the same as the original judge, held that the only substantial question was one of waiver, that the evidence was overwhelmingly against her contentions, that she did in fact understand the charge and the proceedings and "freely, intelligently and knowingly waived her constitutional rights." The case was affirmed by the three judge court of appeals, one judge dissenting.

The Supreme Court reversed the lower court and set the trial court's judgment aside.[53] The case was sent back so that further hearings might be held and more explicit findings of fact made in order to determine whether the prisoner "competently, intelligently, and with full understanding of the implications, waived her constitutional right to counsel." On the remand, the federal judge found against the prisoner and the court of appeals, again by a vote of two to one, upheld the trial judges' findings and affirmed its judgment.[54]

The events leading up to this woman's arraignment and sentence do not constitute one of the bright pages in the history of investigative procedure and law enforcement in this country. Between six and seven o'clock in the morning one day in the middle of the war, six agents of the Federal Bureau of Investigation knocked on the door of her home in Detroit. She was in bed. She was told that she must get up and go with them. The home was searched with the consent of her husband. She was taken to the local office of the F.B.I., fingerprinted and photographed. She was then taken to the Immigration Detention Home, placed in solitary confinement and, except for a message to her husband concerning the care of a sick child, was held incommunicado for four days, during which time she was constantly questioned by two F.B.I. agents from ten o'clock in the morning until 9 o'clock at night. It was more than three weeks after her arrest that she was able to find out the exact offense charged against her.

For several days before her plea of guilty, the prisoner had had many conversations with F.B.I. agents some of whom were lawyers.

But she had no lawyer of her own, dedicated to serve her best interests. There was considerable conflict in the testimony as to what the F.B.I. men told her as to her rights and the implications and effects of a plea of guilty. There was no evidence that they intentionally deceived the prisoner or deliberately misled her. But, as Justice Black observed, "the Constitution does not contemplate that prisoners shall be dependent upon government agents for legal counsel and aid, however conscientious and able those agents may be."[55]

Perhaps the most important factual issue involved in this case was the one Justice Frankfurter put his finger on. "The appropriate disposition of this case," he wrote, "turns for me on the truth of petitioner's allegation that she was advised by an F.B.I. agent, active in the case, that one who merely associated, however innocently, with persons who were parties to a criminal conspiracy was equally guilty." He went on to say, "we are dealing, no doubt, with a person of intellectual acuteness."

> But it would be very rare, indeed, even for an extremely intelligent layman to have the understanding necessary to decide what course was best calculated to serve her interest when charged with participation in a conspiracy. . . . Thus, as may have been true of petitioner, an accused might be found in the net of a conspiracy by reason of the relation of her acts to acts of others, the significance of which she may not have appreciated. . . . Accordingly, if an F.B.I. agent, acting as a member of the prosecution, gave her, however honestly, clearly erroneous legal advice which might well have induced her to believe that she was guilty under the law as expounded to her . . . a person in the petitioner's situation might well have thought a defense futile and the mercy of the court her best hope. Such might have been her conclusion, however innocent she may have deemed herself to be.[56]

This is a case to trouble thoughtful persons, sensitive to invasions of personal liberty. Here was a German-born woman, with application for naturalization pending. In view of her status as an immigrant, the outrageous behavior of the law enforcement officers, the highly conflicting evidence and dissent of two of the six judges of the court of appeals who reviewed the district court's findings, it would appear to be impossible to resolve doubts. After his own careful summary of the evidence, Judge McAllister, in the final court of appeals decision, concluded:

... I am of the opinion that the record shows clearly that appellant did not competently, intelligently and with full understanding of the implications, waive her right to counsel; that her plea of guilty was not understandingly made; and that the findings of the district court to the contrary are not supported by substantial evidence.[57]

In fact, Rutledge apparently felt the same way. When the case was originally before the Supreme Court, he indicated in a handwritten, pencilled opinion, that he thought the judgment below should be reversed and the prisoner released from custody rather than sent back to the lower court for further hearings. He admitted that there was much conflicting testimony but there was one incident, as related by Mrs. Von Moltke, which was not denied by the F.B.I. agent involved. This was the illustration of the "rum runners' conspiracy." In short, it was that if several persons agree to violate the internal revenue law, another who is present but takes no part in the plan or agreement and doesn't even realize what is going on, is also guilty of conspiracy. The prisoner testified that one of the agents who interviewed her gave this example of an unlawful conspiracy. As Justice Frankfurter stated in his opinion, "The law, of course, is precisely to the contrary."[58] Rutledge thought that this was sufficient evidence of the prisoner's lack of understanding of her position before the law, that it might well have misled her into believing that she was guilty of conspiracy and induced her to plead guilty when she in fact and in law was innocent. Where constitutional rights were involved, he thought, "neither this Court nor any other should speculate on whether it [the "rum" illustration] influenced the plea. In the setting of this case, it could not have been without effect." He then concluded:

> It seems to me therefore, that the mandate for further proceedings and findings only requires the trial court to do again what it has already done. And if the assumption is true that the learned trial judge without objection from the District Attorney, so far slipped up in his functions as to ignore or consider irrelevant the bearing of this crucial portion of the evidence upon his ultimate findings and conclusions, that fact only demonstrates how much more the petitioner, unlearned in the law, though intelligent, had need of counsel at the crucial stage of her trial. Ignorance of the law is no excuse. But that does not mean it can be induced by government representatives with the effect of producing and validating a plea of guilty which cuts off all right of trial and defense.

Rutledge's opinion was not published. Indeed, it was not even typed. The reason is clear. Justice Black wrote the plurality opinion, joined in by Rutledge, Murphy and Douglas. It set forth in detail matters from the record to justify a finding that Mrs. Von Moltke was indeed misled and confused and that her waiver of counsel was not made with an adequate understanding of its implication. "Anyone charged with espionage in wartime under the statute in question," Black wrote, "would have sorely needed a lawyer; Mrs. Von Moltke, in particular, desperately needed the best she could get." He thereupon stated that he and the other three Justices would have directed the prisoner's release. He did not represent a majority, however. Justices Burton, Reed and Chief Justice Vinson wanted to affirm the lower court's judgment and Justice Jackson joined Justice Frankfurter in his "separate" opinion and conclusion to remand and direct that findings be made all over again by the trial court on whether the F.B.I. agent had misinformed the prisoner as to the law of conspiracy. Of the total of eighteen judges who had this prisoner's fate in their hands, six were altogether convinced that her right to counsel had been denied in that she had not intelligently and understandingly waived it; twelve were content to accept the contrary conclusion.

Bute v. *Illinois*[59] is a typical example of the right to counsel cases in that state during the decade, 1940-1950. Again, the question was whether the procedure in the state court on the question of counsel shocked the conscience. Again it turned out that it is harder to shock the consciences of some Justices than those of others. The decision in the state court received the blessing of the Supreme Court in a five to four decision with the usual dissenters, Rutledge, Murphy, Black and Douglas. Justice Burton, for the majority, took 33 pages to reaffirm the rule of *Betts* v. *Brady* that the Fourteenth Amendment did not require for the states the same right of counsel rule that the Sixth Amendment required for the national government. The prisoner was a fifty-seven year old man who had been convicted of taking indecent liberties with children, a non-capital offense, for which he was sentenced for from one to forty years in the penitentiary. The Court held that, unlike the rule in capital cases, the state was not required to offer the aid of counsel to this accused, to inquire as to his desire for counsel or as to his ability to employ counsel. Indeed, if the accused realized his need for counsel and had requested it, the state was under no obligation to assign counsel. This system of handling the matter did not, in the words of Justice Cardozo in the *Palko* case[60] violate "the very essence of a scheme of ordered liberty" nor violate a "principle of justice so rooted in the traditions and conscience of our people as to be ranked as fundamental."

The four dissenters thought otherwise. As Justice Douglas pointed out in his opinion, the assumption that the ordinary person knows enough to realize when he needs counsel and that the crime charged in this case was easy for a layman to comprehend and know whether he was guilty or not was naive. "[I]t has long been recognized," he wrote, "that the charge of taking indecent liberties with a child is, like rape, 'an accusation easily to be made and hard to be proved, and harder to be defended by the party accused, tho never so innocent,' " citing Hale's Pleas of the Crown, 1736. Among several examples, that learned author had cited the case of "an ancient wealthy man of about sixty three" who was indicted for rape, "fully sworn against him by a young girl of fourteen years old, and concurrent testimony of her mother and father, and some other relations." Fortunately, the accused was able to gain an acquittal by physically displaying himself to the jury which reported that "his bowels seemed to be fallen down in those parts, that they could scarcely discern his privities, the rupture being fully as big as the crown of a hat."[61]

As to the *Betts* v. *Brady* rule that cases from the state courts must be decided on an *ad hoc* basis on whether an accused is entitled to counsel, the dissenters thought "it might not be nonsense to draw the *Betts* v. *Brady* line somewhere between [the case involving a long prison sentence] and the case of one charged with violation of a parking ordinance. . . . But to draw the line between this case and cases where the maximum penalty is death is to make a distinction which makes no sense in terms of the absence or presence of *need* for counsel." [Emphasis in the original.]

The exhaustion-of-state-remedies rule has had its "ups" and "downs" in the Supreme Court and its exact status is still a matter for argument and disagreement among the Justices. In the case of a Florida prisoner, convicted of a non-capital offense, the Court refused to follow an earlier ruling that a state prisoner, in order to qualify for a federal writ of habeas corpus, must ordinarily have filed a petition in the Supreme Court for review of a state court judgment, notwithstanding such a petition or appeal could hardly be classed as a "state" remedy.[62] Here, the prisoner, a youth charged with breaking and entering, inexperienced in court procedure and without funds, requested the appointment of counsel which was refused. He was then tried, convicted and sentenced to five years imprisonment. Thereafter, the prisoner sought relief in the state courts by habeas corpus. It was denied by the state supreme court on the merits. The prisoner then resorted to the federal district court for a writ of habeas corpus. That court granted the writ and found that the prisoner had been denied his constitutional right to counsel. The Supreme Court agreed, although the prisoner had not sought review in the Supreme Court from the adverse decision of the state supreme court. It was a matter for the lower federal court to consider in the exercise of its discretion. There was no hard and fast rule to bar federal relief. The decision was another five to four one, Chief Justice Vinson and Justices Jackson and Burton joining in Justice Reed's dissent. This was one of the few cases in which Justice Frankfurter joined with Rutledge, Murphy, Black and Douglas to form a majority in a right-to-counsel case.

The 1948 revision of the judicial code of the United States, dealing with the problem of exhaustion of state remedies before the federal courts will issue the writ of habeas corpus, provides: "An applicant shall not be deemed to have exhausted the remedies available in the courts of the State, within the meaning of this section, if he has the right under the law of the State to raise, by any available procedure, the question presented."[63] An explanatory note by the Revisers stated that this was "declaratory of existing law," citing *Ex parte Hawk*. Two years later the Supreme Court held that this means that ordinarily a prisoner must seek review by petition for certiorari in the Supreme Court after denial on the merits by the highest state courts. A failure to do so renders futile a subsequent petition for habeas corpus in the federal courts on grounds of denial of counsel. The *Hawk* case was cited as authority. If some "special circumstances" existed to excuse the prisoner's failure to do so, the burden was on him to prove them. Insofar as the case from Florida implied a deviation from the *Hawk* rule, it is "corrected by this decision."[64] But in 1963, this case, in turn, was overruled. The Court held that it was only necessary that the prisoner exhaust state remedies available to him at the time of his application for habeas corpus in the federal court. In a thorough and scholarly review of the development of the law on this point, Justice Brennan aptly observed: "A defendant by committing a procedural default may be debarred from challenging his conviction in the state courts even on federal constitutional grounds. But a forfeiture of remedies does not legitimize the unconstitutional conduct by which his conviction was procured."[65] The decision in this case represents a long step forward in removing accumulated confusions with regard to habeas corpus in the federal courts and affords an opportunity for vast improvement in the administration of criminal justice in accordance with the law of the land.

Two other cases involving the right to counsel were decided on the same day [June 14, 1948] as the *Wade* case, both from Pennsylvania. In the *Townsend* case the prisoner was convicted without benefit of counsel and given two indeterminate sentences, not exceeding ten to twenty years in the penitentiary. At the time of sentencing the following took place:

> By the Court (addressing Townsend):
> Q. Townsend, how old are you?
> A. 29.
>
> Q. You have been here before, haven't you?
> A. Yes, sir.
>
> Q. *1933, larceny of automobile.* 1934, larceny of produce. 1930, larceny of bicycle. 1931, entering to steal and larceny. *1938, entering to steal and larceny in Doylestown. . . .* That was up on Germantown Avenue, wasn't it? You robbed a paint store.
> A. No. That was my brother.
>
> Q. You were tried for it, weren't you?
> A. Yes, but I was not guilty.
>
> Q. And 1945, this. 1946, entering to steal and larceny, 1350 Ridge Avenue. Is that your brother too?
> A. No.
>
> Q. *1937, receiving stolen goods, a saxophone.* What did you want with a saxophone? Didn't hope to play in the prison band then, did you?
> The Court: Ten to twenty in the Penitentiary. [Emphasis original.]

The conviction was reversed, Justice Jackson, writing for the Court explained:

> The trial court's facetiousness casts a somewhat somber reflection on the fairness of the proceeding when we learn from the record that actually the charge of receiving the stolen saxophone had been dismissed and the prisoner discharged by the magistrate. But it savors of foul play or of carelessness when we find from the record that, on two others of the charges which the court recited against the defendant, he had also been found not guilty. Both the 1933 charge of larceny of an automobile, and the 1938 charge of entry to steal and larceny, resulted in his discharge after he was adjudged not guilty. We are not at liberty to assume that items given such emphasis by the sentencing court did not influence the sentence which the prisoner is now serving.[66]

The other Pennsylvania prisoner did not come off so well. He had been convicted in the state court as a fourth offender and given a life sentence. The record indicated that the trial judge sentenced the prisoner under the misconception that the Pennsylvania Habitual Criminal Act required imprisonment for life as a mandatory sentence. This was not true. The prisoner did not have counsel and none was offered by the judge. Indeed, it did not appear that he was advised of his right to counsel. Justice Jackson, again writing for the Court thought it not altogether clear that the sentencing judge misconstrued the statute but in any event it was matter for the state courts to interpret their own statutes and a mere error in applying state law as such did not constitute denial of due process of law.[67]

Rutledge, again writing for himself, Black, Douglas and Murphy, took the position that the issue was similar to that in the *Townsend* case and should be decided in the same way. Here, as in that case, the lack of counsel almost certainly prejudiced the prisoner with respect to the sentence imposed. The trial judge in both cases imposed sentence apparently under a serious misapprehension—in the one case of fact, in the other of law. Rutledge concluded his opinion by a telling blow at the rule of *Betts* v. *Brady*.

> Perhaps the difference [between misunderstanding of facts and misconception of law] serves only to illustrate how capricious are the results when the right to counsel is made to depend not upon the mandate of the Constitution, but upon the vagaries of whether judges, the same or different, will regard this incident or that in the course of particular criminal proceedings as prejudicial.[68]

The Court divided six to three in reversing still a third Pennsylvania case in which a seventeen year old boy had pleaded guilty to four indictments of burglary and was sentenced to from twenty to forty years imprisonment. He had no counsel and was not told that he was entitled to one. Eight years later he petitioned a lower Pennsylvania court for a writ of habeas corpus, alleging denial of his right to counsel and alleging that, "frightened by threats of dire consequences if he dared to stand trial, relator pleaded guilty under the direction of an assistant district attorney general. . . ." The judge, without a hearing entered an order dismissing the petition and denying the writ. The decision was affirmed by the state supreme court.

Justice Reed wrote for the majority. He explained the current differences in views of the Justices with respect to the right of counsel. Some thought that the services of counsel to protect the accused were guaranteed by the Constitution in every criminal case. This was the "incorporation" view—the Fourteenth Amendment made the Sixth applicable to the states; other Justices believed in the rule of *Betts* v. *Brady*. Only if, in view of the age of accused, seriousness of the offense charged, etc., the result is apt to be an unfair trial, is the accused entitled to counsel in state criminal proceedings. Under either view, Reed wrote, the accused in this case was entitled to counsel.[69]

Justice Frankfurter, with whom Justices Jackson and Burton agreed, believed that the Supreme Court of Pennsylvania was entitled to the benefit of a doubt that it had not flouted the federal Constitution, but that it had affirmed the lower court because the constitutional claim had not been adequately presented. He found that the allegation on which the Court reviewed the decision of the state supreme court had not been before that court when it denied relief to the prisoner. He would have dismissed the case and, as so often happened, forced the prisoner to start all over again in Pennsylvania.

The last of the nineteen right to counsel cases during Rutledge's tenure on the Court involved a man in his thirties who had also been convicted in Pennsylvania for larceny and sentenced to from two and a half to five years in the penitentiary, solitary confinement and hard labor. He had conducted his own defense. There were many errors committed during the trial. Hearsay and other inadmissible evidence was offered and admitted, which was prejudicial to the accused; the judge commented on the prisoner's previous criminal record in the presence of the jury, accused was prevented from proving a fact clearly relevant to his defense, and the judge, in sentencing the prisoner rather clearly displayed an injudicious hostility by remarking, "If I could give you life, I would do it."[70] Before trial, the district attorney had asked the accused if he had a lawyer, to which he replied that he had no money to retain one but wished to have one appointed for him. He did not ask the Court to appoint counsel because he did not know that he was entitled to one. After the evidence was in, but before the jury had retired, the judge explained that "the defendant in this case has not been represented by counsel, but this is not necessary under Pennsylvania law."

Rutledge's conference notes indicated that the tentative disposition of the case was to affirm by a vote of five to four, the state court's denial of habeas corpus. Justice Reed turned out to be the "swing man" here as in several other of these cases. The case was assigned to him to write the opinion for the Court. In less than three weeks, he circulated the first draft with a memorandum of explanation that he had changed his mind and had come to the conclusion that the case should be reversed as a denial of the prisoner's right to counsel under the rule of *Betts* v. *Brady*. It was "lacking [in] fundamental fairness because neither counsel nor adequate judicial guidance or protection was furnished at the trial."[71]

As it turned out, Chief Justice Vinson and Justices Frankfurter, Burton and Jackson also were persuaded that their first position was erroneous. The result was unanimous for reversal. Justices Black and Douglas concurred in the judgment of the court but insisted that *Betts* v. *Brady* should be overruled. Justices Murphy and Rutledge merely noted that they concurred in the result.

The Court had another opportunity to overrule the *Betts* case in 1962, but declined to do so over the protest of Chief Justice Warren and Justices Black and Douglas. The disposition of the specific case, however, satisfied all. An illiterate man had been convicted in a Florida state court of the non-capital offenses of incest and lascivious assault upon a girl under the age of fourteen. Unless intelligently waived, the failure to afford him counsel was held to have denied him a fair trial, as required by the due process clause of the Fourteenth Amendment. In this case, the record did not disclose whether the prisoner had requested counsel or whether he had been offered and had waived counsel. The Court, it appears, took the position that there was, in such cases, a presumption against waiver. This was quite a significant departure from previous "presumptions." "The record must show or there must be an allegation and evidence which show that an accused was offered counsel but intelligently and understandingly rejected the offer."[72] But the Court did not go so far as to hold the Sixth Amendment applicable to state criminal trials.

On March 18, 1963, however, Justice Black had the satisfaction of writing the opinion for a unanimous Court in a decision which overruled *Betts* v. *Brady*. In the *Gideon* case,[73] the prisoner had been convicted by a Florida court of breaking and entering a poolroom with intent to commit a misdemeanor. Under Florida law this is a felony for which the accused was sentenced to five years imprisonment. He had requested the aid of counsel at his trial since he had no money to hire one. The judge said that he was sorry he could not appoint counsel for him because under the law of Florida counsel could be furnished only in capital cases. After his conviction, the prisoner filed a petition for habeas corpus in the supreme court of Florida. That court regarded this as proper procedure and "upon consideration" denied relief without opinion. The Supreme Court granted the prisoner's motion to permit him to proceed *in forma pauperis* and agreed to review the case.[74] It later granted his motion to appoint counsel to represent him, appointed Abe Fortas, prominent Washington attorney, and requested both sides to discuss in their briefs and in their oral arguments whether the decision in *Betts* v. *Brady* should be reconsidered.[75]

As Justice Black pointed out, the facts in the case were strikingly like the facts in the *Betts* case. Both accused had been charged with commission of a felony, both were indigent and had requested counsel, both had been denied counsel, had tried to defend themselves, had been convicted and thereafter sought relief by habeas corpus on the grounds of denial of the constitutional rights to counsel. He reviewed the course of decision as to the "incorporation" of guarantees of the Bill of Rights into the Fourteenth Amendment. He pointed out that the Court in *Betts* had granted that provisions in the Bill of Rights which are "fundamental and essential to a fair trial" are made obligatory on the states by the due process clause, but that the Court was wrong in concluding that the Sixth Amendment's guarantee of counsel to all accused of crime, unless intelligently waived, is not one of these fundamental rights. He concluded: "Florida supported by two other States, has asked that *Betts* v. *Brady* be left intact. Twenty-two States, as friends of the Court, argue that *Betts* was 'an anachronism when handed down' and that it should now be overruled. We agree." Justice Douglas, in a concurring opinion, apparently wanted to make certain that the decision concerning right of counsel did not foreclose the question whether all guarantees and protections of the Bill of Rights were included in the Fourteenth Amendment. He thought that at least ten Justices held the view that this was the case. He named himself, Justices Black, Murphy, Rutledge, the first Justice Harlan, Bradley, Swayne, Field and probably Justices Brewer and Clifford.

Justice Harlan, the second, on the other hand, in his concurring opinion, made it clear that in his view, the decision did *not* "incorporate" the Sixth Amendment, as such, into the Fourteenth. He insisted that the Court had not departed from the theory of Justice Cardozo's opinion in *Palko* v. *Connecticut*[76] but that it had merely decided that the right to counsel was fundamental in "the concept of ordered liberty" and thus guaranteed by the Fourteenth Amendment without regard to the Bill of Rights. He regarded the decision as just another step in the evolution of the right to counsel rule. "The special circumstances rule," Harlan wrote, "has been formally abandoned in capital cases, and the time has now come when it should be similarly abandoned in non-capital cases, at least as to offenses which, as the one involved here, carry the possibility of a substantial prison sentence. (Whether the rule should extend to *all* criminal cases need not now be decided.)" *Betts* v. *Brady* is, indeed, overruled. But there

may still be disagreement as to exactly what it was that was overruled.

The same problem of retroactivity was involved here as in situations involving the overruling in *Mapp* v. *Ohio* of the previous
rule as to the admissibility of unconstitutionally seized evidence in
state criminal trials. Late in 1963, Justice Harlan dissented from the
Court's remand of ten or a dozen cases to the state courts in right to
counsel cases for reconsideration in the light of the Court's latest
decision. Harlan wanted the Court to face up to the question of retroactive application of such decisions rather than shift the onus first
on the state supreme court.[77] The Court in substance did so in 1964.[78]

The materials presented in this chapter involve problems of great
magnitude for democratic man. Although the specific context has
been the right to counsel, there are basic issues which encompass
other matters of equal importance. Justice Rutledge and his fellow
dissenters pointed up most of them in one way or another, while Justice Frankfurter duly stressed another.

As to the right to counsel, there is, of course, the whole "incorporation" doctrine involved. The extent of the application of this principle to other guarantees of the Bill of Rights and particularly of the
Sixth Amendment and the future of the "concept of ordered liberty
doctrine" are yet to be determined, but it may be that the *Gideon*
case will have an important bearing thereon. In any event, the
right to counsel in state criminal trials will no longer depend on the
length of five Justice's feet. So too, the "exhaustion of state remedies"
rubric has been partly alleviated in federal court habeas corpus cases
by Justice Brennan's recent opinion which goes a long distance to meet
the state "merry-go-round" game. It also strikes a blow at the rule in
some states creating a forfeiture of constitutional rights by the selection of the wrong state remedy and the expiration of the statute of
limitation on the right remedy which prevails in some states.

But the problems are only partially solved and there are still
many roadblocks before state prisoners are assured of full vindication of federal constitutional rights. This point was emphasized in an
address by Justice Brennan to the Advisory Council of Judges in
New York on May 30th, 1963. He referred to the problems of "federalism" which so worried Justice Frankfurter. In a large sense, the
"unwanted intrusion" of federal courts into the administration of
criminal justice in the state courts was to be laid at their own door.
It could be minimized by a scrupulous regard for the constitutional
rights of persons accused of the violation of state law. He felt that the
opinion which he had rendered in *Fay* v. *Noia* a few weeks before

had clarified matters somewhat, as indeed it had. He again warned that failure to make state remedies as broad as federal remedies would inevitably force many constitutional claims into federal courts. There must be an adequate post-conviction procedure which would afford the prisoner an opportunity to raise all of his federal constitutional claims, not merely those which may be characterized as "jurisdictional." He warned against technicalities in state procedure which resulted in forfeitures or waiver of rights on the part of prisoners asserting violations of constitutional guarantees. The Justice urged full hearings in state courts on constitutional claims depending on factual issues and, no doubt with the Illinois "common law record" in mind, the compilation of a full and complete record in state proceedings and full opinions by the judges instead of summary dispositions.[79]

The "delicate relation" between the courts of the United States and the courts of the various states is an inescapable problem of federalism. The particular aspect involved in the administration of state criminal law, however, may be over-emphasized. To be sure, any review by the federal courts of state action is capable of creating friction. But the major cries of "states rights" with its occasional acute and embarrassing political and international overtones do not arise from individual criminal cases involving right to counsel, double jeopardy, self-incrimination and the like. Proposals for a "Court of the Union" have a totally different origin and should not be confused with problems of the administration of criminal justice which, as Justice Brennan declared can be much improved in both state and federal courts.

Justice Brennan's suggestions for specific reforms all dealt with matters which Justice Rutledge had faced and urged in the right to counsel cases. He felt strongly about them, in part, it would seem because of his passion for individual, as distinguished from abstract, justice. The problems involved he saw always in the form of a lone prisoner challenging the all powerful state itself, in reliance on the Constitution.

CHAPTER VIII

"ALL PERSONS BORN OR NATURALIZED . . . ."

CITIZENSHIP, like good health, is a possession the value of which is seldom appreciated until one is deprived of it. Imprisoned in concentration camps until and unless some benign nation granted them a haven, hundreds of thousands of stateless persons who survived World War II understood it too well. Probably most Americans would be shocked at the suggestion that in this democratic country there are two levels of citizenship—first class and second class citizens. On the other hand it no doubt seems perfectly reasonable that if the United States grants to a foreigner the privilege of American citizenship, it should have the right and the power to take it away if it had been acquired by fraud or other illegal means. Citizenship revoked, the alien may be deported—sent back "where he came from" or to some other country if one can be found which is willing to admit him. The immigration laws and the cases which have arisen under them present these matters, sometimes in tragic context. The *Schneiderman* case and the opinions of the Justices throw a glaring light on this dilemma.[1]

The law provides for a hearing before a United States district judge in naturalization proceedings in which the Department of Justice may participate and be heard in opposition and present such evidence as there may be that the applicant is not qualified to become a citizen. Among other conditions to be met by the applicant, it must appear to the judge, and he must so find, that during the five years next preceding, the petitioner "has been and still is a person of good moral character, attached to the principles of the Constitution of the United States, and well disposed to the good order and happiness of the United States."[2] If the judge so finds, he enters a judgment to that effect and, other conditions being satisfied, a certificate of naturalization is issued. The alien then becomes a citizen of the United States. The law at that time gave the Government the right and indeed, imposed the duty to institute proceedings to set aside and cancel certificates of naturalization on the grounds of "fraud" or on the ground that they were otherwise "illegally procured." The language but not the substance of this provision has been changed.

The *New York Times* story of February 15, 1943 on the occasion of the swearing in of Rutledge as Associate Justice, contained the following paragraph:

> The . . . order directed rehearing of the undecided case in which Wendell L. Willkie argued on November 9 [1942] that the Government could not legally cancel the citizenship of William Schneiderman, secretary of the Communist Party of California. The order was taken to mean that the presence of Justice Rutledge might resolve a deadlock of ten weeks.

This represented the period when but eight Justices were sitting after the Byrnes resignation.

The man Schneiderman had come to this country from Russia when he was three years old. When he was sixteen, in 1922, he became a member of the Young Workers League in California. At the time of the denaturalization proceedings and for some years before, this organization was merged with the Communist Party of the United States. Schneiderman had been naturalized in 1927. Proceedings to cancel his certificate of naturalization were begun in 1939.

The Government's sole case rested on Schneiderman's membership and activities in the Party and its predecessor organizations. He had not been asked whether he was a Communist at the time of his naturalization and he did not volunteer the information. He had never been arrested and there was no record of his participation at any time in any overt, illegal or violent action or even any disturbance of the peace, before or after he became a citizen. He testified that as a boy, he had been reared in poverty and had joined the Young Workers League to study what light the principles of Communism could throw on the problems of society. He worked his way through night high school and college.

The district court found that he had acquired citizenship illegally. It based its decision that Schneiderman was not attached to the principles of the Constitution at the time of his naturalization on the fact of his membership in the Communist Party and other Communist groups which, the court found, advocated the overthrow of organized government by force. On this point there was conflicting evidence. Two professors who had discussed Marxian theory as evidenced by the writings of Marx, Engells and Lenin, concluded that it did not necessarily and inevitably involve the use of force and violence as a method of attaining its objectives. Schneiderman himself testified that he did not so advocate. As stated in Justice Murphy's opinion, it was a tenable conclusion from the evidence that the Communist Party in 1927 "desired to achieve its purpose by peaceful and democratic means, and as a theoretical matter justified the use of force and violence only as a method of preventing an attempted forcible counter-overthrow once the Party had obtained control in a peaceful manner, or as a method of last resort to enforce the majority will if at some indefinite future time because of peculiar circumstances constitutional or peaceful channels were no longer open." Apparently the Court in 1927 subscribed to some such interpretation of the evidence.

In the denaturalization proceedings the Supreme Court decided to review the case on October 12, 1941. The case was not argued until November 9, 1942. In the meantime Justice Byrnes had resigned. Rutledge replaced Byrnes in February 1943. Apparently it was clear from the beginning that there would be a closely divided Court. Justice Jackson took no part at any time because he had been Attorney General during the denaturalization proceedings. Justice Rutledge had not heard the original argument. For these reasons, no doubt, the case was restored to the docket for reargument on February 15, 1943. The following June, the Supreme Court decided the case, reversing the judgment of the lower court.

Murphy's majority opinion is one of the most convincing of his judicial career. The principal basis for the reversal was that the Government had not proved by "clear, unequivocal and convincing" evidence that Schneiderman was not attached to the principles of the Constitution at the time of his naturalization. He reviewed the evidence thoroughly. He pointed out that it was unsafe to assume that every member of an organization believed everything that other members said or wrote or even that the organization officially proclaimed. He emphasized that a heavy burden rested upon the Government to invalidate a judicial decision conferring citizenship upon an alien and that such a burden had not been met. "The Government," he wrote, "has not proved that petitioner's beliefs on the subject of force and violence were such that he was not attached to the Constitution in 1927." If any provisions of the Constitution required unqualified attachment, "they are the guarantees of the Bill of Rights and especially that of freedom of thought contained in the First Amendment." He declared that the Constitutional fathers "fresh from a revolution, did not forge a political strait jacket for the generations to come." In a footnote, he quoted the famous passage from Jefferson's first inaugural address:

If there be among us those who would wish to dissolve this Union or to change its republican form, let them stand undisturbed as monuments of the safety with which error of opinion may be tolerated where reason is left free to combat it.

Murphy was joined by Douglas, Rutledge, Black and Reed, but Douglas and Rutledge wrote separate concurring opinions. Rutledge's concurrence is important. He was appalled by the implications of a denaturalization decision.

Immediately we are concerned with only one man, William Schneiderman. Actually, though indirectly, the decision affects millions. If, seventeen years after a federal court adjudged him entitled to be a citizen, that judgment can be nullified and he can be stripped of this most precious right, by nothing more than re-examination upon the merits of the very facts the judgment established, no naturalized person's citizenship is or can be secure. If this can be done after that length of time, it can be done after thirty or fifty years. If it can be done for Schneiderman, it can be done for thousands or tens of thousands of others.[3]

He questioned seriously whether Congress had power under the Constitution to provide for the invalidation of a final judgment, years thereafter, on the identical evidence presented in the original proceeding. After all, it was a *judgment* rendered in the exercise of the judicial power created by Article III of the Constitution which was involved. It is true, he admitted, that Congress with some exceptions had power to legislate on the matter of jurisdiction of the federal courts. But to confer jurisdiction and at the same time provide for the complete nullification of the effects of its exercise presented a different problem.

To say therefore that the trial court's function in this case is the same as was that of the admitting court is to ignore the vast difference between overturning a judgment, with its adjudicated facts, and deciding initially upon facts which have not been adjudged.

He here referred to the age-old doctrine of the common law that an issue once decided on the facts before the court becomes *res judicata, i.e.*, finally settled and not subject to future litigation between the same parties.

He doubted seriously that the framers of the Constitution intended to create two classes of citizens, one free and independent, one haltered with a lifetime string tied to its status.

If this is the law and the right the naturalized citizen acquires, his admission creates nothing more than citizenship in attenuated, if not suspended, animation. He acquires but prima facie status, if that. Until the Government moves to cancel his certificate and he knows the outcome, he cannot know whether he is in or out.

"And when that is done, nothing forbids repeating the harrowing process again and again, unless the weariness of the courts should lead them finally to speak *res judicata*."

Chief Justice Stone wrote a long and powerful dissent in which Justices Frankfurter and Roberts joined. "The question then," he wrote, "is not of petitioner's opinions or beliefs—save as they may have influenced or may explain his conduct showing attachment, or want of it, to the principles of the Constitution."

It is not a question of freedom of thought, of speech or of opinion, or of present imminent danger to the United States from our acceptance as citizens of those who are not attached to the principles of our form of government. The case obviously has nothing to do with our relations with Russia, where petitioner was born, or with our past or present views of the Russian political or social system. The United States has the same interest as other nations in demanding of those who seek its citizenship some measure of attachment to its institutions.[4]

As to the constitutionality of the denaturalization law, the Chief Justice declared that there was no question. He cited some previous cases which so indicated in general terms, but he did not answer the specific arguments made by Rutledge as to the finality of judgments. As to the evidence that Schneiderman was not attached to the principles of the Constitution, he went into it in detail, including in an Appendix, several pages of excerpts from Statutes, Theses and Conditions of Admission to the Communist International, from which he concluded that there was ample evidence to support the finding that Schneiderman had not, at the time of his naturalization, the necessary attachment to the principles of the Constitution which the Act of Congress required. The Chief Justice did not discuss the question whether a native born citizen could be denaturalized, if Congress so provided, because he was not attached to the principles of the Constitution and therefore did not meet the issue of first and second class citizenship.

A year after the *Schneiderman* case, the Court reviewed the case of a German immigrant named Baumgartner who had been naturalized in 1932. In 1942, proceedings were brought by the Department of Justice to cancel his naturalization certificate on the grounds of fraud. It was charged that he did not truly renounce his allegiance to Germany and that he did not intend to support the Constitution and the laws of the United States when he swore that he would do so. Judgment of denaturalization was rendered against him by the district court and affirmed by the circuit court of appeals. Again the Supreme Court reversed on the grounds that the Government had failed to prove fraud by "clear, unequivocal and convincing" evidence as required by the *Schneiderman* case.[5]

Baumgartner had repeatedly boasted of the superiority of the German schools and other achievements of his native land. He had spoken slightingly of the United States and declared that its democracy was "a farce." He had expressed pride and joy when Dunkerque fell and great admiration for Hitler and the Nazi program. He was violently anti-Semitic. Many of the pro-Nazi and anti-American expressions were subsequent to his 1932 naturalization.

Mr. Justice Frankfurter wrote the unanimous opinion of the Court. He pointed out that "foreswearing past political allegiance without reservation and full assumption of the obligations of American citizenship" were "not at all inconsistent with cultural feelings imbedded in childhood and youth." In this connection he quoted from a distinguished historian, writing of his own naturalization as an American citizen: "Your pledges are only juridical and political. You are asked to sever your connections with the government of your former country, not with the people and civilization of your former country."[6]

Justice Murphy wrote a concurring opinion in which Rutledge, Black and Douglas joined. The main thrust of this opinion was an attack upon the use of statements and occurrences subsequent to naturalization as evidence of the immigrant's state of mind at that time. This point was particularly relevant in Baumgartner's case since most of his pro-German sympathies were with respect to the Nazi Government, while the Weimar Republic was the German Government when he foreswore allegiance and took the oath to support the Constitution and laws of the United States. Thus Murphy wrote:

American citizenship is not a right granted on a condition subsequent that the naturalized citizen refrain in the future from uttering any remark or adopting an attitude favorable to his original homeland or those there in power, no matter how distasteful such conduct may be to most of us. He is not required to imprison himself in an intellectual or spiritual strait jacket; nor is he obliged to retain a static mental attitude. Moreover, he does not lose the precious right of citizenship because he subsequently dares to criticize his adopted government in vituperative or defamatory terms. It obviously is more difficult to conform to the standard set forth in the Schneiderman Case by mere proof of a state of mind subsequent to naturalization than by proof of facts existing prior to or at the time of naturalization. But that does not excuse a failure to meet that standard. The naturalized citizen has as much right as the natural born citizen to exercise the cherished freedoms of speech, press and religion, and without "clear, unequivocal, and convincing" proof that he did not bear or swear true allegiance to the United States at the time of naturalization, he cannot be denaturalized. . . .[7]

A year after the *Baumgartner* decision another Nazi denaturalization case came to the Supreme Court.[8] Knauer was a notorious Nazi Bundist in Milwaukee who had come to this country in 1925. He took his oath of allegiance and was admitted to citizenship in 1937. Six years later the Government began denaturalization proceedings against him and was successful in obtaining cancellation of his certificate by the district court on the grounds that he had taken a false oath. The evidence against him was vast, convincing and unequivocal. He not only believed in Hitler and the Nazi Party, but declared it was necessary to have the same party in this country because of the Jews and the Communists. He visited Germany and told with pride of meeting Hitler and the offer of a position in the German Government. He said he was opposed to any republican form of government. He emphasized that allegiance to Hitler was a higher obligation than allegiance to the United States. There was no doubt that he was a confirmed Hitlerite and opposed to the principles of the Constitution of the United States at the time of his naturalization.

The case was argued before the Supreme Court in March 1946. Chief Justice Stone died within less than a month thereafter. The case was decided in June of that year by a seven man Court, Justice Jackson not participating in the decision. Justice Douglas wrote the opinion for the Court, affirming the decision of denaturalization, with only Rutledge and Murphy dissenting. Justice Black in a short concurring opinion declared that he, too, would have dissented had the judgment rested only on Knauer's philosophical or political beliefs. He believed, however, that even in obtaining his naturalization and taking the oath of allegiance, that Knauer was "serving the German Government with the same fanatical zeal which motivated the saboteurs sent to the United States to wage war."

Rutledge in his dissent took the firm position that the Constitution did not permit two classes of citizens save for two purposes, one to provide a method for the acquisition of citizenship by aliens, the other to determine eligibility for the presidency. The Constitution provides that the President must be a native-born citizen, *i.e.*, born in the United States or of parents who were both citizens. He did not believe that the Congress had power to take away citizenship once it is conferred, "other than for some sufficient act of forfeiture taking place afterward." He went on to say:

> Naturalized citizens are no more free to become traitors or criminals than others and may be punished as they are when they commit the same offense. But any process which takes away their citizenship for causes or by procedures not applicable to native-born citizens places them in a separate and an inferior class. . . . In my opinion the power to naturalize is not the power to denaturalize. The act of admission must be taken as final, for any cause which may have existed at that time.[9]

This, in substance was the same position he had taken in the *Schneiderman* case, stated unhesitatingly and with conviction.

Rutledge here recognized, of course, that certain behavior could constitute a renunciation of the citizenship of naturalized aliens as well as the native-born. But forfeiture is quite a different matter. Certainly no such drastic penalty could be imposed on native-born citizens by a mere administrative finding. Nor could a native-born American be banished except, perhaps, as a result of a procedure consistent with the protective devices prescribed for serious crimes such as treason or felony.

Mason in his book on Chief Justice Stone, quotes a statement to Stone by an unnamed Justice in connection with the majority decision in the *Schneiderman* case, to which, it will be remembered, the Chief Justice, Frankfurter and Roberts dissented: "It is very painful for me to say so," the Justice said, "but I do not think there is the slightest doubt that if the same kind of record had come up with reference to a Bundist, the opposite result would have been reached."[10] The *Baumgartner* case adequately disposes of this implication as to the political sympathies of the Schneiderman majority while the *Knauer* case emphasizes it as to Rutledge and Murphy.

The last of the denaturalization cases in which Justice Rutledge participated involved one August Klapprott, another German immigrant who had been admitted to citizenship in 1933. During the war with Germany, nine years later, the Government moved against him on the usual grounds that his oath was false, that at the time he took it, he knew that he was not attached to the principles of the Constitution and did not in fact intend to bear true allegiance to the United States. The charges were general, principally that he had evidenced his disloyalty in speeches and writings, that he had been a member of the Bund and other organizations whose teachings were alleged to be inimical to the Constitution and happiness of the people and that these organizations were propagated and encouraged by enemies of the United States.

Under the rules in such cases, the party proceeded against must answer the charges within sixty days. This, Klapprott failed to do, and on motion of the Government, a default judgment was entered against him and his certificate of citizenship cancelled. Some four years later he brought this action to set aside the default judgment. The lower courts refused to consider the merits of his case because, as it found, he had been guilty of "willful and inexcusable neglect" in delaying so long to seek relief from his loss of citizenship. He finally got a hearing before the Supreme Court.

The sequence of events which followed the initiation of the denaturalization proceedings, as alleged by Klapprott and undenied by the Government, are of the utmost importance. A week before the expiration of the period to answer by denying the falsity of his oath and other charges, he was arrested under a federal indictment charging him and others with conspiracy to violate the Selective Service Act. He was imprisoned in New York unable to make bond of $25,-000. He alleged that he had written a letter to the American Civil Liberties Union, requesting legal assistance without fee in his denaturalization trouble. This letter, he said, was taken from him by F.B.I. agents and never mailed. A lawyer was appointed by the Court to defend him in the conspiracy case. He claimed that, although requested to do so, the attorney neglected to help in the denaturalization case. Klapprott was convicted of conspiracy to violate the draft act and in lieu of bail, imprisoned in a Michigan penitentiary pending appeal. Two years later the conviction was reversed by the Supreme Court, but in the meantime Klapprott with twenty-nine others had been charged with sedition and held in jail in the District of Columbia until the sedition case was dismissed in November, 1946, after which, while awaiting deportation on Ellis Island, he began the action to set aside the default judgment depriving him of his American citizenship.

"Thus," as Justice Black pointed out, "this petitioner has now been held continuously in prison by the Government for six and one-half years."

> During that period he served one and one-half years of a penitentiary punishment under a conviction which this Court held was improper. He was also held in the District of Columbia jail two years and ten months under an indictment that was later dismissed. It is clear therefore, that for four and one-half years this petitioner was held in prison on charges that the Government was unable to sustain. No other conclusion can be drawn except that this long imprisonment was wrongful. Whether the judgment by default should be set aside must therefore be decided on the undenied allegations that the Government, largely through the action of FBI agents, wrongfully held petitioner in New York, Michigan, and District of Columbia prisons, while the same Government largely acting through the same or other FBI agents, caused a district court to revoke petitioner's citizenship on the ground that petitioner had failed to make appearance and defend in the New Jersey courts, although petitioner was at the time without funds to hire a lawyer.[11]

The Court reversed the lower courts. It set aside the decree cancelling Klapprott's naturalization certificate and ordered a hearing on the merits of the Government's charges against him. Justice Black announced the judgment of the Court in an opinion in which Justice Douglas joined. He found that Congress had not authorized default judgments without evidence to support the allegations of the Government. He declared that the burden rested on the Government to prove its charges by "clear, unequivocal and convincing evidence," the test laid down in the *Schneiderman* case. He continued:

> ... This burden is substantially identical with that required in criminal cases—proof beyond a reasonable doubt. The same factors that caused us to require proof of this nature as a prerequisite to denaturalization judgments in hearings with the defendant present, apply at least with equal force to proceedings in which a citizen is stripped of his citizenship rights in his absence.

Justice Rutledge concurred in the result in a separate opinion in which Justice Murphy joined. They thought that no judgment of denaturalization could be taken by default under any circumstances and that only under the rules of criminal procedure, with all of their constitutional protection, could any such judgment be rendered. "To treat a denaturalization proceeding," Rutledge wrote, ". . . as if it were nothing more than a suit for damages for breach of contract or one to recover overtime pay [in which default judgments are permitted] ignores, in my view, every consideration of justice and of reality concerning the substance of the suit and what is at stake."

> . . . If, in deference to the Court's rulings, we are to continue to have two classes of citizens in this country, one secure in their status and the other subject at every moment to its loss by proceedings not applicable to the other class [Citing cases], I cannot assent to the idea that the ordinary rules of procedure in civil causes afford any standard sufficient to safeguard the status given to naturalized citizens. If citizenship is to be defeasible for naturalized citizens, other than by voluntary renunciation or other causes applicable to native-born citizens, the defeasance it seems to me should be surrounded by no lesser protections than those securing all citizens against conviction for crime.[12]

Chief Justice Vinson and Justices Jackson and Reed dissented in an opinion written by Reed. Frankfurter wrote his own dissent. All thought that in the absence of congressional action, default judgments without evidence were permissible.

Thus it was that four Justices in two opinions voted to reverse the default judgment, four in two opinions to affirm it. Justice Burton was the ninth—the "swing" Justice. He joined in no opinion but voted with Black, Douglas, Rutledge and Murphy to reverse. We do not know why he abstained from both the Black and Rutledge reasoning.

As noted, the Court vacated the judgment of the lower court and ordered a hearing on the denaturalization complaint giving the Government the opportunity to present evidence of its charges of Klapprott's disloyalty. Later, however, on motion by the Government, the order was modified, directing the district court only to receive evidence on the truth or falsity of Klapprott's allegations in his petition to vacate the original default decree. Black, Douglas, Rutledge and Murphy dissented from this change. It was Burton who switched to join the other four Justices in the modification order.

The change in the order was important. Instead of a hearing on the denaturalization charges, with a heavy burden of proof on the Government, Klapprott must first sustain the burden of convincing the trial judge of the truth of the facts which he alleged as exculpating him from the charge of "willful and inexcusable neglect." In other words, he must verify the facts relied upon by the Supreme Court as a reasonable explanation for waiting four years to ask for a nullification of the default decree of denaturalization.

Whether Klapprott could have prevailed under the original order, *i.e.*, whether the Government would have failed to produce "clear, unequivocal and convincing evidence" to support its charges that he had taken a false oath will never be known. The burden of proof in criminal cases is extremely important and frequently makes the difference between a verdict for or against the accused. After all, he is presumed to be innocent unless the jury is convinced otherwise "beyond a reasonable doubt." Klapprott was unsuccessful under the modified order. The trial judge found that he had knowingly and voluntarily permitted entry of the default judgment and the Court of Appeals affirmed this ruling, holding that there was sufficient evidence to sustain it.[13] The Supreme Court declined to review.[14] The Department of Justice reported, for the year involved, a total of 13,544 deportations. Presumably Klapprott was a datum in that statistic.

As a footnote, it might be added that when the Supreme Court refused to review Klapprott's last effort to avoid deportation, Rutledge and Murphy had died and in the meantime, had been replaced by Justices Minton and Clark. In cases of this type, it requires four Justices to vote to review. Since Justices Black and Douglas, along with Rutledge and Murphy, had dissented from the modified order, it may be assumed that, had the latter two lived, Klapprott would have had another day in the Supreme Court.

It will be noted that the substance of the Rutledge argument in the denaturalization cases was (1) that there was no warrant in the Constitution for believing that it contemplated an inferior status for naturalized citizens otherwise than disqualification for the presidency, and, (2) native-born citizens could not be deprived of their citizenship without compliance with constitutional procedures for the protection of persons accused of crime.

Throughout Rutledge's opinions runs the contention that, to take away one's citizenship is to impose punishment—drastic punishment —and such punishment is a criminal penalty which cannot be inflicted without regard to the protective provisions of the Fifth and Sixth Amendments, which provide for due process of law, notice, confrontation, compulsory process for obtaining witnesses, trial by jury and assistance of counsel. In the *Knauer* case, he wrote:

> No native-born American's birthright could be stripped from him for such a cause or by such a procedure as has been followed here. Nor could he be punished with banishment. To suffer that great loss, he must forfeit citizenship by some act of treason or felony and be adjudged guilty by processes of law consistent with all the great protections thrown around such trials. . . . The right of citizenship is the most precious of all. The penalty for denaturalization is always harsh. Often it is more drastic than any other.[15]

And in the *Klapprott* case, he declared:

> Regardless of the name given it, the denaturalization proceeding when it is successful has all the consequences and effects of a penal or criminal conviction, except that the ensuing liability to deportation is a greater penalty than is generally inflicted for crime.[16]

Since the death of Justice Rutledge, several important cases involving the expatriation of native-born citizens have come before the Court, four decided by a five to four vote of the Justices. A fifth case was left undecided by the Court by a four to four division. The effect was to leave standing the decision of the lower court. Still another case involving a naturalized citizen resulted in a six to three decision.

In 1958, the Court held unconstitutional an Act of Congress imposing loss of citizenship on an American national who deserted from the armed forces in time of war. It upheld a law which forfeited citizenship of one who voted in a foreign election. It will appear odd to many laymen—and, for that matter to lawyers, too—that a deserter during a war should not lose his citizenship, but one who votes in a foreign election in peacetime may become stateless.

In the latter case a Mexican-American named Perez voted in Mexico and was denaturalized.[17] The legislation was held valid on the rather farfetched grounds that it was an exercise of congressional power to regulate foreign relations. It is true, as Justice Frankfurter wrote, that there was historical evidence that American policy and legislation was to some extent prompted by refusal of other nations to recognize American citizenship of their former nationals. It was also true that the practice developed in the State Department, in the management of foreign affairs, to pass on the validity of claims to American citizenship. But it is something of a strain on the imagination to regard it as "necessary and proper," in order to avoid "embarrassment in the conduct of our foreign relations," that Congress should provide for the expatriation of the rare American who votes in a foreign election. Conceding the "importance and delicacy" of our international affairs, one does not readily appraise as "pregnant with the possibility of embroiling" this country in a dispute with Mexico, the fact that an American citizen, born in Texas of Mexican parents, votes in a Mexican election while living in that country. There certainly would be no such "pregnancy" where the vote was entirely legal under the law of the foreign state, and as Justice Whittaker pointed out in his dissent, there was nothing in the record of the *Perez* case to show that the American's vote was not entirely lawful under Mexican law. Aside from the fact that Mexico, under international law, could properly claim that the voter was a Mexican citizen since he was born of Mexican parents, the Chief Justice, in his dissent, observed that in fact for many years aliens had been permitted to vote in presidential elections in the United States.

But the Chief Justice went much farther in his opinion. Indeed, he went quite as far as did Rutledge in his *Knauer* opinion. The latter believed that the Government had no power to take away the citizenship of a naturalized American. "[T]he power to naturalize is not the power to denaturalize." He conceded, however, that a naturalized citizen, like a native-born, might forfeit his rights by renunciation, treason or other criminal acts. The Chief Justice, too, declared that the "Government is without power to take citizenship away from a native-born or lawfully naturalized American."[18] There was, of course, no question that citizenship could be "voluntarily relinquished." He recalled that although seizure of naturalized American sailors of British birth was the precipitating cause of the War of 1812, there was occasional anomalous lip service to the doctrine of perpetual allegiance. But finally the right of voluntary expatriation was recognized by Congress, both with regard to the protection of our naturalized citizens of foreign birth and as to the reciprocal right of American nationals to renounce their citizenship and to abjure their allegiance.[19] The Chief Justice concluded:

> The mere act of voting in a foreign election, . . . without regard to the circumstances attending the participation, is not sufficient to show a voluntary abandonment of citizenship. . . . The basic right of American citizenship has been too dearly won to be so lightly lost.[20]

In the course of his opinion the Chief Justice bolstered his argument with an exposition of his political philosophy which is well worth emphasizing in a period when too many voices raise doubts concerning the basic freedoms which constitute our heritage. Thus Chief Justice Warren wrote:[21]

> ... This Government was born of its citizens, it maintains itself in a continuing relationship with them, and, in my judgment, it is without power to sever the relationship that gives rise to its existence. I cannot believe that a government conceived in the spirit of ours was established with power to take from the people their most basic right.
>
> Citizenship *is* man's basic right for it is nothing less than the right to have rights. Remove this priceless possession and there remains a stateless person, disgraced and degraded in the eyes of his countrymen. He has no lawful claim to protection from any nation, and no nation may assert rights on his behalf. His very existence is at the sufferance of the state within whose borders he happens to be. In this country the expatriate would presumably enjoy, at most, only the limited rights and privileges of aliens, and like the alien he might even be subject to deportation and thereby deprived of the right to assert any rights. This government was not established with power to decree this fate.
>
> The people who created this government endowed it with broad powers. They created a sovereign state with power to function as a sovereignty. But the citizens themselves are sovereign, and their citizenship is not subject to the general powers of their government. Whatever may be the scope of its powers to regulate the conduct and affairs of all persons within its jurisdiction, a government *of* the people cannot take away their citizenship simply because one branch of that government can be said to have a conceivable rational basis for wanting to do so.

(The emphasis is in the original.)

Justice Douglas also contributed a powerful dissent in which Justice Black joined. He, too, emphasized that expatriation, in the words of Chief Justice Hughes is "the voluntary renunciation or abandonment of nationality and allegiance."[22] He declared that the decision taking away Perez' citizenship broke with that tradition by allowing Congress to brand an ambiguous act as a "voluntary renunciation of citizenship" when there was no requirement by the law and no finding by any court that the citizen transferred his loyalty from this country to another. He expressed the fear that if the power of Congress to regulate foreign affairs extends so far as to enable it to withdraw the foreign voter's citizenship, it could as readily do the same to persons engaged in political discussion and criticism of executive or legislative action relating to foreign affairs. Such action, to be sure, would be in the face of the free expression provisions of the First Amendment. But Douglas thought the Court's decision in upholding this Act of Congress was in the teeth of and contrary to the Fourteenth Amendment.

Douglas' argument here is interesting. The first sentence of the Fourteenth Amendment merely states a declarative proposition: "All persons born or naturalized in the United States and subject to the jurisdiction thereof, are citizens of the United States and of the State wherein they reside." This he regarded as an absolute grant of the rights and privileges traditionally associated in International Law with nationality and as such immune to congressional limitation or abridgment. Thus he wrote:

> What the Court does is to make it possible for any one of the many legislative powers to be used to wipe out or modify specific rights granted by the Constitution, provided the action taken is moderate and does not do violence to the sensibilities of a majority of this Court. The examples where this concept of Due Process has been used to sustain state action as well as federal action, which modifies or dilutes specific constitutional guarantees, are numerous. It is used today drastically to revise the express command of the first Clause of § 1 of the Fourteenth Amendment. A right granted by the Constitution—whether it be the right to counsel or the right to citizenship—may be waived by the citizen. But the waiver must be *first* a voluntary act and *second* an act consistent with a surrender of the right granted. When Perez voted, he acted voluntarily. But, as shown, § 401 (e) [the law in question] does not require that his act have a sufficient relationship to the relinquishment of citizenship—nor a sufficient quality of adhering to a foreign power. Nor did his voting abroad have that quality.[23]

Some may question Douglas' treatment of the first sentence of the Fourteenth in the same way that he interprets the prohibition of the First Amendment. ("Congress shall make no law . . . abridging the freedom of speech or of the press.") And indeed, if this were all, it could plausibly be argued that it is more difficult in law and logic to read in exceptions to a prohibition, absolute in terms, than to interpret as qualified a naked grant of individual right. But, in context, Douglas seems to say of the native-born what Rutledge said of the naturalized citizen. It is not that the Constitution in terms prohibits involuntary expatriation, but that it does not authorize it and in view of the seriousness of such action, he is unwilling to stretch the "necessary and proper" clause so far.

> The Fourteenth Amendment grants citizenship to the native-born. . . . That right may be waived or surrendered by the citizen. But I see no constitutional method by which it can be taken from him. Citizenship, like freedom of speech, press and religion, occupies a preferred position in our written Constitution, because it is a grant absolute in terms. The power of Congress to withhold it, modify it, or cancel it, does not exist.[24]

In the second 1958 case,[25] the Chief Justice announced the judgment of the Court in a plurality opinion joined by Justices Black, Douglas and Whittaker. The Act of Congress which forfeited the citizenship of any American, guilty of deserting the armed forces in time of war, if convicted thereof by court-martial and dismissed or dishonorably discharged, was unconstitutional. In addition to the reasoning in his dissent in the *Perez* case, he found not only that the statute imposed punishment, but that it violated the Eighth Amendment as inflicting "cruel and unusual punishment." Justice Brennan who had voted with the majority in upholding the expatriation of *Perez* under the voting-in-a-foreign-election law, switched his vote here, to constitute the majority. His position was that Congress was without power to forfeit citizenship as provided in this law. The only plausible basis, the war power, would not support it because of the tenuous and remote connection between the means and the end. He could find no rational relation between the law and the power to wage war. It is difficult to understand how one taking this position could have discovered a rational relation between foreign policy and an American citizen voting in a foreign election, especially if it was consistent with the foreign law.

In 1963, two cases came to the Court which involved the validity of the Act of Congress providing for divestment of American citizenship for leaving or remaining outside the United States in time of war. In one case, Mendozo Martinez, an American-born son of Mexican parents, left the country in 1942 and went to Mexico, as he admitted, solely to evade military service. He returned after the war, pleaded guilty to a violation of the draft law and served the imposed sentence of a year and a day in prison. Five years later the immigration service sought to deport him as an alien.

In the other case, a man named Cort, born in Boston, brought suit in the District of Columbia through counsel for a declaration that he was a citizen, entitled to a passport to enable him to return to the United States from Czechoslovakia. Cort had been a medical student at Yale University for several years and while there, it seems, had been a member of the Communist Party. He had registered for the draft and under the Doctor's Draft Act, but while living in England late in 1951, had failed to respond to orders to return. His explanation was that he was engaged in important research and teaching at Cambridge and did not wish to subject himself to what he regarded as unlawful political persecution in the United States. He again failed to report after further notices from his draft board and in 1954 was indicted for evasion of his obligations under the Selective Service Act. The indictment was still outstanding at the time of the decision of this case by the Supreme Court, on February 18, 1963. Unlike Martinez, the Mexican-American in the companion case, Cort did not have dual nationality. If deprived of his American citizenship he would be among the stateless—"fair game for the despoiler at home and the oppressor abroad, if indeed there is any place which will tolerate them at all." [26]

Justice Goldberg in an opinion for the Court in which Justices Black, Douglas, Brennan and the Chief Justice joined, held unconstitutional the law forfeiting citizenship of an American who left or remained outside the country at time of war for the purpose of evading military service. The law imposed "punishment" without affording the procedural safeguards guaranteed by the Bill of Rights in the Fifth and Sixth Amendments. The Justice referred to the traditional tests applied to determine the punitive nature of a law—whether the sanction involves an affirmative disability or restraint, whether it has historically been regarded as punishment, whether it is inflicted only on a finding of *scienter*, that is, knowledge of wrongdoing; whether its imposition will promote the traditional objectives of punishment, that is, retribution and deterrence; whether the behavior to which it applies is already a crime, whether there are alternative objectives, etc. He thought, measured by these criteria, the law was clearly punitive. But in addition, he felt that the legislative history of the law and its predecessor which he examined thoroughly, left no doubt whatever that the sanction was intended by Congress as punishment. The reasons were "fundamentally retributive in nature." His conclusion was, therefore, "that Congress . . . decreed an additional punishment for the crime of draft avoidance in the special category of cases wherein the evader leaves the country. It cannot do this without providing the safeguards which must attend a criminal prosecution."[27]

Justice Goldberg recognized that draft evasion, particularly in time of war, was an heinous offense and that, if he remained out of the country, the evader could not be apprehended and tried for his crime. But, as in other situations (for example, the prohibition on the use of evidence obtained in violation of the Fourth Amendment), the Bill of Rights and its procedural guarantees are not to be abrogated because a guilty man may escape punishment. "Dating back to Magna Carta," he concluded, "it has been an abiding principle governing the lives of civilized men that 'no free man shall be taken or imprisoned or disseized or outlawed or exiled . . . without the judgment of his peers or by the law of the land. . . .' What we hold is only that, in keeping with this cherished tradition, punishment cannot be imposed 'without due process of law.' Any lesser holding would ignore the constitutional mandate upon which our essential liberties depend."[28] Justices Stewart and White dissented in an opinion written by the former and Justices Harlan and Clark dissented separately to note a minor objection to the Stewart opinion.

It thus appears that Justice Rutledge's interpretation of the nature and rights of citizenship in the United States is today largely confirmed, although by the slender margin of one Supreme Court Justice's vote. Involuntary expatriation is "punishment" and as such may not be inflicted without due process of law and the other safeguards for persons accused of crime and the administrative "finding" of a Board of Immigration is not sufficient basis for divestment. If it is argued that the 1963 decisions of the Supreme Court must be read as limited by their facts and thus applicable to native-born citizens only, the matter comes to this. Justice Rutledge's position was that native-born citizens may not be deprived of their citizenship without Fifth and Sixth Amendment protections because involuntary expatriation is "punishment" and the proceedings are criminal in nature. The Constitution does not provide for second-class citizenship. Therefore, naturalized citizens are entitled to the same protection as native-born citizens. Certainly the Court has confirmed the major premise of this syllogism. Moreover, the position taken by four members of the Court flatly deny the power of Congress to deprive any American of his citizenship except as the result of his voluntary act as in the *Mackenzie* case,[29] where it was held that a woman's citizenship was "suspended" during coverture to a foreigner, and the *Savorgnan* case[30] in which an American became naturalized in Italy.

Further approval of the Rutledge views of United States citizenship came in a 1964 case involving the Act of Congress providing for the expatriation of naturalized citizens who returned and lived continuously in their native country for three years. In writing for a majority of six, holding the law unconstitutional, Justice Douglas wrote:

> We start from the premise that the rights of citizenship of the native-born and of the naturalized person are of the same dignity and are coextensive. The only difference drawn by the Constitution is that only the "native" born citizen is eligible to be president.[31]

At the same term of Court and on the same day the Court could not muster a majority on the issue of the validity of the Congressional provision providing for loss of citizenship by one who fights in a foreign army. A native-born citizen named Marks had been an active participant in Castro's Cuban rebellion. The Court of Appeals for the Second Circuit upheld the law which thus made Marks stateless. By a four to four vote, Justice Brennan not participating, the Supreme Court failed to disturb the decision below.[32]

These later decisions show how closely the Court is divided on problems of citizenship. During the 1963-64 term only Justices Black and Douglas had sat on the same Court with Justice Rutledge. It would appear that the constitutional philosophy of the latter, largely carried forward by the former two Justices, has come to dominate the thinking of the Court in this highly important matter. Of how great importance, so far as the number of human beings affected and to be affected, we can only speculate. The State Department is reported to have estimated that as many as 40,000 persons have been deprived of the rights of citizenship under the three year residence-in-their-native-land law.[33] Those who are still living may now reclaim American citizenship. For the others, the decision is irrelevant; for them, the issue is moot.

CHAPTER IX

IN THE GREAT TRADITION

The Dedicated Federalist

IN the previous pages almost exclusive emphasis has been placed upon Justice Rutledge and the civil and political rights of the individual. There is little doubt that his name will always be associated with
this phase of public law. But there are other important areas in
which he contributed mightily to the development of a rational and
workable body of constitutional jurisprudence. He was ever aware of
the three vital functions of the Constitution. It sets forth a framework
of government for the national establishment, that is, three departments and the system of checks and balances, each upon the others.
It allocates powers as between the federal government on the one
hand and the states on the other. And it imposes limitations on the
power of both for the protection of individuals and minorities in the
interest of democratic living.

As to the second function, it was the heartbeat of federalism itself
and Rutledge was a dedicated federalist as a matter of political philosophy. He was an avid reader of history and a great admirer of John
Marshall. He was thoroughly familiar with the experience of the
colonists and the states under the Articles of Confederation after the
War for Independence. He knew of the regional economic differences, the commercial rivalries, the jealousies and trade barriers. He
understood the purpose and admired the wisdom of our forefathers in
their efforts to avert economic catastrophe. "They faced the hard facts
squarely," Rutledge wrote in 1947, "a virtue often rejected by ourselves of late."

The founders were not wishful thinkers, seeing nasty facts
and disregarding them. They rather accepted the conclusion
dictated by the facts in most important matters. So by a
stroke as bold as it proved successful, they founded a nation,

although they had set out only to find a way to reduce trade restrictions. So also they solved the particular problem causative of their historic action, by introducing the commerce clause in the new structure of power. . . . Twelve words the founders used: "The Congress shall have Power . . . [3] to regulate Commerce . . . among the several States. . . . " Simple, those dozen words. They do not in terms forbid the states to act. But by negative implication they stripped the states of ability to lay tariffs or otherwise raise barriers against trade crossing state lines.[1]

The commerce clause has been one of the most important sources of expanding federal power. From the Interstate Commerce Act, the Adamson Act regulating wages and hours for railroad employees, the Pure Food and Drug Act to Child Labor legislation, after two adverse Supreme Court decisions, and the National Labor Relations Act, the clause has been the origin of federal power "as broad as the economic needs of the nation."[2] At the same time, the states may also legislate in this area up to a certain point and under certain circumstances. The determination of what and when the states may enact laws for the regulation of interstate commerce has been and continues to present problems, both theoretical and practical, for the decision of the Court as the final arbiter of power in this nation of dual sovereignties. As Professor Powell observed some years ago, "Congress may regulate interstate commerce. The states may also regulate interstate commerce, but not too much."[3]

It is for the Court to determine how much on a case by case basis. "It is," wrote Rutledge, in a major decision involving a state tax on a foreign insurance company measured by the business done within the state without regard to its interstate or local character, "a recurring manifestation of the continuing necessity in our federal system for accommodating the two great basic powers it comprehends."[4] He characterized the commerce clause as "a uniquely federal instrument."

> More than any other provision it has to do with clashes of federal and state power, the lines of their division and their reconciliation in the federal plan. It is, so to speak, a two-edged sword, cutting both ways. One edge is the positive affirmation of national, that is, congressional power. The other, not so smooth or keen, cuts down state power by implied or inferential negation. The process of applying the clause therefore necessitates making accommodation between those competing powers and the interests affected by them.[5]

Referring to the principle of federalism and particularly to the commerce clause, Rutledge declared that "it has made this nation great and at the same time has kept the country democratic." "It may seem strange," he continued, "to think of a purely commercial power as one of the foundations of democratic institutions."

But in my judgment this is just what the commerce clause has turned out to be. It is inherently a federal device. And such a plan, by its very division of powers, creates a safeguard perhaps not otherwise attainable against wholly autocratic action. A democratic nation must have a government endowed with powers sufficient to meet its external and internal needs. These today necessarily must be large. But there is safety now, as there was when our fathers acted and *The Federalist* was being written, in distributing those powers so that they may not be concentrated altogether in one place.[6]

Rutledge decried a literal and myopic attitude toward congressional legislation. He was less interested in an isolated comment of a single congressman or senator as to "legislative intent" than in the broad legislative purpose and he was willing to allow a wide sweep to the law to achieve that end. This was particularly evident in his handling of labor legislation such as the National Labor Relations and Wage and Hours Acts.[7] It was no less so, however, in connection with all commerce clause regulation.

Congressional statutes passed under the commerce clause were not, for Rutledge, conveyancers' instruments to be scanned with a jealous eye and given a niggardly application. In case after case, with statutes and issues the most various, he went on record as favoring that one of the alternative constructions which gave the more extended operation to what Congress had tried to do and had done; and, on occasion, he categorically supported that approach. In the same spirit, his impulse was in general to support the substantive interpretations and the procedural techniques established by the administrative officials or agencies to whom power was delegated under such statutes.[8]

In other words, he would not cripple the instrumentalities which Congress set up to implement its legislation. On the other hand, he would give them the broadest latitude in carrying out the intention of Congress.

As to the power of the states to legislate in the field of interstate and foreign commerce, Rutledge largely accepted the pattern laid down in 1851 in the famous case of *Cooley* v. *Board of Wardens.*[9] He recognized a distinction between matters in which national uniformity is desirable or necessary and those admitting of diversity regulation. As to the first, the states were powerless to act, regardless of federal legislation or its absence. As to the second class of problems, the states could legislate in the absence of congressional action. Thus there were certain areas in which Congress alone could legislate; in others the states had limited regulatory power except where preempted by national legislation. But even though Congress has acted in the second category of cases, there might still be room for state legislation which is not in conflict with the national laws. So too, Congress on occasion has enacted "permissive" legislation, thus allowing, as legitimate, state regulation which otherwise would be in the area exclusively reserved for federal action.

In 1945, the Court held that a state could not constitutionally segregate white and colored passengers on interstate busses. Rutledge concurred.[10] But three years later he wrote the majority opinion in the *Bob-Lo* excursion case.[11] This case upheld the constitutionality of a Michigan civil rights act forbidding racial discrimination in public conveyances as applied to transportation from Detroit to Bois Blanc, a Canadian island, and return. Pleasure trips to the island resort and return were so "completely and locally insulated a segment of foreign or interstate commerce" as to be of primary interest and concern to the state. To Rutledge there was nothing inconsistent here. The cases came well within the flexible formula of the landmark *Cooley* case.[12]

Rutledge was thoroughly in accord with the policy of giving as broad latitude to the state as was consistent with the principle laid down in *Cooley*. As Professor Pritchett has pointed out, "[T]he liberal position was that of justifying a broad extent of federal power under the commerce clause, as against conservative restrictions on federal regulatory authority. But in these federal-state conflicts, the liberal doctrine has called for limiting the inhibitions which the federal commerce clause imposes on the states, while the conservative has emphasized federal power as a limitation on state regulation or taxation."[13] For the conservative, the less government, the better, whether national or state. Thus federal power was minimized but, at the same time, it minimized state power. The wider the vacuum, the better from the conservative point of view.

In 1944, by a divided vote of four to three, the Court held that the insurance business was interstate commerce.[14] Seventy-five years earlier, it had held the opposite.[15] The earlier case involved the validity of a state law requiring a license and the deposit of securities as a condition to foreign incorporated insurance companies to do business in the state. The later decision involved the validity of federal regulatory legislation in a criminal prosecution for violation of the Sherman antitrust law. Justice Rutledge and Justices Douglas and Murphy joined in Justice Black's opinion for the Court. Chief Justice Stone and Justices Frankfurter and Jackson adhered to the earlier characterization that the insurance industry was not a part of interstate commerce.

Two years later, Justice Rutledge wrote the opinion for a unanimous Court in the case which upheld a South Carolina tax of three per cent on all insurance business conducted within the state without reference to whether the transactions were domestic or interstate.[16] The tax applied only to foreign insurance companies. The company, of course, relied heavily upon the 1944 ruling. In the meantime, however, Congress had passed the McCarran Act which authorized state taxation of the insurance business notwithstanding the decision of the Court that it was interstate commerce. Rutledge interpreted the action of Congress as a declaration "that uniformity of regulation, and of state taxation, are not required in reference to the business of insurance, by the national public interest, except in the specific respects otherwise expressly provided for. This," he continued, "necessarily was a determination by Congress that state taxes, which in its silence might be held invalid as discriminatory, do not place on interstate insurance business a burden which it is unable generally to bear or should not bear in the competition with local business."[17] Such "coordinated action taken by Congress and the states" could not be declared unconstitutional. The tax was "reinforced by the exercise of all the power of government residing in our scheme."[18]

On the same day as the decision upholding the South Carolina tax, Rutledge wrote the opinion in *Robertson* v. *California*.[19] It was a criminal case in which an insurance agent had acted for a company incorporated in another state which had not been admitted to do business in California. He also had failed to obtain a license, as required by California law. This was before the enactment of the McCarran Act, but after the decision holding that insurance business was interstate commerce. The California laws were upheld. They did not discriminate against nor substantially obstruct or burden interstate commerce. The Court expressly disregarded the McCarran Act to avoid any problem of the *ex post facto* or retroactive application of that law. The state had not exceeded its powers over interstate commerce and needed no enabling legislation by Congress to legitimize its action.

An example of a situation requiring uniformity and thus excluding state regulation was an Arizona case involving the validity of a state law limiting the length of railroad trains. An Arizona statute supported by the railroad brotherhoods for obvious reasons, limited the length of passenger trains to fourteen coaches and freight trains to seventy cars. It was defended as a safety law to lessen the danger of "slack action." The Court in an opinion by Chief Justice Stone held that the law was an unconstitutional burden on interstate commerce and deprived it of needed uniformity in its regulation. As to the law's merits as a safety measure, the Court found it negligible in that the result would be to create additional risks of more serious train accidents by increasing the number of trains and train operations. Justices Black and Douglas dissented, but Rutledge concurred in the decision.[20]

Throughout Rutledge's commerce clause opinions there can be detected his constant search for a practical accommodation of state and national interests on the basis of a realistic evaluation of the interests involved. Within these limits, he favored a maximum of power in each. He was more interested in facts and results than in words or formulae. Two cases decided in the same day illustrate his invulnerability to labels. In one, the Court held invalid an Arkansas "sales" tax as applied to shipments of goods from Memphis by a Tennessee corporation to customers in Arkansas who had ordered by mail or from a salesman in Arkansas. In another case, however, it upheld an Iowa "use" tax applied to transactions by a Minnesota corporation which shipped goods into Iowa from orders received there. Mr. Justice Frankfurter thought the difference between a tax on the "sales" and one on the "use" of the products of the sale measured the difference between constitutional and unconstitutional taxation of interstate commerce. Rutledge saw little difference except one of words. The effect on interstate commerce was the same whether the tax was on the freedom to buy or to use goods thus purchased.[21] This search for reality largely characterized Rutledge's entire judicial career.[22]

A careful student of the work of the Justice in connection with the commerce clause has written:

> While Justice Rutledge did not introduce any basically new concepts in the sphere of the commerce clause, he forcefully challenged dogmatic theories and pointed the way to a fair and workable solution of the knotty problems presented in this field. . . . His commerce clause opinions serve to clear the ground

for realistic thinking in this critical area of federal-state relationships. In short, Justice Rutledge's philosophy of the commerce clause in its fundamental aspect presents the challenge of a pragmatic jurisprudence.[23]

The second great nationalizing clause of the Constitution is the full faith and credit clause. As Justice Jackson has described it:

By the full faith and credit clause they [our forefathers] sought to federalize the separate and independent state legal systems by the overriding principle of reciprocal recognition of public acts, records, and judicial proceedings. It was placed foremost among those measures which would guard the new political and economic union against the disintegrating influence of provincialism in jurisprudence, but without aggrandizement of federal power at the expense of the states.[24]

The actual wording of the clause is "Full Faith and Credit shall be given in each State to the public Acts, Records and Judicial Proceedings of every other State."[25] It is then provided that Congress may prescribe the manner of proving or authenticating such records and proceedings and their effect, *i.e.*, what "full faith and credit" means. Congress did so in the first Judiciary Act. As revised in 1948, it provides that such "Acts, records and judicial proceedings [judgments] . . . shall have the same full faith and credit in every court within the United States and its Territories and Possessions as they have by law or usage in the courts of such State, Territory or Possession from which they are taken."[26]

The most frequent application of these provisions is in connection with the effect of judgments of sister states and a large body of highly technical law has evolved. Indeed, many lawyers and judges have been confused and even the Supreme Court decisions sometimes have left much to be desired in clarity of reasoning and policy. Justice Rutledge here, too, showed an alert awareness of the clashing interests of the states and the overriding national policy of federalism. To be sure, when a citizen of one state enters or otherwise subjects himself to the power of another state, he must expect to be governed by the laws of that state and if their application to him or to his activities results in a valid and final judgment against him or in his favor, the effect thereof will be the same throughout the nation and will be enforceable everywhere.

For present purposes, attention is called to the first qualification mentioned. The judgment, to receive the constitutional sanction, must be *valid*. The divorce and alimony cases are excellent examples. A *valid* judgment assumes that the state, the court of which rendered the judgment, had "jurisdiction" over the parties and the subject matter of the action in which the judgment was rendered. If the parties had been served with process within the state, they are before the court and it has personal jurisdiction over them. If they "consent" or otherwise "waive" service within the jurisdiction, they are also "in court." Jurisdiction over the subject matter, that is, the marital relation, is acquired if one of the parties is "domiciled" within the state. "Domicile" is a highly technical term, but when reduced to realities, means that it is the present residence of a person who intends to make his "home" there permanently or for an indefinite period of the immediate future.

There are many practical problems here. What is meant by "home" and by "intention?" Home, Professor Beale used to say, was the place one goes back to when he is away from it. "Intention," presumably, is what the person has in mind at a particular moment as to his future behavior.

In any event, the Supreme Court has taken the position, quite plausible if one doesn't think about it too much, that only a state which is the domicile has jurisdiction to render a valid divorce decree. The theory here is that the state of residence—in the sense of "domicile" as a more or less permanent residence—has the greatest interest and therefore should have the final word as to the marital relations of the people who live there and the circumstances under which that relationship can be abrogated. If the Congress does have power, and it has never been decided, to enact a uniform divorce law, no serious effort in this direction has ever been made. Thus, the entire matter of the "grounds" and "procedure" for obtaining a divorce depends upon the law of the state of "domicile."

Now this makes some sense when the spouses have the same "home" and the same "domicile." But when a man deserts his wife, acquires a new "home" and therefore a new "domicile" elsewhere, difficult problems arise. A similar situation is presented when a wife leaves her husband, for his fault or otherwise. May she acquire a domicile of her own which would be recognized for jurisdictional purposes?

It has been decided now, for a number of years, that although there is a presumption that a wife's domicile is that of her husband, she is permitted to prove the contrary—that she left him and established a "home" of her own and intends to live there "permanently" or "indefinitely." In such cases, she may sue for a divorce under the laws of her "residence." Of course, if the husband leaves his wife and establishes a *bona fide* domicile in another state or country, he

may obtain a valid divorce there under the laws of that state or country. Any local rule that, to obtain a divorce, a party must have had a
local "residence" for six weeks, three months, two years, etc., is one the
effect of which is purely domestic and to be determined solely by state
law. If, as for example, in Alabama, there is no state "residence"
requirement, the state may grant a valid divorce to any person who
has acquired a *bona fide* domicile in the state even if it has only been
for twenty-four hours. Does he (or she) intend to make Alabama his
(or her) "home," "permanently or for an indefinite period"? This
is the only issue so far as concerns the power of the state and the
jurisdiction of its courts to render a valid divorce.

If a court in a state which is the domicile of neither spouse
should purport to decree a divorce, the judgment is null and void
for lack of jurisdiction and other states need give it no effect whatever.
A judgment, while immune to attack or challenge on the merits, if it
is valid, is always vulnerable to attack for want of jurisdiction of the
court which rendered it. Thus the Alabama or the Nevada "divorce"
is void if neither party was domiciled in the state at the time. This is
the case where the spouses live in another state and one goes, say, to
Nevada, intending to return as soon as the divorce decree is rendered.
Of course the plaintiff is asked how long he (or she) expects to live
in Nevada and perjury is required if the decree is to be granted. In
such cases, the divorce is invalid.

The *New York Times* for March 17, 1962, reported the divorce decree obtained by Governor Rockefeller's former wife in Nevada. The
newspaper reported the exact timing of the procedure. Mrs. Rockefeller entered the courtroom "on the dot of nine." Prepared documents on findings of fact and judgment were signed by the Judge and
"sent down for recording by the county clerk at 9:23 a.m., just as the
Rockefeller party emerged from the room through a back door and
went down the stairs." The news story went on:

> No details of the testimony were disclosed, but it was au-
> thoritatively indicated that Mrs. Rockefeller, under standard
> procedure, was asked by her lawyer:
> "When you arrived was it your intention to live here in-
> definitely and make Nevada your home?
> "Has that intention abided with you until the present day?
> "Is it still your present intention?"
> Affirmation to these questions, palpably hollow in many Ne-
> vada divorce cases, is traditionally accepted as legally true on
> the ground that a person can change his mind at any time.

After recounting a few further details, the newspaper story continued:

> The property settlement of last November gave Mrs. Rocke-
> feller the occupancy of their home at 812 Fifth Avenue, New
> York City, and of a residence on the Rockefeller estate near
> Tarrytown, New York.

The Rockefeller divorce is "void" like thousands of other Nevada
decrees, but, oddly enough, it is not without effect. It cannot be
attacked by the parties thereto. Thus if the Governor appeared,
personally or by counsel, in the proceeding or if he signed a waiver of
jurisdiction over his person, he has no standing to challenge the validity of the decree on the grounds that Mrs. Rockefeller was not domiciled in Nevada at the time. It is certain that he was "in court" by one
of these devices and therefore had his "day" there. He thus had his
chance to raise this question and failed to do so. It is *res judicata*
in Nevada and therefore in every other "State, Territory and Possession."

It thus appears that if the parties "cooperate" in the business of
obtaining a decree in an "easy divorce state" such as Nevada, about the
only risk incurred is the chance of a prosecution for bigamy in the
case of remarriage to a third person. And this risk, of course, is a
negligible one if the parties are discreet. The "law" in this aspect of the matter is the result of two notorious cases which reached
the Supreme Court in the early forties, both involving a North
Carolina couple each of whom had had the "benefit" of a Nevada divorce from a prior spouse. They were prosecuted for bigamy and found
guilty. The Supreme Court reversed the state court. It assumed
that the parties obtaining the Nevada decrees were domiciled there at
the time, that the judgments were therefore valid and that North
Carolina had failed to accord them "full faith and credit." There
was nothing in the record to indicate that the finding by the Nevada
court that the plaintiffs had been domiciled in the state was erroneous.
This was the much discussed *Williams* case.[27]

On a second trial, the state did attack the Nevada judgments on
the ground that they were invalid because the plaintiffs were not in
fact "domiciled" in the state. The evidence to support the state's
challenge was overwhelming. The plaintiffs had left Nevada as soon
as they had obtained their divorce decrees and returned "home" to
North Carolina. It was quite obvious that they had had no more
intention of making an "indefinite" home in Nevada than did Mrs.
Rockefeller some twenty years later. The second state conviction of
bigamy was affirmed by the Supreme Court.[28]

It seems clear that the "law" and decency are here quite completely at odds. Men are sent to prison time and time again for long terms because they were guilty of "perjury." But "perjury" in a Nevada divorce court is not *perjury*. The parties, the lawyers, the judges, all know that when the plaintiff states that she intends to make Nevada her home "indefinitely" that she has a return ticket and reservation on the next plane "home." It is just a way of talking about things. No one is misled, no one is deceived. It is merely a legal "rite." But it is hypocrisy and it is not good for the law nor for the respect which people are asked to have for "the law."

This was the kind of sham which Rutledge hated. Master craftsman that he was, he knew where to attack the conceptual framework which encouraged such absurd results. It was the notion of "unitary domicile." A person can have one domicile but only one and every person must have one. When he is born, he takes the "domicile" of his father. This continues until he is "capable" of acquiring a domicile on his own—*i.e.,* when he becomes an adult. Thereafter he continues to have his old domicile until he changes it by going to another state, living there with the intention of making it his home "permanently or for an indefinite period."

Rutledge dissented in the second *Williams* case from North Carolina when the Court approved the conviction of the "bigamists" on the ground that their Nevada divorces were void and their subsequent remarriage invalid. "The Constitution," he asserted, "does not mention domicil."

> Nowhere does it posit the powers of the states or the nation upon that amorphous, highly variable common-law conception. Judges have imported it. The importation, it should be clear by now, has failed in creating a workable constitutional criterion for this delicate region. In its origin the idea of domicil was stranger to the Federal system and the problem of allocating power within it. The principal result of transplanting it to constitutional soil has been to make more complex, variable and confusing than need be inherently the allocation of authority in the Federal scheme. The corollary consequence for individuals has been more and more to infuse with uncertainty, confusion, and caprice those human relations which most require stability and depend for it upon how the distribution of power is made.[29]

The Justice was not particularly concerned whether a policy of strict or easy divorce was to prevail. What he resented was the unreality of the domicile idea as the determinant of validity and the confusion and hypocrisy resulting therefrom. "Domicil, as a substantive concept," he wrote, "steadily reflects neither a policy of permanence nor one of transiency."

It rather reflects both inconstantly. The very name gives forth the idea of home with all its ancient associations of permanence. . . . But . . . "home" in the domiciliary sense can be changed in the twinkling of an eye, the time it takes a man to make up his mind to remain where he is when he is away from home. He need do no more than decide, by a flash of thought, to stay "either permanently or for an indefinite or unlimited length of time." No other connection of permanence is required. All of his belongings, his business, his family, his established interests and intimate relations may remain where they have always been. Yet if he is but physically present elsewhere, without even bag or baggage, and undergoes the mental flash, in a moment he has created a new domicil though hardly a home. Domicil thus combines the essentially contradictory elements of permanence and instantaneous change.[30]

Rutledge could not endorse a legal doctrine so unrealistic, so far removed from the facts of modern American life and one so subject to abuse, misuse and distortion. For him it was adherence to an outworn conceptualism which resulted in a mockery of the law and in unnecessary hardship, confusion and uncertainty. It brought both marriage and the law into disrepute.

In the second *Williams* case, Justice Frankfurter appeared to be overconcerned lest "the policy of each State in matters of most intimate concern . . . be subverted by the policy of every other State."[31] Underlying this anxiety are certain assumed values concerning marriage and divorce which may or may not exist—community attitudes assumed but not critically examined—public policies to which lip service is given but which may be more chimerical than real. Can it be that marriage is more sacred in North Carolina than in New York or California where thousands of Nevada, Florida and Mexican divorcees remarry each year and live, undisturbed, in a secondary or tertiary state of marital bliss? It is hard, indeed, to believe that it was North Carolina's abhorrence of out-of-state divorces of its citizens that sent the Williams to the rock pile. One may guess that the vindictiveness of discarded spouses, hillbilly family hostilities and the brazen effrontery with which pious pretentions were disregarded had more to do with this disastrous marital episode than a serious attack of community conscience on "matters of most intimate concern." This, in turn, raises the question whether the failure of North Carolina to give full faith and credit to the judicial proceedings of Nevada was justified.

In Rutledge's view Frankfurter had overemphasized an assumed state policy to the point of subverting the overriding federal policy of national uniformity and certainty in "matters of most intimate concern" to the nation as a whole.

> It is exactly for the situation where state policies differ that
> the clause and the legislation [full faith and credit] were in-
> tended. . . . The very function of the clause is to compel
> the states to give effect to the contrary policies of other states
> when these have been validly embodied in judgment. To this
> extent the Constitution has foreclosed the freedom of the states
> to apply their own local policies. The foreclosure was not in-
> tended only for slight differences or for unimportant matters.
> . . . The Constitution was not dealing with puny matters or
> inconsequential limitations. If the impairment of the power of
> the states is large, it is one the Constitution itself has made.[32]

It was Rutledge's position that "domicile" as developed in the common law must be abandoned as the jurisdictional prerequisite and in its stead, discoverable, objective and easily identified factors adopted. Had this been done, our federalism would have been strengthened and a great deal of dirty family linen quietly laundered.

No doubt it was Rutledge's passion for realities in dealing with the practical politics of the law that induced him to approve Justice Douglas' "divisible divorce."[33] This is the situation in which a husband does in fact acquire a new "domicile" and obtains a "valid" divorce there in proceedings in which the defendant wife does not participate and is not "in court" by reason of an effective service of process. The question thereafter arises as to the effect of the decree on a prior valid order of the court at the previous domicile that the husband pay periodically a fixed sum for his wife's support. If by the law of that state the support order survives the out-of-state divorce decree, the man will have to continue the payments to his ex-wife. The Supreme Court has held that although the divorce is good, the duty to support the divorced woman cannot be so easily avoided. Otherwise, if she were destitute, the burden of her support would fall upon the state in which she continues to have her home and "domicile." In this way, a compromise is attained between the policies of the two states in "matters of most intimate concern"—what Rutledge called the accommodation of the interests of the two sovereignties in a manner entirely consistent with our federal union.

Justice Rutledge voted many times, either with a majority of the Justices or in dissent, to invalidate state legislation or to reverse decisions of the highest state courts in criminal cases. He believed in judicial review and regarded it, perhaps, as the greatest bulwark of federalism.   He was adamant in his conviction that the Court should not shrink from its responsibilities as determined by Chief Justice Marshall and his colleagues.   It should not be supposed, however, that he was insensitive to its implications or naive as to the nature of federal-state relations.   He was no federal bull in a state china shop.   Several contrasting cases indicate his approach to these problems and his lack of dogmatism, in handling them when he felt that judicial discretion was indicated as an appropriate constitutional tool.

In 1946, the Illinois election districts were entirely out of balance. As in so many states then and now, they were grossly unequal in population with the result that the votes of some citizens, mostly in urban areas, counted far less than others in the democratic process. Three qualified voters from large election districts sought to restrain state officials from holding congressional elections according to a forty-five year old law determining congressional districts. Relief was denied by the three-judge federal court before which the case was heard and the Supreme Court affirmed.   This was *Colegrove* v. *Green*.[34]

Justice Frankfurter wrote the opinion which reflected the "law" in such cases until the famous malapportionment case of *Baker* v. *Carr*, decided in 1962.[35]   "Of course," wrote Frankfurter, "no court can affirmatively re-map the Illinois districts so as to bring them more in conformity with the standards of fairness for a representative system. At best we could only declare the existing electoral system invalid. The result would be to leave Illinois undistricted and to bring into operation, if the Illinois legislature chose not to act, the choice of members for the House of Representatives on a state-wide ticket."[36]

The Justice thought the Court was asked to do something which was "beyond its competence to grant."   The issue was one "of a peculiarily political nature and therefore not meet for judicial determination."   In answer to the argument that the situation was intolerable, morally and constitutionally, he declared that proper regard for the Constitution as a "viable system," whatever he meant by that, "precludes judicial correction."   If the states failed to provide fair apportionment based on population, the Constitution gave Congress "exclusive authority" to correct the situation.   If Congress failed, the remedy, in some way or other, lay with "the people."   So far as courts were concerned, the whole business was a "political thicket" to be kept out of.

Justice Jackson, absent on War Crimes business, took no part in this decision.   The decision was handed down on June 10, 1946 and Chief Justice Stone had died in the evening of April 22, preceding, after being stricken on the bench during the same day.   Justices Black, Murphy and Douglas dissented while Justice Rutledge concurred in a separate opinion. Frankfurter's opinion thus reflected the views only of himself and Justices Burton and Reed. But it was Rutledge who cast the deciding vote not to enter the Illinois "political thicket." He took the position that the Court had already decided that Congress did not have exclusive authority in the matter in issue, that the question was "justiciable" and that the Court had jurisdiction. Recognizing the principle that the Court should use discretion in exercising its jurisdiction and should decline to do so if there was a satisfactory alternative, he thought the gravity of the questions involved were so great and the possibilities of collision with the political departments of the Government so likely that the Court should abstain from action. Jurisdiction should be exercised in such matters "only under the most compelling circumstances." The case was decided in June and the immediate election involved was to be held in November. The shortness of time in which the Illinois legislature could act also argued against interference, Rutledge thought. To require the complaining voters to share in an election at large might bring equality of voting rights but "it would also deprive them and all other Illinois citizens of representation by districts which the prevailing policy of Congress commands." And after pointing out that there could not possibly be a right to precise and exact equality in voting and that rough approximation was possible only at best, he concluded, pragmatically, "the right here is not absolute. And the cure sought may be worse than the disease."[37]

Much has been written about *Baker* v. *Carr* and the extent to which it deviates from the decision, reasons and philosophy of the Illinois apportionment case.[38] But whatever else it decides, it certainly determines the justiciability and the power of the federal courts to intervene in state congressional malapportionment situations. Rutledge was in accord on the basic constitutional issue.

At the same term of Court in which *Colegrove* v. *Green* was decided, an appeal was taken from a three-judge federal court in Georgia in which the county unit voting system in that state was challenged as unconstitutional under the equal protection and privileges and immunities clauses of the Fourteenth Amendment. The lower court had relied largely on the Illinois case. The Supreme Court refused to review the issues, over objection by Black, Murphy and Rutledge.[39] The latter wrote an opinion in which he explained that a majority of the Justices participating in the *Green* case had refused to find that the Court did not have jurisdiction. His own position, he again pointed out, was that the Court should exercise its discretion to decline to interfere in view of the special circumstances there presented. That case was not controlling of this one and the appeals should be allowed and decided after full argument. He even went so far as to suggest that if the Georgia case were to be so treated, perhaps it would be wise to grant the petition for rehearing, then pending in *Colegrove* v. *Green*.[40]

In two other cases, Rutledge wrote the opinion for the Court declining to interfere with judgments of the Supreme Court of California which dealt with constitutional issues by denying rights claimed by litigants. In both cases, however, the state decisions were not final in the sense that further state proceedings were called for and it was possible that the cases might be disposed of without the necessity of reviewing the constitutional issues.[41]

Throughout his brief years on the Court, Justice Rutledge demonstrated repeatedly his profound understanding of our federal system. His was not blind admiration. He knew its strength and its vulnerable spots as well. He was never deluded by catch phrases such as "states' rights," "centralization," "bureaucracy" and other such political clichés. He did not believe that that government is best which governs least nor the one which governs most. He had broad fundamental principles but few dogmas. He, too, believed in crossing constitutional bridges when he came to them, but not before.

Defender of Liberty

There is some truth in the cynical remark that "courts love liberty most when it is under pressure least."[42] Not so, however, with Rutledge. "Where the basic values of democratic life were concerned," Professor Rockwell has written,[43] "Rutledge's interest in a pragmatic adjustment of competing claims evaporated."

If, as he once observed, federalism was the unique institutional core of American democracy, the rights of persons provided the human core. They transcended all else. Nothing less than a rigorous protection of all personal rights on a uniform national scale would satisfy his interpretation of the constitutional mandates. Thus he voted to uphold the claim of personal rights in 84% of all the non-unanimous decisions involving civil liberties—including both procedural and substantive ones. Excluding the war cases, he so voted in 87% of the cases.

Although he consistently asserted that the guarantees of the First Amendment occupied a preferred position, this did not mean that he thought guarantees of procedural rights occupied a deferred position. As a matter of cold statistics he voted to uphold the claim of criminal defendants in 91% of all the non-unanimous decisions involving procedural rights. When rights guaranteed by the First Amendment were involved, he voted to uphold the right in 79% of the non-unanimous decisions. These figures alone would therefore imply a preferred position in his mind for procedural rights. This, of course, is deceptive. There was no hierarchy of values among civil liberties for Rutledge. They were all primary, for they were all bulwarks of human dignity.

No doubt because of his brief period of service and lack of flamboyance of literary style, Rutledge's work and influence on the law was well known and understood during his lifetime only by close students and observers of the Court and its decisions. But there were a number of significant editorial and other comments on the nation's loss by his death. "The measure of a Supreme Court Justice," a sophisticated editor wrote, "is in the stand which he takes and the way in which he takes that stand. In his short span of six years on our highest court, Mr. Justice Rutledge stood out as one of the freest men ever to serve on that level."[44] This thought was echoed by Judge Henry Edgerton who had sat with Rutledge on the Court of Appeals for the District of Columbia. Writing in the *Harvard Law Review*, he quoted from Justice Brandeis that if we would be guided by the law of reason, we must let our minds be bold. "Few judges in our time," Edgerton wrote, "have done this so notably as Rutledge. In boldness and imagination, in sense and defense of democracy, he was in the great tradition."[45] Similarly in the *Post-Dispatch*, "neither public opinion nor any other pressure could sway him from what he believed to be right."[46] The newspaper then put the rhetorical questions: "Will Tom Clark be another Murphy? And will President Truman find another Wiley Rutledge?"

These questions have been answered fully and in detail by writer after writer. After observing that the substitution on the Court of Clark and Minton for Murphy and Rutledge seemed "to introduce another epoch in civil liberty litigation," Professor Mendelson has pointed out that in the term of Court beginning in 1949, the Court rejected all freedom of expression claims in the six relevant cases to come before it.[47]

Perhaps as good answers as could be found are those of my colleague Rodell and my ex-colleague Frank, both gifted students and critics of the Court. In his recent book, Frank, in referring to the Court under Chief Justice Vinson, wrote:

In these post-war years the Court again experienced a shift of personnel, Chief Justice Vinson taking the place of Chief Justice Stone and Justices Burton, Clark and Minton succeeding Justices Roberts, Murphy and Rutledge. The result, with rare exceptions on the part of Justice Burton and even rarer ones on the part of Justice Clark, was to remake the bench into a body that exhibited no real objection to the trend of the times and certainly had no intention to do anything about it. The deaths in 1949 of the strong civil-libertarians Rutledge and Murphy ensured that there would be no judicial objections to the course of events.

Indeed, as the author stated a few pages later "the McCarthy-McCarran era could scarcely roll the repression along fast enough to keep pace with the Vinson Court's approval of it."[48]

Professor Rodell in his Supreme Court study, *Nine Men,* has summarized it this way:

> The ten years stretching from Butler's death and Murphy's appointment as the fifth Roosevelt Justice up to the summer of 1949—when those consecrated co-champions of civil liberties, Murphy and Wiley Rutledge, suddenly and almost simultaneously died (and their close associate, Douglas, was almost killed in a mountain accident)—were the years of the New Deal Court. Not merely that a majority of the Justices, throughout that decade, had been Roosevelt-chosen; that fact remained true of the Court for five subsequent years, until Justice Jackson's death in 1954. Rather that the Court's political and constitutional slant remained, for just that long—and despite incessant and increasing internecine warfare—a New Deal slant.[49]

After referring to what he regarded as the rivalry between Justices Jackson and Douglas for the position of Chief Justice on Stone's death, Rodell continued:

> President Truman compromised by appointing that long-time laborer in the Democratic vineyard and top utility-man for the New Deal, Fred Vinson of Kentucky—with the hope that Vinson's conciliatory talents and slow patience might settle or smother the feuds within the Court. Vinson was Truman's second appointee, Harold Burton of Ohio having been named to the "Republican seat" a year earlier, at Robert's why-bother-to-stay-on retirement. Three years later—when Murphy and Rutledge died, and Truman chose Tom Clark of Texas and Sher-

man Minton of Indiana—the New Deal Court, as a Court, with all its conflicts, its contradictions, its personal spats, and its splintered brilliance, passed into history. An era was ended.

At the time of the appointment Rutledge had expressed his view that Vinson would be an excellent choice to succeed Stone. He made the same mistake as to Minton. On the retirement of Justice Roberts, Brant wrote to his fellow Missourian, Harry Truman,[50] as follows:

> I spent last evening with Wiley Rutledge, who has just returned from Colorado. Although nothing was said about passing anything along to you and it may be that he would not want me to, I feel sure that you would like to know what he thinks about the Supreme Court vacancy. To summarize four points: (1) Top notch men: . . . Minton. . . .

Justice Burton got the appointment and, ironically enough, as we know, Minton took the place vacated by Rutledge.

Irving Dilliard, another fellow Missourian, writing in *The Atlantic* in December, 1949, attempted to assess the effect of Rutledge's replacement by Minton. He was not too sanguine but, as it turned out, he was slightly overly optimistic:

> Minton probably feels closer to Black than to any other Justice. Black was in the Senate when Minton arrived there. They served in the Roosevelt ranks until Black was appointed to the supreme bench in 1937. The prospect is that the newest Justice will be looking to the senior member for at least some measure of guidance in his first term. Beyond that it would be foolish to forecast. But even if Minton should agree with Black in every split civil rights case, still the Rutledge replacement would not equal the Rutledge impact in these cases in the past.[51]

As it turned out, it appeared that Justice Minton looked to Black for "some measure of guidance" less than to any other Justice on the Court. Professor Braden, writing in the *Indiana Law Journal*[52] summarized Justice Minton's first year on the Court and the effect of his appointment along with those of Chief Justice Vinson and Justices Burton and Clark—the "Truman bloc" as he characterized them. "To anyone who follows the Court closely," he wrote, "it is obvious that the Court changed its direction markedly."

> It seems fairly clear that a goodly number of cases decided during the past year would have gone another way had both

Justices Murphy and Rutledge lived. In fact, many of these same cases would have gone another way had only one of the late Justices lived. Hence one can argue that Mr. Justice Minton was an important factor in the shift in direction. . . . The effect of his votes and those of the other members of the Truman bloc is an abandonment of the great tradition of an independent and spirited judiciary. The only hope is that as conditions get worse, the Court will shift again and once more become a defender of the American faith.[53]

It is gratifying indeed, that it can be said that Professor Braden's "only hope" has been largely fulfilled.

In support of Braden's conclusions as to the effect on the Court's direction were Frank's statistics for the term on non-unanimous civil rights cases.[54] According to his appraisal, of 15 such cases, Minton supported the claimed constitutional right 3 times, Clark 1, Burton 3 and Vinson 2 as compared to Black 15, Frankfurter 11 and Jackson 6. Douglas was absent most of the term with an injury received when he was thrown from a horse. As to Justice Minton looking to his old senatorial colleague, Black, for guidance, Frank's data showed that in major and important cases Minton voted with Black 16 times, but with Burton 18 and Vinson 19. Frank concluded his article with the observation made by so many students of the Court. "[T]he New Deal era in jurisprudence is gone." As to Justice Clark's first year performance, there was much significance in the observation of another writer in the *Indiana Law Journal,* that " (1) he cast no dissenting vote whatsoever [and] (2) he has shown an almost unbelievable unanimity of opinion with his Chief [Vinson]."[55]

Throughout his six and a half years on the Court Rutledge wrote a total of 171 opinions or an average of 26 per year. Of the 171, 65 were majority, 45 concurring and 61 dissenting. His rate of agreement with his colleagues is interesting but not surprising. He sat with Justice Roberts for 2-1/2 terms, with Chief Justice Vinson for 3 terms, with Chief Justice Stone 3-1/2, with Burton 4, and with Jackson 5-1/2. With the other Justices, Douglas, Black, Frankfurter and Murphy, he sat the full period of his tenure. It is not believed that the variations in the length of service with the Justices materially affected his rate of agreement and disagreement with them. Rutledge voted with Roberts less than with any other Justice, an average of 31%. He agreed with Murphy more than with any other. The average here was 74.7%. With the other Justices in descending order: Black, 70.6%; Douglas, 65%; Stone, 53.3%; Reed, 51.6%; Frankfurter, 43.6%; Jackson, 43.3%; Burton, 38.5%; and Vinson, 38.3%.[56]

The reason for his high percentage of agreement with Justices Black, Douglas and Murphy of course is obvious. All four Justices adhered closely to the same principles and their application in cases involving civil and political rights. This is slightly more true of Rutledge and Murphy than with Rutledge and the other two "libertarians" as they have sometimes been called. The data here is most revealing. In his study of the last three terms of Court before the deaths of Rutledge and Murphy, Dilliard using Frank's and his own criteria, tabulated the votes of the various Justices in 57 civil rights cases in which the Court was divided.[57]

Here is his box score for the years 1946-1949:

Justice	For claimed right	Against claimed right
Murphy	53	3
Rutledge	52	4
Douglas	47	10
Black	39	17
Frankfurter	23	34
Jackson	14	41
Burton	10	47
Reed	8	49
Vinson	8	49

It is not difficult to get some idea of the place which Rutledge and Murphy had occupied on the Court in the discharge of its obligation to apply the Constitution "equally in war and in peace" and to insure that it "covers with the shield of its protection all classes of men, at all times, and under all circumstances." Dilliard had reason to declare "that the death of Rutledge so soon after the death of Murphy just doubles the loss to citizens who invoke the guarantees of the Bill of Rights."[58]

But, as we have seen, it was not only Rutledge's votes but his opinions, majority, concurring and dissenting which place him among the foremost of the defenders of liberty in the nation's history. His opinions in *Everson, Thomas, United Mine Workers, Yamashita* and many others will be read, reread, studied and cited as long as the Republic endures. A careful student of Justice Rutledge and his judicial career has written:

> Although his contributions in other fields—particularly with respect to the commerce clause—may be significant, it was in the field of civil liberties that he concentrated his efforts and thereby gave the Court—and the nation—what may come to be

some of the greatest essays in American constitutional history.[59]

Rutledge and His Brethren

About a year after Rutledge joined the Court, newspapers carried lurid stories about a rift between Justices Black and Murphy on the one hand and Justice Frankfurter on the other. The occasion was a concurring opinion by Justice Black in a patent case in which Justice Frankfurter had dissented.[60] The case involved the principle of contributory infringement, that is, an action by a patent licensee against one or more firms for contributing to infringement by still another firm. The Court found that there had been none. Frankfurter in his dissent wrote that the doctrine involved both "law and morals." He thought that the doctrine had been misconceived and misapplied.

> That is the fate of all shorthand statements of complicated ideas, whether in law or in the natural sciences. But the misapplication of a formula into which a complicated idea is compressed and thereby mutilated is a poor excuse for rejecting the idea. It will be time enough to define the appropriate limits of the doctrine of contributory infringement when we are required to deal with the problem. Until then litigants and lower courts ought not to be embarrassed by gratuitous innuendoes against a principle of the law which, within its proper bounds, is accredited by legal history as well as ethics.

Black's opinion, in which Murphy joined, was principally devoted to "silencing" the views expressed in Frankfurter's dissent. He thought that the issue of discussing the formula of contributory infringement at an inopportune time was much less important than Frankfurter's characterization of the formula. "It seems to me," he continued, "that the judicial error of discussing abstract questions is slight compared to the error of interpreting legislative enactments on the basis of a court's preconceived views of morals and ethics. . . . And for judges to regard their interpretations of statutes on nothing but their own conceptions of 'morals' and 'ethics' is, to say the least, dangerous."

This particular chicken recently came home to roost from the most unlikely source. The *New York Times* for June 3, 1963 reported certain oral observations made from the bench by Justice Douglas concerning Justice Black's opinion in the Colorado River case involving disputed claims by Arizona and California. It also noted Douglas' written dissent in which he wrote: "The present case will, I think,

"HOW ARE YOU GETTING ALONG, MR. CHIEF JUSTICE,
WITHOUT US OLD FOGIES?"

be marked as the baldest attempt by judges in modern times to spin their own philosophy into the fabric of the law in derogation of the will of the legislature."[61]

Shortly after this bit of judicial repartee in the patent infringement case, Black, again joined by Murphy, referred, somewhat acidly, we may assume, to another "patently . . . gratuitous assertion as to constitutional law" by Frankfurter.[62]

Evidences of disagreements no sharper than these would go unnoticed if occurring in the legislature, and would cause a bare ripple in the executive branch of the Government. Coming from the Justices, however, they put the Court on the front pages of the newspapers. "Supreme Court Divided as Seldom in History," "High Court Feud Widened," "High Court Rift on Frankfurter" were sample headlines. Of course, it was recognized that such exchanges reflected rather fundamental differences of viewpoint which carried with them personal overtones. But the differences and personal innuendoes were magnified out of all proportion and, in some quarters, made the occasion for nasty digs at "New Deal Judges" and a Roosevelt "packed" Court.

To be sure, judicial behavior of this sort leaves something to be desired as a matter of public relations, if for no other reason than taste. The effect, however, if not negligible, is entirely transitory insofar as it concerns Court performance or prestige. Such disagreements, openly aired or discovered by probing reporters had occurred before and were to recur again.

Perhaps the most sensational episode of this kind, again involving Justice Black, was the bitter attack on him by Justice Jackson while the latter was absent from his judicial duties acting as war crimes prosecutor in Germany. On Tuesday, June 11, 1946, the United Press reported from Nürnberg the text of a statement by Mr. Justice Jackson, then chief American war crimes prosecutor, which he had cabled to the Chairmen of the Senate and House Judiciary committees, presumably precipitated, although not motivated, by the nomination of Chief Justice Vinson. He thought the Chief Justice "an upright, fearless, and well qualified man for the position." He thought it important that the "magnitude and nature of the task which faces him should not be minimized." He then referred to what he said was the impression that there was a mere "personal vendetta among justices." Many assumed that these tensions might be dissolved or at least weakened by tactful handling by the presiding officer. "This is utterly false," he declared, "the controversy goes to the reputation of the Court for nonpartisan and unbiased decision." Congress had a right to know the facts and issues involved and "this was an appropriate occasion" for him to reveal them. He then referred to an article in the *Washington Star* of May 15, 1946, which purported to express Justice Black's complaint of Jackson's opinion on the denial of a rehearing in the *Jewel Ridge* portal-to-portal pay case as reflecting upon Black's personal and judicial honor. The Court had held that the miners were entitled to be paid for their underground travel. It was a five to four decision, Justices Murphy, Rutledge, Douglas, Reed and Black constituting the majority.

Jackson thereupon explained that counsel for the United Mine Workers, the ultimately successful litigant, had been Black's former law partner in Alabama; that when the defeated parties applied for a rehearing, they asked that Justice Black disqualify from participation in the decision. This the Justice declined to do. Since all members of the Court were agreed that the petition for rehearing should be denied, Jackson wanted an explanation that the question of disqualification was solely a matter of decision for the individual Justice concerned. For some curious reason, he thought that the usual announcement, merely that the petition was "denied," would be thought "an endorsement by the whole Court of Justice Black's participation." He declared that "neither I, nor any of the other Justices who had dissented, wanted to lend our names to a blind and unqualified approval." He then said that Black had "become very angry" and announced that "any opinion which discussed the subject at all would mean a declaration of war." Jackson then told the congressional committees that "if war is declared on me, I propose to wage it with the weapons of the open warrior, not those of the stealthy assassin."

Jackson then expressed the view that to encourage the employment of ex-partners of a Justice to argue close cases before the Court would tend to bring it into disrepute. "I wanted that practice stopped," he wrote. "If it is ever repeated while I am on the bench, I will make my *Jewel Ridge* opinion look like a letter of recommendation by comparison."

Naturally Jackson's outbreak was front page news and grist for much editorial comment. The *Washington Post* carried the United Press story under a three-line headline across the entire front page of the newspaper for June 11. The *Washington Star* carried the full text of Jackson's blast. Although Senator Lucas declared that both Jackson and Black should resign, Jackson received the brunt of editorial denunciation. The idea of a Supreme Court Justice airing such a controversy, whether from personal pique or from deep-seated disagreement on matters of policy, was shocking to most serious-minded citizens. The *St. Louis Post-Dispatch* labelled it as "lamentably far from a judicial document." It was, the newspaper thought, "an angry outburst, impetuous and almost incoherent. . . . He could not wait until his return from Germany, but humiliated the country in the eyes of its enemies by disclosing the discord in its highest tribunal."[63] Drew Pearson in his "Washington Merry-Go-Round"[64] attributed much of Jackson's emotional explosion to a series of political disappointments, the two most recent ones being his two-time failure to be appointed to the Chief Justiceship, *i.e.*, the occasions for the appointment of Stone and Vinson. Many other observers shared Pearson's view and so expressed themselves at the time. The ill-tempered attack upon Black was the more unpardonable inasmuch as the decision would have been the same even if Black had disqualified himself. The result would have been a four to four vote which would have had the effect of confirming the decision below in favor of the union.

Most of the press comments expressed deep regret at the back fence back-biting that had been going on in the Court and particularly that it should be made public. After Jackson's Nürnberg outburst, the editor of the *St. Louis Star-Times* wrote:

> Disagreements among Justices of the United States Supreme Court are inevitable, and it is not inconceivable—men being what they are—that they should sometimes lead to personal animosities. However, not in a long time—if ever—has the dignity of the Court been threatened by a public blast such as that in which Justice Jackson has just denounced Justice Black.[65]

Undignified, intemperate and unjust as such tirades of a Supreme Court Justice against a colleague are, it is a matter of great satisfaction that public confidence in the Court and its place in the scheme of national government was and continued to be unshaken. The Court, as an institution, is something far greater than the sum total of the Justices who compose it at any one time. Nor can its status be impaired by public reaction to a particular decision whether a *Dred Scott* or a *Brown* (school segregation) case. Indeed, the same is true of a series of unpopular decisions. Although a popular President could not obtain authority from a popularly elected Congress to interfere with an unpopular Supreme Court, he could be re-elected by the largest electoral vote in our history. It is an amazing fact that the Court, with Justices appointed for life and with neither the "purse nor the sword" to gain compliance with its decisions, probably stands higher in public confidence and esteem than any other agency of government. If, from time to time, some of the Justices are influenced in their vote on controversial issues by their guess as to immediate public reaction as distinguished from long range social policy, it is because they underestimate the strength of the great institution which they serve.

In a speech in Colorado in the late summer of 1963, Justice Brennan warned that the Court's survival was imperilled by ill-informed criticism by irresponsible persons who had not even read the opinions.

> There is sectional opposition because of the desegregation cases; state opposition because of recent decisions involving state powers as they relate to aspects of criminal law; rural opposition because of the reapportionment cases, and church opposition because of the prayer case.

The *New York Times* made two well-taken points in its editorial observations on the Brennan complaint:

> Warranted as is his irritation on this score, it scarcely supports his apprehension about the Court's basic security. The only real threat to its authority as supreme arbiter is the proposed "Court of the Union" amendment to the Constitution. This plan to empower the chief justices of the 50 states to review Supreme Court decisions has been approved by the Legislatures of only five states—Alabama, Arkansas, Florida, South Carolina and Wyoming. Most of the steam went out of the drive for this and other "states' rights" amendments once they were exposed to the full light of publicity.[66]
> Unlimited public discussion is a primary safeguard of our democracy, even when many of those who are talking loudest do not know what they are talking about. The decisions of the Supreme Court are written by men on paper, not by gods in letters of fire across the sky. Critics may distort them. But the Court will have to trust the good sense of the people, just as the people trust the good sense of the Court.[67]

Despite posters on billboards to "Impeach Earl Warren" and crackpot proposals for a "Court of the Union" endorsed by a few lobby-controlled legislatures, there is strong reason to believe that the Supreme Court of the United States stands higher in the esteem of the people than ever before in the nation's history. The integrity with which the Court has handled the problems most threatening to our internal peace and most humiliating in our relations with other nations cannot help but command the deep respect of all intelligent citizens. When other departments of the Government are timid, the Court stands firm. As the *New York Times* pointed out[68] "of the three branches of government, it is the judicial that has shown the greatest awareness that the time is *now* in civil rights." It might well have added that major crises inevitably reach a point where the entire issue turns on recognition of the fact that the "time is now."

Actually, the more asinine the proposals for "reform" of the Supreme Court, the more readily and quickly they are laid to rest. In 1946, Senators Eastland and Bridges reached what, at least to date, was an all time low. They devised a scheme to limit Presidents to the appointment of three Justices. In some way or other, the House of Representatives was to have a share in the appointing power of Justices. Such rabble-rousing suggestions have little effect beyond making their sponsors look ridiculous. Much' the same can be said for Senator Jenner's proposal to restrict the Court's jurisdiction in cases relating to "subversion" and contempt of congressional committees and the resolution of the Georgia legislature in 1957 calling for the impeachment of the Chief Justice and Justices Black, Douglas, Reed, Frankfurter and Clark.

The Court consisting of mortals and, as Holmes observed, constitutional law being a "mortal contrivance," a good many mistakes are made. But so long as the Supreme Court continues to face its obligations squarely and deal with them forthrightly, we can justly hope that our federalism and the liberties of our citizens, if not adequately, are as well-protected as we could hope for in this imperfect and largely unhappy world.

The matter of the disqualification of Justices touched off a quixotic suggestion in the fertile brain of Rutledge's friend Irving Brant. A few months after the Jackson-Black episode, from his satirical pen came a letter with the following observations:

> . . . I want to put a disturbing thought before you, based on the super-conscientious tendency toward disqualification when personal economic interests are involved. Every member of the Court, as nearly as I can figure it while running this typewriter, has had about a forty percent salary cut in the last few years through inflation, this being taken out of the sixty percent or thereabouts which remains after paying taxes. That leaves them about 36 percent of their total salaries, and completely defeats the purpose of the original munificence, which was to place them beyond temptations of economic self-interest. As I see it, every member of the Court would have to disqualify

himself in any case involving the inflationary or deflationary spiral. And how could any member sit if some lower court held, as some readily might, that the Sixteenth Amendment [authorizing the income tax] is unconstitutional? . . . .

Throughout these and other intra-Court squabbles, Rutledge confined his energy to the business of judging and refused to dilute his effectiveness by personal partisanship. As remarked by a contemporary student of the Court:

> Throughout the bickering on the Court, Rutledge has kept out of the crossfire. Equally important, he has not been mentioned in the public argument about it. Whether this was due to his determination to remain aloof or was due to the circumstance of his having been brought in from a zone of no politics does not matter. His personal prestige is unsullied and he can go right on with his liberal law . . . without pulling punches.[69]

This is not to say that he was insensitive to his relations with his colleagues. But he seldom showed rancor. Although Rutledge sympathized deeply with Black after Jackson's explosion, his remark to his law clerk expressed his tolerance for a colleague's weakness: "Too bad, but it's just like Bob. I'm not surprised." Another significant instance was the occasion on which Justice Roberts insisted that the Chief Justice disqualify himself in a number of holding company cases. Mason reports that "Roberts' suggestion, apparently querying the Chief Justice's honor and implying that he would discuss in an opinion the propriety of Stone's sitting, brought on a heated debate."[70] There is no evidence that Rutledge contributed to the heat, but he later wrote the Chief Justice a personal note registering his indignation at the veiled challenge to Stone's integrity, for which he received a grateful acknowledgment.

It is true that although Rutledge and Stone were in agreement on many controversial cases, they also differed sharply on a number of others, some of them of great importance. The most important case, of course, was *Yamashita*. But there is no reason to believe that either took their differences personally even though both were greatly distressed by them.

On the day after the death of the Chief, Rutledge wrote to his long-time friend, Luther Ely Smith in St. Louis, revealing sentiments about his relationship with Stone.

> There is nothing I can say that will add to your understanding of my feeling for this great man. Recently I have been

saddened by the fact that more and more we have come to vote differently on many matters. I am not altogether clear about the reason for this, but sometime I want to talk it over with you. . . . It has been a great privilege for me to have had the opportunity to work with him even so briefly and in his declining years. . . . Notwithstanding our increasing differences, there was always about him a calm poise combined with firmness and tolerance which gave real balance to our discussions. Of the several who may succeed him, I hope it will be someone of that temperament. We need it perhaps more than anything else at this stage of the Court's history. . . . I have no idea about who may come in, though I have definite ideas about some who may try very hard. I am not anxious for any of those to take over.

Those who have followed the Court's history have some fairly definite ideas as to the persons Rutledge referred to, "who may try very hard to come in." He confided to the writer that Vinson was his personal choice. The two had sat together on the Court of Appeals for the District of Columbia for several years and had formed a close friendship. But in the few years in which they served together on the High Court, Rutledge must again have been saddened at the frequency with which he disagreed with his Chief in cases of great importance. Nevertheless, there is no evidence that their personal friendship and mutual esteem was lessened.

My colleague and former student, Professor Louis Pollack, Rutledge's last law clerk, tells of an incident which reflects the warmth between the two Justices as well as interesting aspects of their characters. It seems that the Court had reviewed a case from the Court of Appeals of the District of Columbia which was extravagantly absent of any legal merit. It was the emphatic view of all the Justices that the case must be reversed. The opinion below was an unusually long one, written by a judge with whom both Rutledge and Vinson had sat and for whom they obviously had both respect and affection.

At the conclusion of the conference, Pollack reported, the Chief Justice came into Rutledge's office with a request that he write an opinion for the Court reversing the decision below, but somehow making it appear that there had been at least some merit in the position taken by the judge of the lower court. "We do not want to hurt his feelings, or embarrass him in any way," Vinson explained. Rutledge said he understood and would do the best he could. When the Chief Justice had left, Rutledge turned to Pollack and said, "You have heard the instructions, do you want to take a try at a first draft?" Pollack did, and produced an eleven page opinion for the Justice. "Well, you have certainly followed the Chief's instructions," he said smilingly, "but you did not have to go to the length of writing 11 pages." Rutledge took the draft home with him that night, Pollack recalls, and returned the next morning with a draft of eighteen pages.

In his syndicated column, "Washington Calling" for June 15th, 1946, after the Jackson-Black incident, Marquis Childs wrote:

> With the summer recess the Supreme Court quarrel will be in abeyance, but the long summer vacation will not heal a feud that in its current phase has torn the veil of illusion from the venerable institution. A little background helps to explain the extraordinary bitterness that pervades the conference room of the Court. About a year after Justice Hugo Black was appointed to the Court I unintentionally contributed toward fanning the bitterness. It came about this way.

Childs then proceeded to explain how a magazine article which he had written had produced considerable consternation in Supreme Court circles.

It seems that the columnist had become quite intimate with Chief Justice Stone with whom he had frequent talks in morning walks on the way to their respective offices. In the course of these conversations it appears that the Chief Justice somewhat indiscreetly made certain observations concerning Justice Black which formed the basis of an article published by Childs in *Harper's Magazine* in the May issue for 1938. The gist of Childs' article was that the Chief Justice and some other members of the Court were unhappy because of what seemed to them to be a lack of craftsmanship on the part of the new Roosevelt appointee. Childs at first prepared his article as a bit of inside dope on the Court for the *St. Louis Post Dispatch* for which he was a Washington correspondent. As a careful newspaper man, he took the article to the Chief Justice for his approval which he readily obtained. In fact, the Chief Justice indicated that the article should have a wider public than a midwestern newspaper with only a local circulation. Childs replied that he had written several articles for *Harper's Magazine* and he thought the editor would be glad to have this one if properly expanded. The Chief Justice readily agreed, with the result that the article so appeared.

Naturally, Childs did not in his piece reveal the source of his information, but, also indiscreetly, he revealed this to a fellow em-

ployee of the St. Louis newspaper. Unfortunately, his confidant
proved untrustworthy in that after losing his job for overindulgence
in alcohol, he overindulged again at the National Press Club and
revealed the secret to anyone who would listen. After the story appeared in the gossip columns the following morning, Childs received
a call from the Chief Justice's secretary saying "The story is out.
What shall we do?" To which Childs replied, "There is only one
thing that can be done. The Chief Justice must deny it."

Another aspect of the story comes from a letter by Irving Brant to
Rutledge dated November 26, 1938:

> It was very unfortunate that after Black began to make his
> record on the bench, *Harper's* should have come along with
> that article by Marquis Childs. He told *Harper's* that he got it
> from Justice Stone. The fact is that he completely misunder-
> stood everything Stone said. I know this because I talked with
> Stone for a couple of hours about Black within a week of the
> time Childs did. What he was worried about was fear that
> Black's method in aiming at a common objective would be
> wasted effort. He objected to disregard of established meth-
> ods of modifying the Court's position, disregard of historical
> perspective. My own impression is that Black has a deeper
> knowledge of economic and social facts than anyone else on the
> Court, and I think it highly significant that the first subject
> to be taken up by the monopoly investigators is the bearing of
> the patent laws upon monopoly, which has been the subject of
> two dissents by Black.

It is not at all unlikely that Child's interpretation of Stone's attitude was less erroneous than Brant thought. Childs later referred to
another incident which insured the sharp disapproval of Jackson and
contributed little to peace and tranquility among the Justices. In
the Winter of 1944 the Washington Chapter of The National Lawyers' Guild gave a dinner in honor of Justice Black which was
attended by several hundred prominent lawyers and government
officials. All members of the Supreme Court were invited and the
majority attended. The Chief Justice and Justices Frankfurter and
Jackson did not attend. Senator Alben Barkley served as Toast-
master and in the course of the evening introduced two speakers who
appeared before the Court on behalf of their clients within the next
few days. Jackson is reported to have regarded this as grossly improper. Childs reports him as saying to friends:

What if in the old days of the Court when the conservative Justices were under fire, one of the big business associations had given a dinner in honor of one of the conservative Justices with appropriate eulogies by a corporation lawyer. Then the speaker making the eulogy would appear in Court to argue a case the following day. Why every liberal in the country would have screamed his head off over it.[71]

At the end of his article Childs suggested that perhaps both Jackson and Black should resign. "Then the unhappy effects of this feud might be erased. Under the administration of Fred Vinson, the new Chief Justice, the Court might again achieve working harmony and repair the damage done in loss of public esteem." Here even an experienced newspaperman overestimated and exaggerated the effect on the public of such disagreements, in terms of "public esteem" for the Court. Expressing a different view of this intramural heat behind the purple curtain, the *Portland Oregonian* observed after the Frankfurter-Black-Murphy spat in 1944:

Some may regret such public revelation of a break within the Court. We find it most reassuring. It always has been our suspicion that honest men, even though they may have run high temperatures when engaged in partisan politics, would come to their senses and become Americans rather than partisans once they were appointed to the Supreme Bench.[72]

As another astute observer put it in 1948:

Despite the unjudicial antics of some of them [Justices] and the record breaking number of dissenting opinions that have poured from the Court in the last few years, its authority has never been more conclusive. There are two major reasons for this. One is the overall outstanding caliber of the Justices. As a whole, they average in ability, breadth, and stature with the very best in the history of the Court. In legal brilliance and literary quality some of their decisions and dissents, are in the noblest tradition. The other factor is the relative youthfulness and vigor of the group. . . . In recent years, the Court has not only considered more cases and handed down more decisions than ever before, but has closed with a clear docket, when it shut down for its annual four months summer recess. In the days of the more sedate Nine Old Men, the Court was as much as three years behind on its docket.[73]

Rutledge always carried his share of the work load. For the two terms preceding the above article, he had written a total of sixty-two opinions, majority, dissenting and concurring. Frankfurter led all the Justices with seventy-two. Douglas was a close second with seventy-one. Jackson delivered seventy; Murphy fifty; Reed thirty-nine; Vinson twenty-eight and Burton nineteen.

Another intra-Court irritant occurred in connection with a case involving rate-fixing for the interstate marketing of natural gas. A landmark case, and a highly controversial one[74] decided in 1898, had held that among a number of factors to be considered in determining the "fair value" of utility property for purposes of rate-fixing, "the present as compared with the original cost of construction" should be included. It is obvious that, over a period of rising prices, the extent to which reproduction cost is a factor, the utility is favored, perhaps in many instances, by a rate utterly beyond any rational degree. The rate bases would fluctuate along with the price of labor and materials and indeed also with the interest rate on money.

The *Hope Natural Gas Company* case put an end to this fiction by holding that the Federal Power Commission need not take into account the "reproduction cost new" factor. The Court approved the Commission's action in relying primarily upon the "prudent investment" or "actual legitimate cost" criterion. Although the case was decided in 1944, by a curious coincidence the Hope Natural Gas Company was organized in 1898, the year of the original (*Smyth* v. *Ames*) decision. The Company was a West Virginia corporation and a wholly owned subsidiary of the Standard Oil Company of New Jersey. It produced, bought and marketed natural gas in West Virginia. However, most of its products were sold to local companies in Ohio and Pennsylvania.

In 1938 the cities of Akron and Cleveland filed complaints with the Power Commission charging that the rates collected by Hope were excessive and unreasonable. In March of the following year the Public Utility Commission of Pennsylvania filed a similar complaint. Although the federal Commission had no authority to order reparations for past over-charges, it nevertheless made a finding that the rates charged Ohio distributing companies had resulted in unjustifiable costs to consumers in excess of several million dollars a year. The Commission thereupon established an interstate rate base and fixed what it regarded as a reasonable rate of return thereon. In so doing, it refused to consider the "reproduction cost new" theory. It also ruled out what the Company called "trended 'original cost.'" This formula consisted in calculating " 'what the original cost of the property would have been if 1938 material and labor prices had prevailed throughout the whole period of the piecemeal construction of the company's property since 1898.' " This struck the Commission as

being basically "irrational" in its results. The difference in the rate
base allowed by the Commission on the prudent investment theory
and that contended for by the Company was approximately $32,000,-
000. The Company contention was almost 100% greater than that
allowed by the Commission. The Commission's order allowed a
yield of 6-1/2% on an evaluation of slightly more than $33,000,000.
The Company had demanded a rate of 8% on a base of $66,000,000.
Under the Commission's order the Company would earn $2,191,314
annually as compared with its immediate past income of close to
$6,000,000.

The Circuit Court of Appeals had set the Commission's ruling aside as erroneous in that it failed to take into account reproduction cost. It also held that the "actual legitimate cost" was not a
proper measure of "fair value" when price levels had substantially
changed. The Supreme Court by a divided vote reversed the Court
of Appeals and reinstated the Commission's order. It held that the
validity of the order was to be determined by whether its impact or
total effect was just and reasonable. "[I]t is the result reached, not the
method employed which is controlling."[75]

Writing for the Court, Justice Douglas pointed out that over the
forty years of its operation, Hope had earned the amount of total
investment in the Company nearly seven times over. Down to 1940, it
had earned over 20% per year on the average annual amount of its
capital stock issued for cash or assets and, in addition, had accumulated reserves for depletion and depreciation of $46,000,000. Chief
Justice Stone and Justices Black, Murphy and Rutledge concurred in Douglas' opinion. Mr. Justice Roberts took no part in the
decision. Justices Reed, Jackson and Frankfurter wrote separate
dissents. Frankfurter's dissent is particularly interesting in that he
deviated from the rate philosophy of his beloved Brandeis who consistently championed the "prudent investment" doctrine.

This was an important case and attracted widespread attention
not only in financial circles but elsewhere, because of the obvious
significance for the average consumer of utility products as well as
for the investors. What created a heightened interest, particularly in
Supreme Court circles, was a radio broadcast by Drew Pearson on
Sunday, January 2, the day before the opinion was rendered. Pearson
had a popular weekly broadcast entitled "Predictions of Things to
Come." On this occasion, he stated:

> Tomorrow the Supreme Court will split wide open on
> one of the most important economic questions of the country
> —the fixing of gas and electric rates. The case involves a

Standard Oil of New Jersey subsidiary, which supplies natural gas to Cleveland and Akron, but the issue of rate-fixing affects gas and electric consumers of the entire country. Yesterday the Court was split four to four, with the ninth Justice trying to make up his mind by today.

It was reliably reported that several members of the Court were incensed at what they thought was an obvious "leak." Since Rutledge was the newest member of the Court at that time, it seems that in some quarters, at least, he or his clerk was suspect. It has since been clearly established that neither was involved.

It appeared that Justice Roberts was particularly disturbed at this incident. It may be recalled that the Justice resigned in July 1945 after several terms in which a number of personal grievances had developed. It was reported that after the *Hope Natural Gas* case Roberts declined to join the Justices for lunch during the recess on days in which the Court heard oral arguments. It seems that it was a long-standing tradition that the Justices should shake hands with each other in the robing room immediately before appearing on the bench. In the latter months of service, it is said that Roberts declined to shake hands on this occasion with at least one of his colleagues. The feelings generated by these recurring incidents culminated in the unfortunate disagreement among the Justices concerning the letter to be sent Roberts after his resignation.[76]

In retrospect, it appears that Pearson in his broadcast, though literally erroneous in detail, may have sensed a touch-and-go situation. He was wrong, of course, in his assertion that the ninth member of an evenly divided Court was trying to make up his mind. There were in fact only eight Justices who participated in the case. It is possible, however, that Rutledge may at first have been indecisive in which event, had he voted with the dissenters, the Court would have been equally divided and the decision of the Circuit Court of Appeals in favor of the Hope Company would have prevailed.

It is unlikely, however, that Rutledge ever seriously considered joining Frankfurter, Jackson and Reed. His files on the case disclose a handwritten concurring opinion in which he pointed out that the most troublesome matter in rate cases was what the courts regarded as "the necessity for finding a rate base." This, he thought, was a search "for a mythical value found independently of earnings, to be attributed to property which itself has no market and enjoys monopoly of the market it serves." This search for a "will-o'-the-wisp," he thought had resulted in extreme confusion which made more difficult the underlying problem. It is possible, of course, that there was no "leak" at all. Close followers of the Court might well have guessed, from previous positions taken by the Justices, that the decision would be a close one and that one Justice might have the deciding vote. Why Roberts failed to participate in the decision is not known, and whether his failure to participate in it affected his reaction to the Pearson broadcast is also purely speculative.

In any event, Pearson was altogether correct in stressing the importance of the case to the consumer. Indeed it was of no less importance for the utilities. The financial writer for the *Baltimore Sun*[77] pointed out:

> With the FPC sustained in its employment of the principle of "prudent investment," it is expected that public utilities carrying inflated values must now write them down. This list would include the properties of some of the largest holding companies in the power and light field. A number of the operating companies which have adjusted their capital accounts to the "prudent-investment" form will not be affected.

He then quoted the dire prophecy of the *Wall Street Journal* that:

> Ultimately this question must be dealt with through legislation; if an act of Congress will not do it, then a constitutional amendment will be required, unless the system of private ownership of property dedicated to the public use is to be thrown overboard.

No congressional action and no constitutional amendment has changed the rate-making principle of the case and the system of privately owned utilities has not yet collapsed.

Instead of contributing to tensions among the Justices, Rutledge did all he could to relieve and avoid them. A good example is the situation which developed around a case involving the Securities and Exchange Commission. Early in 1943 the Court had refused to uphold an order of the Commission which required directors of a public utilities holding company who had purchased preferred stock of their company while plans for reorganization were pending, to surrender such stock at cost plus interest. The directors, of course, had planned to convert the stock into securities of the reorganized company, as all other holders would be permitted to do. In so ruling, the Commission had specifically found that the directors were guilty of no fraud and that they had not misused their managerial positions. It based its holding on what it regarded as general, equitable principles "judicially established." The Supreme Court held that there were no equitable principles established by judicial decision to support the ruling of the Commission in the absence of some inequitable conduct. Justice Frankfurter wrote the opinion of the Court. Justices Black, Murphy and Reed dissented. Justice Douglas, perhaps because of his former connection with the Commission, took no part in the consideration of the case, and Justice Rutledge had not yet taken the oath of office. The decision thus was by a vote of four to three.[78] The matter was remanded to the Commission for further proceedings.

Three years later the case again came before the Court. The Commission had reached precisely the same result but this time on different grounds. It held, on the basis of its "experience as a regulatory commission," that the proposed plan would not be in accord with the standards set forth in the Holding Company Act. It would not be "fair and equitable" to all persons affected, and the securities of the new company issued to the directors of the old would, in the circumstances, be "detrimental to the public interest or the interest of investors." Moreover, it would result in an "unfair or inequitable distribution of voting power."

The Court upheld this order. Justice Murphy wrote the majority opinion in which Justices Black, Reed and Rutledge joined. Justice Burton concurred in the result. Justice Douglas again did not take part, nor did Chief Justice Vinson who in the meantime had replaced Stone and, of course, had not participated in the prior case. Justice Jackson dissented, joined by Justice Frankfurter.

In his opinion, Jackson noted that the order approved was identical with the one disapproved in the earlier case. The Commission had merely "recast its rationale." He proceeded, "there being no change in the order, no additional evidence in the record and no amendment of relevant legislation, it is clear that there has been a shift in attitude between that of the controlling membership of the Court when the case was first heard and that of those who have the power of decision on this second review." Jackson then went on to analyze what he regarded as the change in "prevailing philosophy," and the reasoning of the majority in upholding the Commission's second order. He was unconvinced. "I give up," he wrote, "now I realize fully what Mark Twain meant when he said, 'the more you explain it, the more I don't understand it.' "[79]

None of this was particularly startling. Reversals by a closely divided Court of a previous position after change of personnel was by no means unprecedented. The Jehovah's Witnesses cases after Rutledge joined the Court were notable examples. It was clear also that Rutledge's was the controlling vote here. Even if Burton had adhered to his former view along with Frankfurter and Jackson, the same decision would have been reached by a vote of 4 to 3—exactly as in the first case. Jackson's comment on the situation was not calculated to raise eyebrows to any extent. There was, however, trouble in the air before the decision was announced on June 23rd, near the end of the term.

It seems that Murphy's opinion was circulated for the first time on June 17th, just six days before decision day with the end of the term at hand. Apparently, this irritated Frankfurter who promptly circulated a short statement of dissent in which he referred to "the unavoidable lateness of the decision" as precluding before adjournment, opportunity for the preparation of an adequate answer to the argument of the majority. Murphy immediately sent out a "memorandum for the conference" objecting to any reference to the "lateness of the decision." The case had been assigned to him not more than two weeks before the distribution of his opinion. Rutledge sought to avoid what he sensed as trouble by writing a personal letter to Frankfurter as follows:

June 18, 1947

Dear Felix:

I have just seen your circulation in Chenery, Nos. 81 and 82; and I am going to take whatever onus there may be in making the following suggestions to you.

I am fully in sympathy with your situation insofar as it involves the necessity on your part of following either one of two courses; namely, writing an inadequate dissent under impossible limitations of time (such as I faced in the *Yamashita* case) or of filing your dissenting opinion after the case comes down. I do not like either choice. On the other hand, there are times when one or the other becomes necessary. . . .

You will recall that in the *Yamashita* case my dissenting opinion contained a very general reference to the shortness of time which the Court had taken to dispose of the case. You will recall also that you specifically suggested to me that I should eliminate that rather soft statement of the actual situation, and I did so in compliance with the suggestion.

The basis for it was that you felt neither the Court nor any of its members should ever disclose or specifically acknowledge such a situation even though the acknowledgment was in accordance with the actual fact. I thought your suggestion both proper and right. I therefore followed it.

All of which comes down to a return by me of the same suggestion to you in this instance, made in all sincerity and friendliness. . . . [W]hat you have written will have either one or the other effect. It will put two men on this Court in a very bad light. One is Burton, ... It was assigned to him in the course of our regular routine. It remained under that assignment until June 3rd, when Murphy took it over, not by request but by the Chief's assignment. He of course will appear, if your circulation goes down, in the light of having caused all of the delay. I do not think either implication is fair, that is, I do not think it is quite fair to Harold, nor do I think it is fair to Frank. . . . I therefore earnestly and sincerely urge in the interest of the Court, as well as of the relations of its members, that you withdraw the circulation. . . .

As always,

We do not know the tenor of Frankfurter's reply, if he made one, but we do know that the final brief notice of dissent and forthcoming opinion, signed by both Frankfurter and Jackson was devoid of implied rebuke to anyone. It may be of significance that on October 6, 1947, at the beginning of the 1947 term, Jackson announced that *he* had filed the dissenting opinion "in which Mr. Justice Frankfurter joins."

Although there is no evidence that he employed any but the kindliest methods to dissuade Frankfurter from publishing his initial barb, Rutledge contemplated, if necessary, publicly coming to the defense of Murphy and Burton in a concurring opinion. Although he would do what he could to preserve harmony on the Court, he would tolerate injustice toward a colleague no more than toward anyone else. The following typed opinion appears in his files:

Mr. Justice RUTLEDGE, concurring.

Although I concur in the opinion of the Court, in view of certain statements appearing in another opinion concerning the confidential course of the Court's business, I think it necessary to point out that this case was argued on Friday, December 13, and Monday, December 16, 1946. It was thereafter considered at conference and assigned for writing of the opinion.

Because of the extraordinary pressure of the Court's work during this term, the case was reassigned to another Justice on June 3, 1947, and the opinion now presented is written substantially in accordance with the views of the majority expressed at the conference prior to the first assignment. . . .

This is not the first time in which for one reason or another dissenting Justices have been confronted with the necessity of stating their views inadequately because of considerations of time or, in the alternative, of setting them forth after the opinion comes down. . . . It is the first time when such a situation has brought forth an official disclosure of the Court's confidential procedures.

Fortunately, as the result of Frankfurter's amenability to the reasoned appeal of a trusted colleague, this opinion was not published. The incident, as in many other exchanges between the two Justices, reflects credit to both.

Shortly after Justice Rutledge took his seat, there occurred another behind-the-scenes episode involving himself and Justice Frankfurter in which their roles were the reverse of those in the *Security and Exchange Commission* case. It was Frankfurter trying to persuade Rutledge to cut out a portion of his opinion in the *Galloway* case which involved the respective functions of the judge and the jury in civil cases. It will be remembered that the Seventh Amendment guarantees the right to trial by jury in civil cases in the federal courts where the amount involved is twenty dollars or more.

In this case a young veteran sued the government in a federal court under a war risk insurance policy seeking benefits for total and permanent disability by reason of insanity which he claimed existed on the day his renewable term policy lapsed for nonpayment of premium. At the close of all the evidence, the trial court granted the government's motion for a directed verdict in its favor on the grounds that should the jury find for the plaintiff on the issue of fact as to the plaintiff's insanity at the time alleged, the verdict could not stand because there was not legally sufficient evidence to support it. The Court of Appeals affirmed the decision and the plaintiff obtained a review by the Supreme Court claiming, as he had claimed all along, that he had produced substantial evidence from which a jury could reasonably find that the facts which he had alleged were true and that he was entitled to have a jury pass on the issue.

The case raised the question of the validity of the judicial process which had been in operation in common law courts for centuries. Early in the history of trial by jury, a distinction was assumed between "questions of law" and "questions of fact," the former being matters for the judge to deal with, the latter for the jury. Some—indeed many issues—can be characterized as one or the other. The practice developed, in cases where the facts were in dispute, that after the evidence on both sides was presented to the jury it was instructed by the judge as to the legal points involved. He explained the issues and instructed it as to what ultimate finding of facts it must reach in order to return a verdict for either party. Under strict rules, which prevail in most common law jurisdictions today, the judge determines what evidence is admissible but he may not comment on it, either as to its probative value or on the credibility of the witnesses. If the evidence is "all one way" and there is no substantial conflict, the judge may render judgment accordingly, notwithstanding a jury verdict to the contrary. The practice also developed for the judge in such cases to "instruct" the jury to return a verdict which the evidence thus required. Under such an instruction, of course, the jury's function is purely nominal. In certain courts in England, the plaintiff who has the burden of proof as to the facts on which he relies for a recovery, may be "non-suited" at the conclusion of his presentation if, in the judge's opinion, there is no substantial evidence—not merely a scrap or "scintilla"—upon which the jury could find in his favor even in the absence of any evidence by his adversary. If, however, each party presents substantial evidence as to his side of the story so that reasonable men might find either way, the case is one for the jury and the jury's verdict is final.

In this state of affairs, the judges have evolved the euphemism that where the evidence is in substantial conflict, its resolution is a "matter of fact," otherwise it is one "of law." As Justice Holmes put it, if the case is an easy one, the judge decides it as a "question of law"; if it is a hard one, it is a "question of fact" for the jury. It is obvious, of course, that this is merely a way of talking about the situation. A more accurate way of putting it would be that questions which the judge decides are *called* questions of law; those left to the jury, questions of fact. Thus it is that the trial judge exercises control over the jury by determining whether the disputed factual issues lie in that area where, on consideration of the evidence on both sides, in the light of experience, reasonable men might differ by coming to different conclusions. On appeal, it is the trial court's judgment on this point which is under review.

In the *Galloway* case, the Supreme Court decision was handed down on May 24, 1943. The veteran's insurance policy had expired on May 31, 1919, after he had been in the service exactly one year and seven months. This was about a month after he had been discharged. He subsequently enlisted in the army and deserted. A series of examinations by physicians of the Veterans' Administration from 1930 to 1934 found serious mental illness. It was conceded that he was hopelessly insane at the time of the Supreme Court decision but that he had been of sound mind when he first enlisted in 1917. The question was whether the medical and other evidence adduced eleven to fifteen years later was sufficient to support a finding that he had been insane on May 31, 1919. The Supreme Court agreed with the Court of Appeals that such "long range retroactive diagnosis" on such a delicate question of insanity was insufficient to satisfy a reasonable mind.[80] A directed verdict was proper.

Justices Black, Murphy and Douglas dissented. They accepted the veteran's claim that the decision deprived him of a jury trial as guaranteed by the Seventh Amendment. Rutledge rejected the argument in a long and scholarly opinion for the Court. He was challenged by an equally scholarly and even longer opinion by Black who had consistently objected to what he regarded as a gradual process of erosion by judges invading the province of juries in admiralty, diversity and Federal Employers Liability Act cases which come before the Court each year. Black thought it very seldom that a judge should substitute his judgment for that of the jury on the issue whether the evidence was such as to require a verdict on one side or the other.[81] Inconsistently or not, he has been one of the chief proponents of a scrupulous examination by the Court of jury verdicts in criminal cases.[82]

While the draft opinions were circulating among the Justices for their comments, a brief but interesting exchange took place between Justices Rutledge and Frankfurter. The latter sent a kind and congratulatory letter to the new Justice on his position, acknowledging "the arduous and painstaking labor" which went into the opinion. Curiously, however, he was unhappy about the thoroughness with which Rutledge sought to justify the Court's decision. He thought the matter already settled beyond argument and that Rutledge should treat Black's attack "with intelligent neglect." He saw nothing to be gained, except confusion and unsettlement, by treating the matter as something to be argued and discussed at this late date. Frankfurter concluded his memorandum by apologizing for the "brutality" of asking Rutledge to omit material on which he had spent so much time and effort. He quoted the classic remark of Holmes who, when some trusted colleague persuaded him to omit a part of an opinion, remarked: "Very well, I'll take it out but I'll use it in a letter to a friend." This time Rutledge did not "take it out" as he did, at Frankfurter's urging in his *Yamashita* dissent—and then in fact used it in "a letter to a friend," John Frank.[83]

What explanation Rutledge made to Frankfurter we do not know. Dated May 21, 1943, a handwritten note addressed to "Mr. Justice Frankfurter" is marked in red crayon "not sent." It is as follows:

> In re Galloway.
>
> 5-21, 1943
>
> Dear Frankfurter,
>
> There's nothing either brutal or unkind in your suggestion for treating the dissent summarily. I debated doing so before submitting recirculation, with inclination toward that treatment. But I came out convinced the matter should not be brushed aside.
>
> 1. This is an old ghost, with more than feline capacity for returning to life.
> 2. Previous discussions here, especially more recently, seem to me to generate more heat than light.
> 3. Probably mine does not do better, nevertheless I am better satisfied than with the previous treatments. Van Devanter was not quite willing to come out squarely & say he was wrong before. The last pronouncement here was a sort of dodge.
> 4. The dissent is forceful—and plausible in some respects. It will carry more weight, unanswered, with some than if answered now. This, contrary to your view, might invite further raising of the question.
> 5. I do not agree that an honest view concurred in by three brethren, on a matter of such importance, should be "intelligently neglected."
>
> Not pride of authorship, but belief the ghost will be more securely laid, is the reason I think the collision should be head-on.
>
> W.R.

Here were two great minds at odds as to how to treat the arguments of a third. There was much to be said for Frankfurter's advice, as a matter of judicial strategy. As it turned out, Rutledge was right. The "feline capacity" of this ghost has brought it up many times in the past twenty years, and as late as the new Supreme Court Rules of Civil Procedure adopted by the Court in January, 1963. A statement in the nature of a dissent was made by Justices Black and Douglas, in part, as follows:

(1) (a) Rule 50 (a) is amended by making the order of a judge granting a motion for a directed verdict effective without submitting the question to the jury at all. It was pointed out in *Galloway* v. *United States,* 319 U. S. 372, 396, 401-407, 63 S. Ct. 1077, 87 L. Ed. 1458 (dissenting opinion), how judges have whittled away or denied the right of trial by jury through the devices of directed verdicts and judgments notwithstanding verdicts. Although the amendment here is not itself a momentous one, it gives formal sanction to the process by which the courts have been wresting from juries the power to render verdicts. Since we do not approve of this sapping of the Seventh Amendment's guarantee of a jury trial, we cannot join even this technical *coup de grace.*

The rule in question merely made the order of a judge granting a motion for a directed verdict effective without going through the useless motion of submitting it to the jury which would have no choice but to obey instructions.

The Later Years

There is evidence, a little here, a little there, that Justice Rutledge during the last half of his Court service became increasingly unhappy with its decisions. How far this went toward hastening his death, we shall never know. But it appears that he worked harder and longer and the pressure was unquestionably there. One might easily hazard the guess that it took its first toll on his strength and tolerance with the wartime cases, culminating in *Yamashita*, and gradually sapped away at his physical and emotional resistance thereafter. Note has been taken of Rutledge's expressions of disappointment in some of Stone's positions during his later years. He was soon to be further grieved by the performance of Stone's successor. As early as December, 1946, he wrote to his friend Brant that "F.V. is starting off well as C.J.—but votes the other way too often for my comfort. He's finding this is no Treasury Department or Office of Stabilization." (Vinson had been head of both at one time.) The three succeeding years were to find Rutledge increasingly uncomfortable. In July, 1947, in a letter to his friend Irving Dilliard, he referred sadly to the anti-Bill of Rights decisions of the term just completed as a "deluge of disaster."

A suggestion of depression may also be detected in his reaction to an Oklahoma case involving segregation of Negroes in the public schools. In the *Sipuel* case[84] the Court ordered the state of Oklahoma to give a Negro girl applicant an opportunity for a legal education equal to that afforded white students. This was during the "separate but equal" era of civil rights in education—six years before the *Brown* case which invalidated segregation in public schools. The exact language of the Court was as follows: "The State must provide it [opportunity for legal education] for her in conformity with the equal protection clause of the Fourteenth Amendment and provide it as soon as it does for applicants of any other group."

After the Oklahoma courts purported to issue orders to the Regents in conformity with the Supreme Court's opinion, Miss Sipuel (then Mrs. Fisher) thought the state court had not complied with the Supreme Court's mandate but had left loopholes to avoid it. The order directed the Regents either to:

> (1) enroll plaintiff, if she is otherwise qualified, in the first-year class of the School of Law of the University of Oklahoma, in which school she will be entitled to remain on the same scholastic basis as other students thereof until such a separate law school for Negroes is established and ready to function, or (2) not enroll any applicant of any group in said class until said separate school is established and ready to function.

The Court in a *Per Curiam* opinion held that: "It is clear that the District Court of Cleveland County [Oklahoma] did not depart from our mandate." To Justice Rutledge, it was just as clear that the state court had so departed in that, under its order, the Regents could establish a law school for Negroes overnight which obviously could not be "equal" to the highly respected law school of the State University, or by refusing all applications to the first year class but continuing the education of the other classes.[85]

While the first *Sipuel* appeal was pending, Rutledge received a form letter, presumably sent to all the Justices, with the overworked warning that "well-known Communists" in Oklahoma were responsible for most of the public agitation in Sipuel's case. The writer signed the letter as "spokesman" but there was no suggestion by letterhead or otherwise, to explain for whom or for what he was "spokesman." The Justice received a number of other letters commenting on his dissenting opinion, some favorable, some otherwise. His answer to one carries some significance. His friend, Aubrey Williams, wrote a congratulatory note, expressing astonishment that the Court could have come to such a conclusion after the earlier decision. "I feel like saying," he concluded, "God help us, with the Court fading in and out like that, what have we to hold to?" To which Rutledge replied:

I was not greatly surprised at the outcome in the second *Fisher* case, though at the time of the first opinion, I had some hope it might be different. It is not for me to criticize the action of my brethren, at any rate in any public way other than by speaking in dissent, but I can say to you in confidence that this is not the only time this term when I have felt great discouragement from action taken by the Court.

We also know that the Justice was much distressed over the turn of world events after the war. The foreign policy of the United States worried him and especially the so-called "Truman policy" of encircling and containment. In answering a letter from a friend on the *St. Louis Star-Times* after the *United Mine Workers* case, he complained of "news-management" at home and our national behavior abroad.

Thanks a lot for your note of March 27th. I can well understand why you might not be wholly free to write your views about the Lewis business. I suspect there have been others in your boots in that respect. The other day when I picked up the *Washington Post* I had to hunt for about five minutes before I spotted the very short and hidden news item about the Chicago municipal election. The significant thing to me lay in the fact that I well knew that if the result had been the other way it would have been splurged all over the front page of the paper. And then they say we have a free press!

I frankly admit that this is a time when one has to steel himself to see anything bright on either the world or the national horizon. Things have already gone so far in wrong directions, both domestically and internationally, that I can't be sure the works are not pretty well shot, especially for any prospect of real peace through the United Nations or other international relationships.

In an address to the Oregon State Bar Association in the fall of 1946, his concern over the international situation was further evident.

The period following armistice is always one of relief and usually, at the beginning, of hope for victor and vanquished. But such months are also pregnant with danger. Vengeance still rides high, without opposition of arms to check its course. Not all men or leaders have the Godlike magnanimity of Lincoln's Second Inaugural. Unities forged by comradeship-in-arms dissolve and are replaced by competitive grasping among allies for the fruits of victory. Nationalistic aims and attachments come to outweigh considerations for the common good of all nations and peoples. Reversions to old ways of thinking outmoded by war's effects come easily and often, it seems inevitably. The time after armistice, a time neither of war nor of peace, is always one of hope mixed with fear, of struggle to find the tenable bases for peace mingled with effort to secure national advantages which make its achievement impossible. . . . Rare has been the instance in which the end of war has not merely set the stage for another and more horrible conflict, or, if not so, brought for millions conditions of living which only decades could soften.

The same ominous note was sounded in a speech at the University of Iowa.

Strange is the paradox which makes men bent on killing more brotherly than when walking together in peace. Now those compelling unities have dissolved. Now the bonds tying us to other nations and other races have been loosened. Now we see slipping away the dream of what we and they fought to save, in pullings apart over things which in war we mastered together.

But during these years, Justice Rutledge, while discouraged and frequently depressed, was not without hope. His hope was that mankind might still seize upon the rule of law as a substitute for the rule of force before he destroyed himself. "In this aftermath of war," he told the Federal Bar Association late in 1947, "many of us, sensitive to this necessity, have become discouraged, disillusioned, even hopeless."

Some, indeed impatient with our snail's progress openly call for taking the plunge that would end all progress. I am fully conscious of the great facts tending to create that outlook. It is, nevertheless, one to which men and women devoted to the rule of justice under law dare not surrender.

Rutledge's insight into the ways of men and nations was frighteningly accurate. One of the great historians of our times has only recently sounded the same warning:

Today [November 3, 1963] we are living in a world in which nationalism is effervescing all around us. We do not need to be told of its existence and its power. It thrusts itself on our attention. . . . It is a state of mind in which we give our paramount political loyalty to one fraction of the human race—to the particular tribe of which we happen to be tribesmen.[86]

Arnold Toynbee is not talking only of the tribesmen of newly liberated and underdeveloped countries of Africa. He includes the "tribesmen" of Western Europe, Asia and the Americas. Nationalism, he declares, is "one of the most potent forces in the modern world." French nationalism "incarnated in the personality of Charles de Gaulle" is obstructing "deliberately" the political unification of the Western peoples. But neither the British, the Americans nor the Russians are free from what Toynbee fears might be the end of what we call civilization. Particularly the United States and the Soviet Union are in a nationalistic state of mind "inspired by the ambition to become the one supreme power in the world by definitely getting the better of the other." Perhaps the Peoples Republic of China should now be included in this race for human extinction.

And so, if Justice Rutledge had lived fifteen years longer, he would have found, in the international arena, little to encourage him other than the fact that mankind had not yet committed suicide. His appraisal of the domestic situation and the image it creates in other countries and cultures would not have made him happy. His hopes and aspirations for an era of the brotherhood of man, in any practical, realistic sense, which is the only way in which his mind worked, would have been made no brighter by the situation as he would find it.

Although there was no hint in the summer of 1949 of the weapon which Death would suddenly seize to overcome him, Rutledge worried his family and his friends both by his physical and emotional condition. The incessant, continuous hard driving over the years was taking its toll and after the death of Murphy to whom he was devoted, his despondence increased. Less than two weeks before he was stricken, Brant wrote to him (August 30, 1949): "During this transitional period on the Court, the best service you can render is to help decide cases. To hell with writing opinions. . . . You are needed on the Court more now than at any previous time, but your first duty is to remain on earth." This was one duty Wiley Rutledge was unable to discharge.

Shortly after the Justice's death, Brant wrote to the widow, Annabel, a letter containing a remark by former Secretary Ickes: "Harold Ickes told me a few days ago that he felt Wiley's death in the same way that he did F.D.R.'s, mostly personally and in the sense of loss to the country." This was a feeling shared by many others who knew the Justice. Because, as the late Reverend A. Powell Davies of All Souls' Unitarian Church said at the memorial meeting for the Justice, he was a man of natural kindness, of gentleness, of ready comprehension and flashes of humor, of quick sympathy, warm humanity, directness of thought and purity of action. He was a man both of humility and dignity.

Add to these qualities a passion for justice, and the words of the Chief Justice at the Supreme Court Memorial take on additional meaning. "The very factors which made Wiley Rutledge a great man made him a great judge." Every case which came before him was a challenge but it was also a deep emotional experience. It was not abstract justice that he sought. He was not interested in a form of words. It was not justice in the air but in this very case, between man and man—between man and the state. But not only was he concerned with the fate of the particular petitioner or appellant but in the significance of the case for others who might be affected by the result. "Immediately we are concerned with only one man, William Schneiderman. Actually, though indirectly, the decision affects millions." One can sense and almost share the agony the Justice must have felt at the appalling thought of thousands of naturalized immigrants who might be put in peril if the Court affirmed Schneiderman's denaturalization, seventeen years after he thought he had become a citizen.

Although his life was all too short, it was, for the most part, a full and happy life. He was happy with his family, and the association with his friends and colleagues, and with his work. His life was full—full of gratifying experiences and achievement, as educator, scholar and judge. It was also full of love—love for his wife and children, for his country and for his work. But for Wiley Rutledge, the tragedy of his life was that there was something which he passionately wanted but could not obtain. With all the satisfactions and enjoyment which he found in his work, there was always the haunting thought that he should have done better. He was not content with having done his best and that it was effective. "Wiley was a great addition to the Court," wrote one of the Justices who sat with him the entire period of his tenure.

[H]e went at writing an opinion pretty much as a law professor goes to work writing a Law Journal article. So he exhausted himself unnecessarily, doing more than deciding a particular case and trying to work out the total mosaic in which the case appeared in legal literature. His mill ground slowly and very fine. He probably put more actual energy and concentration into each of the several cases that came across his desk than anyone in modern history.

But after driving himself, day and night, to produce an opinion which will be read and bear fruit so long as men love liberty, he would be tortured with the feeling that it might have been improved. Nothing was good enough unless it was perfect and like all others, however gifted, he never achieved perfection. The Chief Justice was right, "the qualities which made him a great man made him a great judge." And in the words of a former president of the University of Colorado written after Rutledge's death: "Such men are seldom."[87]

Such Men are Seldom, indeed.

UNITED STATES COURT OF APPEALS FOR THE
DISTRICT OF COLUMBIA, 1940

Henry W. Edgerton   Fred M. Vinson   Wiley Rutledge

Harold M. Stephens   D. Lawrence Groner   Justin Miller

RUTLEDGE WITH SENATORS NORRIS AND O'MAHONEY
AFTER SENATE CONFIRMATION, 1943

Reproduced here by permission of the Associated Press, Copyright © 1943.

THE STONE COURT, 1943

Stanley Reed   Owen J. Roberts   Harlan F. Stone   Hugo L. Black   Felix Frankfurter

Robert H. Jackson   William O. Douglas   Frank Murphy   Wiley Rutledge

THE VINSON COURT, 1948

Felix Frankfurter   Hugo L. Black   Fred M. Vinson   Stanley Reed   William O. Douglas

Wiley Rutledge   Frank Murphy   Robert H. Jackson   Harold H. Burton

CHAPTER X

EPILOGUE

JUDGES, like most people, behave in a more or less predictable way. Whether more or less depends upon many variables. Prediction here is hazardous and one reason is a failure accurately to appraise the political and economic environment of past actions upon which future judicial behavior is predicted. Justice McReynolds with a trust-busting reputation, for example, appointed by a liberal president, will probably be thought of as one of the Court's most conservative Justices of all times. Justice Minton is another case in point. As a New Deal Senate whip, he was, by many, mistaken as an appropriate successor to Justice Rutledge. But he turned out to be no Rutledge. Free from the limitations of political pressures, the judicial performance of these two Justices was at complete variance from normal expectations. Chief Justice Vinson might also be included in this category. On the other hand, Justice Black has, to a large extent followed, as a judge, the liberal economic philosophy which he revealed as a senator.

Predictions based on past judicial attitudes may be a more accurate index to future decisions. Close students of the Supreme Court can frequently make reasonably accurate predictions of things to come. It requires no crystal ball to guess, generally, where Chief Justice Warren and Justices Black and Douglas will stand on civil liberty cases resulting in a divided Court. Much the same can be said of Justice Brennan who more often than not will be found voting with the other three in such cases. And yet, strange diversions and groupings are not uncommon.

A striking recent example is the Connecticut birth control case of 1961 in which the Court, after full briefing and oral arguments, declined to pass on the constitutionality of a Connecticut law which made it a criminal offense to "use any drug, medicinal article or instrument for the purpose of preventing conception." Because the law had not been enforced, the Court declared the case not "justiciable."[1]

The issue arose when an obstetrician and two of his patients brought a declaratory judgment action to determine the constitutionality of the law. Justices Frankfurter, Clark, Whittaker, Brennan and the Chief Justice dismissed the appeal. Justices Black and Stewart dissented, declaring that the case should be decided, one way or the other. Justices Douglas and Harlan dissented in separate opinions in which they not only insisted that the case should be decided but that the decision should hold the Connecticut law unconstitutional. These were not the usual groupings of the Justices on highly controversial social and political issues. The Court avoided the substantive problem of determining the validity of a criminal law in a procedure especially designed, among others, to enable citizens to obtain a constitutional ruling on it without taking the risk of violation. The Court took the position that there was no real risk involved because no one had ever been caught and punished.

Again, many would not have predicted that former Attorney General, Justice Tom Clark, would have written the powerful opinion in *Mapp* v. *Ohio*,[2] raising to the constitutional level the rule excluding unconstitutionally obtained evidence in criminal trials in state courts, thus overruling *Wolf* v. *Colorado*[3] and making Justice Rutledge's dissent in that case the law of the land.

The war cases also produced a number of strange alignments. Rutledge's concurrence in the Japanese exclusion[4] case can be explained only by the climate of opinion created by Pearl Harbor and the natural reluctance of the Justices to review the acts of the military in the midst of a war when the nation was fighting desperately for survival. We know now that he came to regret his stand in this case. No more unpredictable division of the Justices could be imagined than in the *Bundists* case in which leaders of the Bund were indicted for conspiracy to counsel evasion of the Selective Service Act. This case came on at the height of the war although the decision did not come down until June, 1945. The convictions were reversed. Justice Roberts wrote an opinion the substance of which was that counseling a refusal to *serve* in the armed forces after registration was not a violation of the Selective Service law. Justices Frankfurter and Murphy joined in the opinion with Black and Rutledge concurring in separate opinions. Chief Justice Stone wrote a vigorous dissent in which Douglas, Reed and Jackson concurred.[5]

A committee of the American Bar Association, at its 1962 meeting in San Francisco, made a report on the possibilities of the computer as an aid to the bar. The committee appeared to be fascinated with the idea that a lawyer could feed the facts of his case into the machine, push a button and get the exact vote of each of the Justices.

The secret of such an enterprise, it was explained, was the consistency of the Justices in previous cases of similar factual content.

The theory here is not that judges with definite social, philosophical and economic views may be expected to follow a certain pattern of decision. It is difficult to believe that any machine could function in this manner. The theory is the naive one that a judge who decides a case one way today will decide a case with more or less similar facts the same way tomorrow. This is a sort of personal *stare decisis*. It does not take into account the almost limitless capacity of lawyers, and especially judges to "distinguish" cases on the basis of their factual content and their ideational overtones. This is to say nothing about the capacity of good minds to see both sides of controversial issues where there are valid interests and values of high order in close competition. Good examples are Justice Douglas' and Justice Black's votes in the two flag salute cases—the first in which they voted to uphold the constitutionality of the compulsory ceremony, the second in which they joined the majority to hold that it violated the First Amendment guarantee of free speech and the free practice of religion.[6] Equally in point is Justice Black's reversal of his original position in a Jehovah's Witness case, involving the peddling of religious literature on the streets and ringing doorbells, by joining with Rutledge and others in holding the city ordinance unconstitutional. All predictions of Supreme Court decisions must allow for a definite margin of error, but the most reliable predictions will not be made by a mechanical operation. A machine cannot take into account the process of decision-making which occurs in important cases within the walls of that marble hall.

It is probably true, as most citizens believe, that they know much more about how important decisions are made in the highest legislative and executive branches of the government than in the judiciary. This may be the case with the Congress, although the considerations which motivate senators in executive session and representatives on the Rules Committee of the House are hardly matters of public record. Nevertheless, published reports, legislative debates and recorded votes afford considerable reliable information on how this phase of democracy works. Decision-making in the Executive Departments is something else. We do know that the President sits down with his cabinet officers to discuss national problems. We do not know the extent to which collective judgments are made there or how often the President, the next day, meets with a special assistant or personal advisor and makes his own decision on matters vital to the nation. Nor do we know the extent to which one part of the executive establishment understands what another is doing or what it is telling the public that it is doing. The recent barrage of ambiguous and even misleading statements resulting from a policy of "managed news" in regard to the Bay of Pigs fiasco and the South Vietnam crises is not calculated to inspire confidence in what the public is told, or in the responsibility of the decision-makers.

Even less information is available about the process of decision in the Supreme Court. There are no press releases, there is no record of debates. All conferences are "executive sessions." There are official opinions of the Justices—and "leaks." And no good usually comes from the gossip. Speculation as to how important decisions are made and not made may do more harm than good by creating a false image of the Court and an erroneous impression of the judicial process at its highest level. The official opinions set forth the legal rationalization for the decision of the Court or the vote of the particular Justice. But they do not describe how that decision was reached. The opinions, of course, are invaluable to other courts, the entire legal profession and, for that matter, to the public at large. Justice Brennan recently emphasized that "unlike the case of a Congressional or White House decision, Americans demand of their Supreme Court judges that they produce a written opinion, the collective judgment of the judges subscribing to it, setting forth the reasons which led them to the decision."[7] It might be more accurate to say that the opinion demanded is one setting forth a justification in legal terms for the decision.

A few years ago, Professor Hart complained that many of the Court's opinions were written too fast. After a series of arithmetical assumptions he concluded that an average of twenty-four hours was about the allowance of time per opinion. This will do, as he put it, for "a superficially plausible rationalization of what is in substance an *ipse dixit*." But it is not enough for the evolution and presentation of "ideas which will stand the test of time for the solution of hard problems." Ideas of this magnitude "have ordinarily to be hammered out by a process of collective deliberation. . . ." Hart thought that in many instances the Court was falling down on its job and that these failures were "threatening to undermine the professional respect of first-rate lawyers for the incumbent Justices of the Court. . . ."[8] He advocated fewer cases decided by full opinions after oral argument in order to increase the "twenty-four hour" average.

There is no doubt that from time to time superficial opinions have been handed down by the Supreme Court. And there has probably been no extended period in which professional respect for one or more of the "incumbent Justices" has not been undermined by their sloppy performance. But it is submitted that there is little evidence that respect for the Court, as an institution, has been substantially undermined, at least within the present century.

Commenting on Professor Hart's conclusions, Thurman Arnold took a totally different view of decision-making on the Court. As for the "maturing of collective thought" which Hart thought would improve the Court's opinions, Arnold declared that "there is no such process as this, and there never has been; men of positive views are only hardened in those views by such conferences."[9]

There is something to be said for and against both views. It may be that the Court has a heavier case load than it should have and the Justices are overworked, although there is authoritative opinion to the contrary.[10] But it is also quite plausible that Hart has overworked his arithmetic as an explanation for an occasional slipshod opinion. As Judge Charles Clark once pointed out:

> There are vast and important areas of the law where there is little debate as to the substantive principles, and the cases, if not foredoomed from the start, deal only with the procedure or the settling of the facts for the ready application of these principles. On the appellate level all observers place the number of cases of a predestined outcome at a very high level; Cardozo eventually went so far as to place it at nine-tenths, perhaps more.[11]

As for Thurman Arnold, a former judge, he knows that collective judgments do not derive entirely from "conferences." The exchange of views by the constantly circulated opinions, revised and re-revised to meet objections and incorporate suggestions may be far more important.

Justice Brennan recently has described the "decisional process" in some detail but in abstract terms. "We follow a schedule of two weeks of argument from Monday through Thursday," he told the Florida Bar Association,[12] "followed by two weeks of recess for opinion writing and the study of appeals and certiorari petitions."

> The argued cases are listed on the Friday conference agenda of the Friday following argument. . . . Not infrequently discussion of particular cases may be spread over two or more conferences. Not until the discussion is completed and a vote is taken is the opinion assigned.

The Justice then described the agonizing and sometimes frustrating experience of the opinion writer:

When the author of an opinion feels he has an unanswerable document he sends it to the print shop, which we maintain in our building. The printed draft may be revised several times before his proposed opinion is circulated among his brethren. Copies are sent to each member of the Court, those in the dissent as well as those in the majority. Now often comes the time when the author discovers that his work has only begun. He receives a return, ordinarily in writing, from each Justice who voted with him and usually also from the Justices who voted the other way. He learns who will write the dissent if one is to be written. But his particular concern is whether those who voted with him are still of his view and what they have to say about his proposed opinion. Often some who voted with him at conference will advise that they reserve final judgment pending the circulation of the dissent. It is a common experience that dissents change votes, even enough votes to become the majority. I have converted more than one proposed majority opinion into a dissent before the final decision was announced. I have also, however, had the more satisfying experience of rewriting a dissent as a majority opinion for the Court. Before everyone has finally made up his mind a constant interchange among us by memoranda, by telephone, at the lunch table, continues while we hammer out the final form of the opinion. I had one case during the past Term in which I circulated 10 printed drafts before one was approved as the Court opinion.

. . .

The point is that each Justice, unless he disqualifies himself in a particular case, passes on every piece of business coming to the Court. The Court does not function by means of committees or panels. Each Justice passes on each petition, each item, no matter how drawn, in longhand, by typewriter, or on a press. Our Constitution vests the judicial power in only one Supreme Court. This does not permit Supreme Court action by committees, panels, or sections. The method that the several Justices use in meeting an enormous caseload varies. There is one uniform rule: Judging is not delegated. Each Justice studies each case in sufficient detail to resolve the question for himself. So that in a very real sense, each decision is an individual decision of every Justice. . . .[13]

A few actual examples will highlight Justice Brennan's description of the process of decision. The *Thomas* case,[14] was decided in the Supreme Court of Texas on October 27, 1943. The appeal to the United States Supreme Court was under consideration until the following March when the Court ruled that it would hear oral arguments. Rutledge was assigned to write the opinion. Apparently, the case was the subject of repeated discussion in the Friday conferences and was restored to the docket for rehearing during the 1944 term which began in October. It was not until the following January that the final decision was handed down, reversing the state court.

No less than seventeen opinions were circulated during the months in which the matter was under consideration, twelve by Rutledge, two each by Roberts and Jackson and one by Douglas. The first of Rutledge's was originally designated by him as "dissenting" which suggests that in the earlier stages it appeared that a majority of the Justices would uphold the Texas statute as constitutional. In the copy of this opinion in the Justice's files, the word "dissenting" is penciled out and the word "memorandum" substituted. Several of the subsequent revisions were made to satisfy Douglas who, at one point, wrote Rutledge that he could not join him. He finally did, of course, although as indicated above, he wrote a concurring opinion on his own.

In the *Malinski* case[15] Justice Douglas wrote the plurality opinion, holding Malinski unconstitutionally convicted by the admission in evidence of a coerced confession, but affirming the conviction of Rudish who was tried with Malinski. In the first draft of his opinion, Douglas would affirm both convictions. He later changed his mind as to Malinski and was joined by Black, Murphy and Rutledge on that part of his opinion. Douglas wrote and circulated five drafts in all. Rutledge, dissenting as to Rudish, revised his opinion nine times. On his tenth draft, he was joined by Murphy who also dissented in a separate opinion. Frankfurter's concurrence went through three circulations compared to two of Justice Stone's dissent as to both prisoners, in which Roberts, Reed and Jackson joined.

Sometimes unanimity or near unanimity in decision and reasoning is regarded by an opinion-writer as more important than at others. Indeed, in his conception of judicial strategy, to keep dissents and concurrences to a minimum may be more important than the soundness of the opinion. Again, concessions may be made to avoid a delay perhaps even to the following term of Court with possibilities of an adverse decision. Some such situation involving an opinion by Justice Holmes is related by Justice Frankfurter in his *Reminiscences*.[16] In this case, it appears that Holmes signed an opinion which he himself regarded as altogether unsatisfactory because he feared the case might be carried over to the following term, and perhaps decided the other way.

The case involved the constitutionality of an Act of Congress known as the Hepburn Act which subjected a monopolistic network of pipelines owned by the Standard Oil Company to regulation by the Interstate Commerce Commission.[17] This, then, was a law checking economic power, legislation sure to be challenged by great interests and their spokesmen. It raised an issue which, in the first quarter of the century, was likely to invite division among the Justices either as to result or the reasons therefor.

The law actually was upheld, with only Justice McKenna dissenting. Holmes' opinion for the Court was an anemic affair not calculated to elicit admiration from his admirers or respect from his detractors. It seems that Professor Powell, who taught constitutional law, had twitted Frankfurter about his "hero," Holmes, for writing what Powell called a question-begging opinion, failing to discuss the basic economic reasons for the law. After Holmes' death, his Supreme Court files were made available to Justice Frankfurter who explained the case as follows:

. . . When I came into possession of the papers, the opinion as originally circulated in the *Pipeline* case and the opinion that finally became the opinion of the Court, the documents revealed that Holmes did go on this essentially economic justification for Congressional interference, but the boys wouldn't stand for it. In all the years Holmes was on the Court, from 1902 to 1932, in no other case did he write and rewrite and circulate and recirculate with a view to getting an agreement on the part of the Court, and the opinion that now appears is an eviscerated document—a castration really, not an evisceration, a castration of his original opinion. And in his own annotation on his copy of the opinion that Powell dealt with in class as "question-begging," Holmes wrote in his own handwriting, "This is a wholly unsatisfactory opinion," and then stated why it was unsatisfactory. I don't think there's another instance—well, I can't say that, but I should be greatly surprised—yes, I don't believe that there is another instance in which a member of the Supreme Court, or for that matter any court, analyzed and characterized with such naked candor an opinion of his own as "unsatisfactory" and gave the reasons why it was and why he yielded to having his name put to such an opinion; namely, that if he hadn't done that, the case would not have been decided that Term with the risk of being adversely decided later. . . .

The New Jersey school bus case certainly throws light on decision-making by the High Court. It was argued on the twentieth of November, 1946. Printed briefs, of course, had been filed several months before. The Court's decision was handed down February 10th, 1947 —approximately three months later. During that period, fifteen different opinions were circulated among the Justices, eight by Rutledge, six by Black, one by Jackson, and one by Frankfurter which was never published.

Rutledge's files disclose several handwritten notes from Frankfurter. One stressed the importance of Rutledge's dissenting opinion in which he expressed his desire to join, which he did. He indicated his reluctance, because of his own religion to write an opinion. As noted, he did in fact write one but it never got as far as the printer. Another scribbled note discussed the apparent line-up of the Justices and a third referred to Rutledge's own religious upbringing. A handwritten note from Murphy raised the question of the qualification of both himself and Rutledge to participate on account of Rutledge's Baptist background and Murphy's Catholic affiliation.

As usual Rutledge made his own conference notes as to the initial reaction of his brethren. Jackson and Burton, both of whom eventually joined him in dissent, were at first in favor of affirming the New Jersey Supreme Court which had upheld the law. Murphy "passed" —a term Rutledge, a veteran bridge player, invariably used to indicate indecision or noncommittal attitude of a colleague at the conference.

Black's first circulated draft is quite different from the finished product. He made no mention of the possible vulnerability of the New Jersey law on equal protection grounds in that it expressly excluded transportation payments for children attending private schools operated for profit. In his final opinion he disposes of the point quite satisfactorily. The issue had not been raised in the state court nor in the Supreme Court and for all that appeared in the record there were no New Jersey children attending such schools. He stated in his first opinion that neither federal nor state government could prefer one religion over another. In his final opinion he adds that neither may pass laws aiding all religions. This is one of the most sweeping statements in the majority opinion and, if applied literally, would forbid tax exemption to religious organizations and many other collateral benefits enjoyed by them. Also, at this stage

Black appeared to be more willing to call a spade a spade. He admitted that the parochial schools derive an "indirect benefit," but this is not "support." Under the hammering of Rutledge's early drafts, Black in the end does not admit (although he does not deny) that the church schools are benefited indirectly. It is the *children* who are benefited. Rutledge argued that there could be no valid criteria to distinguish "direct" from "indirect" benefits for constitutional purposes since the establishment clause was absolute in its prohibition.

In two or three of his earlier circulations, Black made some kind of a point that the state had not entered into any kind of partnership with the church. Rutledge hit this point hard. The First Amendment is not directed merely at partnerships, limited or unlimited. It forbids any kind of relationship involving aid, support or benefit, direct or indirect. Black's next draft omitted all references to the "partnership" idea.

And so it went, as Rutledge pecked away at his arguments, Black tightened them up, revised them to reduce their vulnerability or dropped them altogether. Apparently, however, Black never wavered in his conviction that the New Jersey statute had not passed through the "verge" and over the brink into unconstitutionality. But something persuaded Jackson and Burton from their original view and it may be surmised that the power and persistency of Rutledge's arguments played a large part. In spite of a personal note, expressing admiration for his opinion, Rutledge's arguments failed to convince his close friend Murphy who "passed" at the original conference but in the end voted with the majority.

One reason for the large number of revisions by Rutledge was that he too, of course, was benefiting from comments from Frankfurter, Burton and Jackson. Copy after copy was returned to him by these three, raising doubts, making criticisms and suggestions. Indeed, it was not until his sixth revision that Jackson indicated that he would join. Noted improvement appears from draft to draft, both in force and scholarship. His masterly discussion of the history and scope of the establishment clause does not appear until after the third draft circulation.

As in the *Everson* school bus case a period of three months elapsed between the oral arguments and decision day in the Illinois release time school case. Here, too, a total of fifteen opinions were circulated by Justices Black, Reed, Frankfurter and Jackson, although Reed was the only dissenter.

In his first draft opinion, Black attempted to recapitulate the holding in the New Jersey bus case and to imply that there was no inconsistency between the decision in that case and this one. This created a minor disturbance. Three days later Frankfurter called a conference among the dissenters in the earlier case (himself, Rutledge, Burton and Jackson) to consider the position they should take in this case. It was clear that Frankfurter wanted to continue the ideological fight of the school bus case. Three weeks and another Black opinion later, he circulated his first concurrence draft only "to the anti-*Everson* lads" suggesting that he hoped he could speak for all, and inviting comments. Apparently upset by Black's reference to the school bus case, Frankfurter was at pains to point out that the *Everson* dissenters are still in disagreement with that decision and to deny that their concurrence here is to be taken as a modification of their earlier views or that they regard that decision as in any way leading to this one. Actually in a note to Frankfurter, making suggestions, Rutledge referred to the opinion as a "dissent."

As revision of the various opinions followed revision, Frankfurter was succeeding in holding the "anti-*Everson* lads" together by generously adopting their suggestions and modifications. During these early circulations, only three other Justices were going along with the Black opinion. There was a prospect of one dissent and two opinions representing four Justices each, holding the Illinois law unconstitutional for reasons on which they could not agree. Not only would there be no majority but there would be no plurality opinion.

At this point, which was February 7th, Burton addressed a letter to "dear Hugo and Felix" expressing the view and hope that their respective opinions were close enough together to make possible an opinion of the Court by seven members *plus* a concurring opinion on behalf of Frankfurter, Rutledge, Jackson and himself. He thought it would be of great value to have agreement among seven rather than have two four-and-four opinions, leaving to the bar and the public the task of discovering the differences, if they could, or leaving it to their imagination. He suggested the deletion from Black's opinion of any restatement of the reasoning in the school bus case. He suggested some relatively slight changes in Frankfurter's.

Shortly thereafter, Frankfurter, in a brief memorandum, indicated that if all references to the *Everson* case were omitted from the opinion of the Court, he would omit any such reference in his concurring opinion but time had only confirmed his conviction that the decision in that case was wrong and "mischief-breeding." On the same day Black sent out a memorandum in answer, stating that he would not join in any opinion which did not make reference to the *Everson* case and that time had only confirmed *his* conviction that the decision in that case was right. He added that it was not unusual for one to think that constitutional views contrary to his own were mischievous. To Burton and Frankfurter, Black wrote that he would agree to any opinion which disposed of the case on the basis of those principles on which the majority opinion and Rutledge's dissent in *Everson* had agreed. He did not desire to continue the school bus fight into this case.

This suggestion of Black's was finally carried out. He omitted some *Everson* material which he had originally included and, in his final published opinion, carefully correlated in text and footnotes, references to the Court's and Rutledge's discussion of First Amendment principles. Frankfurter also, at Burton's request, made several substantial changes in his opinion. The result was that Rutledge and Burton felt that they could consistently join in the Black opinion as well as in Frankfurter's concurrence. Thus the opinion of the Court, while not representing seven Justices, as Burton had hoped, reflected the views of six, a substantial majority.

The thoughtful reader will not confuse these exchanges as the petulant quibbling of small minds. On the contrary, they represent the clash of views of dedicated men of deep-seated convictions, sensitive to the effect of their decisions and opinions on important issues of national policy. Future generations of judges and lawyers will be looking to what they do and say for guidance and enlightenment. It is important that so far as possible, they concur in decision and agree on rationale. But these are also men of rigorous intellectual honesty. They can subscribe to an opinion only if they endorse its implications as well as its explicit arguments and its conclusion.

There will always be strong differences among the Justices. They must interpret and apply legal and political principles often expressed in the broadest terms, in the light of history. But the application is to the often unprecedented conditions of the present, and the Justices may not be unmindful of the problems of tomorrow or the claims of future generations.

To be sure, by far the majority of cases which reach the Court are of "predestined outcome." They require a minimum of time for decision or opinion. But there are enough "school bus," "release time" and other types of situations loaded with constitutional complications creating many torturing problems which the Justice must work out with his eight colleagues and with his own conscience. And in so doing, there will always be limits to his capacity to emancipate himself from his intellectual and cultural heritage. But it is all a part of the arduous and painful process of decision.

Referring to cases under the commerce clause and judicial review under the due process clause, Justice Frankfurter once wrote:

Judicial judgment in these two classes of the most difficult cases must take deep account, if I may paraphrase Maitland, of the day before yesterday in order that yesterday may not paralyze today, and it must take account of what it decrees for today in order that today may not paralyze tomorrow.

A judge whose preoccupation is with such matters should be compounded of the faculties that are demanded of the historian and the philosopher and the prophet. The last demand upon him—to make some forecast of the consequences of his action—is perhaps the heaviest. To pierce the curtain of the future, to give shape and visage to mysteries still in the womb of time, is the gift of imagination. It requires poetic sensibilities with which judges are rarely endowed and which their education does not normally develop. These judges, you will infer, must have something of the creative artist in them; they must have antennae registering feeling and judgment beyond logical, let alone quantitative, proof.[18]

It may well be said of Frankfurter himself and of Rutledge, as well as of most of the Justices who sat with them, that these qualities were abundantly manifested in their opinions. Yes, even the power "to pierce the curtain of the future." But alas, behind that curtain different things were revealed to different Justices.

APPENDIX

SIX UNPUBLISHED OPINIONS BY JUSTICE RUTLEDGE

(Numbered footnotes are the Justice's; Bracketed material is the Author's)

SUPREME COURT OF THE UNITED STATES
No. 142.—OCTOBER TERM, 1946.

―――――――

State of Louisiana, ex rel. Willie Francis, Petitioner, v. E. L. Resweber, Sheriff of the Parish of St. Martin, Louisiana, et al.	On Writ of Certiorari to the Supreme Court of the State of Louisiana.

[December—1946.]

[Willie Francis, a colored citizen of Louisiana, was convicted of murder in 1945 and sentenced to death in the electric chair. He was fifteen years old at the time of the crime. Several months later (May 3, 1946) the boy was prepared for electrocution, blindfolded and strapped in the chair. The wiring and switches had been tested and the generator voltage set at 2500. In fact the generator previously had been operated for a few minutes to make sure that everything was working. Willie's father was at the jail with a coffin. A priest administered the last rites of the Roman Catholic Church. Everything was ready. The executioner threw the switch. As described by Judge Prettyman in an article adapted from his book, *Death and the Supreme Court*:* "For a fraction of a second nothing happened. Then Willie jumped. He strained against the straps. He groaned. But even those witnessing their first execution knew something was wrong. . . . Those closest Willie heard him strain out the words, 'Let me breathe'." The death hood was removed, the electrodes unfastened. The equipment, for some reason, had failed to perform its lethal function although it appeared that a charge of electricity had passed through Willie's body.

―――――――

* New York, 1961.

The youth was returned to the death cell. A new death warrant was prepared and Willie was to be "electrocuted" all over again six days later. But his lawyers immediately filed motions for all sorts of writs—mandamus, prohibition, certiorari, *habeas corpus*—and the execution was stayed. All relief was denied in the state courts and review was sought in the Supreme Court of the United States on the grounds that federal constitutional rights would be invaded by putting Willie through another ordeal of electrocution, whether successful or not.

In the Supreme Court, Willie relied on the "due process" clause of the Fourteenth Amendment, the provision of the Fifth Amendment, " . . . nor shall any person be subject for the same offense to be twice put in jeopardy of life or limb," and the Eighth Amendment forbidding "cruel and unusual punishment."

Mr. Justice Reed in his opinion for the Court affirming the decision of the state court, held that Willie had not been put in double jeopardy in the sense that it applies to the states under the "due process" clause. In a previous case, the Court had so held when the state had sought and had obtained a new trial for errors in law which resulted in a death sentence instead of imprisonment for life. The Justice thought that the case was dispositive of Willie's case. Although the "due process" clause of the Fourteenth Amendment would, according to the Reed opinion, prevent execution by a state in a cruel manner with unnecessary suffering, a subsequent execution, after the aborted one, would not be cruel "in the constitutional sense." There was no purpose to inflict unnecessary pain. The distinction between cruelty "in the constitutional sense" and the kind to which Willie Francis was subjected undoubtedly failed to satisfy the boy and, as it turned out, Justice Rutledge. Several minor contentions were also disposed of summarily by the opinion.**

Justice Frankfurter wrote a concurring opinion which carried his frequently repeated argument that the states were not subjected to the specific limitations of the first eight amendments by reason of the "due process" clause of the Fourteenth. That clause prohibits a state from depriving a person of life, liberty or property by means which offend principles of justice "rooted in the traditions and conscience of our people." But such was not the case here. Justice Burton wrote a dissent in which he declared that the Louisiana Supreme Court had not actually passed on the federal questions involved. He would remand the case to give that court an opportunity to do so while expressing the opinion that if the facts in the case

---

** Louisiana ex rel. Willie Francis v. Resweber, 329 U.S. 459 (1947).

were substantially as related above, the punishment was "cruel and unusual" in "the constitutional sense." Justice Douglas and Murphy joined in this opinion as did Justice Rutledge eventually, but not until after writing the following dissent. It had been sent to the printer but whether it was ever circulated among the other Justices is not clear. Slightly more than a year after he had first thrown the switch to the electric chair in which Willie Francis was strapped, the executioner repeated the operation. The result this time was different.]

MR. JUSTICE RUTLEDGE, dissenting.

No one would hold, I think, that Louisiana would be free deliberately to place a convicted man in the electric chair, turn on the current, cut it off before death, remove him and later reelectrocute him. That would be sheer torture. Due process outlaws this barbarism in our scheme, whether as contravening the most elementary standards of decency in dealing with persons charged with crime, *Malinski* v. *New York,* 324 U.S. 401, or as incorporating the commands against cruel and unusual punishments and punishing a man twice for the same offense. See *In re Kemmler,* 136 U.S. 436. Here this trinity comes to the same thing.

I do not think the element of torture is removed because the state acts carelessly rather than deliberately. This is the crucial question. The majority say the failure was due to accident.[1] I find no basis for this view in the record, except that the failure was not intended or foreseen. Even so, it was not shown to be due to causes over which the state had no control. Its duty is to see that such failures do not occur. It has no right to take chances with faulty or antique equipment, low current or any other risk likely to produce such horror. Torture, for the victim, is not a matter of the executioner's state of mind. It may be inflicted as much by carelessness and bungling or taking a chance as by design. The facts of this electrocution are more consistent with such a cause than any other,[2] if only

---

[1] The Court also regards what occurred in this case as equivalent to what happens when the state secures a new trial. Palko v. Connecticut, 302 U.S. 319. The analogy is one I neither accept nor understand.

The Palko case held "that kind of double jeopardy . . . [which is] so acute and shocking that our polity will not endure it" within the protection of the due process clause of the Fourteenth Amendment. 302 U.S. at 328.

[2] The state stated in its answer to the petition for habeas corpus that there was a "latent electrical defect." In its brief submitted to this Court it also has attached a record of the testimony given at a hearing before the Pardon Board on May 31, 1946. It appears from the uncontradicted testimony that a portable electric chair was used. The electric chair was in-

by the absence of any showing that the failure was due to factors beyond the state's control. That showing at the least should be compelled in such a case as this, before a second or perchance a third electrocution is attempted.

I do not think the states are free to take chances in any way with such a consequence as took place here. I am unwilling to indulge the presumption on this record that it did not do so. Men's lives should not hang upon a thread so slender. I know of no way to force the states to forego such risks and the horrors both of cruel and of multiple punishments they entail, other than by applying strictly the constitutional prohibitions against them. Willie Francis cannot be electrocuted again without undergoing a second time the death pangs he already has suffered and which now I think the state has no right to reinflict. Needless to add, I am in substantial agreement with the views expressed by my brothers, Murphy and Burton.

[Although the *Francis* case is referred to as without precedent in Anglo-American law, the statement is not entirely accurate. At least there was a close analogy in the execution of Captain Kidd in 1701 by hanging. It is reported authoritatively that "the rope broke and he had to be raised from the ground and hanged again."]***

SUPREME COURT OF THE UNITED STATES
No. 870.—October Term, 1942.

Gordon Kiyoshi Hirabayashi	On Certificate from the United
vs.	States Circuit Court of Appeals
The United States of America	for the Ninth Circuit.

[Some hint of Justice Rutledge's doubts and pangs of conscience can be gathered from this attempt to unburden his inner struggle. The opinion was typed but apparently never sent to the printer and never

---

stalled in the St. Martin Parish Prison by a prison inmate, an assistant to the electrician at the penitentiary where the chair is normally kept and from where it was brought for the purpose of this execution. It was installed about 8:30 a.m. on the day of the execution. The wires ran from a truck outside the prison through a window to the switchboard connected with the electric chair. After the chair was installed it was tested. No further test was made prior to the actual electrocution, which occurred between 12:00 noon and 1:00 p.m. There was also testimony that the cause of the partial or total failure of the electricity was that a wire had come loose. The wire was apparently one between the truck and the switchboard.

*** Radzinowicz, History of English Law, 185 (1948).

circulated among the other Justices. The changes, alterations, omissions, marginal scribbles reveal a great deal. I have tried to reproduce this aborted opinion as nearly as I can from the Justice's corrections and ambiguous marginal marks. Material marked for omission is as he indicated. There was no date on the manuscript. The treatment of this case by the Court will be found in Chapter VI, pp. 174-76, *supra*.]

Mr. Justice RUTLEDGE, concurring.

~~Generally I think the Court should speak with one voice when substantial agreement is possible. And this ordinarily is the more appropriate the more important the case. Especially is the obligation of modesty, in expressing individual variation, compelling upon the junior member. But occasionally a situation presents issues of delicacy where individual shading becomes important and the practice of another place not inappropriate. In my view this is such a case, and therefore I add what follows.~~

I have strong sympathy with Mr. Justice MURPHY's views. Unrestrained personal authority go to the heart of Nazi-Fascist totalitarianism we now fight. And, as he says, we shall not win the war against them if in securing military victory we break down the barriers our tradition has built against both evils. On the face of the statute, and the Executive order, there is ~~here both~~ a delegation of concentrated, unconfined power over civilian citizens. As construed and applied they result in a kind of discrimination only war's highest emergency could sustain. Beside the former the *Panama Refining Company* and *Curtis-Wright* situations instanced normal authority, while alongside the latter the policies of the Thirteenth and Fourteenth Amendments, won by civil war, fade out in the national wartime picture. ~~Accordingly, one sensitive to our tradition in both respects could only be torn to disagree with the dissenting conclusion.~~

That is one side of the shield. The other is that there must be power to preserve the nation when it is in peril ~~at whatever cost.~~ To this every individual right must yield when the urgencies of war create the necessity. And war in our time creates necessities undreamed of a century ago. We have here therefore something approaching the ultimate strain total war puts upon constitutionally established democratic principles and institutions.

In this emergency the function of the judiciary is indeed limited. Ours is not the primary office to see to the nation's safety. And more than the usual self restraint is to be exercised that we do not impede those whose duty that is. But however pressing the necessity is claimed to be, and however deferential, because of that, we must be to the judgment of those whose function it is to preserve the nation at this time, we can neither abandon our office nor ignore the dictates of the Constitution and the democratic principles on which the nation is founded by approving measures which it is clear necessity does not require.

In view of the known perils and the even greater uncertainties prevailing when the action now questioned was taken, I cannot bring myself to believe it was not or may not have been justified when it was done, as a measure necessary for the time being to preserve the nation. ~~And, taking account of the possible consequences of failure at that time to guard against any risk I cannot say the extreme method used was not necessary to the country's safety~~.

We cannot know all the facts, much less the fears grounded in vast uncertainties, themselves generative of duty, which gave anxiety to the authorities charged with the nation's protection. But we do know too much was then uncertain and too much was at stake for taking any chance which offered or reasonably may have been felt to offer a substantial threat. The unusual circumstances, even for this country in war, required the maximum of precaution. ~~And there was not time, if these were to be secured, to deal individually with all who might be sources of danger~~.

I do not know whether there was greater danger in fact from our Japanese citizens as a class than there was from other classes, selected by race, nationality of descent, by organizational affiliations or other criteria. As processes of proof usually go in judicial proceedings, especially when they involve a citizens's liberty, nothing in this record proves to me there was greater evidence of sabotage, espionage, fifth column activity or disloyalty among our Japanese citizens than there was or may have been among other racial groups in our citizenry or perhaps in the body of it at large. So far as proof of specific acts of this character is concerned, this record is almost barren. And it may be added, though no question concerning it is now directly before us, that it is doubtful whether any other group, similarly selected, would have accepted with as little outcry as did this one the uprooting from home, livelihood, property and freedom which we all know followed later in the progression of steps which began with the order now in review. This much these citizens are entitled to have said for them here and now, in recognition of the sacrifice many loyal ones have made. And there can be no doubt that the manner in which many, perhaps most of them, accepted the upheaval was proof of their consummate attachment to this nation, its institutions and principles. ~~Next to our men in the armed-forces,~~

~~the loyal citizens in this group have made the greatest sacrifice the country has required in this war.~~

~~But all I have said does not negative the danger, the uncertainty, the need for speed or the disability of civil and military authorities in the region to deal individually with the large and concentrated population of Japanese descent.~~ We need not determine the causes for their segregation, allocate blame for it or, indeed, imply it was blameworthy. Regardless of these things, we cannot ignore it as a fact or the difficulties and risks it created. We do not know that there were more disloyal citizens of Japanese origin, possible sources of the dangers sought to be averted, than in some other groups. But we do know there was danger from some, and the life apart which the group as a whole led made unusually difficult the task of separating the bad from the good.

Responsible authorities were thus faced with a situation where incalculable and imminent danger from an external enemy was rightly feared, where the uncertainties both with respect to that enemy and the enemy within were harrowing, and where the difficulties of ferreting out the disloyal in an ununderstood group required time and energy which were not available. Under those circumstances I cannot say that the action taken was not justifiable or that it transgressed constitutional limitations.

I go no further than the necessity of this case. The curfew order gives me little concern. Obeying that was a small sacrifice for any citizen to pay for preservation of his heritage. But I cannot view this case, in its possible implications, as stopping there. All of us know that much more followed. I cannot ignore this fact. But because we are not compelled now to decide more, I indicate no further views than this. Emergency, I think with deference, does create power, for that comes to the same effect as creating new and broader occasions for its exercise. Power equal to emergency is not wanting. But the converse also is true. When the emergency narrows or recedes, so does the extraordinary reach of power. That may be true in some instances, even while war continues. For it does not follow, from the fact war itself creates a vast expansion, that its widely varying fortunes may not create further ones or, when the extreme perils have passed, bring the farthest reaches of authority back to more normal areas of wartime operation. I pass no judgment further than that the emergency existing when the action taken, and now questioned here, justified what was done. Whether and how far subsequent steps have been justified, either when taken or in their continuance, and to what extent they may be reviewable here, I do not intimate. We are on strange, delicate and dangerous ground. Our duty is to tread carefully, in what we do, in what we imply and in what we leave open to inference.

SUPREME COURT OF THE UNITED STATES
Nos. 239 Misc. and 240 Misc.—OCTOBER TERM, 1948.

Koki Hirota, Petitioner, 239 Misc.

v.

General of the Army Douglas MacArthur, et al.

Kenji Dohihara, Petitioner, 240 Misc.

v.

General of the Army Douglas MacArthur, et al.

Motions for Leave to File Petitions For Writs of Habeas Corpus.

[December 6, 1948.]

[This opinion, when written intended as a dissent to a Court order summarily denying a hearing to a condemned war criminal, was withheld for reasons explained in Chapter VI, beginning at p. 196, *supra.*]

MR. JUSTICE RUTLEDGE.

The applications seek writs of *habeas corpus* to review sentences of death by hanging pronounced upon these former Japanese officials[1] by the International Military Tribunal for the Far East. The convictions of Hirota and Dohihara were mainly for "Crimes against Peace," including "Crimes against Humanity," "waging aggres-

---

[1] The application alleges that Hirota has always been a career diplomat, never holding military office or position. He was "Foreign Minister of the Japanese Empire from September, 1933, until March, 1936, when he became Prime Minister. From the fall of his cabinet in February, 1937, for four months he held no public office. He was Foreign Minister again in the first Konove Cabinet until May 10, 1938, at which time he resigned his last public office and retired to private life. He had no connection with the Pacific war proper or anything which transpired in connection with the Japanese prosecution of that war. The petitioner, together with other former Prime Ministers of Japan, was called before the Emperor of Japan on November 29, 1941, to express his opinion as a senior statesman of Japan with respect to the position of the Tojo Government that the Pacific war was 'inevitable' from the standpoint of the national defense of Japan and on that occasion he expressed a dissuading point of view with respect to the Japanese participation in the Pacific war proper."

sive war," and conspiring to wage such wars from 1928 to 1945.[2]
Those offenses were defined exclusively and for the first time, in relation to possible application to these applicants, in the Tribunal's
Charter promulgated by General MacArthur in 1946.[3] That document
also defined the procedures to be followed, especially in relation to
the rules of evidence to be applied.[4]

The applications attack the validity of the Tribunal's constitution,
in respect to the authorizations by which it was established, and
of its Charter, as well as the conduct of the trial pursuant to its provisions. The challenge goes both to the question of the Tribunal's constitution and character as an international tribunal and to the validity of our participation in its organization and conduct. So far as our
participation is concerned, reliance is placed in part upon various
provisions of the Constitution. Among these it is said the issuance of
the Charter was repugnant to and in violation of Art. I, § 8, cl. 10,

---

2 Hirota, *e.g.*, was convicted under Counts 1, 27 and 55. Count 1 charged
conspiracy of all the accused and others in a common plan "between
the 1st January, 1928, and the 2nd September, 1945" with the object "that
Japan should secure the military, naval, political and economic domination
of East Asia and of the Pacific and Indian Oceans . . ." and, for that purpose, "that Japan should . . . wage declared or undeclared war or wars
of aggression. . . ." Count 27 charged that the accused between the 18th September, 1931, and the 2nd September, 1945, waged aggressive war against
China. Count 55 charged neglect of duty in securing observance of Con-
ventions, and the laws and customs of war respecting armed forces in specified countries, prisoners of war and civilians, specifying China beginning
in 1931 in relation to Hirota. See note 3.

3 The Charter was promulgated by General MacArthur on April 26,
1946, by his General Orders No. 20, amending General Orders No. 1 previously issued, pursuant to his Special Proclamation of January 19, 1946, as
"General of the Army, United States Army, and Supreme Commander for the
Allied Powers," for the Establishment of an International Military Tribunal
for the Far East. Section II, Art. 5, of the Charter defined the Tribunal's jurisdiction and the offenses of (a) Crimes against Peace, including "the
planning, preparation, initiation or waging of a declared or undeclared war
of aggression . . ." and conspiracy to any of those ends; (b) Conventional War
Crimes, "namely, violations of the laws or customs of war"; and (c) Crimes
against Humanity, including "other inhumane acts committed before or
during the war."

4 The provisions of Art. 13 authorized the Tribunal to "admit any evidence which it deems to have probative value," including for example "a
report which appears . . . to have been signed or issued . . . by an investi-
gator or intelligence officer . . ." and "a diary, letter or other document,
including sworn or unsworn statements, which appear to the Tribunal to
contain information relating to the charge."

which gives Congress sole power "to define and punish . . . offenses against the laws of nations," Congress having not done so. Reliance also rests on Art. I, § 9, cl. 3, forbidding *ex post facto* laws.

It is not necessary to state the objections in further detail. For me they raise important questions concerning the Tribunal's jurisdiction and also concerning this Court's power to act upon the applications. The cases differ from those of *In re Yamashita,* 327 U.S. 1, and *In re Homma,* 327 U.S. 759, in some important respects. They were enemy belligerents, combatants in the late war. Here Hirota, at any rate, was never such. He served Japan in important civilian posts and that service terminated prior to December 7, 1941.[5] Yamashita and Homma were able to invoke the jurisdiction of an inferior court subject to our review.[6] These applicants have had no such forum available.

If the *Yamashita* and *Homma* cases determined, as I thought, that enemy belligerents have none of our constitutional protections, it does not follow that they held enemy civilians to occupy the same denuded status. Nor has this Court yet decided that such persons or others, including our own citizens, but excepting perhaps enemy combatants, having access to no inferior court, can have no remedy for reviewing action by an American military tribunal in disregard of all constitutional limitations or like action of any such tribunal in which our officials may participate.

For me the applications set forth serious challenges to the validity of the Tribunal's constitution and jurisdiction. Thereby in turn they raise grave questions concerning this Court's power to act in review of what has been done. If the Tribunal is in fact a validly constituted international one, presumably its action is beyond our reach. If it is in fact a political body, exercising power under forms of legal procedure strange to our institutions and traditions, established wholly or in part by the political departments of our Government by action our judicial institutions have no authority or power to check, the same consequences must follow. These consequences however are not for me either self-evident or frivolous matters, to be decided without hearing or argument.

The questions presented raise doubts so serious that in conscience I cannot join my brethren in summary denial. Accordingly, I think the applications should be set for argument and determined only

---

[5] See note 1.

[6] One application was for certiorari from the denial of *habeas corpus* by the Supreme Court of the Philippines. Other applications, however, came directly to this Court in the first instance and were considered in the same hearing.

after full hearing and consideration. Being so far at odds with my brethren, in a matter of this nature and public importance, I have felt called upon to state this much in explanation of thus recording my vote.

SUPREME COURT OF THE UNITED STATES
No. 20.—OCTOBER TERM, 1946.

United Public Workers of America (C. I. O.), et al., Appellants, v. Harry B. Mitchell, Frances Perkins and Arthur S. Fleming.	Appeal from the District Court of the United States for the District of Columbia.

[February 10, 1947.]

[This case is dealt with in detail in Chapter IV, beginning at p. 141, *supra*. It is not clear why Rutledge withheld this opinion expressing his views about judicial self-restraint.]

Mr. Justice RUTLEDGE, dissenting.

My views on the declaratory judgment phase of this case differ somewhat from those expressed in the other opinions. Accordingly, I shall state them briefly.

The purpose of the Declaratory Judgments Act, Judicial Code § 274 d, was to overcome limitations which had surrounded other forms of legal proceedings in the federal courts. These arose from the necessity of asking for specific relief beyond determining and declaring rights, and the consequent necessity for making the various showings required to secure the particular type of relief sought.[1]

These limitations frequently worked to prevent parties to controversies from securing determination of their rights not only until they had reached a stage of serious and concrete difference, but until actual harm was impending or immediately incident. In numerous instances persons having vital interests at stake were left for long periods suspended not only in controversy but also in gross uncertainty concerning their rights without any available mode of relief.[2]

---

[1] S. Rep. 1005, 73d Cong., 2d Sess.

[2] See Borchard, Declaratory Judgments (2d ed.) 931. In the federal courts conceptions derived from the "case or controversy" limitation upon federal jurisdiction were influential in some instances to magnify the difficulties arising from the necessity of seeking specific and conventional relief. Cf. Willing v. Chicago Auditorium Assn., 277 U.S. 274 with Nashville, C. & St. L. Ry. v. Wallace, 288 U.S. 249. See Borchard, supra, 172-203.

To provide a means for escape from these consequences Congress in 1934 enacted:

> "In cases of actual controversy the courts of the United States shall have power upon petition, declaration, complaint, or other appropriate pleadings to declare rights and other legal relations of any interested party petitioning for such declaration, whether or not further relief is or could be prayed, and such declaration shall have the force and effect of a final judgment or decree and be reviewable as such."[3]

By thus dispensing with the requirement of any prayer calling for relief beyond declaring the rights of the parties, Congress broadened the field for federal adjudication of rights previously dependent for enforcement upon classification remedially in the historic categories of common law and equity jurisdiction. Rights which had been enforceable only at law, others only in equity, and still others at law or in equity were included, as were many previously not enforceable at all. The statute was not therefore merely an extension of the earlier existing jurisdictional categories. A new and broadly inclusive type of federal jurisdiction, as related to the enforcement of substantive rights, was created.

But in two important respects, both pertinent here, pre-existing doctrines continued to prevail. One was of course the constitutional limitation, repeated for emphasis in the statute itself, of the jurisdiction to "cases of actual controversy." The other was an incorporation into the entire declaratory jurisdiction, for exercising it, of the large discretionary element which historically had characterized the exercise of equity jurisdiction, but not that at law. The language of the Act is permissive, not mandatory: " . . . the courts of the United States shall have power . . . to declare rights. . . ."

This discretionary element is as yet largely an undefined one, although it is without question a large one. See Borchard, "Discretion to Refuse Jurisdiction of Actions for Declaratory Judgments" (1942) 26 Minn. L. Rev. 677. At the least it is comparable in scope with the similar element inherent in the equity jurisdiction.[4] But

---

[3] Provisions for granting further relief "based on a declaratory judgment or decree . . . whenever necessary or proper" and for jury trial when issues of fact so triable are presented are contained in subsequent subsections. Judicial Code § 274 d; 28 U.S.C. § 400.

[4] Cf. Borchard, Declaratory Judgments (2d ed.) 312: "The declaratory remedy is not like an ordinary equitable remedy in which the federal courts have on occasion remarked that when the plaintiff has the right to invoke the federal jurisdiction, the court is bound to take the case and proceed to

because the declaratory proceeding is itself freed from other limitations which characterize the exercise of equitable jurisdiction, for example the necessity for showing irreparable injury in order to secure injunctive relief, it presents quite different and broader problems for determining when the discretion to decline to exert it may itself be appropriately exercised. And many of these problems of late have arisen in relation to the determination of constitutional matters.[5]

It is in this respect that the declaratory proceeding in the federal courts presents peculiar problems of its own, as distinguished from nonconstitutional determinations in those courts and declaratory suits in state courts. These arise not only from the case and controversy limitation but also from other historic policies relating to constitutional adjudications in the federal courts. Compare the controversy as to declaratory judgments in relation to constitutional questions in (1932) 45 Harv. L. Rev. 1089; (1932) 41 Yale L. J. 1195; (1938) 51 Harv. L. Rev. 1267.

Many in the profession regarded the declaratory jurisdiction askance at the time of its acceptance by Congress and widely in the states,[6] as well as afterward. But, as often happens when a new legal institution is born, only a short time has been acquired to bring a complete about-face. Not only has the proceeding acquired general acceptance at both federal and state levels. It has come to be used by some, perhaps many, lawyers as a method freely available for securing determination of controversies in some instances highly abstract in character, in others wholly premature.[7]

This tendency has its clearest and most widespread effect in the federal courts in relation to adjudication of constitutional questions. Not only is the proceeding utilized at times in a manner which, if permitted, would surmount the case and controversy limitation. It is also used in obvious efforts to secure adjudications which, again if allowed, would break down other historic policies relating to the

---

judgment. Nor does the fact that the Report of the Judiciary Committee of the Senate makes no direct reference to the discretionary exercise of the powers granted by the Federal Act militate against the rule of discretion."

For present purposes it is unnecessary to distinguish between "discretionary" equitable jurisdiction and "discretionary" equitable relief. Great Lakes Dredge & Dock Co. v. Hoffman, 319 U.S. 293; Alabama State Fed. of Labor v. McAdory, 325 U.S. 450.

[5] Alabama State Fed. of Labor v. McAdory, 325 U.S. 450; cf. Colegrove v. Green, 328 U.S. 549; Note (1946) 56 Yale L.J. 139; dissenting opinion in Cook v. Fortson, 329 U.S. 675.

[6] Largely in the decade 1930-1940. Forty states and territories have enacted declaratory judgment statutes. Borchard, Judgments (2d ed.) 1933.

[7] Cf. note 4.

determination of constitutional questions. And it is just at this point that I think the greatest care must be taken to see that those policies are not overthrown. Here accordingly is the place for a liberal exercise of the discretion to decline exercize of the jurisdiction.

It is much too late now to consider whether the policy underlying the case and controversy limitation, settled to require the federal courts not to render advisory opinions, and underlying also the long tradition of conservatism about deciding constitutional issues, is wise. History and experience have committed us to the policy in both respects. See Frankfurter, "A Note on Advisory Opinions," (1924) 37 Harv. L. Rev. 1002. The tradition is applicable within, as well as in finding, the limits of the case and controversy principle. It forbids deciding cases on constitutional grounds when other adequate or sufficient ones may be found. It is reflected in jurisdictional statutes. It dictates refusal to exercise equity jurisdiction in instances where its peculiar restrictions may be satisfied. In general it defers constitutional determinations until necessity forces them.[8] And this is true although the case and controversy limitation may be fully satisfied.

The declaratory judgment procedure had no purpose to change this policy. It has been useful, and will continue to be, in presenting constitutional issues in many situations where formerly the limitations it was intended to discard prevented this. But that it may properly be so used does not mean that it should become a vehicle for forcing or securing decision on the validity of long parades of statutory provisions in a single suit prior to their application or on whole masses of possible applications of a single statutory provision broadly applicable to many situations. The sheer quantity of decision called for if nothing else, taxes judicial capacity. It imposes also a job of evasion or reduction of issues to bring the issues within manageable scope, which ought not to characterize any process of judicial decision, much less one of constitutional effect. It invites as an alternative to these escapes, broadside decision, equally inappropriate for such determinations.[9]

---

[8] See Alma Motor Co. v. Timken-Detroit Axle Co., 329 U.S. 129, and authorities.

[9] Compare Frankfurter and Fisher, "The Business of the Supreme Court at the October Terms, 1935 and 1936" (1938) 51 Harv. L. Rev. 577, 624: "Just as equity, at common law, created its own jurisdictional problems with special reference to the avoidance of friction between two tribunals, so resort to equity for invalidating legislation generates its special problems, if needless friction between the judiciary and other branches of government is to be avoided. The evasion of the requirement for damage that cannot be compensated has a pungency of consequence in these public law controver-

Moreover it forestalls the possibility that many of the anticipated applications will never occur, and thus the necessity for adjudicating them will not arise. And the inevitable effect is to present the issues, or many of them, in much less definitely chiseled form, on the facts and on the law, than is consistent with the most careful determination of constitutional effects.

All these things are true, or may be, even though all requirements of the case and controversy limitation are met. All of them bear strongly on the question whether the broad discretionary power implicit in the procedure should be exercised for declining to exert the jurisdiction. It is not enough therefore in a case of this sort to find merely that the requirements of the case and controversy limitation have been met. The further question remains, once that has been decided, whether the jurisdiction should be exercised to permit such a broadside determination of constitutional matters.

This case peculiarly illustrates effort to secure such a decision. A multiplicity of statutory provisions and regulations are challenged on half a dozen or more constitutional provisions, affecting possible future applications to hundreds of thousands of persons.

I am not sure whether, apart from Poole, the Court is simply exercising its discretion to refuse exerting the declaratory jurisdiction; is reading into it the limitations characteristic of equity jurisdiction for securing injunctive relief; or is finding that the case and controversy limitation has been exceeded. There are, I think, strong reasons for thinking that the latter requirements are fulfilled concerning others affected than Poole, set forth by Mr. Justice Black and Mr. Justice Douglas. And, if so, the jurisdiction exists. But there are also strong reasons, in the considerations I have stated relating to historic conservative policy in reaching constitutional questions, why exercise of the jurisdiction should be declined.

As to Poole, however, those considerations do not apply. His case is concrete, definite, limited, and the issues not only are thus chiseled but fall within manageable scope. I am brought therefore to the merits in his situation. Upon them I am in accord with the views stated by Mr. Justice Black, although I would not extend their application in this case to others than Poole.

---

sies which strikingly underlines traditional equity practice. Public interest, however, exerts contradictory pressures. Considerations for abstention from decision, unless technical equity requirements are satisfied, are met with the temptation to make use of the flexible facilities of equity for prompt allaying of uncertainty. And so the cases reflect an oscillation between a very strict and a very easy-going attitude toward taking equity jurisdiction to decide constitutionality."

SUPREME COURT OF THE UNITED STATES
No. 238.—OCTOBER TERM, 1942.

Thelma Martin, Appellant,	On Appeal from the Supreme
vs.	Court of the State of
City of Struthers, Ohio	Ohio.

[The somewhat unusual circumstances which led Justice Rutledge to write but withhold this opinion, intended as a dissent, are described in Chapter III, p. 54, *supra*.]

Mr. Justice RUTLEDGE.

In my opinion the Struthers ordinance is infected with more than one vice. I agree with the CHIEF JUSTICE and Mr. Justice MURPHY that it invades the old and till now hardly questioned rights to engage in house-to-house evangelism and pamphleteering. It also usurps the householder's right to control his property; and, if for no other reason, would be void on its face for unreasonable classification. It singles out the evangelist and the pamphleteer, along with the small advertiser, for a prohibition it places on no others, though many create in greater degree the disturbance it is aimed to prevent. It makes criminals of persons who do not trespass and nuisances of people who commit no offensive act. Innocent and offending are lumped together.

An ordinance of such scope and effects has no right to favorable presumption. It is necessary first to get the record straight. It contains no proof of "swing shifts," twelve-hour shifts, or the number of night workers and day sleepers in Struthers. These suggestions come from the argument. Nor is there evidence that Struthers has been flooded with peddlers, canvassers, solicitors, crooks, thugs or criminals descending on its doorbells, leaflets in hand. We may take common knowledge that some persons may abuse the implied general invitation to enter; and, on that basis, sustain legislation reasonably adapted to prevent the abuse. But this ordinance is not limited to abuse. And neither common knowledge nor unsupported assertions of counsel can supply foundation in fact for belief that handbill distributors are more disturbing bell ringers than many others. Something more is necessary to sustain an edict so devastating of ancient rights and of wholly harmless conduct indiscriminately with real annoyance and peril.

The ordinance is not aimed at thugs, crooks or criminals, seeking entry for unlawful purposes. Nor is it directed at breaches of the peace or public nuisance. The bearing of handbills alone hardly marks off

such offenders from others. The sole claimed purpose is to protect
the individual householder in the enjoyment of his personal quiet
and privacy at home. That object is laudable. But relevant to its
accomplishment by valid legal means are the existence of a real, not
merely a fancied disturbance, the accommodation of his right to the
rights of others, and the reasonableness of the means, including the
classifications of persons inhibited, taken in securing it.

I.

A glance at the ordinance discloses its arbitrary character. It is
at once too broad and too narrow. It excludes too many who create
no greater or different disturbance than do those inhibited. Conversely,
it restricts too few, who do no more than others are left free to do.
And the crux of distinction has no substantial relation, more particularly in the absence of proof, to the evil proscribed.

The ordinance, as written, includes everyone who knocks or rings
the bell, with paper in hand and intent to give it to the occupant.
It excludes all who come without the circular. The prohibition is not
confined to the nuisance who rings pestiferously or persistently. One
knock is enough. And only the handbill bearer must not ring. The
Fuller brush man, the Good Housekeeping salesman, and solicitors
for the Red Cross, the Community Fund and the Salvation Army may
knock and ring as often and as long as they please. But they must
[not] leave behind War Cry and the literature that tells about the
brushes and the campaigns. The newsboy can collect for the paper,
but cannot leave it when he collects, unless it is summer and the sub-
scriber is sitting on the porch. Churches, labor unions, the Chamber
of Commerce, Boy Scout troops, and air raid wardens cannot send
notices of meetings from house to house. And the candidate for public
office would run afoul the law by sending his card or campaign literature from door to door. All these must observe the householder's
peace by calling him on the telephone, littering up his yard, or
putting upon the mailman the onus of delivery. But for his federal
function, he too well might hesitate before touching the buzzer.
Examples need not be multiplied. The short story is that everybody can
bother the householder in Struthers, by ringing the bell he has put
there for the purpose, if he does not bring along a leaflet. But no
one who goes from house to house, for whatever cause, beneficent
or fraudulent, welcome or distasteful, can summon the owner from
his rocking chair without becoming a misdemeanant, if he has and
intends to leave a circular.

This law singles out the distributor of literature more sharply than
did the tax in *Grosjean* v. *American Press Co.*, 297 U.S. 233. It does

so without evidence, and against common knowledge, that he more than others creates the proscribed disquiet. It makes him criminal, when the peddler, the solicitor, the beggar and the crook are left free to come and ring at will. An ordinance which ostensibly seeks to prevent annoyance, but leaves so much untouched, is not a means of protecting the householder's privacy or rest. It is an instrument of petty tyranny. And it extinguishes rights which should be the last, not the first, to fall before such a weapon.

It does not lessen the discrimination against the disseminator of opinion and information that the small advertiser is included with him. That only adds another victim. Still too many circulating bell ringers are left out. The application of the ordinance to any one within its terms is in itself an invalid discrimination. It does not matter that within the narrowly selected class other such discriminations might be, but are not shown to have been made.[1]

Classification, to be constitutional, must be reasonable in fact. This requires that it be both relevant and reasonable in relation to the evil for which cure is sought. And, where an accommodation of rights must be made, the evil must justify both invading the one to protect the other and the selected classification of persons whose rights are thus restricted. It is not reasonable to select one group from many for subjection to criminal sanction, when it no more than the others causes the prohibited act. And the Struthers householder has it largely, if not entirely, within his own power to prevent the annoyance at which this ordinance was aimed. For that reason there cannot have been compelling cause for relief by public action. But if there had been, it could not justify the arbitrary discrimination Struthers makes.

Finally, it does not lessen the discriminatory effect that the Struthers edict bears most heavily on persons and groups without funds for purchasing radio time or newspaper space and whose principal avenues for reaching other persons, whether for advertising or to spread news and opinion, are by approaching them in public places and at their homes. The ordinance, therefore, in my opinion combines the vice of invading rights heretofore established in a preferred constitutional protection with that of unreasonable and invalid discrimination against persons who hold and assert them.

II.

These invasions are justified as amounting to no more than repeal of the owner's implied invitation to enter. And to sustain this we

---

[1] During its forty years of history Struthers must have suffered thousands of violations of this ordinance. It is significant the first case to reach this Court is one involving Jehovah's Witnesses.

have counsel's opinion, unsupported by Ohio decision, that it does not apply to persons previously invited. Its terms clearly include them. And in this case it has been applied to one whom the owner has not forbidden to come, did not order to depart, and to whom by her conduct at the door she gave license for all that had been done. Judged by all known standards of trespass, there was none here, unless the ordinance is effective to make trespass what the owner has licensed. On the facts, there was license, if not invitation.

But it would make no difference if petitioner had been invited indoors. The officer arrested her without knowing whether she came from within or only from the door. And it has not been admitted that the ordinance does not apply to one who, having rung the bell, but without previous explicit license, is invited inside and treated as a guest; in other words, that the owner's invitation, given on responding to the bell, would wipe out the trespass or the criminal offense. Exactly the opposite is the theory of this law and this case. Only previous explicit invitation, given before the bell is rung, can wipe out the criminal effect. That is the sum of the view that all the ordinance does is to "revoke the owner's implied invitation to enter."

One trouble with this is that the revocation by the ordinance is irrevocable by the owner. It deprives him of the right to say who shall or shall not freely enter his premises. The ownership of land comprehends the right not only to say beforehand who shall come upon it for lawful purposes, but also to waive and license what may have been technically or substantially trespass when the entry was made. That right is taken away, and persons are made criminals for entering who, but for the law and perhaps even under it, could not be sued for trespass or annoyance. This makes crime of what amounts to invasion of neither public nor private right. If these are not the ordinance's effects, then the conviction in this case was wrong since in no sense was it made to hang on whether the owner at the door gave license for the entry or in effect repudiated it. Without that determination the conviction cannot stand, unless it is to stand for ringing the bell regardless of the owner's assent and attitude.

Other difficulties arise, including the question, What is previous invitation? Must it be express, and if so standing or specific for each occasion? May it be implied from previous acquaintance or friendship? Not all handbill distributors are strangers, and the ordinance is not limited to them. How long standing and intimate must the friendship be? These and other inquiries which might be made are not answered by counsel's concession.

It merely rephrases, but obscures the issue. That is, Who has the right to extend the invitation, determine how and when it shall be given, revoke it, and take advantage of it? Are these rights of the property owner and his visitor or do they belong to state legislatures and town councils? This ordinance either takes away the owner's right to give license to persons who have come without his previous invitation or it has been misapplied in this case. It strikes at his visitor, regardless of his consent. It runs contrary to universal custom men have followed for ages in licensing approach to their homes. It does all this to protect the householder, not against crime, nuisance or trespass, but against annoyance (if it be that, by one class) which it permits and he accepts from all others and which, as to all, he can prevent in his own way, if he will.

It is true today, as it was yesterday, that a man's house is his castle. But, for that reason, it is for him, not the town council, to say who may approach and enter for lawful purpose. And, for the same reason, it is not for the council to punish his visitor, when the owner receives him, whether his assent is given before or after the entry. The state puts all its authority behind the man who seeks his own privacy. It should not force the same seclusion upon others who do not want it. It may be doubted that all householders in Struthers object to having circulars left by persons who summon them to the door.

A final word remains. It is said this ordinance is narrow. The pamphleteer is not prohibited to enter the premises. The evangelist may leave his tract. The advertiser can distribute his handbills. All the ordinance does is prohibit them to touch the bell. If so, it does not revoke the implied license to enter as is claimed. It merely prohibits an act after entry, amounting heretofore neither to trespass *ab initio* nor to *nuisance*. But this is not the conclusion drawn. It is rather that, with so much freedom left untouched, this prohibition cannot invade the great freedoms of the press and religion. Until today it has been argued likewise that the evangelist and the pamphleteer can be driven from the streets by taxation. And one ground for this has been that they are left access to the home by house-to-house distribution.

Such piecemeal alternatives have no place in the conception of these liberties. They lead only to ultimate and total destruction. If access to the home can be denied because the particular enactment does not forbid it on the street and if the right to distribute on the street can be taxed away because the ordinance does not forbid house-to-house distribution, these heritages have vanished. The power to tax can destroy the one and the power to prohibit can nullify the other. If distributors of information and opinion can be forbidden to knock at the door, they can be ordered not to enter or litter the premises. The sum of these separate, and therefore (it is claimed) valid, erosions would be annihilation of pamphleteering and printed evangelism. These ancient freedoms are not so to be chipped away. One invasion is not validated because another is not made or is made by a separate act. Now, if ever, the great freedoms of the mind and heart are to be guarded. They can be lost by the erosions of legal refinement as by less subtle attack. I cannot assent to the one made in this case.

Nos. 34 & 35. Federal Power Commission v. Hope

[This opinion, intended by the Justice to be concurring, never got to the typewriter. It was found in his files, written out in his own hand, as all his first drafts were. There was no date to indicate at which stage of the case's consideration it was written. His enthusiasm for expressing his somewhat unorthodox views on the judicial treatment of reviewing rate-schedules was, for some reason, dampened.]

RUTLEDGE, concurring:

I concur in the result and in the opinion of the Court. But I add what, in view of the tortuous history of the subject, I think should be put in the plainest terms.

The major thing, which may be minimized in the conflict of discussion about less important matters, is putting an end, for purposes of judicial review of rate orders, to the necessity for finding a rate-base. From 1898, when *Smyth* v. *Ames* was decided, until recently, perhaps today, the search of courts and commissions has been for a mythical value, found independently of earnings, to be attributed to property which itself has no market and enjoys monopoly of the market it serves, for use in measuring what the industry may be allowed to earn.

The search has been for a will-o-the-wisp. "Fair value" has a fair sound. But forty years have shown it is the confusion of sounding brass and tinkling cymbal. Except in one respect it makes little difference whether "fair value" is modified by adding "present" or is translated into "prudent investment." Under the translation, a rate-base generally can be found once and for all, and then can be kept up-to-date by yearly adjustments. It therefore provides what "present fair value" or "reproduction new" cannot give, namely, escape from the vicious circle that a base cannot be found and validated, in our fluctuating price system, before the process must, or should, begin all over again. This difference is real. And it is important. Hence, if the choice were solely between "reproduction new" and "prudent investment," considerations of stability in economic relationships, as well as the necessity of escape from the vicious circle in which "reproduction new" casts all concerned would turn the scales for "prudent investment." The Constitution does not guarantee a never-ending process of litigation.

But the choice is not so limited. And to select either of those alternatives infects the whole business of rate regulation with a deeper vice than the one which represents the difference between them. Neither the Constitution nor a statute which requires a utility to give service at "just and reasonable" rates contemplates that the rates shall be founded upon and measured by speculation. Even if eminent domain principles could be applied, as was attempted in *Smyth* v. *Ames* and the decisions which have followed it, values which rest only in speculative imagination should be eliminated.

But the vice of the rule of *Smyth* v. *Ames,* that is, of "present fair value" or "reproduction new" is in applying eminent domain principles where they can have no application. In taking property for public use, the applicable standard is (1) what the property will bring in the market, if one exists; or, if there is none, what the property is reasonably capable of earning. But neither of these criteria can be used in arriving at the "value" of property for rate-making purposes. There is no market for the property. Earnings cannot be used to determine value, when earnings are in issue. Hence the criteria of valuation for a taking by eminent domain are unavailable.

But escape is sought in the speculative venture of deciding what it would cost to reproduce a plant which need not and cannot be reproduced. And generally the effort is made when the cost of producing what would take its place (but will not do so) is higher than the cost has been of building what exists. The result is that the present hypothetical cost of a hypothetical plant becomes the "value" of an existing plant built yesterday or long years ago at greatly different price levels and in an entirely different state of the art.

Furthermore, "prudent investment," in this aspect, is only "reproduction new" in reverse gear. What was prudently invested yesterday or twenty or forty years ago may be and often is waste today, regardless of change in price levels or because of them. Apart from the merit of stability and the consequent escape from never-ending, never complete rate-making, "prudent investment" brings with time elements of fiction and speculation in the base almost as gross as when "reproduction new" performs the office. True, there is the tie to history. But history as "present value" hardly measures to a presently realistic standard.

Regulation of late has steered from the Charybdis of reproduction new to the Scylla of prudent investment. The Court's opinion as I take it veers away from both. The test is pragmatic. It is based on experience. First, this shows what it costs, with reasonable margin for foreseeable contingencies, to operate the business. This the utility is allowed. And perhaps the allowance is generous. But if so, that is for the Commission. Then to costs of operation is added a return, which is reasonable, upon the par value of all outstanding securities representing original investment in cash or in property. The two items make up what the Commission allowed. Their sum guarantees two things: that the business will continue a going concern; that all investment interests will receive a reasonable return. And if the items of expense permitted is adequate, provision for replacement of the equipment as it is consumed in use will have been made. The overall effect is one which, neither by the company's history, its policy when free from regulation, nor its presently foreseeable requirements for the future, can be found to be either confiscatory or unreasonable. This being true, there is an end to judicial inquiry.

With this I agree. And I do so regardless of the fact that if I were bound by either of the formulae which heretofore have prevailed, I would feel obligated to cast my vote for returning the case to the Commission for correction in detail. It did not follow "prudent investment" consistently. There were some variations hard to justify if that theory were binding exclusively as the standard. But the Constitution does not require either "prudent investment" or unvarying consistency in its application. Nor, as I read it, does the statute do so. What is prohibited is confiscation and arbitrary action. Confiscation there is none. Procedural requirements have been observed. Errors of substance in detail, if there were any, are offset by liberality in making other allowances for individual items, and wash out in the net result as tested by the only criteria we can apply without becoming involved in speculations we have no right to make or to require others to make. No deviation from the standard the Commission applied in general rises to the degree of arbitrary action and none had an effect upon the end result which made it arbitrary or unreasonable. This being true, there is no warrant for us to return the case to the Commission to consider making changes in detail we cannot, in view of the record and the result, say are necessary in order to make what the Commission has done reasonable and just.

A different question would be presented, if in respect to any detail it were shown that the Commission had acted arbitrarily and that action had affected the net result. But that has not been shown. At most, as has been said, there appears an apparent inconsistency in respect to some details, which in its effect upon the net result makes that neither confiscatory nor arbitrary.

I add two further words. I do not impute to the decision the effect of requiring rate-making bodies to discard entirely consideration of "prudent investment" or, for that matter, of "reproduction new." My understanding is it leaves them free to consider and apply these theories, when they may be helpful in fixing the just and reasonable rate the statute requires. And this accords with my understanding of the statute, at any rate so far as "prudent investment" is concerned. But I do impute to the decision, and on that understanding I join in it, the intent to relieve the Commission and others with it of the hitherto assumed constitutional burden of applying either theory, whether one or the other, when the criteria the Court itself employs can be applied to the facts with similar consequences. Probably for a time yet Commissions and other rate-making bodies will give lip-service to "considering" reproduction new or perhaps move often to applying "prudent investment," both because habit is strong, especially when formed on a constitutional plane, and because, in view of the long history of variation if not of conflict in the decisions of this Court, the fear may remain that not to do so would result in invalidation of orders. But, if the shackles of theories of valuation are loosened somewhat and the determinations are made more with an eye to the facts of economic life than to them, the results will be at once more consistent with the constitutional and statutory mandates and more in accord with economic realities.

In this case there is no evidence that the outstanding securities, upon which the return in addition to operating expense is allowed, do not represent actual original investments equal to the par value of the stock. What adjustments might be required if this were not true or if the outstanding securities were shown clearly to represent fictitious investments, may be left for the future.

I agree with much that is said in the dissenting opinion of Mr. Justice Jackson. But, with the majority, I cannot find in the statute authority which would enable us to return the case to the Commission solely to consider questions of conservation or matters of discrimination not raised before it. The statute empowers the Commission to decrease rates which are not "the lowest reasonable rates." Sec. 5 (a). And in this respect it makes no explicit distinction between domestic and industrial uses. The statute also expressly provides: "No objection to the order of the Commission shall be considered by the Court unless such objection shall have been urged before the Commission in the application for rehearing unless there is reasonable ground for failure so to do." Sec. 19 (b). No objection on the score of undue discrimination between domestic and industrial users was urged before the Commission and no reasonable ground for failure to do so has been assigned. In the face of these explicit statutory provisions, I am unable to agree that we should return the matter to the Commission with instructions to find that any rate which does not require industrial users to pay more than domestic users per identical unit consumed is an unduly discriminatory and hence an unreasonable rate. Such an instruction, in my opinion, would invade the Commission's function and perhaps require it to violate the express prohibition of Section 19 (b). Without such an instruction, it is at least doubtful that the effort at conservation through rate differentials would be achieved, even if we make the assumption that such differentials could accomplish that result appreciably and at the same time remain just and reasonable. Accordingly, I agree with the conclusion that the Commission's function, in so far as it relates to conservation, is to be achieved primarily, if not exclusively, in other ways.

NOTES

Chapter I

1 For a full account of this episode, see C. Warren, *The Supreme Court in United States History* (Boston: Little, Brown, 1932), pp. 128-41.

2 *Hamilton* v. *Alabama*, 376 U.S. 647, 11 L. Ed. 2d 979, 84 Sup. Ct. 982 (1964).

3 *Des Moines Register*, February 26, 1939.

4 Resolutions presented by Solicitor General Perlman, Proceedings Before the Supreme Court of the United States, April 10, 1951.

5 Speech delivered at Indiana University, July 5, 1946.

6 *The Reader's Digest*, January, 1950, "The Most Unforgettable Character I've Ever Met," as told to John Herling.

7 *Bakery Sales Driver's Local Union No. 33* v. *Wagshal*, 333 U.S. 437, 92 L. Ed. 792, 68 Sup. Ct. 630 (1948).

8 Letter from Professor Morris to the author.

Chapter II

1 A. T. Mason, *Harlan Fiske Stone: Pillar of the Law* (New York: Viking Press, 1956), pp. 592-93.

2 F. Biddle, "The Wartime Cabinet," *American Heritage,* pp. 65, 76 (June 1962).

3 Letter to the author, October 29, 1963, from John P. Frank, former clerk to Justice Black.

4 *St. Louis Globe Democrat,* January 12, 1943, commenting on Rutledge's appointment to the Supreme Court.

5 I. Brant, "Mr. Justice Rutledge—The Man," 25 *Indiana Law Journal* 424, 432 (1950).

6 H. B. Phillips, ed., *Felix Frankfurter Reminisces* (New York: Reynal, 1960), pp. 281-82.

7 *Id.* at p. 282.

8 *Bridges* v. *California*, 314 U.S. 252, 86 L. Ed. 192, 62 Sup. Ct. 190, 159 A.L.R. 1346 (1941), was the more important.

9 January 12, 1943.

10 January 18, 1943.

11 *Chattanooga News-Free Press,* January 12, 1943.

12 January 12, 1943.

Chapter III

1 *United States* v. *Ballard,* 322 U.S. 78, 94-95, 88 L. Ed. 1148, 1158, 64 Sup. Ct. 882, 890 (1944) (dissenting opinion).

2 Justice Miller in *Watson* v. *Jones,* 80 U.S. (13 Wall.) 679, 728, 20 L. Ed. 666, 676 (1872).

3 M. Cole, *Jehovah's Witnesses* (New York: Vantage, 1955), p. 106.

4 H. H. Stroup, *The Jehovah Witness* (New York: Columbia University, 1945), p. 61.

5 *Id.* at p. 62.

6 *Qualified to be Ministers* (New York: Watchtower Bible and Tract Society, 1942), p. 324.

7 *Id.* at pp. 277-78.

8 *Minersville School Dist.* v. *Gobitis,* 310 U.S. 586, 84 L. Ed. 1375, 60 Sup. Ct. 1010, 127 A.L.R. 1493 (1940).

9 *The Persecution of Jehovah's Witnesses* (American Civil Liberties Union, 1941), p. 27.

10 *Cantwell* v. *Connecticut,* 310 U.S. 296, 84 L. Ed. 1213, 60 Sup. Ct. 900, 128 A.L.R. 1352 (1940); *Schneider* v. *Irvington,* 308 U.S. 147, 84 L. Ed. 155, 60 Sup. Ct. 146 (1939); *Lovell* v. *Griffin,* 303 U.S. 444, 82 L. Ed. 949, 58 Sup. Ct. 666 (1938).

11 Under the by-line of Thomas Wood.

12 *Jones* v. *Opelika,* 316 U.S. 584, 86 L. Ed. 1691, 62 Sup. Ct. 1231, 141 A.L.R. 514 (1942).

13 *Jones* v. *Opelika,* 319 U.S. 103, 87 L. Ed. 1290, 63 Sup. Ct. 890 (1943).

14 *Jones* v. *Opelika, supra* n. 12, at 596-98, 86 L. Ed. at 1701-02, 62 Sup. Ct. at 1231.

15 *Lovell* v. *Griffin, supra* n. 10.

16 *Murdock* v. *Pennsylvania,* 319 U.S. 105, 87 L. Ed. 1292, 63 Sup. Ct. 870, 146 A.L.R. 81 (1943).

17 *Id.* at 127-28, 87 L. Ed. at 1306, 63 Sup. Ct. at 896.

18 *Id.* at 112, 87 L. Ed. at 1298, 63 Sup. Ct. at 874.

19 *Martin* v. *Struthers,* 319 U.S. 141, 87 L. Ed. 1313, 63 Sup. Ct. 862 (1943).

20 319 U.S. 157, 87 L. Ed. 1324, 63 Sup. Ct. 877 (1943).

21 *Prince* v. *Massachusetts,* 321 U.S. 158, 88 L. Ed. 645, 64 Sup. Ct. 438 (1944).

22 *Commonwealth* v. *Prince,* 313 Mass. 223, 229, 46 N.E.2d 755, 758 (1943).

23 321 U.S. at 165-66, 88 L. Ed. at 652-53, 64 Sup. Ct. at 442.

24 *Id.* at 168-70, 88 L. Ed. at 653-54, 64 Sup. Ct. at 443.

25 *Id.* at 177, 88 L. Ed. at 658, 64 Sup. Ct. at 445.

26 *Id.* at 171, 88 L. Ed. at 655, 64 Sup. Ct. at 444.

27 *Commonwealth* v. *Prince, supra* n. 22, at 228-29, 46 N.E.2d at 758.

28 "Note," 32 *Georgetown Law Journal* 309, 312 (1944).

29 *Follett* v. *McCormick,* 321 U.S. 573, 88 L. Ed. 938, 64 Sup. Ct. 717 (1944).

30 *Id.* at 579, 88 L. Ed. at 942, 64 Sup. Ct. at 720.

31 P. B. Kurland, *Religion and the Law* (Chicago: Aldine, 1962), pp. 67-68.

32 *E.g., Gabrielli* v. *Knickerbocker,* 306 U.S. 621, 83 L. Ed. 1026, 59 Sup. Ct. 786 (1939); *Hering* v. *State Board of Education,* 303 U.S. 624, 82 L. Ed. 1087, 58 Sup. Ct. 748 (1938); *Leoles* v. *Landers,* 302 U.S. 656, 82 L. Ed. 507, 58 Sup. Ct. 362 (1937).

[33] *Johnson* v. *Deerfield,* 306 U.S. 621, 83 L. Ed. 1027, 59 Sup. Ct. 786 (1939), *decision below,* 25 F. Supp. 918 (D. Mass. 1939).

[34] 319 U.S. 624, 87 L. Ed. 1628, 63 Sup. Ct. 1178, 147 A.L.R. 674 (1943).

[35] *Jones* v. *Opelika, supra* n. 12, at 623-24, 86 L. Ed. at 1715, 62 Sup. Ct. at 1251.

[36] *West Virginia State Board of Education* v. *Barnette, supra* n. 34, at 641, 87 L. Ed. at 1639, 63 Sup. Ct. at 1187.

[37] *Id.* at 642, 87 L. Ed. at 1639, 63 Sup. Ct. at 1187.

[38] June 29, 1942.

[39] June 22, 1942.

[40] "Recent Cases," 91 *University of Pennsylvania Law Review* 75, 76 (1942).

[41] "Recent Decisions," 42 *Columbia Law Review* 1200, 1201 (1942).

[42] "Recent Decisions," 29 *Virginia Law Review* 339, 340 (1942).

[43] *Ibid.*

[44] M. R. Lazere, "Comments," 11 *Fordham Law Review* 304, 310 (1942).

[45] "Notes," 52 *Yale Law Journal* 168, 174 (1942).

[46] W. F. Anderson, "Recent Decisions," 39 *Michigan Law Review* 149, 152 (1940).

[47] "Recent Decisions," 18 *New York University Law Review* 124, 127 (1940).

[48] W. G. Fennell, "The 'Reconstructed Court' and Religious Freedom: The Gobitis Case in Retrospect," 19 *New York University Law Review* 31, 42 (1941).

[49] *State* v. *Lefebvre,* 91 N.H. 382, 385, 20 A.2d 185, 187 (1941).

[50] *In re Reed,* 262 App. Div. 814, 28 N.Y.S.2d 92 (1941).

[51] May 24, 1943.

[52] May 5, 1943.

[53] May 4, 1943.

[54] May 5, 1943.

[55] *City of Chicago* v. *Tribune Co.,* 307 Ill. 595, 139 N.E. 86 (1923).

[56] *Near* v. *Minnesota ex rel. Olson,* 283 U.S. 697, 75 L. Ed. 1357, 51 Sup. Ct. 625 (1931).

[57] *Busey* v. *District of Columbia,* 129 F.2d 24 (D.C. Cir. 1942).

[58] *Jehovah's Witnesses in the Divine Purpose* (New York: Watchtower Bible and Tract Society. Brooklyn: International Bible Students Association, 1945), p. 209.

[59] C. A. Beard, *The Republic; Conversations on Fundamentals* (New York: Viking Press, 1943), p. 173.

[60] *Everson* v. *Board of Education,* 330 U.S. 1, 91 L. Ed. 711, 67 Sup. Ct. 504, 168 A.L.R. 1392 (1947).

[61] *Cochran* v. *Louisiana State Board of Education,* 281 U.S. 370, 74 L. Ed. 913, 50 Sup. Ct. 335 (1930).

[62] Frankfurter, J., in *Olberding* v. *Illinois Central R.R.,* 346 U.S. 338, 98 L. Ed. 39, 74 Sup. Ct. 83 (1953).

[63] See E. Cahn, "On Government and Prayer," 37 *New York University Law Review* 981, 984 (1962).

64 J. Madison, *Letters and Writings,* Vol. 1 (Philadelphia: Lippincott, 1885), p. 16.

65 J. Madison, "Memorial and Remonstrance Against Religious Assessments" in *The Writings of James Madison,* Vol. 2 (New York: Putnam, 1901), pp. 183-91.

66 *Everson* v. *Board of Education, supra* n. 60, at 8-9, 91 L. Ed. at 720, 67 Sup. Ct. at 508.

67 *Id.* at 15-16, 91 L. Ed. at 723, 67 Sup. Ct. at 511.

68 *Id.* at 18, 91 L. Ed. at 725, 67 Sup. Ct. at 513.

69 Letter from Vancouver Island, British Columbia, March 11, 1947.

70 *Everson* v. *Board of Education, supra* n. 60, at 19, 91 L. Ed. at 725, 67 Sup. Ct. at 513.

71 See E. S. Corwin, "The Supreme Court as National School Board," 14 *Law and Contemporary Problems* 3 (1949).

72 *Everson* v. *Board of Education, supra* n. 60, at 42, 91 L. Ed. at 737, 67 Sup. Ct. at 524.

73 *Id.* at 44-46, 91 L. Ed. at 738-39, 67 Sup. Ct. at 526.

74 *Id.* at 63, 91 L. Ed. at 748, 67 Sup. Ct. at 534.

75 February 13, 1947.

76 *Illinois ex rel. McCollum* v. *Board of Education,* 333 U.S. 203, 92 L. Ed. 649, 68 Sup. Ct. 461, 2 A.L.R.2d 1338 (1948).

77 *Zorach* v. *Clauson,* 343 U.S. 306, 96 L. Ed. 954, 72 Sup. Ct. 679 (1952).

78 *Engel* v. *Vitale,* 370 U.S. 421, 8 L. Ed. 2d 601, 82 Sup. Ct. 1261 (1962).

79 *Id.* at 426-27, 429, 8 L. Ed. 2d at 605-07, 82 Sup. Ct. at 1265.

80 *Id.* at 443-44, 8 L. Ed. 2d at 615-16, 82 Sup. Ct. at 1274.

81 R. F. Drinan, "Comment A", *America,* p. 593 (March 1949).

82 T. R. Powell, "Public Rides to Private Schools", *Harvard Educational Review,* Vol. XVII, p. 82 (1947).

83 *Chattanooga News-Free Press,* March 10, 1948.

84 *St. Louis Post-Dispatch,* December 7, 1947.

85 See the sampling of editorial comment in *Liberty Magazine,* Third Quarter, 1948.

86 S. Corwin, "The Supreme Court as National School Board", *Thought,* p. 681 (December 1948).

87 *New York Times,* June 30 and July 1, 1962.

88 P. B. Kurland, "Of Church and State and the Supreme Court," 29 *University of Chicago Law Review* 1, 4 (1962). Also published as a book, *op. cit. supra* n. 31.

89 *Id.* at 5.

90 Pfeffer, "Book Review," 15 *Stanford Law Review* 389, 400 (1963).

91 *Everson* v. *Board of Education, supra* n. 60, at 16, 91 L. Ed. at 724, 67 Sup. Ct. at 512.

92 *Engel* v. *Vitale, supra* n. 78, at 430, 8 L. Ed. 2d at 607, 82 Sup. Ct. at 1267.

93 *McGowan* v. *Maryland,* 366 U.S. 420, 453, 6 L. Ed. 2d 393, 414-15, 81 Sup. Ct. 1101, 1119 (1961).

94 *Braunfeld* v. *Brown,* 366 U.S. 599, 605, 6 L. Ed. 2d 563, 567, 81 Sup. Ct. 1144, 1147 (1961).

95 *Id.* at 607, 6 L. Ed. 2d at 568, 81 Sup. Ct. at 1148.
96 *Id.* at 613, 6 L. Ed. 2d at 572, 81 Sup. Ct. at 1151.
97 Conway, "Religion and Public Education in the States," *International Journal of Religious Education* (March, 1956).
98 R. B. Diernfield, *Religion in American Public Schools* (Washington: Public Affairs Press, 1962), Chs. III, IV.
99 *School District of Abington Township* v. *Schempp,* 374 U.S. 203, 10 L. Ed. 2d 844, 83 Sup. Ct. 1560 (1963).
100 *Id.* at 219, 10 L. Ed. 2d at 856, 83 Sup. Ct. at 1569.
101 *Id.* at 222, 10 L. Ed. 2d at 860, 83 Sup. Ct. at 1573.
102 *Hamilton* v. *Regents of the University of California,* 293 U.S. 245, 79 L. Ed. 343, 55 Sup. Ct. 197 (1934).
103 June 19, 1963.
104 July 1, 1962.
105 *Sherbert* v. *Verner,* 374 U.S. 398, 10 L. Ed. 2d 965, 83 Sup. Ct. 1790 (1963).
106 *Id.* at 410, 10 L. Ed. 2d at 974, 83 Sup. Ct. at 1797.
107 *Id.* at 412, 10 L. Ed. 2d at 975, 83 Sup. Ct. at 1798.
108 *Braunfeld* v. *Brown, supra* n. 94, at 611, 6 L. Ed. 2d at 571, 81 Sup. Ct. at 1150.
109 *Sherbert* v. *Verner, supra* n. 105, at 416, 10 L. Ed. 2d at 977-78, 83 Sup. Ct. at 1799.
110 Kurland, *supra* n. 88, at 96.
111 *The Writings of Thomas Jefferson* (Memorial Edition, 1904), pp. 414-18.
112 *School District of Abington Township* v. *Schempp, supra* n. 99, at 234, 10 L. Ed. 2d at 865-69, 83 Sup. Ct. at 1578-81.

Chapter IV

1 *Gitlow* v. *New York,* 268 U.S. 652, 69 L. Ed. 1138, 45 Sup. Ct. 625 (1925).
2 F. Frankfurter, "Constitutional Opinions of Justice Holmes," 29 *Harvard Law Review* 683, 686 (1916).
3 *Lochner* v. *New York,* 198 U.S. 45, 49 L. Ed. 937, 25 Sup. Ct. 539 (1905).
4 *Id.* at 75-76, 49 L. Ed. at 949, 25 Sup. Ct. at 546.
5 *United States* v. *Carolene Products Co.,* 304 U.S. 144, 82 L. Ed. 1234, 58 Sup. Ct. 778 (1938).
6 *Jones* v. *Opelika,* 316 U.S. 584, 86 L. Ed. 1691, 62 Sup. Ct. 1231 (1942).
7 *Murdock* v. *Pennsylvania,* 319 U.S. 105, 87 L. Ed. 1292, 63 Sup. Ct. 870, 146 A.L.R. 81 (1943).
8 *West Virginia State Board of Education* v. *Barnette,* 319 U.S. 624, 87 L. Ed. 1628, 63 Sup. Ct. 1178, 147 A.L.R. 674 (1943).
9 *Schneider* v. *Irvington,* 308 U.S. 147, 161, 84 L. Ed. 155, 165, 60 Sup. Ct. 146, 151 (1939).
10 *West Virginia Board of Education* v. *Barnette, supra* n. 8, at 648, 87 L. Ed. at 1643, 63 Sup. Ct. at 1190.

11 *Schenck* v. *United States,* 249 U.S. 47, 52, 63 L. Ed. 470, 474, 39 Sup. Ct. 247, 249 (1919).

12 C. H. Pritchett, *The American Constitution* (New York: McGraw-Hill, 1959), p. 389.

13 *Abrams* v. *United States,* 250 U.S. 616, 63 L. Ed. 1173, 40 Sup. Ct. 17 (1919).

14 *Id.* at 628, 63 L. Ed. at 1179, 40 Sup. Ct. at 21.

15 *Whitney* v. *California,* 274 U.S. 357, 71 L. Ed. 1095, 47 Sup. Ct. 641 (1927).

16 *Id.* at 376, 71 L. Ed. at 1106, 47 Sup. Ct. at 648.

17 P. A. Freund, *On Understanding the Supreme Court* (Boston: Little, Brown, 1949), p. 27.

18 *Bates* v. *Little Rock,* 361 U.S. 516, 524, 4 L. Ed. 2d 480, 80 Sup. Ct. 412, 417 (1960).

19 *Poe* v. *Ullman,* 367 U.S. 497, 6 L. Ed. 2d 989, 81 Sup. Ct. 1752 (1961).

20 *Id.* at 544, 6 L. Ed. 2d at 1026, 81 Sup. Ct. at 1782.

21 *Dennis* v. *United States,* 341 U.S. 494, 95 L. Ed. 1137, 71 Sup. Ct. 857 (1951).

22 *Id.* at 505-06, 95 L. Ed. at 1150-51, 71 Sup. Ct. at 865.

23 *Id.* at 509-10, 95 L. Ed. at 1152-53, 71 Sup. Ct. at 867.

24 *Id.* at 589, 95 L. Ed. at 1193, 71 Sup. Ct. at 907.

25 *Id.* at 526-27, 95 L. Ed. at 1161-62, 71 Sup. Ct. at 876.

26 *Id.* at 539-40, 95 L. Ed. at 1168, 71 Sup. Ct. at 883.

27 W. Mendelson, "Clear and Present Danger—From Schenk to Dennis," 52 *Columbia Law Review* 313 (1952).

28 H. Kalven, review of W. Mendelson, "Justices Black and Frankfurter: Conflict in the Court," 37 *Indiana Law Journal* 572 (1962).

29 L. Hand, *The Bill of Rights* (Cambridge: Harvard University Press, 1958), pp. 29-30.

30 *Id.* at p. 42. The Judge made a slight concession as to issues involving freedom of speech. See p. 69.

31 See L. H. Pollak, "Racial Discrimination and Judicial Integrity: A Reply to Professor Wechsler," 108 *University of Pennsylvania Law Review* 1 (1959).

32 See Clark, "A Plea for the Unprincipled Decision," 49 *Virginia Law Review* 660 (1963).

33 M. P. Golding, "Principled Decision-Making and the Supreme Court," 63 *Columbia Law Review* 35 (1963).

34 H. Wechsler, *Principles, Politics and Fundamental Law* (Cambridge: Harvard University Press, 1961), pp. xiii-xiv.

35 A. M. Bickel, *The Least Dangerous Branch—The Supreme Court at the Bar of Politics* (Indianapolis: Bobbs-Merrill, 1962), pp. 24-25.

36 E. V. Rostow, *The Sovereign Prerogative—The Supreme Court and the Quest for Law* (New Haven: Yale University Press, 1962), Chs. 5, 6.

37 E. Cahn, *The Predicament of Democratic Man* (New York: MacMillan, 1961).

38 Hand, *op. cit. supra* n. 29, at p. 66.

39 Rostow, *op. cit. supra* n. 36, at p. 136, n. 22.

40 C. E. Clark, "The Limits of Judicial Objectivity," 12 *American Law Review* 1, 9, 13 (1963).

41 *Perez* v. *Brownell,* 356 U.S. 44, 2 L. Ed. 2d 603, 78 Sup. Ct. 568 (1958).

42 *Id.* at 79, 2 L. Ed. 2d at 625, 78 Sup. Ct. at 586.

43 L. Pollak, "Constitutional Adjudication: Relative or Absolute Neutrality," 11 *Journal of Public Law* 48, 49 (1962).

44 302 U.S. 319, 82 L. Ed. 288, 58 Sup. Ct. 149 (1937).

45 C. H. Pritchett, *Civil Liberties and the Vinson Court* (Chicago: University of Chicago, 1954), p. 33.

46 *Kovacs* v. *Cooper,* 336 U.S. 77, 93 L. Ed. 513, 69 Sup. Ct. 448 (1949).

47 *Id.* at 95, 93 L. Ed. at 527, 69 Sup. Ct. at 458.

48 Justice Rutledge, concurring (Black, Murphy and Douglas joining) in *United States* v. *C. I. O.,* 335 U.S. 106, 140, 92 L. Ed. 1849, 1870-71, 68 Sup. Ct. 1349, 1366 (1948).

49 See A. Meiklejohn, "The First Amendment is an Absolute," *Supreme Court Review* 245 (1961).

50 Holmes, dissenting in *Gitlow* v. *New York,* 268 U.S. 652, 673, 69 L. Ed. 1138, 1149, 45 Sup. Ct. 625, 632 (1925).

51 See *Roth* v. *United States,* 354 U.S. 476, 514, 1 L. Ed. 2d 1498, 1523, 77 Sup. Ct. 1304, 1324 (1957) (dissenting opinion); *Schenck* v. *United States, supra* n. 11, at 52, 63 L. Ed. at 473, 39 Sup. Ct. at 249.

52 Quoted by Justice Rutledge in his dissenting opinion in *Everson* v. *Board of Education,* 330 U.S. 1, 32, n. 9, 91 L. Ed. 711, 732, 67 Sup. Ct. 504, 519 (1947).

53 J. Madison, *The Federalist,* No. 37 (Cooke ed.), p. 236.

54 T. I. Emerson, "Toward a General Theory of the First Amendment," 72 *Yale Law Journal* 877, 955 (1963).

55 *Terminiello* v. *Chicago,* 337 U.S. 1, 37, 93 L. Ed. 1131, 69 Sup. Ct. 894, 911 (1949).

56 *Id.* at 4, 93 L. Ed. at 1134, 69 Sup. Ct. at 896.

57 323 U.S. 516, 89 L. Ed. 430, 65 Sup. Ct. 315 (1945).

58 *Id.* at 529-30, 89 L. Ed. at 440, 65 Sup. Ct. at 323.

59 *Id.* at 540, 89 L. Ed. at 445, 65 Sup. Ct. at 327.

60 *Id.* at 545, 89 L. Ed. at 448, 65 Sup. Ct. at 329.

61 *Saia* v. *New York,* 334 U.S. 558, 92 L. Ed. 1574, 68 Sup. Ct. 1148 (1948).

62 *Cantwell* v. *Connecticut,* 310 U.S. 296, 84 L. Ed. 1213, 60 Sup. Ct. 900, 128 A.L.R. 1352 (1940), *Hague* v. *C. I. O.,* 307 U.S. 496, 83 L. Ed. 1423, 59 Sup. Ct. 954 (1939); *Lovell* v. *Griffin,* 303 U.S. 444, 82 L. Ed. 949, 58 Sup. Ct. 666 (1938).

63 *Saia* v. *New York, supra* n. 61, at 571, 92 L. Ed. at 1583, 68 Sup. Ct. at 1155.

64 I. Dilliard in the *St. Louis Post-Dispatch,* June 7, 1948.

65 June 8, 1948.

66 *Zorach* v. *Clauson,* 343 U.S. 306, 96 L. Ed. 954, 71 Sup. Ct. 679 (1952).

67 *Kovas* v. *Cooper, supra* n. 46.

68 *Id.* at 94-95, 93 L. Ed. at 526, 69 Sup. Ct. at 457.

69 *Id.* at 106, 93 L. Ed. at 532, 69 Sup. Ct. at 463.

[70] *Musser* v. *Utah,* 333 U.S. 95, 96-97, 92 L. Ed. 562, 565, 68 Sup. Ct. 397, 398 (1948).

[71] *Id.* at 101-02, 92 L. Ed. at 567-68, 68 Sup. Ct. at 400.

[72] *State* v. *Musser,* 118 Utah 537, 223 P.2d 193 (1950).

[73] *Pennekamp* v. *Florida,* 328 U.S. 331, 90 L. Ed. 1295, 66 Sup. Ct. 1029 (1946).

[74] *Bridges* v. *California,* 314 U.S. 252, 86 L. Ed. 192, 62 Sup. Ct. 190, 159 A.L.R. 1346 (1941).

[75] *Toledo Newspaper Co.* v. *United States,* 247 U.S. 402, 62 L. Ed. 1186, 38 Sup. Ct. 560 (1918).

[76] *Nye* v. *United States,* 313 U.S. 33, 85 L. Ed. 1172, 61 Sup. Ct. 810 (1941).

[77] *Craig* v. *Harney,* 331 U.S. 367, 375, 91 L. Ed. 1546, 1551, 67 Sup. Ct. 1249, 1254 (1947).

[78] *Palko* v. *Connecticut, supra* n. 44.

[79] R. C. Donnelly and R. Goldfarb, "Contempt by Publication in the United States," 24 *Modern Law Review* 239, 248 (1961).

[80] *R.* v. *Editor of New Statesman,* 44 T.L.R. 301 (1928).

[81] U. S. CONST. art. III, § 2.

[82] *United Public Workers* v. *Mitchell,* 330 U.S. 75, 91 L. Ed. 754, 67 Sup. Ct. 556 (1947).

[83] *McAuliffe* v. *New Bedford,* 155 Mass. 216, 29 N.E. 517 (1892).

[84] *United Public Workers* v. *Mitchell, supra* n. 82, at 122-26, 91 L. Ed. at 781-87, 67 Sup. Ct. at 581.

[85] *Id.* at 102, 91 L. Ed. at 774, 67 Sup. Ct. at 570.

[86] *Id.* at 111, 91 L. Ed. at 779, 67 Sup. Ct. at 575.

[87] *United States* v. *C. I. O.,* 335 U.S. 106, 92 L. Ed. 1849, 68 Sup. Ct. 1349 (1948).

[88] *Ashwander* v. *Tennessee Valley Authority,* 297 U.S. 288, 80 L. Ed. 688, 56 Sup. Ct. 466 (1936).

[89] C. E. Hughes, *The Supreme Court of the United States* (New York: Garden City Pub. Co., 1928), p. 32.

[90] U. S. CONST. art. 1, § 4.

[91] June 22, 1948.

[92] T. I. Emerson, "Toward A General Theory of the First Amendment," 72 *Yale Law Journal* 877, 955 (1963).

Chapter V

[1] 116 U.S. 616, 29 L. Ed. 746, 6 Sup. Ct. 524 (1886).

[2] *Works of John Adams,* Vol. 2 (Boston: Little, Brown, 1856), p. 521 and reprinted in *Quincy's Reports of the Superior Court of Massachusetts,* pp. 1761-72.

[3] *Quincy's Reports,* p. 472, n. 15.

[4] *Harris* v. *United States,* 331 U.S. 145, 155, 91 L. Ed. 1399, 1408, 67 Sup. Ct. 1098, 1104 (1947).

[5] *Id.* at 160-61, 91 L. Ed. at 1411, 67 Sup. Ct. at 1106.

[6] 339 U.S. 56, 94 L. Ed. 653, 70 Sup. Ct. 430 (1950).

7 *Trupiano* v. *United States,* 334 U.S. 699, 92 L. Ed. 1663, 68 Sup. Ct. 1229 (1948).

8 *United States* v. *Rabinowitz, supra* n. 6, at 72, 94 L. Ed. at 663-64, 70 Sup. Ct. at 437.

9 *Johnson* v. *United States,* 333 U.S. 10, 16-17, 92 L. Ed. 436, 442, 68 Sup. Ct. 367, 370 (1948).

10 *Miller* v. *United States,* 357 U.S. 301, 308, 2 L. Ed. 2d 1332, 1337-38, 78 Sup. Ct. 1190, 1195 (1958).

11 *Ker* v. *California,* 374 U.S. 23, 10 L. Ed. 2d 726, 83 Sup. Ct. 1623 (1963).

12 338 U.S. 25, 93 L. Ed. 1782, 69 Sup. Ct. 1359 (1949).

13 232 U.S. 383, 58 L. Ed. 652, 34 Sup. Ct. 341 (1914).

14 *Yonkers* v. *United States,* 320 U.S. 685, 694, 88 L. Ed. 400, 405, 64 Sup. Ct. 327, 332 (1944) (dissenting opinion).

15 *Elkins* v. *United States,* 364 U.S. 206, 224-25, 4 L. Ed. 2d 1669, 1682-87, 80 Sup. Ct. 1437, 1453 (1960).

16 *Wolf* v. *Colorado, supra* n. 12, at 47, 93 L. Ed. at 1795-96, 69 Sup. Ct. at 1372.

17 *Rochin* v. *California,* 342 U.S. 165, 96 L. Ed. 183, 72 Sup. Ct. 205, 25 A.L.R.2d 1396 (1952).

18 *Irvine* v. *California,* 347 U.S. 128, 98 L. Ed. 561, 74 Sup. Ct. 381 (1954).

19 *Breithaupt* v. *Abram,* 352 U.S. 432, 1 L. Ed. 2d 448, 77 Sup. Ct. 408 (1957).

20 367 U.S. 643, 6 L. Ed. 2d 1081, 81 Sup. Ct. 1684 (1961).

21 *Id.* at 657, 6 L. Ed. 2d at 1091-92, 81 Sup. Ct. at 1693.

22 F. A. Allen, "Federalism and the Fourth Amendment," *The Supreme Court Review,* pp. 1, 23 (1961).

23 *Elkins* v. *United States, supra* n. 15, at 214, 215, 4 L. Ed. 2d at 1676, 80 Sup. Ct. at 1443.

24 *Olmstead* v. *United States,* 277 U.S. 438, 72 L. Ed. 944, 48 Sup. Ct. 564, 66 A.L.R. 376 (1928).

25 *Rea* v. *United States,* 350 U.S. 214, 100 L. Ed. 233, 76 Sup. Ct. 292 (1956).

26 *People* v. *Reilly,* 200 Misc. 1086, 1089, 105 N.Y.S.2d 845, 847 (1951).

27 *People* v. *Gonzales,* 20 Cal. 2d 165, 124 P.2d 44 (1942).

28 Comment, "Wolf v. Colorado and Unreasonable Search and Seizure in California," 38 *California Law Review* 498 (1950).

29 *People* v. *Cahan,* 44 Cal. 2d 434, 282 P.2d 905 (1955).

30 *Id.* at 445, 282 P.2d at 911-12.

31 *People* v. *Defore,* 242 N.Y. 13, 21, 150 N.E. 585, 587 (1926).

32 Trayner, J., "Mapp v. Ohio at Large in the Fifty States," 1962 *Duke Law Journal,* 319, 322.

33 *Id.* at 320.

34 See N. Redlich, "Survey of the Law, Constitutional Law," 36 *New York University Law Review* 1417 (1961), for discussion.

35 *People* v. *Loria,* 10 N.Y.2d 368, 179 N.E.2d 478 (1961).

36 *Id.* at 374, 179 N.E.2d at 482.

37 *State* v. *Valentin,* 36 N.J. 41, 174 A.2d 737 (1961).

38 For further discussion, see P. Bender, "The Retroactive Effect of an Overruling Constitutional Decision: Mapp v. Ohio," 110 *University of Pennsylvania Law Review* 650 (1962).

39 *Eskridge* v. *Washington State Board,* 357 U.S. 214, 2 L. Ed. 2d 1269, 78 Sup. Ct. 1061 (1958).

40 *In re Harris,* 56 Cal. 2d 879, 366 P.2d 305, 308 (1961).

41 *Petition of Dirring,* 344 Mass. 522, 183 N.E.2d 300 (1962); *State* v. *Kaiser,* 80 N.J. Super. 176, 193 A.2d 270 (1963).

42 *Gaitan* v. *United States,* 295 F.2d 277 (10th Cir. 1961), *certiorari denied,* 369 U.S. 857 (1962).

43 *Mikeleich* v. *Wainwright,* 375 U.S. 2, 11 L. Ed. 2d 41, 84 Sup. Ct. 80 (1963) (dissenting opinion). The Courts of Appeal have come to contrary conclusions. See *Sisk* v. *Lane,* 331 F.2d 235 (7th Cir. 1964) and cases cited.

44 *Lanza* v. *New York,* 370 U.S. 139, 8 L. Ed. 2d 384, 82 Sup. Ct. 1218 (1962).

45 *Id.* at 150, 8 L. Ed. 2d at 392, 82 Sup. Ct. at 1224.

46 See *infra,* p. 308.

47 *Lanza* v. *New York, supra* n. 44, at 147, 8 L. Ed. 2d at 390, 82 Sup. Ct. at 1223.

48 *Wong Sun* v. *United States,* 371 U.S. 471, 485, 9 L. Ed. 2d 441, 454, 83 Sup. Ct. 407, 416 (1963).

49 *Elkins* v. *United States, supra* n. 15.

50 See Redlich, *supra* n. 34, at 1424-25.

51 J. H. Wigmore, *Evidence,* Vol. 8 (Boston: Little, Brown, 1961, McNaughten rev.), p. 31,n.

52 Y. Kamisar, "Wolf and Lustig Ten Years Later," 43 *Minnesota Law Review* 1083 (1959).

53 See Notes, "Philadelphia Police Practice and the Law of Arrest," 100 *University of Pennsylvania Law Review* 1182, 1206, 1207 (1952).

54 See also Comment, "Search and Seizure in Illinois: Enforcement of the Constitutional Right to Privacy," 47 *Northwestern University Law Review* 493, 497 ff. (1952).

55 *Brinegar* v. *United States,* 338 U.S. 160, 181, 93 L. Ed. 1879, 1893, 69 Sup. Ct. 1302, 1313 (1949) (dissenting opinion).

56 A. Barth, *The Price of Liberty* (New York: Viking Press, 1961), pp. 109, 110.

57 F. A. Allen, *supra* n. 22, at p. 40.

58 *New York Times,* August 13, 1963.

59 L. G. Rockwell, "Justice Rutledge on Civil Liberties," 59 *Yale Law Journal* 27, 58 (1949).

Chapter VI

1 *Hirabayashi* v. *United States,* 320 U.S. 81, 87 L. Ed. 1774, 63 Sup. Ct. 1375 (1943).

2 A. T. Mason, *Harlan Fiske Stone: Pillar of the Law* (New York: Viking Press, 1956), pp. 674-75.

3 *Korematsu* v. *United States,* 323 U.S. 214, 89 L. Ed. 194, 65 Sup. Ct. 193 (1944).

4 *Id.* at 230, 232, 89 L. Ed. at 206-07, 65 Sup. Ct. at 200.

5 *Id.* at 245, 89 L. Ed. at 214, 65 Sup. Ct. at 207.

6 *Id.* at 225, 89 L. Ed. at 203, 65 Sup. Ct. at 198.

7 *Ex parte Endo,* 323 U.S. 283, 89 L. Ed. 243, 65 Sup. Ct. 208 (1944).

8 E. V. Rostow, "The Japanese American Cases—A Disaster," 54 *Yale Law Journal* 489, 490-92 (1945).

9 *Harper's Magazine,* Vol. 191, p. 193 ff. (1945).

10 March 30, 1944.

11 June 25, 1943.

12 June 22, 1943.

13 December 30, 1944.

14 January 3, 1945.

15 *In re Yamashita,* 327 U.S. 1, 90 L. Ed. 499, 66 Sup. Ct. 340 (1946).

16 *Ex parte Quirin,* 317 U.S. 1, 87 L. Ed. 3, 63 Sup. Ct. 1 (1942).

17 *In re Yamashita, supra* n. 15, at 14, 90 L. Ed. at 509, 66 Sup. Ct. at 347.

18 *Id.* at 22-23, 90 L. Ed. at 513, 66 Sup. Ct. at 351.

19 *Id.* at 41, 90 L. Ed. at 523, 66 Sup. Ct. at 359.

20 *Id.* at 49-50, 90 L. Ed. at 527-28, 66 Sup. Ct. at 363.

21 *Id.* at 60-61, 90 L. Ed. at 533-34, 66 Sup. Ct. at 368.

22 *Id.* at 76, 90 L. Ed. at 542, 66 Sup. Ct. at 376.

23 *Id.* at 78-79, 90 L. Ed. at 543, 66 Sup. Ct. at 377.

24 *Homma* v. *Patterson,* 327 U.S. 759, 90 L. Ed. 992, 66 Sup. Ct. 515 (1946).

25 *Washington Star,* February 13, 1946.

26 January 14, 1946.

27 February 6, 1946.

28 February 6, 1946.

29 February 6, 1946.

30 Recent Decisions, "Trial by Military Commission of Enemy Combatant after Cessation of Hostilities," 44 *Michigan Law Review* 855, 861 (1946).

31 Comments, "Due Process and the Military Commission," 30 *Marquette Law Review* 190, 192 (1946).

32 K. C. Davis, "Review of Administrative Action," 44 *Illinois Law Review* 598, n. 202 (1946).

33 J. P. Frank, *The Marble Palace—The Supreme Court in American Life* (New York: Knopf, 1958), p. 135.

34 J. T. Ganoe, "The Yamashita Case and the Constitution," 25 *Oregon Law Review* 143, 158 (1946).

35 F. Reel, *The Case of Yamashita* (Chicago: University of Chicago Press, 1949).

36 *Hirota* v. *MacArthur,* 335 U.S. 876, 880, 93 L. Ed. 418, 69 Sup. Ct. 157 (1948).

37 *Hirota* v. *MacArthur,* 338 U.S. 197, 93 L. Ed. 1902, 69 Sup. Ct. 197 (1948).

38 Fairman, discussing the German cases in "Some New Problems of the Constitution Following the Flag," 1 *Stanford Law Review* 587, 590-603 (1949).

39 *Hirota* v. *MacArthur, supra* n. 37, at 215, 93 L. Ed. at 1913, 69 Sup. Ct. at 198.

40 December 7, 1948.

41 January 11, 1949.

42 *In re Oliver*, 333 U.S. 257, 264, 92 L. Ed. 682, 689-90, 68 Sup. Ct. 499, 503 (1948).

43 *Ex parte Terry*, 128 U.S. 289, 32 L. Ed. 405, 9 Sup. Ct. 77 (1888).

44 *Id*. at 307, 32 L. Ed. at 410, 9 Sup. Ct. at 80.

45 See C. B. Swisher, *Life of Stephen J. Field* (Washington: The Brookings Institute, 1930), p. 321.

46 333 U.S. at 274-75, 92 L. Ed. at 695, 68 Sup. Ct. at 508.

47 *Fisher* v. *Pace*, 336 U.S. 155, 93 L. Ed. 569, 69 Sup. Ct. 425 (1949).

48 *Id*. at 169, 93 L. Ed. at 577, 69 Sup. Ct. at 431.

49 *United States* v. *Sacher*, 182 F.2d 416 (2d Cir. 1950).

50 *Sacher* v. *United States*, 341 U.S. 952, 95 L. Ed. 1374, 71 Sup. Ct. 1010 (1951).

51 See F. V. Harper and D. I. Haber, "Lawyer Troubles in Political Trials," 60 *Yale Law Journal* 1 (1951), for a full discussion of this case.

52 *In re Oliver, supra* n. 42, at 285, 92 L. Ed. at 701, 68 Sup. Ct. at 513.

53 *Id*. at 280-82, 92 L. Ed. at 698-99, 68 Sup. Ct. at 511.

54 332 U.S. 261, 91 L. Ed. 2043, 67 Sup. Ct. 1613 (1946).

55 *Malinski* v. *New York*, 324 U.S. 401, 89 L. Ed. 1029, 65 Sup. Ct. 781 (1945).

56 302 U.S. 379, 82 L. Ed. 314, 58 Sup. Ct. 275 (1937).

57 *Malinski* v. *New York, supra* n. 55, at 415, 89 L. Ed. at 1038, 65 Sup. Ct. at 788.

58 *Adamson* v. *California*, 332 U.S. 46, 91 L. Ed. 1903, 67 Sup. Ct. 1672 (1947).

59 *Den* v. *Hoboken Land & Improvement Co.*, 59 U.S. (18 How.) 272, 15 L. Ed. 372 (1856).

60 W. W. Crosskey, "Constitutional Limitations on State Authority," 22 *University of Chicago Law Review* 1, 6-7 (1954).

61 Quoted from Congressman Bingham's Speech in the House by Justice Black in the Appendix to his opinion in *Adamson* v. *California, supra* n. 58.

62 *Butcher's Benevolent Ass'n* v. *Crescent City Live-Stock Landing & Slaughter House Co.*, 83 U.S. (16 Wall.) 522, 21 L. Ed. 395 (1873).

63 *Twining* v. *New Jersey*, 211 U.S. 78, 53 L. Ed. 97, 29 Sup. Ct. 14 (1908).

64 *Adamson* v. *California, supra* n. 58.

65 A question still to be raised is the extent to which the Ninth Amendment is applicable as a limitation on state authority.

66 *United Mine Workers* v. *United States*, 330 U.S. 258, 342, 91 L. Ed. 884, 938, 67 Sup. Ct. 677, 720 (1947).

67 *Ex parte Milligan*, 71 U.S. (4 Wall.) 2, 18 L. Ed. 281 (1866).

68 *United Mine Workers* v. *United States, supra* n. 66, at 274, 91 L. Ed. at 903, 67 Sup. Ct. at 687.

69 *Id*. at 310-11, 91 L. Ed. at 921-22, 67 Sup. Ct. at 704.

70 See R. Watt, "The Divine Right of Government by Judiciary," 14 *University of Chicago Law Review* 409 (1947).

71 *United States* v. *Shipp,* 203 U.S. 563, 51 L. Ed. 319, 27 Sup. Ct. 165 (1906).

72 *Cooke* v. *United States,* 267 U.S. 517, 537, 69 L. Ed. 767, 774, 45 Sup. Ct. 390, 395 (1925).

73 March 8, 1947.

74 March 8, 1947.

75 March 7, 1947.

76 See Notes, "United States v. United Mine Workers," 47 *Columbia Law Review* 505 (1947).

77 American Federation of Labor v. American Sash & Door Co., 335 U.S. 538, 93 L. Ed. 222, 69 Sup. Ct. 258 (1949); Lincoln Federal Labor Union v. Northwestern Iron & Metal Co., 335 U.S. 525, 93 L. Ed. 212, 69 Sup. Ct. 251 (1949).

78 January 5, 1949.

79 *Lochner* v. *New York,* 198 U.S. 45, 49 L. Ed. 937, 25 Sup. Ct. 539 (1905).

Chapter VII

1 See *Betts* v. *Brady,* 316 U.S. 455, 466, 86 L. Ed. 1595, 62 Sup. Ct. 1252 (1942), citing Chitty on Criminal Law (5th Am. ed.), Vol. I, 407.

2 See W. M. Beaney, *The Right to Counsel in American Courts* (Ann Arbor: University of Michigan Press, 1955), Ch. II, for an excellent review; also see, *Powell* v. *Alabama,* 287 U.S. 45, 77 L. Ed. 158, 53 Sup. Ct. 55, 84 A.L.R. 527 (1932).

3 Z. Swift, *A System of the Laws of the State of Connecticut* (Windham: John Byrne, 1795), Vol. II, pp. 398-99, quoted by Mr. Justice Sutherland in *Powell* v. *Alabama, supra* n. 2, nn. 63-64.

4 See *Betts* v. *Brady, supra* n. 1.

5 *Johnson* v. *Zerbst,* 304 U.S. 458, 82 L. Ed. 1461, 58 Sup. Ct. 1019, 146 A.L.R. 357 (1938).

6 316 U.S. 455, 86 L. Ed. 1595, 62 Sup. Ct. 1252 (1942).

7 *Id.* at 462, 86 L. Ed. at 1602, 62 Sup. Ct. at 1256.

8 *Powell* v. *Alabama, supra* n. 2.

9 Beaney, *op. cit. supra* n. 2, at p. 155.

10 *Carnley* v. *Cochran,* 369 U.S. 506, 519, 8 L. Ed. 2d 70, 79, 82 Sup. Ct. 884, 892 (1962).

11 *Williams* v. *Kaiser,* 323 U.S. 471, 89 L. Ed. 398, 65 Sup. Ct. 363 (1945).

12 *Powell* v. *Alabama, supra* n. 2.

13 *Id.* at 71, 77 L. Ed. at 172, 53 Sup. Ct. at 65.

14 *Tompkins* v. *Missouri,* 323 U.S. 485, 487, 89 L. Ed. 407, 413, 65 Sup. Ct. 370, 372 (1945).

15 J. Allison and W. Seymour, "The Supreme Court and the Doctrine of the Right to Counsel," 46 *Journal of the American Judicature Society* 259, 265 (1963).

16 *House* v. *Mayo,* 324 U.S. 42, 46, 89 L. Ed. 739, 742, 65 Sup. Ct. 517, 520 (1945).

17 *Rice* v. *Olson,* 324 U.S. 786, 789, 89 L. Ed. 1367, 1369, 65 Sup. Ct. 989, 991 (1945).

18 *Ex parte Hawk,* 321 U.S. 114, 88 L. Ed. 572, 64 Sup. Ct. 448 (1944).
19 *Hawk* v. *Olson,* 326 U.S. 271, 278, 90 L. Ed. 61, 67, 66 Sup. Ct. 116, 120 (1945).
20 *Hawk* v. *Olson,* 146 Neb. 875, 22 N.W.2d 136 (1946).
21 *Fay* v. *Noia,* 372 U.S. 391, 445, 9 L. Ed. 2d 837, 873, 83 Sup. Ct. 822, 852 (1963).
22 *Carter* v. *Illinois,* 329 U.S. 173, 176, 91 L. Ed. 172, 175, 67 Sup. Ct. 216, 219 (1946).
23 *Id.* at 176, 91 L. Ed. at 175, 67 Sup. Ct. at 219.
24 *Williams* v. *Kaiser, supra* n. 11.
25 *Marino* v. *Ragen,* 332 U.S. 561, 92 L. Ed. 170, 68 Sup. Ct. 240 (1947).
26 *Id.* at 567, 92 L. Ed. at 175, 68 Sup. Ct. at 244.
27 Comment, "A Study of the Illinois Supreme Court," 15 *University of Chicago Law Review* 107, 120 (1947).
28 *Id.* at 129, n. 98.
29 *Marino* v. *Ragen,* 333 U.S. 852, 92 L. Ed. 1133, 68 Sup. Ct. 729 (1948).
30 *Illinois ex rel. Marino* v. *Ragen,* 336 U.S. 969, 93 L. Ed. 1120, 69 Sup. Ct. 929 (1949).
31 *People ex rel. Marino* v. *Ragen,* 404 Ill. 35, 88 N.E.2d 7 (1949).
32 *Illinois ex rel. Marino* v. *Illinois,* 339 U.S. 921, 94 L. Ed. 1345, 70 Sup. Ct. 608 (1950).
33 *Ex parte Hull,* 312 U.S. 546, 85 L. Ed. 1034, 61 Sup. Ct. 640 (1941).
34 See Comments, "Procedural Due Process in Criminal Cases," 47 *Michigan Law Review* 73, 76 (1948).
35 December 26, 1947.
36 *De Meerleer* v. *Michigan,* 329 U.S. 663, 91 L. Ed. 584, 67 Sup. Ct. 596 (1947).
37 *Canizio* v. *New York,* 327 U.S. 82, 90 L. Ed. 545, 66 Sup. Ct. 452 (1946).
38 *Glasser* v. *United States,* 315 U.S. 60, 76, 86 L. Ed. 680, 702, 62 Sup. Ct. 457, 467 (1942).
39 *White* v. *Maryland,* 373 U.S. 59, 10 L. Ed. 2d 193, 83 Sup. Ct. 1050 (1963).
40 *Hamilton* v. *Alabama,* 368 U.S. 52, 7 L. Ed. 2d 114, 82 Sup. Ct. 157 (1961).
41 *Adamson* v. *California,* 332 U.S. 46, 91 L. Ed. 1903, 67 Sup. Ct. 1672, 171 A.L.R. 1223 (1947).
42 *Foster* v. *Illinois,* 332 U.S. 134, 91 L. Ed. 1955, 67 Sup. Ct. 1716 (1947).
43 *Id.* at 141, 91 L. Ed. at 1960, 67 Sup. Ct. at 1720.
44 *Id.* at 142, 91 L. Ed. at 1960, 67 Sup. Ct. at 1720.
45 Beaney, *op. cit. supra* n. 2, at p. 197.
46 *Griffin* v. *Illinois,* 351 U.S. 12, 100 L. Ed. 891, 76 Sup. Ct. 585, 55 A.L.R.2d 1055 (1956).
47 March 18, 1963.
48 *Douglas* v. *California,* 372 U.S. 353, 358, 9 L. Ed. 2d 811, 815, 83 Sup. Ct. 814, 817 (1963).
49 *Id.* at 359, 9 L. Ed. 2d at 816, 83 Sup. Ct. at 818.
50 *Lane* v. *Brown,* 372 U.S. 477, 9 L. Ed. 2d 892, 83 Sup. Ct. 768 (1963).
51 *Draper* v. *Washington,* 372 U.S. 487, 9 L. Ed. 2d 899, 83 Sup. Ct. 774 (1963).

52 *Gayes* v. *New York,* 332 U.S. 145, 91 L. Ed. 1962, 67 Sup. Ct. 1711 (1947).

53 *Von Moltke* v. *Gillies,* 332 U.S. 708, 92 L. Ed. 309, 68 Sup. Ct. 316 (1948).

54 *Von Moltke* v. *United States,* 189 F.2d 56 (6th Cir. 1951).

55 332 U.S. at 725, 92 L. Ed. at 322, 68 Sup. Ct. at 324.

56 *Id.* at 727, 92 L. Ed. at 328, 68 Sup. Ct. at 325.

57 *Von Moltke* v. *United States, supra* n. 54, at 76.

58 332 U.S. at 728, note, 92 L. Ed. at 323, note, 68 Sup. Ct. at 325, note.

59 333 U.S. 640, 92 L. Ed. 986, 68 Sup. Ct. 763 (1948).

60 *Palko* v. *Connecticut,* 302 U.S. 319, 82 L. Ed. 288, 58 Sup. Ct. 149 (1937).

61 *Hale's Pleas of the Crown* (Stokes and Ingerson ed., 1847), Vol. I, p. 636.

62 *Wade* v. *Mayo,* 334 U.S. 672, 92 L. Ed. 1647, 68 Sup. Ct. 1270 (1948).

63 28 U.S.C. § 2254 (June 25, 1948, c. 646, § 1, 62 Stat. 967).

64 *Darr* v. *Burford,* 339 U.S. 200, 94 L. Ed. 761, 70 Sup. Ct. 587 (1950).

65 *Fay* v. *Noia, supra* n. 21, at 428, 9 L. Ed. 2d at 862, 83 Sup. Ct. at 843.

66 *Townsend* v. *Burke,* 334 U.S. 736, 739-40, 92 L. Ed. 1690, 1693, 68 Sup. Ct. 1252, 1254 (1948).

67 *Gryger* v. *Burke,* 334 U.S. 728, 92 L. Ed. 1683, 68 Sup. Ct. 1256 (1948).

68 *Id.* at 736, 92 L. Ed. at 1689, 68 Sup. Ct. at 1260.

69 *Uveges* v. *Pennsylvania,* 335 U.S. 437, 93 L. Ed. 127, 69 Sup. Ct. 184 (1948).

70 *Gibbs* v. *Burke,* 337 U.S. 773, 779, note, 93 L. Ed. 1686, 1690, 69 Sup. Ct. 1247, 1250 (1949).

71 *Id.* at 781, 93 L. Ed. 1686, 1692, 69 Sup. Ct. 1247, 1251.

72 *Carnley* v. *Cochran,* 369 U.S. 506, 516, 8 L. Ed. 2d 70, 77, 82 Sup. Ct. 884, 890 (1962).

73 *Gideon* v. *Wainwright,* 372 U.S. 335, 9 L. Ed. 2d 799, 83 Sup. Ct. 792, 93 A.L.R.2d 733 (1963).

74 *Gideon* v. *Cochran,* 370 U.S. 908, 8 L. Ed. 2d 403, 82 Sup. Ct. 1259 (1962).

75 370 U.S. 932, 82 Sup. Ct. 1587 (1962).

76 302 U.S. 319, 82 L. Ed. 288, 58 Sup. Ct. 149 (1937).

77 375 U.S. 25, 26, 11 L. Ed. 2d 43, 44, 84 Sup. Ct. 89, 90 (1963).

78 See *Doughty* v. *Maxwell,* 376 U.S. 202, 11 L. Ed. 2d 650, 84 Sup. Ct. 702 (1964). See also *United States ex rel. Durocher* v. *La Vallee,* 330 F.2d 303 (2d Cir. 1964).

79 Reported in the *New York Times,* May 31, 1963.

Chapter VIII

1 *Schneiderman* v. *United States,* 320 U.S. 118, 87 L. Ed. 1796, 63 Sup. Ct. 1333 (1943).

2 8 U.S.C. § 1427 (a) (3) (June 27, 1952, c. 477, Title III, subchap. 2, § 316, 66 Stat. 242).

3 *Schneiderman* v. *United States, supra* n. 1, at 165, 87 L. Ed. at 1823, 63 Sup. Ct. at 1356.

4 *Id.* at 171, 87 L. Ed. at 1826, 63 Sup. Ct. at 1358.

5 *Baumgartner* v. *United States,* 322 U.S. 665, 88 L. Ed. 1525, 64 Sup. Ct. 1240 (1944).

6 G. Salvemini, Radcliffe Quarterly, August, 1941, p. 9.

7 *Baumgartner* v. *United States, supra* n. 5, at 679-80, 88 L. Ed. at 1534, 64 Sup. Ct. at 1247.

8 *Knauer* v. *United States,* 328 U.S. 654, 90 L. Ed. 1500, 66 Sup. Ct. 1304 (1946).

9 *Id.* at 677, 90 L. Ed. at 1514, 66 Sup. Ct. at 1316.

10 A. T. Mason, *Harlan Fiske Stone: Pillar of the Law* (New York: Viking Press, 1956), p. 689.

11 *Klapprott* v. *United States,* 335 U.S. 601, 607, 93 L. Ed. 266, 274, 69 Sup. Ct. 384, 387 (1949).

12 *Id.* at 616, 619, 93 L. Ed. at 278-79, 69 Sup. Ct. at 391-92.

13 *Klapprott* v. *United States,* 183 F.2d 474 (3d Cir. 1950).

14 340 U.S. 896, 95 L. Ed. 649, 71 Sup. Ct. 238 (1950).

15 *Knauer* v. *United States, supra* n. 8, at 676, 679, 90 L. Ed. at 1513, 1515, 66 Sup. Ct. at 1316-17.

16 *Klapprott* v. *United States, supra* n. 11, at 619, 93 L. Ed. at 280, 69 Sup. Ct. at 392.

17 *Perez* v. *Brownell,* 356 U.S. 44, 2 L. Ed. 2d 603, 78 Sup. Ct. 568 (1958).

18 *Id.* at 77, 2 L. Ed. 2d at 624, 78 Sup. Ct. at 586.

19 *Id.* at 67, 2 L. Ed. 2d at 619, 78 Sup. Ct. at 580.

20 *Id.* at 78, 2 L. Ed. 2d at 625, 78 Sup. Ct. at 586.

21 *Id.* at 64, 2 L. Ed. 2d at 617, 78 Sup. Ct. at 579.

22 *Perkins* v. *Elg,* 307 U.S. 325, 334, 83 L. Ed. 1320, 1326, 59 Sup. Ct. 884, 889 (1939).

23 *Perez* v. *Brownell, supra* n. 17, at 82, 2 L. Ed. 2d at 677, 78 Sup. Ct. at 588.

24 *Id.* at 83, 2 L. Ed. 2d at 628, 78 Sup. Ct. at 589.

25 *Trop* v. *Dulles,* 356 U.S. 86, 2 L. Ed. 2d 630, 78 Sup. Ct. 590 (1958).

26 Judge Clark, dissenting, in *Trop* v. *Dulles,* 239 F.2d 527, 530 (2d Cir. 1956).

27 *Kennedy* v. *Mendozo Martinez,* 372 U.S. 144, 184, 9 L. Ed. 2d 644, 670, 83 Sup. Ct. 554, 575 (1963).

28 *Id.* at 186, 9 L. Ed. 2d at 671, 83 Sup. Ct. at 577.

29 *Mackenzie* v. *Hare,* 239 U.S. 299, 60 L. Ed. 297, 36 Sup. Ct. 106 (1915).

30 *Savorgnan* v. *United States,* 338 U.S. 491, 94 L. Ed. 287, 70 Sup. Ct. 292, 15 A.L.R.2d 538 (1950).

31 *Schneider* v. *Rusk,* 377 U.S. 163, 12 L. Ed. 2d 218, 84 Sup. Ct. 1187 (1964).

32 *Marks* v. *Esperdy,* 375 U.S. 810, 12 L. Ed. 2d 292, 84 Sup. Ct. 1224 (1964).

33 *New York Times,* May 19, 1964.

Chapter IX

1 W. Rutledge, *Declaration of Legal Faith* (Lawrence: University of Kansas Press, 1947), pp. 26, 28-29.

2 *American Power & Light Co.* v. *Securities & Exchange Comm'n,* 329 U.S. 90, 104, 91 L. Ed. 103, 115, 67 Sup. Ct. 133, 141 (1946).

3 T. R. Powell, *Vagaries and Varieties in Constitution Interpretation* (New York: Columbia Press, 1956), p. ix.

4 *Prudential Insurance Co.* v. *Benjamin,* 328 U.S. 408, 412-13, 90 L. Ed. 1342, 1351, 66 Sup. Ct. 1142, 1146 (1946).

5 Rutledge, *op. cit. supra* n. 1, at p. 33.

6 *Id.* at 74-75.

7 N. Nathanson, "Statutory Interpretation and Mr. Justice Rutledge," 25 *Indiana Law Journal* 462 (1950).

8 A. Abel, "The Commerce Power: An Instrument of Federalism," 25 *Indiana Law Journal* 498, 500 (1950).

9 53 U.S. (12 How.) 299, 13 L. Ed. 996 (1851).

10 *Morgan* v. *Virginia,* 328 U.S. 373, 90 L. Ed. 1317, 66 Sup. Ct. 1050, 165 A.L.R. 574 (1946).

11 *Bob-Lo Excursion Co.* v. *Michigan,* 333 U.S. 28, 92 L. Ed. 455, 68 Sup. Ct. 358 (1948).

12 *Cooley* v. *Board of Wardens, supra* n. 9. And see L. Mosher, "Mr. Justice Rutledge's Philosophy of the Commerce Clause," 27 *New York University Law Review* 218, 220-21 (1952).

13 C. H. Pritchett, *The American Constitution* (New York: McGraw-Hill, 1959), pp. 265-66.

14 *United States* v. *South-Eastern Underwriters Ass'n,* 322 U.S. 533, 88 L. Ed. 1440, 64 Sup. Ct. 1162 (1944).

15 *Paul* v. *Virginia,* 75 U.S. (8 Wall.) 168, 19 L. Ed. 357 (1869).

16 *Prudential Ins. Co.* v. *Benjamin, supra* n. 4.

17 *Id.* at 431, 90 L. Ed. at 1361, 66 Sup. Ct. at 1156.

18 *Id.* at 435-36, 90 L. Ed. at 1363, 66 Sup. Ct. at 1158.

19 328 U.S. 440, 90 L. Ed. 1366, 66 Sup. Ct. 1160 (1946).

20 *Southern Pacific Co.* v. *Arizona,* 325 U.S. 761, 89 L. Ed. 1915, 65 Sup. Ct. 1515 (1945).

21 *General Trading Co.* v. *State Tax Comm'n,* 322 U.S. 335, 88 L. Ed. 1309, 64 Sup. Ct. 1028 (1944); *McLeod* v. *J. E. Dilworth Co.,* 322 U.S. 327, 88 L. Ed. 1304, 64 Sup. Ct. 1023 (1944).

22 See D. Levitan, "Mr. Justice Rutledge," 34 *Virginia Law Review* 393 (1948).

23 See Mosher, *supra* n. 12, at p. 247; and see Remarks by Fuchs in *Proceedings of the Bar and Officers of the Supreme Court in Memory of Justice Rutledge,* p. 31 (1951).

24 Justice Jackson, "Full Faith and Credit—The Lawyer's Clause," 45 *Columbia Law Review* 1, 17 (1945).

25 U. S. CONST. art. I, § 1.

26 28 U.S.C. § 1738 (June 25, 1948, c. 646, § 1, 62 Stat. 947).

27 *Williams* v. *North Carolina,* 312 U.S. 287, 87 L. Ed. 279, 63 Sup. Ct. 207, 143 A.L.R. 1273 (1942).

28 *Williams* v. *North Carolina,* 325 U.S. 226, 89 L. Ed. 1577, 65 Sup. Ct. 1092, 157 A.L.R. 1366 (1945).

29 *Id.* at 255, 89 L. Ed. at 1595, 65 Sup. Ct. at 1107.

30 *Id.* at 257-58, 89 L. Ed. at 1596, 65 Sup. Ct. at 1107-08.

31 *Id.* at 231, 89 L. Ed. at 1582, 65 Sup. Ct. at 1096.

32 *Id.* at 254, 89 L. Ed. at 1594, 65 Sup. Ct. at 1106.

33 *Estin* v. *Estin,* 334 U.S. 541, 92 L. Ed. 1561, 68 Sup. Ct. 1213, 1 A.L.R.2d 1412 (1948); *Esenwein* v. *Pennsylvania,* 325 U.S. 279, 89 L. Ed. 1608, 65 Sup. Ct. 1118, 157 A.L.R. 1396 (1945) (concurring opinion).

34 328 U.S. 549, 90 L. Ed. 1432, 66 Sup. Ct. 1198 (1946).

35 369 U.S. 186, 7 L. Ed. 2d 663, 82 Sup. Ct. 691 (1962).

36 328 U.S. at 553, 90 L. Ed. at 1434, 66 Sup. Ct. at 1200.

37 *Id.* at 566, 90 L. Ed. at 1443, 66 Sup. Ct. at 1209.

38 See *e.g.,* the "Symposiums on Baker v. Carr," 72 *Yale Law Journal* 7 (1962).

39 *Cook* v. *Fortson,* 329 U.S. 675, 91 L. Ed. 596, 67 Sup. Ct. 21 (1946).

40 *Id.* at 678-79, 91 L. Ed. at 598, 67 Sup. Ct. at 22.

41 *Rescue Army* v. *Municipal Court,* 331 U.S. 549, 91 L. Ed. 1666, 67 Sup. Ct. 1409 (1947); *Gospel Army* v. *Los Angeles,* 331 U.S. 543, 91 L. Ed. 1662, 67 Sup. Ct. 1428 (1947).

42 J. Frank, in E. Cahn ed., *Supreme Court and Supreme Law* (Bloomington: Indiana University Press, 1954), p. 114.

43 L. G. Rockwell, "Justice Rutledge on Civil Liberties," 59 *Yale Law Journal,* 27, 58 (1949).

44 *St. Louis Post-Dispatch,* September 13, 1949.

45 H. Edgerton, "Mr. Justice Rutledge," 63 *Harvard Law Review* 293, 298 (1949).

46 September 12, 1949.

47 W. Mendelson, "Clear and Present Danger—From Schenck to Dennis," 52 *Columbia Law Review* 313, 328 (1952).

48 J. P. Frank, *The Marble Palace—The Supreme Court in American Life* (New York: Knopf, 1958), pp. 190, 252.

49 F. Rodell, *Nine Men: A Political History of the Supreme Court of the U. S. from 1790 to 1955* (New York: Random House, 1955), pp. 255-56.

50 September 17, 1946.

51 I. Dilliard, "Truman Reshapes the Supreme Court," *The Atlantic Monthly,* pp. 30, 32 (December 1949).

52 G. Braden, "Mr. Justice Minton and the Truman Bloc," 26 *Indiana Law Journal* 153, 160-61 (1951).

53 *Id.* at 160-61, 168.

54 J. Frank, "The United States Supreme Court: 1949-1950," 18 *University of Chicago Law Review* 1, 38 (1950).

55 C. Dutton, "Mr. Justice Tom C. Clark," 26 *Indiana Law Journal* 169, 174 (1950).

56 These data taken from Dean Canon's study, "Mr. Justice Rutledge and the Roosevelt Court," 10 *Vanderbilt Law Review* 167, 191 (1957).

57 Dilliard, *supra* n. 51, at p. 32.

58 *Id.* at p. 33.

59 Canon, *supra* n. 56, at 184.

60 *Mercoid Corp.* v. *Mid-Continent Investment Co.,* 320 U.S. 661, 88 L. Ed. 376, 64 Sup. Ct. 268 (1944).

61 *Arizona* v. *California,* 373 U.S. 546, 566, 10 L. Ed. 2d 542, 581, 83 Sup. Ct. 1468, 1512 (1963).

62 *Federal Power Comm'n* v. *Hope Natural Gas Co.,* 320 U.S. 591, 619, 88 L. Ed. 333, 354, 64 Sup. Ct. 281, 296 (1944).

63 June 12, 1946.

64 June 14, 1946.

65 June 12, 1946.

66 *New York Times,* August 30, 1963.

67 September 2, 1963.

68 May 28, 1963.

69 W. McCune, *The Nine Young Men* (New York: Harper & Bros., 1947), p. 211.

70 A. T. Mason, *Harlan Fiske Stone: Pillar of the Law* (New York: Viking Press, 1956), p. 641.

71 Child's column for June 15, 1944.

72 January 5, 1944.

73 R. S. Allen, "The Nine Embattled Men," *Pic Magazine,* pp. 32, 113 (1948).

74 *Smyth* v. *Ames,* 169 U.S. 466, 42 L. Ed. 819, 18 Sup. Ct. 418 (1898).

75 *Federal Power Comm'n* v. *Hope Natural Gas Co., supra* n. 62, at 602, 88 L. Ed. at 345, 64 Sup. Ct. at 287.

76 Reported in Mason, *op. cit. supra* n. 70, p. 765 ff.

77 January 12, 1944.

78 *Securities & Exchange Comm'n* v. *Chenery Corp.,* 318 U.S. 80, 87 L. Ed. 626, 63 Sup. Ct. 454 (1943).

79 *Securities & Exchange Comm'n* v. *Chenery Corp.,* 332 U.S. 194, 214, 91 L. Ed. 1995, 2008, 67 Sup. Ct. 1575, 1760, 1762 (1947).

80 *Galloway* v. *United States,* 319 U.S. 372, 87 L. Ed. 1458, 63 Sup. Ct. 1077 (1943).

81 See C. A. Reich, "Mr. Justice Black and the Living Constitution," 76 *Harvard Law Review* 673, 678 (1963).

82 *Id.* at 679.

83 See Frank, *op. cit. supra* n. 42, p. 114.

84 *Sipuel* v. *Board of Regents,* 332 U.S. 631, 92 L. Ed. 247, 68 Sup. Ct. 299 (1948).

85 *Fisher* v. *Hurst,* 333 U.S. 147, 92 L. Ed. 604, 68 Sup. Ct. 389 (1948).

86 *New York Times Magazine,* November 3, 1963, p. 23.

87 R. L. Stearns, *The Colorado Alumnus,* p. 2 (October 1949).

Chapter X

1 *Poe* v. *Ullman,* 367 U.S. 497, 6 L. Ed. 2d 989, 81 Sup. Ct. 1752 (1961).

2 367 U.S. 643, 6 L. Ed. 2d 1081, 81 Sup. Ct. 1684, 84 A.L.R.2d 933 (1961).

3 338 U.S. 25, 93 L. Ed. 1782, 69 Sup. Ct. 1359 (1949).

4 *Hirabayashi* v. *United States,* 320 U.S. 81, 87 L. Ed. 1774, 63 Sup. Ct. 1375 (1943).

5 *Keegan* v. *United States,* 325 U.S. 478, 89 L. Ed. 1745, 65 Sup. Ct. 1203 (1945).

6 *West Virginia Board of Education* v. *Barnette,* 319 U.S. 624, 87 L. Ed. 1628, 63 Sup. Ct. 1178, 147 A.L.R. 674 (1943); *Minorsville School Dist.* v. *Gobitis,* 310 U.S. 586, 84 L. Ed. 1375, 60 Sup. Ct. 1010, 127 A.L.R. 1493 (1940).

7 *New York Times Magazine,* October 6, 1963, pp. 35, 103.

8 "The Supreme Court, 1958 Term," 73 *Harvard Law Review* 84, 99-100 (1959).

9 T. Arnold, "Professor Hart's Theology," 73 *Harvard Law Review* 1298, 1312 (1960).

10 See W. O. Douglas, "The Supreme Court and Its Case Load," 45 *Cornell Law Quarterly* 401 (1960).

11 C. Clark, "The Limits of Judicial Objectivity," 12 *American University Law Review* 1, 3-4 (1963).

12 "State Court Decisions and the Supreme Court," reprinted in A. F. Westin, *An Autobiography of the Supreme Court* (New York: MacMillan, 1963), p. 299.

13 Some of this material also appeared in the magazine section of the *New York Times* for October 6, 1963.

14 Discussed at pp. 118-22, *supra.*

15 Discussed at pp. 210-12, *supra.*

16 H. B. Phillips ed., *Felix Frankfurter Reminisces* (New York: Reynal, 1960), pp. 294-99.

17 The Pipeline Cases, *United States* v. *Ohio Oil Co.,* 234 U.S. 548, 58 L. Ed. 1459, 34 Sup. Ct. 956 (1914).

18 Justice Frankfurter, in the *Proceedings of the American Philosophical Society,* Vol. 98 (1954), reprinted in Westin, *op. cit. supra* n. 12, at pp. 267, 274.

A Bill of Rights

as provided in the Ten Original Amendments to

The Constitution of the United States

in force December 15, 1791.

Article I

Congress shall make no law respecting an establishment of religion, or prohibiting the free exercise thereof; or abridging the freedom of speech, or of the press; or the right of the people peaceably to assemble, and to petition the Government for a redress of grievances.

Article II

A well regulated Militia, being necessary to the security of a free State, the right of the people to keep and bear Arms, shall not be infringed.

Article III

No Soldier shall, in time of peace be quartered in any house, without the consent of the Owner, nor in time of war, but in a manner to be prescribed by law.

Article IV

The right of the people to be secure in their persons, houses, papers, and effects, against unreasonable searches and seizures, shall not be violated, and no Warrants shall issue, but upon probable cause, supported by Oath or affirmation, and particularly describing the place to be searched, and the persons or things to be seized.

Article V

No person shall be held to answer for a capital, or otherwise infamous crime, unless on a presentment or indictment of a Grand Jury, except in cases arising in the land or naval forces, or in the Militia, when in actual service in time of War or public danger; nor shall any person be subject for the same offence to be twice put in jeopardy of life or limb; nor shall be compelled in any Criminal Case to be a witness against himself, nor be deprived of life, liberty, or property, without due process of law; nor shall private property be taken for public use, without just compensation.

Article VI

In all criminal prosecutions, the accused shall enjoy the right to a speedy and public trial, by an impartial jury of the State and district wherein the crime shall have been committed, which district shall have been previously ascertained by law, and to be informed of the nature and cause of the accusation; to be confronted with the witnesses against him; to have compulsory process for obtaining witnesses in his favor, and to have the Assistance of Counsel for his defence.

Article VII

In Suits at common law, where the value in controversy shall exceed twenty dollars, the right of trial by jury shall be preserved, and no fact tried by a jury shall be otherwise re-examined in any Court of the United States, than according to the rules of the common law.

Article VIII

Excessive bail shall not be required, nor excessive fines imposed, nor cruel and unusual punishment inflicted.

Article IX

The enumeration in the Constitution, of certain rights, shall not be construed to deny or disparage others retained by the people.

Article X

The powers not delegated to the United States by the Constitution, nor prohibited by it to the States, are reserved to the States respectively, or to the people.

Index